Applied Pedagogies for Higher Education

Dawn A. Morley • Md Golam Jamil
Editors

Applied Pedagogies for Higher Education

Real World Learning and Innovation across the Curriculum

palgrave
macmillan

Editors
Dawn A. Morley
School of Sport, Health and Social Sciences
Solent University
Southampton, UK

Md Golam Jamil
Bristol Institute for Learning and Teaching
University of Bristol
Bristol, UK

ISBN 978-3-030-46950-4   ISBN 978-3-030-46951-1   (eBook)
https://doi.org/10.1007/978-3-030-46951-1

Cover illustration: © BlackJack3D / Getty

This Palgrave Macmillan imprint is published by the registered company Springer Nature Switzerland AG.
The registered company address is: Gewerbestrasse 11, 6330 Cham, Switzerland

Preface

This edited collection was instigated in response to the groundswell of applied learning expertise that was apparent through talking to academics teaching and researching at Solent University, UK. This spark for the book, and related research, mirrors an awareness across higher education for curriculum and pedagogies that have greater alignment with students' future work readiness.

The editors would like to thank Professor Catherine Lee for her support on making this the first open access, edited collection through Solent University, UK.

A special thanks must also go to Barry Summerton (Dawn's Dad) who meticulously checked all the chapter references and fed back to the editors in such a timely way.

Southampton, UK   Dawn A. Morley
Bristol, UK   Md Golam Jamil

Contents

1 Introduction: Real World Learning—Recalibrating the Higher Education Response Towards Application to Lifelong Learning and Diverse Career Paths   1
Dawn A. Morley and Md Golam Jamil

Part I   Emerging Responses in Real World Learning   19

2 Internal Knowledge Transfer: Professional Development Programmes and Embedding Real World Learning for Full-Time Undergraduates   21
David Perrin, Connie Hancock, and Ruth Miller

3 The Role of Professional Networks in Supporting and Developing Real World Learning   41
Joanne Brindley and Stuart Sims

4 Real World Learning Through Civic Engagement: Principles, Pedagogies and Practices   63
Kristine Mason O'Connor and Lindsey McEwen

5 Working and Learning Through the Local Community:
   Four Case Studies from Higher Education That Promote
   Civic Engagement   91
   Dawn A. Morley, Tracey Gleeson, Kerstin Mey, Anne Warren-
   Perkinson, Tracey Bourne, Amy E. King, Linda Cooper, and
   Duncan Reavey

6 Real World Learning and the Internationalisation of
   Higher Education: Approaches to Making Learning Real
   for Global Communities   107
   Md Golam Jamil, Nazmul Alam, Natascha Radclyffe-Thomas,
   Mohammad Aminul Islam, A. K. M. Moniruzzaman Mollah,
   and Annajiat Alim Rasel

Part II Moving Learning into Real World Practice: Extending
         Student Opportunities in Higher Education   133

7 Designing and Supporting Extraordinary Work
   Experience   135
   Dawn A. Morley, Paul Marchbank, Tony Steyger, Lesley Taylor,
   Anita Diaz, and Pauline Calleja

8 Making Projects Real in a Higher Education Context   163
   Roy Hanney

9 Real World Learning: Simulation and Gaming   187
   Jonathan Lean, Jonathan Moizer, Cathrine Derham, Lesley
   Strachan, and Zakirul Bhuiyan

10 Learning Enterprise and Entrepreneurship Through Real
   Business Projects   215
   Lucy Hatt

11 The Journey of Higher Degree Apprenticeships   243
   Claire Hughes and Gillian Saieva

Part III   Future Higher Education Direction: Engaging Real World Learning Through Innovative Pedagogies   267

12   **Making Inspiration Mainstream: Innovative Pedagogies for the Real World**   269
     Carina Buckley and Maria Kukhareva

13   **'Getting to the Soul': Radical Facilitation of 'Real World' Learning in Higher Education Programmes Through Reflective Practice**   299
     Jo Trelfa

14   **Real World Learning and Authentic Assessment**   323
     Melenie Archer, Dawn A. Morley, and Jean-Baptiste R. G. Souppez

15   **Using Educational Technology to Support Students' Real World Learning**   343
     Edward Bolton and Roger Emery

16   **Real-Time, Real World Learning—Capitalising on Mobile Technology**   371
     Keith D. Parry, Jessica Richards, and Cameron McAuliffe

17   **Conclusion: Real World Learning—Researching and Co-constructing Working Definitions for Curriculum Development and Pedagogy**   395
     Dawn A. Morley

Index   413

Notes on Contributors

Nazmul Alam is an Associate Professor and Head of Public Health Department at Asian University for Women (AUW), Bangladesh. He has doctoral degree from the University of Alabama at Birmingham (UAB), USA, and postdoctoral training from the University of Montreal, Canada. He is a recipient of the National Institute of Health (NIH) Fogarty International Centre fellowship.

Melenie Archer is Lecturer in Festival and Event Management at Solent University, UK. With over 15 years' experience in the live events industry she also supervises student work placements at major UK music festivals as part of the course delivery.

Zakirul Bhuiyan has over 30 years of maritime industry experience and his time at sea was mainly spent in worldwide trade. He has been working as Senior Lecturer and Course Leader, Maritime Bridge Simulation at Solent University, since 2006. He is a member of UK Marine Autonomous Systems Regulatory Working Group (MASRWG), Merchant Navy Training Board (MNTB) and International Maritime Organisation's (IMO's) Human Element, Training and Watchkeeping (HTW) sub-committee sessions.

Edward Bolton is a Learning Technologist at Solent University responsible for researching and investigating how digital technologies can be best used for pedagogical benefits of both students and staff. His specialisms include audience response systems promoting student engagement in the classroom, use of e-Portfolio and supporting academics in their design and use of Solent Online Learning.

Tracey Bourne is the module lead for Principles of Football Development and Applied Football Development at Solent University. Tracey is qualified as a Football Association (FA) Futsal tutor and works with prospective tutors training them to achieve their license to deliver coach education for the FA.

Joanne Brindley is Senior Lecturer in Education and the academic practice lead in the School of Education and Sociology at University of Portsmouth, where she is the course leader for the Academic Professional Apprenticeship and Postgraduate Certificate in Higher Education. Her doctoral thesis focused on reflective practice, mentorship and the development of communities of practice.

Carina Buckley is the Instructional Design Manager at Solent University and is responsible for leading on the design and development of blended online learning environments for flexible learners or distance learners and supporting and leading institutional projects to implement effective teaching and learning strategies. Carina is the chair for the Association for Learning Development in Higher Education.

Pauline Calleja is a Senior Lecturer at CQUniversity in Cairns, Australia. Pauline's clinical speciality is emergency nursing and rural and remote practice with her research expertise in mixed methods and qualitative design projects that encompass clinical intervention, practice improvement, teaching and learning in clinical environments and simulation settings. Pauline's area of research focus is to improve rural and remote communities' local access to high-quality emergency and trauma care.

Linda Cooper has worked in education as a teacher and teacher educator for the past 20 years. She currently works in the Institute of Education, Health and Social Sciences at University of Chichester and coordinates the Education Studies courses there. Her research interests and publications include creative learning strategies, history education in primary schools and using technology with primary children

Cathrine Derham is a Principal Teaching Fellow in the School of Health Sciences and Associate Dean (Education) in the Faculty of Health and Medical Sciences at University of Surrey. Her research and interests focus upon feedback and simulated practice.

Anita Diaz is a conservation ecologist at Bournemouth University where her research projects include collaboration with wildlife conservation organisations forging an innovative landscape-scale conservation vision for the Purbeck Heaths. Students have integral roles in the project, co-creating long-term monitoring of ecological change. Similarly, Anita's collaborations in Spain provide student co-researchers with different perspectives on wildlife conservation of mountain meadow ecosystems.

Roger Emery is Head of Learning Technologies, responsible for the online learning and digital education provision for Solent University. Roger is a regular contributor to sector bodies including Association for Learning Technology (ALT), Heads of e-Learning Forum (HeLF) and the Moodle and Mahara communities.

Tracey Gleeson is the senior coordinator of the Limerick Inside Out International Practica Programme at University of Limerick. She has worked with the Irish Peace Institute, Co-operation Ireland and the Centre for International Co-operation on cross-border and cross-community national and international projects.

Connie Hancock is an Associate Professor at University of Chester Business School where she heads up the Department of Enterprise, Leadership and Management. Her research principally focuses on entrepreneurship education and entrepreneurial endeavour in a Higher Education context.

Roy Hanney is the course leader for Media Production at Solent University, specialising in communications, media production, producing and project development. Roy's practice interests include documentary filmmaking, arts and heritage, audio-visual performance and immersive story experiences. Roy has widely published on the topic of project-based learning, and he is currently registered as a PhD student at University of Portsmouth, investigating project-based learning in media practice education.

Lucy Hatt is a Senior Lecturer at Newcastle Business School, Northumbria University, and leads the Entrepreneurial Business Management programme where students set up and run their own business projects in teams. She is also a doctoral researcher at the School of Education, Durham University, researching entrepreneurship education through the lens of threshold concepts and transactional curriculum inquiry, expecting to graduate in 2020. She was highly commended as an Enterprise Catalyst in the National Enterprise Educator Awards 2016.

Claire Hughes is the inaugural Chartered Manager Degree Apprenticeship (CMDA) programme manager and course leader for the BA (Hons) Business Management and BA (Hons) Business Enterprise and Entrepreneurship degree courses at Solent University. Having come from industry, working for global market leaders and worldwide partners, she draws upon these experiences to inform her teaching.

Mohammad Aminul Islam is a Senior Lecturer at the Institute of Languages, BRAC University, Bangladesh. He has extensive training and educational programme development experience with the Ministry of Education, Bangladesh; Open University, UK; BRAC; Save the Children and International Labour Organisation. He has been a member of the 'English Language Fellow Program' run by the US Department of State and has received Commonwealth Distance Learning Scholarship in 2017.

Md Golam Jamil is a Pedagogic Researcher at University of Bristol. He has taught academic programmes and managed a professional development unit at BRAC University in Bangladesh. His research interests include applied pedagogies, research-informed teaching, technology-enhanced learning and language education.

Amy E. King is the Health and Exercise Development Officer at Solent University where she studied Health, Exercise and Physical Activity. Her work focuses on health promotion with a strong emphasis on physical activity and nutrition. Amy is a strong advocate for real world learning experience and provides students with various opportunities alongside supporting students through the Community Innovation Programme.

Maria Kukhareva works at Centre for Learning Excellence, University of Bedfordshire, where she leads on staff development and innovative practice. Her interdisciplinary work includes developing effective teaching approaches grounded in drama pedagogy, object-based learning and visual pedagogy. Maria is the chair of the Research and Development working group for the Association for Learning Development in Higher Education (ALDinHE).

Jonathan Lean is Associate Professor of Strategic Management at Plymouth Business School, University of Plymouth, UK, with over 20 years' experience in teaching strategic management, entrepreneurship and research methods. He has published widely on topics including management learning and development, entrepreneurship and the use of simulation games in education and training. Jonathan is associate editor of the *International Journal of Management Education* and an Honorary Fellow of Enterprise Educators UK, the UK's national network for entrepreneurship educators.

Paul Marchbank is an Associate Professor and Dean of the School of Media Arts and Technology at Solent University, Southampton, UK. Paul has been instrumental in the introduction of vocational and work-based learning pathways throughout the school and university and has developed innovative vehicles for students to gain real world experience—such as enterprise businesses harnessing work-experience opportunities across the media and digital industries.

Kristine Mason O'Connor is Professor Emerita of Higher Education Development at University of Gloucestershire and a UK Higher Education Academy National Teaching Fellow. Her fellowship at the university's Centre for Active Learning enabled her to research university-community engagement. She has served as co-chair of the Staff and Educational Development Association, chair of the Association's National Conference Committee and as a council member of the International Consortium for Educational Development. Her publications include biography, educational development and university-community engagement.

Cameron McAuliffe is Senior Lecturer in Human Geography and Urban Studies at Western Sydney University. Cameron is an urban, social and cultural geographer and a member of the Urban Research Program, where his research engages with the regulation of difference and the way cities govern 'marginal' bodies. His research includes projects on the negotiation of national and religious identities among Iranian migrant communities; policy research on graffiti management; and the geographies of kerbside waste.

Lindsey McEwen is Professor of Environmental Management in the Centre for Water, Communities and Resilience, University of the West of England, Bristol. Her specialisms include water risk management, water education, community-based research and community-based learning. Her research publications are both subject-based and pedagogic, with interest in Education for sustainable development (ESD), citizenship and learning for resilience. Lindsey is a UK Higher Education Academy National Teaching Fellow.

Kerstin Mey is the Vice President of Academic Affairs and Student Engagement and Professor of Visual Culture at University of Limerick, Ireland. She has sustained a scholarly interest and publications in contemporary art practices, public pedagogies and arts as research.

Ruth Miller is the Director of Programmes for Accreditation, recognition of prior learning (RPL) and Work Based Learning in the School of Health and Education, Middlesex University. She has extensive experience of accrediting both organisational staff development programmes and individual's own work-based learning, thereby developing flexible progression pathways for a range of practitioners. She has a particular interest in how work-based projects undertaken as part of academic awards can have real impact on the development of practice in the workplace.

Jonathan Moizer is an Associate Professor of Business Operations and Strategy at University of Plymouth Business School. His research interests include both serious games and their applications in education and training, as well as simulation modelling for learning, insight and prediction. Jonathan has published widely in these fields. He recently acted as President of the UK Chapter of the System Dynamics Society and sits on the committee of the European Conference on Games Based Learning.

A. K. M. Moniruzzaman Mollah is Professor of Biological Sciences and the Head of Science and Math Programmes at Asian University for Women (AUW), Bangladesh. He holds a BA in Biology from Illinois Wesleyan University, USA, and a PhD in Molecular Biology from University of Notre Dame, USA. He continued his academic career as a postdoctoral fellow in the Department of Biochemistry at Albert Einstein College of Medicine, USA, and as an assistant professor in the Biology Department at Yeshiva University, USA. He also taught at Stony Brook University, USA.

Dawn A. Morley is a Postdoctorate Researcher at Solent University and Principal Academic in adult nursing at Bournemouth University. Dawn specialises in how students' learning at university can be connected to greater work readiness and is the lead editor of two previously published edited collections related to work-based learning.

Keith D. Parry is a Senior Lecturer at the University of Winchester and an associate fellow at Western Sydney University. His research interests are based on the sociology of sport, with a focus on sports fandom, health and the spectator experience. His knowledge and expertise have also been recognised with invitations to write for websites such as The Conversation and News.com.au. He is an award-winning teacher and writer, receiving a UN Day Media Award for a co-authored media piece: *Pushing casual sport to the margins threatens cities' social cohesion.*

David Perrin is Director of the Centre for Work Related Studies and an associate professor at University of Chester, UK. He runs one of Europe's largest work-based learning frameworks for undergraduate and postgraduate students. He has published widely in the field, with specialism in the accreditation of prior learning.

Natascha Radclyffe-Thomas is an Higher Education Academy (HEA) National Teaching Fellow and Professor of Marketing and Sustainable Business at the British School of Fashion, Glasgow Caledonian University. Natascha's extensive international teaching experience informed her innovative collaborative online international learning project linking students in Asia to peers in London. An award-winning case study author writing on ethical business (The Case Centre) and co-author of *Fashion Management: A Strategic Approach* (2019) (Palgrave Macmillan). Natascha is the Vice Chair of the Costume Society and Fellow of the Royal Society of Arts.

Annajiat Alim Rasel is the Undergraduate Programme Coordinator at the Department of Computer Science and Engineering, BRAC University, Bangladesh. He holds BSc and MSc degrees in Computer Science and Engineering from BRAC University. Prior to joining as a faculty member in the Computer Science and Engineering Department, he worked as a research intern at the Centre for Research on Bangla Language Processing (CRBLP) lab at the same university.

Duncan Reavey is Principal Lecturer in Learning & Teaching at University of Chichester. His interests and publications include ecology, innovations in undergraduate learning and teaching, science education and learning benefits of Forest Schools. He is a National Teaching Fellow, has won the national TEAN Commendation for Innovative Practice in Teacher Education (with Linda Cooper) and was shortlisted as Most Innovative University Teacher at the national Times Higher Education Awards.

Jessica Richards is Lecturer in Sport Management in the School of Business, Western Sydney University. Her research and teaching interests focus on the sociology of sport and sport business management with an emphasis on sport fandom and stadium geography. She has published on sports fandom, gender and research ethics.

Gillian Saieva is Senior Lecturer in Human Resource Management (HRM) at Solent University, UK, Course Leader Business and Head of Business, Finance & Accountancy and Higher & Degree Apprenticeships. Her international industry experience and passion for learning and teaching have enabled the development of the school's work-based learning strategy in areas of work placement design, collaborative delivery and higher and degree apprenticeships.

Stuart Sims is Senior Lecturer in Higher Education in the Academic Development team at University of Portsmouth. His remit is around student-staff co-creation and teaching on the Academic Professional Apprenticeship and PgCert in Higher Education. Stuart completed a doctorate at Cardiff University exploring pedagogy, student experience and the labour market.

Jean-Baptiste R. G. Souppez previously at Solent University, is a Senior Teaching Fellow in Mechanical Engineering and Design at Aston University. His pedagogical research focused on innovative use of technology in higher education, real world learning and students as researchers. He is also a visiting professor at the University of Liege, the UK Principal Expert in Small Craft Structures and the deputy editor-in-chief of the SNAME *Journal of Sailing Technology*.

Tony Steyger is a documentary maker and teaches MA and BA levels for Solent University in Television Production. He heads up Solent Productions, the university's media centre, making professional and award-winning projects for broadcasters and clients. Tony continues to make broadcast content, documentaries and experimental work, often working alongside students and graduates in a skills chain.

Lesley Strachan is the Learning & Development Manager of SimVenture. For the past 15 years she has been embedding business simulation games into modules across the UK higher education sector to fast-track learning via the immersive experience of running a virtual company online. Lesley also conducts empirical research into the awareness and development of learners' employability skills so that students become more aware of the skills and behaviours they are developing whilst operating their virtual business.

Lesley Taylor is a Senior Lecturer at Solent University, working as the academic lead for the Re:So store (The Retail Solent Initiative). Lesley has presented at Interior Educators and Advance HE conferences in the

UK. In 2018–2019, she led an outward-facing project for Crawley Town Council as a collaboration with the Chichester College group, giving students the opportunity to work as researchers and trainers to small businesses in the town over a six-month period.

Jo Trelfa is Head of Academic Professional Development and Assistant Director of the Winchester Institute for Contemplative Education and Practice at the University of Winchester. Jo is a skilled facilitator working with individuals, groups of all sizes and communities around capacity building and developing connection with themselves, each other and wider societies/other communities. Her area of specialism is reflective practice.

Anne Warren-Perkinson is a PhD candidate at University of Limerick and holds a BA in Political Science from University of Canterbury and an MA in International Relations from University of Kent. Over the last three years she has become increasingly involved in innovation and transformation initiatives in higher education, with an interest in socially engaged learning.

List of Figures

Fig. 2.1   Concept map from the authors   22
Fig. 3.1   The role of professional networks in supporting and
             developing real world learning   43
Fig. 3.2   Creating a culture of shared understanding within a
             professional community of practice. (Adapted from Davies
             & Kremer, 2016)   46
Fig. 4.1   Real world learning (RWL) through civic engagement
             concept map   64
Fig. 4.2   Ten principles of real world learning through
             civic engagement   75
Fig. 6.1   Concept map on real world learning and internationalised
             academic programmes   111
Fig. 7.1   Concept map from the authors   137
Fig. 8.1   Agile learning through PjBL concept map   164
Fig. 9.1   Concept map from the authors   188
Fig. 9.2   Change in self-perceived employability skills   196
Fig. 11.1   Concept map from the authors   245
Fig. 12.1   Concept map from the authors   271
Fig. 12.2   Model for the dynamic interdependence of learning spaces
             and sites of innovation   275
Fig. 12.3   Reiterative process of workshop development   283
Fig. 12.4   Task-based reflection for assessment   284
Fig. 12.5   The SOL Baseline   287

Fig. 13.1   Concept map from the author   304
Fig. 14.1   Concept map from the authors   325
Fig. 15.1   Concept map from the authors   346
Fig. 16.1   Concept map from the authors   372

List of Tables

Table 3.1   Agreed list of staff and student responsibilities   56

Table 4.1   Real world learning through civic engagement—principles into practice   76

Table 4.2   Real world learning through civic engagement—four case studies   77

Table 8.1   Contrasting views of a project adapted from Svejvig and Andersen (2015, p. 280)   166

Table 11.1   Profile of degree and master's level apprentices at University of Chester   249

1

Introduction: Real World Learning—Recalibrating the Higher Education Response Towards Application to Lifelong Learning and Diverse Career Paths

Dawn A. Morley and Md Golam Jamil

Reviewing Current Higher Education Provision for Employability

Over the last 20 years, higher education has been increasingly audited for its relevance to the student population—whether this is for the quality of its provision, the ability to place students in employment with meaningful 'learning gain', or its response to the student voice. Historically, there has been a split between higher education curricula, employment sectors and students' career objectives (Finch, Falkenberg, McLaren, Rondeau, & O'Reilly, 2018; Miles, 2017). Many profession-focused academic

D. A. Morley (✉)
School of Sport, Health and Social Sciences, Solent University, Southampton, UK

M. G. Jamil
Bristol Institute for Learning and Teaching, University of Bristol, Bristol, UK

© The Author(s) 2021
D. A. Morley, M. G. Jamil (eds.), *Applied Pedagogies for Higher Education*,
https://doi.org/10.1007/978-3-030-46951-1_1

1

programmes often fail to stay relevant with the rapid transformation of global labour market and the demands of new skill sets from employees (Trilling & Fadel, 2009). This creates the risk of outdated academic practice, leading to potential talent gaps in industries, indicated by the wide selection of degree apprenticeship programmes that have been developed in response (Morley, 2017).

Measurement of student outcomes, the longer tradition of grafting employability skills into courses (Atkins, 2009; Bridgstock, 2009; Mason, Williams, & Cranmer, 2009) or adding placements into the student experience highlights the increasing recognition that students' graduation is the first step, and not the destination, in their learning and working trajectories. To address the shortfall of employability attributes among university students, many universities have begun both academic and non-academic interventions, such as job-focused academic programme design and faculty development with enhanced industry exposures (Nguyen, Tran, & Le, 2019). However, most of these initiatives have failed to demonstrate positive learning outcomes in terms of preparing job-ready graduates (Woodside, 2018). There is a criticism that vocationally oriented curricula are 'dumbing down', causing the 'loss of critical mission' (Turner, 2011). Traditional learning and teaching practices, which are generally academic skills–oriented and content-based, are not always appropriate to prepare students as global citizens and job-ready graduates (Woodside, 2018). These two contrasting and challenging areas in higher education curricula demand a proper balance between academic rigour and work-related competencies in teaching and learning. On the one hand, university students need academic rigour in their learning to expand and renew strategic capabilities. On the other, they require instituting real-life connections and competencies transferable to future profession and work.

In contemporary economic and educational policies, graduate employability has emerged as a defining factor for the overall enhancement of human capital and economy (Tomlinson, 2017). The European Commission in its Education and Training Monitor 2014 report calls for enhancing graduate employability skills that can benefit the society and labour market (European Commission, 2014). Australian higher education has adopted a 'demand driven system' investing a significant amount of funding for universities to respond to the needs of efficient workforce

(Bridgstock & Cunningham, 2016). In UK higher education, an emphasis has been placed on the application of learning to academic and professional areas. The National Student Survey (NSS), a key indicator to measure student satisfaction and teaching quality in UK universities, contains questions such as 'my course has provided me with opportunities to apply what I have learnt' to gauge the extent of real world rigour and academic-industry links in the academic programmes (Office for Students, 2019).

UK higher education institutions have responded proactively to improve their performance in the annual NSS particularly as results feed into the core metrics of the university's Teaching Excellence Framework (TEF) ratings. Most notably, the work on learning gain and the TEF in the UK has more recently unravelled as too difficult or statistically flawed (Kernohan, 2018; Shah, 2018) to continue in its present form, bringing into question the ability to measure a correlation between learning and postgraduation employment. Added to the question of the viability of employment measures in higher education, the new Graduate Outcomes Survey, the largest social survey outside of the ten-year census, relies on students to complete the survey 15 months after graduation. Already there are concerns that the survey will attract response rates up to 20% below its predecessor, the Destination of Leavers from Higher Education (DLHE) Survey (Grey, 2018).

It seems that time is of the essence to revisit the appropriateness of modern curriculum to deliver student learning that has relevance after graduation. The Inaugural Global Learner's survey (Pearson, 2019), of 11,000 learners between 16 and 70 years old in 19 countries, acknowledges that the 40-year career has now gone and needs to be replaced by educating for lifelong learning and diverse career paths.

Using Theory to Elicit a Changing Pedagogy for Employability and Lifelong Learning

Knud Illeris, publishing in the 1990s, foresaw an approaching juxtaposition between the way students learnt and the way they were taught that insufficiently prepared them for the changing postgraduate landscape.

> Changes of late modernity are fundamentally changing the conditions of learning, and if politicians, administrators and educators are to cope adequately with this, as educational researchers we must be able to develop adequate theories matching the problems experienced at all levels. (Illeris, 2003, p. 404)

He argues (Illeris, 2003) that learning cannot be straightjacketed into a curriculum but requires a broader foundation to be responsive to the wider goals of learning. Billett (2010) supports this view that higher education's emphasis on educational provision privileges more traditional learning. By doing so, transformative opportunities for learning, such as those found outside of the curriculum and more creatively added to the curriculum, may be overlooked.

The question arises as to whether higher education pedagogy risks being out of sync with students' immediate and postgraduate needs. Higher education continues to make a distinction between the students' own personal cognitive learning processes and socio constructivist learning where students' learning is situated from their own experience and that of others (Wenger, 1998). Illeris (2003) argues that assimilated learning, which adds to previous knowledge and experience, is common but realises greater learning impact occurs when the process is disrupted, and the student must struggle to accommodate new learning into their existing schema.

Heath and Heath (2017) advocate transforming the flat landscape of experience by punctuating it with memorable events that have impact for the individual. This is not to be confused with 'being entertained', and both academics and students often comment on the acceleration of skills and development that occur during student placement opportunities (Morley et al., 2017). There is no coincidence that the type of learning that students experience in the world of work is fundamentally different from that experienced at university—theoretical knowledge is applied and challenged, expectations on standards and performance are constant and students work up against experts who can be questioned and, in their turn, give feedback in real time. Overall, learning is much more organic, exposed and dependent on students' own individual effect. Much can be learnt from the area of work-based learning which Lester and Costley (2010) argue has a particular pedagogy to support its learners.

An innovative approach to learning 'break(s) the script' (Heath & Heath, 2017) that can be memorable both during and after the event. By making a personal connection with students, in either their present or their future selves, personalises their learning, for example, resonance with an outside presenter or greater accessibility to learning materials sympathetic to students' own learning preferences, increases students' understanding and ability to question. The recognised barrier of the gulf between the learning at university and its application, 'the theory-practice gap', can start to be addressed by stimulating students' curiosity and giving them the confidence to ask questions. Arguably, a curriculum that encourages the use of innovative pedagogies, such as inquiry and peer-based learning, may provide a stronger lead to social models of learning and the development of both individual and team learning skills. A piquancy is added by a third factor; stakes are heightened by learning strategies that aim to make the learning event crucial through, for example, links to assessments or the opportunity for public scrutiny such as student-led journals or retail initiatives.

Carefully considered curriculum design that addresses the impact of learning through novelty, application and personal development is arguably more attuned to students' current needs for higher education and later employment. The challenge is to move real world learning into a robust, research-informed position so its implementation does not occur by accident, but it is considered against the more traditional taxonomies of learning and established pedagogic theory. University structures, more reflexive to a process-led curriculum with an emphasis on personalised and appropriate support structures, may also do better to resituate learning in higher education institutions to a real world ethos.

Theorists, influential to practice pedagogy, look closely as to how learning is situated and how the environment can be altered to promote higher level learning. Fuller and Unwin's (2003) research of apprenticeships identified a 'restrictive-expansive continuum' that classified the type of learning environment presented in the workplace. Crucially, expansive learning encouraged a supportive environment for students to learn higher level skills such as dialogue, problem solving and reflexive forms of expertise. What could be isolated as soft skills, important for employability, are highly valued and explicitly incorporated within the learning.

Ellstrom (2011) also makes a similar distinction between an enabling and constraining learning environment whereby the structures in the practice setting impact on how easily a student can move between adaptive (skills acquisition) and developmental (professional critique) learning. A constraining working environment can prioritise adaptive learning, or be detrimental to the development of both, with students displaying the attributes of acquiescence. Although the prioritisation of adaptive or developmental learning may naturally and appropriately occur during their learning, students need encouragement to be able to question what and how they are being taught. The interdependency between knowledge and practice where one promotes the other (Schön, 1983) advances this learning further.

The strong emphasis on the learning application and graduate employability suggest modernising the existing educational objectives and pedagogic approaches in higher education curricula. *Applied Pedagogies for Higher Education. Real World Learning and Innovation Across the Curriculum* responds to this call and provides an evidence-driven discussion linked to different academic disciplines. The curricular approaches are centred on real world learning pedagogy which demonstrates strengths to improve deep learning and graduate employability skills.

The Emerging Power of Real World Learning

Real world learning is a developing educational concept in the higher education literature. The approach contains the ethos of deep, experiential, personalised and applied learning experiences (Boss, 2015; Rau, Griffith, & Dieguez, 2019; Sharma, Charity, Robson, & Lillystone, 2018). There are several pedagogic proposals, reaching from academic programme to sector levels, suggesting curricular tactics that can facilitate real world learning in higher education and, at the same time, minimise theory-practice gaps. Examples of recommendation include university-industry partnership (Finch et al., 2018), civic engagement (Jacoby, 2009), collaboration and reflection (Herrington, Reeves, & Oliver, 2010; Schön, 1983), and using authentic content and assessment in teaching and learning (Remington-Doucette et al., 2013).

Real world learning has not yet emerged as a distinct pedagogic model or approach, but in many teaching and learning discourses, the expression is used to refer to students' positive learning experiences and gains. For example, the term 'real world learning' has been used to describe long-term, experiential and applied learning (Rau et al., 2019; Sharma et al., 2018). It has also been portrayed as interdisciplinary and competence-based learning which can equip students with applied knowledge and skills, such as problem-solving, decision-making and planning to handle real world challenges as well as accomplish real world tasks (Holley, 2009; Moore, 2011).

The aim of this book is to address the shortfalls that currently exist in developing graduates' work readiness. Currently real world learning lacks definitional clarity and evidence-based descriptions, particularly when linked to higher education settings, and the intention is that this edited collection addresses these gaps. The chapters are centred on the case studies of 'real world learning' in different academic disciplines where students gain opportunities to focus on not only their present learning but how they can develop attributes and identities that equip them to progress following graduation. The book explores how higher education can be 'recalibrated' so the student experience becomes more orientated towards students' long-term development starting on day one of their higher education studies.

Up to this point, real world learning has established itself in primary and secondary education as a means for children to develop confidence and self-esteem in the compulsory education curriculum (Laur, 2013; Lucas & Guy, 2013; Maxwell, Stobaugh, & Tassell, 2015). Real world learning is now positioning itself in higher education academic programmes that are 'applied' where the need for an agile and authentic curriculum takes precedent (Marris, 2018).

It seems critical that real world learning, like other areas of academic development and pedagogy within higher education, is scrutinised and debated. To date, very little is written on real world learning in higher education apart from a focus on project work (Boss, 2015). The ethos and branding of real world learning need to be clear to both students, who are studying courses described under this banner, and academics who are designing real world curricula from a currently under-researched position. The book questions whether higher education curricula that link to work experience or applied examples are only accessing part of the potential of real world learning to help students learn in both their immediate and long-term development.

A qualitative research study complements the book chapters and is presented in the conclusion. Each chapter's authors formed their own focus group facilitated by the lead editor to explore real world learning through the methodology of concept mapping. The authors' individual maps and accompanying narrative are presented in each chapter. Concept mapping can portray the perceptions of the group, and the facilitating researcher, through interrogating the map that the participants provide, can enable the group to provide deeper and clearer links between concepts (Kinchin et al., 2018). For potentially complex and unexplored topics, such as real world learning in higher education, the method drew out ideas that participants used to contextualise the written narrative of the theme for their chapter.

The book has taken an approach aimed at addressing the areas found to be missing within the current literature. It critiques real world learning across the wide spectrum of both the curriculum and extracurricular activities. A cross-disciplinary approach draws on expertise from disciplines such as business, health, fashion, sport, media, sociology and geography. In this book, authors, and case study contributors, from 23 universities have shared their own expertise in 15 wider collaborative chapters on real world learning. While the book draws mainly on examples and case studies from modern UK universities, they are applicable to all vocational and professional degrees and will have resonance internationally. International evidence of real world learning in practice is drawn from the USA, Bangladesh and Australia.

The chapters are divided into three parts that reflect different aspects of this development.

Part I: 'Emerging Responses in Real World Learning' consists of five chapters, and both the authors and those academics that have provided case studies represent 12 universities from the UK, Ireland and Bangladesh. This part examines the broader application of real world learning across university ethos and policy. Chapter 2, 'Internal Knowledge Transfer: Professional Development Programmes and Embedding Real World

Learning for Full-Time Undergraduates,' sets the scene, and Perrin, Hancock and Miller provide a discussion of the distinctive features of negotiated work-based learning frameworks that help capture and develop learning for part-time students who are professional practitioners. They demonstrate their established experience as to how approaches to teaching, learning and assessment in these frameworks can also be leveraged for programmes aimed at full-time undergraduate students wishing to engage with real world learning.

Chapter 3, 'The Role of Professional Networks in Supporting and Developing Real World Learning,' by Brindley and Sims, provides insight into how professional learning networks can be effectively implemented to encourage sharing of good practice and developed to support a real world learning context within higher education. Their case studies are drawn from practice team meetings and partnership learning agreements.

Chapter 4, 'Real World Learning Through Civic Engagement: Principles, Pedagogies and Practices,' argues for alternative transformational opportunities for students to experience real world learning through civic engagement. Mason O'Connor and McEwen present changing drivers to community-based learning from local to global, including newer imperatives of learning for sustainability, citizenship education and building resilience. It concludes by reflecting on the means by which radical real world learning through civic engagement can advance and thrive. This chapter is supported by case studies from Irish and UK universities in Chapter 5, which provide innovative evidence of civic engagement in action. Chapter 5, 'Working and Learning Through the Local Community: Four Case Studies from Higher Education That Promote Civic Engagement' (by Morley, Glesson, Mey, Warren-Perkinson, Bourne, King, Cooper and Reavey) illuminates different aspects of civic engagement with international students, through sport and health initiatives and as an extension of a teaching degree. Each case study demonstrates best practice recognised by their sustainability, growing reputation and ongoing positive impact on students' alternative real world learning experiences.

Chapter 6, 'Real World Learning and the Internationalisation of Higher Education: Approaches to Making Learning Real for Global Communities,' is authored by Jamil, Alam, Radclyffe-Thomas, Islam,

Mollah and Rasel. Inquiry and application lie at the heart of real world learning, and the internationalisation of academic programmes are expected to equip learners with diverse learning styles and global citizenship skills. However, combining these two sets of educational objectives for pedagogic success is challenging, mainly because of learners' academic, social and cultural differences. The chapter addresses this problem theoretically and with the help of three real cases drawn from the UK and Bangladesh.

Part II: 'Moving Learning into Real World Practice: Extending Student Opportunities in Higher Education' examines pedagogy and strategy to enhance the impact of students' direct experience of practising in a real world setting. It consists of five chapters drawn from 13 universities in the UK and Australia. All the chapters provide examples of the theory and practice of implementing examples of real world learning pedagogies, or particular programme design, within authors' own disciplines that contribute significantly to the building of students' attributes. Part II reflects on the impact of students' direct experience of practising in a real world setting.

Morley, Marchbank, Steyger, Taylor, Diaz and Calleja, in Chapter 7, 'Designing and Supporting Extraordinary Work Experience,' recognise that real world learning experienced by students on placement is highly significant. The chapter explores emerging areas of practice pedagogy and how innovative design can bridge the theory-practice divide and support structures between university and work. Focus is placed on how these experiences can be accelerated from being part of courses to a pivotal event towards students' future development.

Chapter 8, 'Making Projects Real in a Higher Education Context,' by Hanney, draws on the work of the 'critical projects movement' framing the use of live projects as a mode of real world learning that generates encounters with industry professionals and provides real-value outputs for clients. The chapter explores the challenges that face educators who wish to foreground 'social learning' and engagement with communities of practice as a means of easing the transition for students from education to the world of work.

In Chapter 9, 'Real World Learning: Simulation and Gaming,' Lean, Moizer, Derham, Strachan and Bhuiyan present how simulations and games are being used across a variety of subject areas as a means to provide insight into real world situations within a classroom setting; they offer many of the benefits of real world learning but without some of the associated risks and costs. The nature of simulations and games is discussed with reference to a variety of examples in higher education. Their role in real world learning is evaluated with reference to the benefits and challenges of their use for teaching and learning in higher education.

Hann presents Chapter 10, 'Learning Enterprise and Entrepreneurship Through Real Business Projects,' which describes an experiential, real world approach to entrepreneurship education in HE known as 'Team Academy' and suggests a complementary conceptual grounding to the accepted curriculum using candidate entrepreneurship threshold concepts and pedagogical approaches identified from doctoral research. Four case studies are taken from the two oldest and largest UK Team Academy programmes to illustrate the approach and highlight the way in which an understanding of a selection of candidate entrepreneurship threshold concepts have been successfully developed in the students.

Hughes and Saieva, in Chapter 11, 'The Journey of Higher Degree Apprenticeships (HDAs),' outline the history and rationale of the development of higher degree apprenticeships (HDAs) as well as explore how to embed the real-world ideologies to innovate curriculum. The necessity of strong support structures across the tripartite relationship to best meet the requirements of both apprentices and employers is emphasised. The chapter will also review the added value that HDAs bring, not only to the individual apprentices but to the organisations too, with the use of case studies and feedback from employers on the impact of the apprentice's work-based learning journey.

Part III: 'Future Higher Education Direction: Engaging Real World Learning Through Innovative Pedagogies' is drawn from nine universities in the UK, USA and Australia. It analyses the use of learning strategies, such as reflection and technology, on students' experience of real world learning.

Chapter 12, 'Making Inspiration Mainstream: Innovative Pedagogies for the Real World,' presents pedagogies that are flexible and student-centred and focus on authentic, situated, real world tasks which are complex and non-linear. Buckley and Kukhareva argue for a higher education model that focuses on the 'beyondness' of learning and allows for alternative ways of seeing through the cross-pollination of disciplinary approaches, interactivity outside the subject group and flexibility in teaching spaces. The model makes explicit a learning community that exists beyond the immediate experience of the student with case studies that include a writing café, drama-based pedagogies and a virtual learning environment.

Trelfa, in writing Chapter 13, 'Getting to the Soul': Radical Facilitation of Real World Learning in Higher Education Programmes Through Reflective Practice,' foregrounds reflective practice as integral to real world learning in higher education. Concerning the development of professional 'artistry' of and for post-degree life, literature focusses on the nature and form of reflective activities to foster student scrutiny and therefore control of self and situation whilst engaged in real world learning. Yet, Trelfa's doctoral research suggests the only real 'learning' is correct performance to pass their course. Reflective practice, and real world learning, has 'lost its soul'. Drawing on Lefebvre's (1992/2004) concept of 'breaking-in' to understand this soul-less situation, Trelfa calls for it to be radically different: if real world learning is to live up to its name, then its reflective practice needs to be authentic.

Chapter 14 examines the context of 'real world learning and authentic assessment', and Archer, Morley and Souppez critique the value of building authentic assessment to reflect better a real world learning approach that prepares students more explicitly for employment after graduation. The two case studies within the chapter are drawn from the different disciplines of festival and event management, and yacht design; both aim to prepare students for their respective industries from the onset of their degree programmes. The case studies present how the use of well-managed pedagogic strategies, such as peer review and assessment, reflective practice and the use of formative feedback, can prepare students successfully for authentic and high-risk summative assessments.

The final two chapters of the book specifically focus on the role of technology in real world learning. Bolton and Emery, in Chapter 15, 'Using Educational Technology to Support Students' Real World Learning,' makes the case for students developing a wider skill set for an increasingly digitalised world. This chapter explores technologies such as social media, e- portfolios and recording simulations that augment students' experience, development and readiness for employability. Bolton and Emery look at how educational technology is used to simulate the workplace by capturing and reflecting on actions in real world situations, while recognising that using technology of the workplace can facilitate learning outcomes.

Chapter 16, 'Real Time, Real World Learning—Capitalising on Mobile Technology,' critiques an active learning approach that makes use of mobile technology and augmented reality to enhance students' real world learning. Students are now bringing a variety of mobile technology into the classroom, and Parry, Richards and McAuliffe discuss the challenge of maintaining students' interest and engagement when they can be connected to the world outside the classroom via electronic devices.

The book concludes with a presentation of the research in Chap. 17: 'Conclusion: Real World Learning—Researching and Co-constructing Working Definitions for Curriculum Development and Pedagogy,' co-constructed with the book authors. Through the method of concept mapping, the authors discuss their views and experience of 'real world learning'. A thematic analysis of the author focus groups identifies three themes of fidelity, individuality and mutuality. A discussion of the themes applies the authors' experience of real world curriculum planning and pedagogy in higher education and the future implications that this may entail.

References

Atkins, M. J. (2009). Oven-ready and self-basting: Taking stock of employability skills. *Teaching in Higher Education, 4*(2), 267–280. https://doi.org/10.1080/1356251990040208

Billett, S. (2010). The perils of confusing lifelong learning and lifelong education. *International Journal of Lifelong Education, 29*(4), 401–413. https://doi.org/10.1080/02601370.2010.488803

Boss, S. (2015). Real-world projects: How do I design relevant and engaging learning experiences?. ASCD.

Bridgstock, R. (2009). The graduate attributes we've overlooked: Enhancing graduate employability through career management skills. *Studies in Higher Education, 28*(1), 31–44. https://doi.org/10.1080/07294360802444347

Bridgstock, R., & Cunningham, S. (2016). Creative labour and graduate outcomes: Implications for higher education and cultural policy. *International Journal of Cultural Policy, 22*(1), 10–26. https://doi.org/10.1080/1028663 2.2015.1101086

Ellstrom, P.-E. (2011). Informal learning at work: Conditions, processes and logics. In M. Malloch, L. Cairns, K. Evans, & B. O'Connor (Eds.), *The Sage handbook of workplace learning* (pp. 105–119). London/California/New Delhi/Singapore: Sage.

European Commission. (2014). Educating and training monitor 2014. Retrieved from http://ec.europa.eu/education/library/publications/ monitor14_en.pdf

Finch, D., Falkenberg, L., McLaren, P. G., Rondeau, K. V., & O'Reilly, N. (2018). The rigour–relevance gap in professional programmes: Bridging the 'unbridgeable' between higher education and practice. *Industry and Higher Education, 32*(3), 152–168. https://doi. org/10.1177/0950422218768205

Fuller, A., & Unwin, L. (2003). Learning as apprentices in the contemporary UK workplace: Creating and managing expansive and restrictive participation. *Journal of Education & Work, 16*(4), 407–426. https://doi. org/10.1080/1363908032000093012

Grey, M. (2018, December 27). Graduate outcomes: Necessity is the mother of invention. *Wonkhe.* Retrieved from https://wonkhe.com/blogs/ graduate-outcomes-necessity-is-the-mother-of-invention/

Heath, C., & Heath, D. (2017). *The power of moments: Why certain experiences have extraordinary impact.* London/Toronto/Sydney/Auckland/Johannesburg: Bantam Press.

Herrington, J., Reeves, T. C., & Oliver, R. (2010). *A guide to authentic e-learning.* New York: Routledge.

Holley, K. A. (2009). Understanding interdisciplinary challenges and opportunities in higher education. *ASHE Higher Education Report, 35*(2), 1–131.

Illeris, K. (2003). Towards a contemporary and comprehensive theory of learning. *International Journal of Lifelong Learning, 22*(4), 396–406. https://doi. org/10.1080/02601370304837

Jacoby, B. (2009). *Civic engagement in higher education: Concepts and practices.* John Wiley and Sons.

Kernohan, D. (2018). Plenty ventured, but what was gained?. Retrieved from https://wonkhe.com/blogs/plenty-ventured-but-what-was-gained/

Kinchin, I., Heron, M., Hosein, A., Lygo-Baker, S., Medland, E., Morley, D. A., & Winstone, N. E. (2018). Researcher-led academic development. *International Journal for Academic Development, 23*(4), 339–354. https://doi.org/10.1080/1360144X.2018.1520111

Laur, D. (2013). *Authentic learning experiences: A real-world approach to project-based learning*. Routledge.

Lefebvre, H. (1992/2004). *Rhythm analysis: Space, time and everyday life* (Trans. S. Elden & G. Moore). London: Continuum.

Lester, S., & Costley, C. (2010). Work based learning at higher education level: Value, practice and critique. *Studies in Higher Education, 35*(5), 561–575. https://doi.org/10.1080/03075070903216635

Lucas, B., & Guy, L. (2013). *Expansive education: Teaching learners for the real world*. McGraw-Hill Education.

Marris, P. (2018). *The experience of higher education* (Vol. 17). Routledge.

Mason, G., Williams, G., & Cranmer, S. (2009). Employability skills initiatives in higher education: What effects do they have on graduate labour market outcomes. *Education Economics, 17*(1), 1–30. https://doi.org/10.1080/09645290802028315

Maxwell, M., Stobaugh, R., & Tassell, J. L. (2015). *Real-world learning framework for secondary schools: Digital tools and practical strategies for successful implementation*. Solutions Tree.

Miles, E. W. (2017). Historical context and insights for criticisms of the 21st century business school. *Journal of Education for Business, 92*(5), 245–254. https://doi.org/10.1080/08832323.2017.1335277

Moore, T. J. (2011). Critical thinking and disciplinary thinking: A continuing debate. *Higher Education Research & Development, 30*(3), 261–274. https://doi.org/10.1080/07294360.2010.501328

Morley, D. A. (2017). Degree apprenticeships are a ray of light in a gloomy sector. Retrieved from https://www.timeshighereducation.com/blog/degree-apprenticeships-are-ray-light-gloomy-sector

Morley, D. A., Archer, L., Burgess, M., Curran, D., Milligan, V., & Williams, D. (2017). *A panel discussion—The impact of the university student placement experience on both students and academics*. Paper presented at the ExCiTes Teaching and Learning conference, 5 January 2017, University of Surrey, Guildford, UK.

Nguyen, N. T., Tran, T. L., & Le, T. T. T. (2019). Work-integrated learning for enhancing graduate employability: Moving from the periphery to the Centre of the curriculum. In *Reforming Vietnamese higher education* (pp. 113–132). Singapore: Springer.

Office for Students. (2019). NSS questionnaire 2019. Retrieved from https://www.officeforstudents.org.uk/media/ceed008b-1f02-48ad-b566-d9ca7080376f/nss-2019-questionnaire.pdf

Pearson. (2019). *The global learner survey*. Retrieved from https://www.pearson.com/corporate/news/global-learner-survey.html

Rau, K., Griffith, R. L., & Dieguez, T. A. (2019). Out of the classroom and into the deep end: Real world learning at ICCM. In M. A. Gonzalez-Perez, K. Linded, & V. Taras (Eds.), *The Palgrave handbook of learning and teaching international business and management* (pp. 159–184). Palgrave Macmillan.

Remington-Doucette, S. M., Connell, K. Y. H., Armstrong, C. M., & Musgrove, S. L. (2013). Assessing sustainability education in a transdisciplinary undergraduate course focused on real-world problem solving. *International Journal of Sustainability in Higher Education, 14*(4), 404–433. https://doi.org/10.1108/IJSHE-01-2012-0001

Schön, D. (1983). *The reflective practitioner: How professionals think in action*. Aldershot: Ashgate Publishing Limited.

Shah, H. (2018). Awarding university subjects gold medals is deeply flawed. *The Guardian*. Retrieved from https://www.theguardian.com/higher-education-network/2018/jun/01/awarding-university-subjects-gold-medals-is-deeply-flawed

Sharma, S., Charity, I., Robson, A., & Lillystone, S. (2018). How do students conceptualise a 'real world' learning environment: An empirical study of a financial trading room? *The International Journal of Management Education, 16*(3), 541–557. https://doi.org/10.1016/j.ijme.2017.09.001

Tomlinson, M. (2017). Introduction: Graduate employability in context: Charting a complex, contested and multi-faceted policy and research field. In M. Tomlinson & L. Holmes (Eds.), *Graduate employability in context* (pp. 1–40). London: Palgrave Macmillan.

Trilling, B., & Fadel, C. (2009). *21st century skills: Learning for life in our times*. San Francisco: John Wiley and Sons.

Turner, G. (2011). Surrendering the space: Convergence culture, cultural studies and the curriculum. *Cultural Studies, 25*(4–5), 685–699. https://doi.org/10.1080/09502386.2011.600556

Wenger, E. (1998). *Communities of practice: Learning, meaning and identity.* New York: Cambridge University Press.

Woodside, J. M. (2018). Real-world rigour: An integrative learning approach for industry and higher education. *Industry and Higher Education, 32*(5), 285–289. https://doi.org/10.1177/0950422218784535

Part I

Emerging Responses in Real World Learning

2

Internal Knowledge Transfer: Professional Development Programmes and Embedding Real World Learning for Full-Time Undergraduates

David Perrin, Connie Hancock, and Ruth Miller

Introduction

Negotiated work-based learning (NWBL) frameworks have existed in higher education (HE) in the UK for around 30 years. Thousands of students who are part-time learners at work have gained undergraduate or postgraduate awards through their study on them (Major, 2016; Talbot, 2017). They have involved a particular set of approaches to learning, teaching and assessment for experienced adult professional practitioners, many of which have been distinct from the more traditional pedagogic approaches used for students studying on full-time

Case Studies: Connie Hancock and Ruth Miller

D. Perrin (✉) • C. Hancock
University of Chester, Chester, UK
e-mail: d.perrin@chester.ac.uk

R. Miller
School of Health and Education, Middlesex University, London, UK

© The Author(s) 2021
D. A. Morley, M. G. Jamil (eds.), *Applied Pedagogies for Higher Education*,
https://doi.org/10.1007/978-3-030-46951-1_2

21

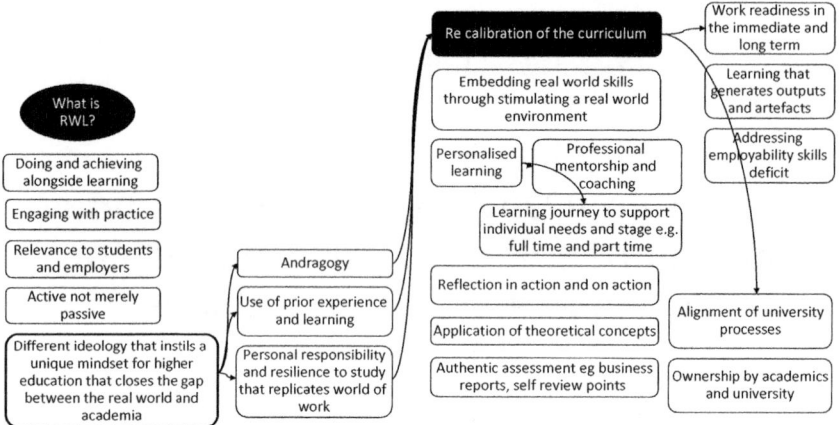

Fig. 2.1 Concept map from the authors

undergraduate programmes (Wall & Perrin, 2015). Some attempts in recent years have been made to 'leverage' the academic practice deployed on negotiated work-based learning frameworks for other purposes, specifically including the fostering of 'real world learning' for full-time undergraduates. The chapter examines how this leveraging can theoretically happen—and is now also happening in practice—to meet the needs of the economy and wider society for 'work-ready' graduates who are able to apply their learning in real world scenarios as well as critically reflect on this. Key concepts and issues related to this have been identified in the associate concept map (Fig. 2.1).

NWBL: Characteristics

NWBL involves the creation of a distinct and ragogic learning culture which in many respects is different to 'traditional', didactic higher education. Philosophically, its starting point is that much of the knowledge capital in society exists outside of the academy and resides in workplaces and with the professionals that work in them (Boud & Symes, 2000; Garnett, Comerford, & Webb, 2001; Talbot, 2017). In this respect, it draws its inspiration and approaches to learning from outside of the academy in large part too, being focused on the development and enhancement of professional knowledge across a range of practice areas. Its progressive view of education is thus associated with the ideas articulated by Dewey (1897) concerning the need to integrate learning and experience.

NWBL does not intrinsically relate to a particular subject discipline or set of disciplines, and is essentially trans-disciplinary in approach (Nicolescu, 2002). Nevertheless, it has common features wherever it is found that make it distinctive and different to more traditional, didactic higher education. In this respect its key features can be identified as being:

- academic recognition for work-based, experiential learning and associated critical reflection on this;
- an andragogic methodology of learning facilitation rather than a pedagogic method of didactic instruction;
- personal and professional skill audits to help inform the choice and planning of development opportunities;
- enabling participants to negotiate key aspects of their learning in ways that reflect their area of practice (including their learning outcomes, methods of assessment and, in some cases, even award titles);
- the intrinsic and conscious embedding of professional skills and capabilities within the curriculum;
- an emphasis on inquiry-based learning, designed to address practical, real-work problems and issues;
- a curriculum that is driven by workplace and professional requirements rather than one pre-configured by the academy according to prevalent academic subject expertise and interests;
- assessment that is work-based and/or work-related, allowing artefacts principally created in and through work to be included for the purposes of academic reward;
- the opportunity to recognise, enhance and build on relevant prior learning (whether certificated or experiential).

Some of these approaches are also used on occasion in more general professional practice programmes and contexts where NWBL frameworks are not necessarily in operation. However, NWBL typically brings together *all* the features above in a unique way and in this respect exists as an exemplar of how learning can be fostered and captured in HE by using innovative, non-traditional methods (if modern HE teaching, learning and assessment can be seen as a spectrum, NWBL occupies one end of it—arguably the most vivid). Indeed, for similar reasons NWBL frameworks have sometimes been at the forefront of other new initiatives in HE too such as developments in online and distance learning (Stephenson & Saxton, 2005). Staff involved in them therefore have a tendency to develop an ideological cohesion around their educational practice that helps foster distinct communities of practice around these approaches to teaching, learning and assessment (Talbot, Perrin, & Meakin, 2019).

NWBL: Approaches and Practices for 'Real World Learning'

NWBL is, in essence, based on what has been termed Mode 2 learning rather than Mode 1 learning; that is, it is learning largely generated and held in professional contexts that is typically not aligned to conventional conceptions of academic disciplines (Gibbons et al., 1994). Being mainly experiential and underpinned by reflective practice, it needs expression outside of classroom environments—in real world situations and practices. Only then can the interplay between learning that is taught and learning that is experienced and applied be readily identified and assimilated. The process of critical reflection is able to reveal this process and in doing so deepen and enhance the learning further (Brookfield, 1991).

It would be near impossible to draw up an exhaustive list of what this might entail, but typical examples of the types of knowledge and skill involved from a variety of areas of professional practice would include thinking strategically; applying or adapting learning to new contexts; solving problems so as to create a positive impact; working with other people effectively; communicating professionally; transcending disagreement or conflict; managing and delivering specific tasks and projects to schedule; allocating limited resources effectively.

Many, if not most, of these attributes are difficult to learn outside of professional contexts—for instance, while a full-time undergraduate student may learn to solve certain types of problems and be confronted by many of these in formal examinations that test them, problem-solving in a real work context is a different matter. It is one thing to solve a mathematical problem but quite another to apply it to an unfamiliar (and possibly changing) context where it becomes just one factor to consider among many others, such as in a situation of resource allocation where supply is limited and demand is uncertain.

Because of this, while traditional learning in undergraduate programmes has value, this value is necessarily limited and constrained. It is only through application and contextualisation in real world situations that it can be truly tested and where its impact can be assessed in the round (Boud & Symes, 2000). This is where much traditional HE learning is perceived as falling short, even vocational learning fostered by business schools with 'work-ready' graduates very much in mind (Bennis & O'Toole, 2005; Jackson, 2013).

One way in which more traditional programmes aimed at full-time undergraduates can seek to address this issue is by incorporating methods and approaches developed by staff engaged in NWBL more widely, most productively by rewriting and recalibrating undergraduate programmes where possible to enable real world learning using these methods. There are a number of ways in which this can happen—some fundamental and distinctive, others more subtle.

Some of these methods involve a replication or simulation of real world scenarios and work processes (refer to Chap. 9). But others involve learners engaging at a fundamental level in experiential learning that intrinsically involves the principles and practices of NWBL. For this to happen, learners need to have access to experiential learning opportunities, and this can happen in a variety of ways—through part-time work, through volunteering or through placement opportunities arranged by the university itself (Helyer & Lee, 2014).

Significant examples of ways this can happen include the following:

1. Introduction of learning agreements: learning agreements (or contracts) can be used to allow learners flexibility in terms of curriculum design. This can exist both at a programme level and at a module level (such as where there are negotiated learning opportunities like work-based projects). A particular curriculum may involve a number of prede-termined modules but may allow flexibility in terms of other academic credits so as to enable the reward of situated, experiential learning that is negotiated between students, tutors and—where relevant—employers. Learning agreements are designed to empower students to see the work-place as both the site of knowledge generation and the motor-force for designing the 'real world' curriculum and so constitute an important way of facilitating this within HE (Knowles, 1986; Major, 2016; Stephenson & Laycock, 1993; Talbot, 2017).

2. Use of skills audit and programme planning modules: these are designed to enable learners to develop an awareness of their personal and professional development, their progress in this regard and the opportu-nities that can be identified for future enhancement and academic reward. In addition, they often encourage students to uncover their preferences and filters through engagement with concepts such as learning styles and personality type, helping students develop a consideration of what Eraut has described as personal knowledge (Eraut, 2010). These processes can then feed into the curriculum design itself to address gaps in skills and knowledge while building on—and enhancing—identified preferences. The results of these processes will typically vary from student to student and will form the basis of the creation of the negotiated curriculum and the personalised learning agreement that captures this in HE (Talbot, 2017; Willis, 2008).

3. Integration of WBL project modules into the curriculum: many, if not most, NWBL frameworks use 'shell' or 'template' modules which are characterised by generic aims, learning outcomes and assessment methods, and which can then be customised for specific circumstances by learners. This typically involves work-based projects, or else experiential learning which may cross-cut individual projects but relate to a learning theme (such as presentation skills or effective web design). This approach encourages learners to specifically relate their real world experiential learning to academic process and development, and allows the confer-ment of academic credit for this (Little & Brennan, 1996).

4. Systematic integration of reflective practice into the curriculum: there is a huge body of literature on the use of reflective practice for educational purposes, and NWBL uses this as a key method for surfacing deep learning and tacit knowledge (Raelin, 2008). This can be embedded not just in work-based experiential learning such as project modules or similar, but also in those instances where students take learning that has sometimes been introduced in more traditional ways (marketing, resource allocation, etc.) and then learn more deeply by applying this learning and critically reflecting on the learning processes and achievements (Talbot, 2017).

5. Embedding opportunities for the recognition of prior experiential learning, where relevant: allowing room in the curriculum for germane experiential learning also opens up the possibility of allowing students with considerable prior workplace experience and learning to claim credit for this and to deepen the learning by reflecting on it. Opportunity for this in traditional HE courses is often limited because work-based experiential learning is 'messy' (Raelin, 2008) and does not often map easily into predetermined module learning outcomes. However, incorporating shell modules such as work-based projects into the curriculum allows students to compile claims, where relevant, for their prior experiential learning and in doing so draw parallels and meaning from this and their more formal taught learning (Perrin & Helyer, 2015).

6. Incorporation of assessment methods typical to NWBL programmes: this enables students to integrate artefacts and activities linked to the workplace as a legitimate means of demonstrating knowledge and capability. This could range from physical artefacts such as reports produced, or digital media created, through to assessment of presentations given to colleagues. These can be used towards the notional word count of modules and can allow learners to see the academic relevance and currency of workplace learning (Boud, 2000; Brodie & Irving, 2007; Talbot, 2017).

Case Studies of Real World Learning

There are clearly a variety of ways in which 'leveraging' of NWBL approaches can occur, and we explore two case studies of where this has been happening in practice. Both of these are from universities with well-known NWBL frameworks and which have had sizeable numbers of students across a wide range of professional practice areas—and for many years. Staff involved in the facilitation of learning and assessment on them have built up considerable expertise in these fields and have developed genuine communities of academic practice (Major, Meakin, & Perrin, 2011; Workman & Garnett, 2009) that have helped foster and disseminate these practices—including internally at the universities concerned.

For over two decades the Centre for Work Related Studies (CWRS) at the University of Chester and what became the Institute for Work Based Learning (IWBL) at Middlesex University have been prominent exponents of NWBL in HE. Both have recruited significant numbers of students (typically with over a thousand part-time learners at any one time in each case) and have developed their NWBL expertise in a wide range of fields ranging from business and management through to health and education (Talbot et al., 2019). They have also disseminated their practice in developing pioneering approaches to experiential learning, negotiated learning and prior learning, among others (Garnett, Costley, & Workman, 2009; Perrin, Weston, Thompson, & Brodie, 2010; Talbot, 2017).

On a practical level—and driven by what could be called an ideological commitment to these types of HE learning—this has sometimes involved assisting other universities develop their own WBL frameworks. Latterly, this has also involved helping full-time undergraduate courses address the criticism that they are not producing 'job-ready' graduates and are not fully enabling students to claim academic reward for learning outside of traditional pedagogic environments. In each instance, the universities concerned have leveraged the skills and knowledge of their staff involved in NWBL to create alternative learning opportunities that can be embedded in full-time undergraduate curricula.

The first case study is from Chester, where the university developed the Work Based and Integrative Studies (WBIS) framework from 1998 onwards, housed and managed in the Centre for Work Related Studies. Over a period of years, CWRS worked closely with Chester Business School in the University to recalibrate the undergraduate offer for full-time business and management students, including those in specific fields such as events management and tourism management. The following case study explores one of the main ways in which this has been approached.

Case Study 1

Leveraging NWBL in the Business School at the University of Chester (Connie Hancock, Head of Department for Enterprise, Leadership and Management, University of Chester, UK)

What follows is a discussion relating to applied research that was undertaken in the Business School to make provision for a partnership approach with business to support pragmatic assessment and formal acknowledgement of skills and learning acquisition gleaned through a 12-month undergraduate industrial placement for full-time students. This used many of the principles and approaches to learning, teaching and assessment developed within the University's NWBL framework.

There were 1.77 million undergraduate students, according to the Higher Education Statistics Agency, that were studying at UK institutions in 2017–2018, the majority of whom will amass significant debt towards securing a first rung on the career ladder. It is seen as an essential responsibility of higher education to prepare and equip these graduates for the workplace environment (CBI, 2009; Jackson & Chapman, 2012). Nevertheless, embedding real world business skills into a business degree programme and immersing undergraduates in the authentic, dynamic world of business is acknowledged as providing a source of challenge in HE. In response to this, institutions, practitioners and theorists alike see work-related placements and experiential, career-focused learning as fostering an informed approach to students' career planning and thinking (Morley, 2018; Wilson, 2012). To this end, business undergraduates at Chester, having completed the first two years of their degree programme, are now offered the opportunity to undertake an experiential learning placement year in industry, either in the UK or abroad.

The Business School has cultivated a range of relationships with external businesses and organisations with the objective of building sustainable links for mutually beneficial partnerships. Assessment of student placement activities drove dialogue with placement providers and led to opportunities for research into client and student needs and the development of an innovative approach to assessing experiential learning.

Sandwich placements and internships provide experiential interventions that make provision for the application of formal learning in a pragmatic, work-related environment (Edwards, 2014; Paglis Dwyer, 2013). The methodology through which this work-related experiential learning is assessed is a formal, academic system that lays greater emphasis on the formulating of the experience into what is an accepted traditional academic assignment that obscures the action orientation of the workplace. At Chester Business School, making provision for an assessment methodology that permits a more work-related, attitudinal, action- and behavioural-focused exploration of the student's performance as an employee in a work-based environment has been a challenge. It is this objective to align relevant assessment with student outputs in an industrial setting that prompted this research.

The interviewing by staff of 64 Chester Business School sandwich placement students and 58 workplace supervisors over the course of the industrial placement year 2017–2018 enabled the development of an innovative 'Action Portfolio' as the key point of assessment for experiential learning.

Student placements aid the acquisition of attributes, responses, behaviours, competencies and skills likely to significantly impact on student career insight (Edwards, 2014; Major, 2016). Placements secure links between institution and external agencies and organisations and support and build student competencies that aren't simply connected to career and employability development (Boud, Keogh, & Walker, 1985; Edwards, 2014). Undergraduates returning after industrial placement at Chester displayed and referred to personal achievement systematically, with these typical responses:

> I have delivered presentations and coordinated so many events and talks that nothing fazes me now. I can present to anyone and any number. I feel I have gained confidence for myself. (Student A)

> I knew what was needed and I was confident that I could deliver. (Student B)

> I know I can handle things now and I didn't know that before. (Student C)

Whilst the development of such core skills are key in the development of work-ready graduates, the assessment of these outcomes is typically formal and inert in HE, with students being required to demonstrate their academic articulation as opposed to work competence. A lack of scholarly dexterity in the formulation of an assessment does not necessarily correlate with the level of performance in the work-focused environment. The relevant assessment of experiential learning is vital in establishing work-related competencies, responsiveness in the workplace and the capacity to undertake appropriate actions and carry out key tasks, and as such it should not simply be associated with demonstrating academic prowess. Therein lay the challenge faced by Chester Business School. The data from our study indicated that high-performing interns were not necessarily reflecting their work-related competencies to a commensurate level in written format.

Following an analysis of the interviews and subsequent findings of the data gleaned from both students and workplace supervisor respondents, the Sandwich Placement Support Team set about designing a new assessment that would empower students to more effectively demonstrate high-level workplace experiential learning.

An Action Portfolio emerged from this study as a methodology of students being able to effectively communicate workplace experiential competencies. The portfolio consists of components established through research with placement providers, tutors and student interns and draws on approaches from the University's WBIS framework for part-time learners. This includes many of the nine key characteristics of NWBL listed above. In this way, comprehensive analysis of the data emanating from the study led to the establishment of a six-component Action Portfolio that is student and employer centred:

- **A learning agreement** consisting of ten learning objectives set after commencement of the placement via triangulated discussion between workplace supervisor, tutor and student intern. This sets the context for the mapping of the experiential learning journey; what skills and competencies the student has acquired and how they have been secured. Additions and amendments to the learning objectives may be recorded and discussed as the placement trajectory progresses. This component of the portfolio makes provision for planned and unplanned experiential learning and minimises the role of the tutor. Placement provider and student are best placed through an understanding of role and responsibility to draw up the learning objectives. The tutor's role is one of facilitation in this process.

- **Two workplace observations** of the intern, with two pre- and post-observational discussions carried out by the supporting tutor where the application of formal learning to a practical task is considered by the student. Both of these 'observations' are documented and included in the final portfolio as evidence of learning, with annotations by the student and, when appropriate and available, the workplace supervisor.
- **Two feedback sessions** with the workplace supervisor, with each of these discussions set into a report format that is either written by the supervisor or captured by the supporting tutor. This narrative may include any performance ratings, personal development reviews and skills audits, comments on progress or simply general comments and observations on the student's contribution to the organisation. These feedback sessions may take place at the time of the workplace observations.
- **Delivery of a presentation** within a 'mid-term conference', taking place, as the name suggests, halfway through their placement. The presentation is delivered to workplace representatives, Level 4 students who—the following year—will be applying for sandwich placements and current Level 5 students who will be currently making applications. The presentation deals with placement acquisition, organisation, and role, learning to date, negotiated learning objectives and how this learning will be utilised. Together with the question and answer phase, the presentation is recorded for portfolio submission and post-event critical reflection.
- **A critically reflective commentary** on practice that is underpinned with supporting academic references and evidence in the appendix. Supporting evidence of action, workplace output and competency level may be included with organisational approval.

- **Two curriculum vitae** are required to form a component of the portfolio: one from the time of application of the placement and the other written at the time of placement completion. This inclusion, together with an annotated comparison of the two, emphasises the skills audit element helping to identify the 'transformation' taken place during the 12-month industrial placement.

The Action Portfolio components are mapped to employer needs in the business environment and research undertaken with students and tutors. This assessment strategy was deployed as a way of assessing students in the academic year 2018–2019 with significant success and resulted in an 18% increase in marks awarded to placement students. The external examiner acknowledged the results of this innovative assessment methodology, and the organisations continue to be involved in the partnership to empower interns to demonstrate experiential learning.

Case Study 2

Middlesex University 'Volunteering Module' (Ruth Miller, Director of WBL Programmes, School of Health and Education, Middlesex University, London)

The second case study is from Middlesex University and examines the creation of the University's volunteering module for full-time undergraduates. This utilises the negotiated and experiential learning approach specifically developed in the University's work-based learning framework for professional practitioners.

Opportunities for real world and work-based learning have a significant contribution to make in developing the employability and transferable skills that are now required outcomes for all graduates through the UK Teaching Excellence Framework (Department of Education, 2017). Although professional degrees such as nursing and social work already involve well-developed work placements, these are primarily for the enhancement and assessment of specific skills and competencies. More flexible work-based modules can provide an opportunity for students to develop (and have recognition for) wider personal, professional and transferable attributes valued by employers and society.

During the recent revalidation of the negotiated work-based programmes for part-time professional practitioners within the School of Health and Education at Middlesex University, the work-based project and professional development modules were specifically validated so they could also be applied within full-time undergraduate degree programmes. This opportunity has been recently adopted in the newly validated BSc Mental Health Nursing degree, where a small 15-credit work-based project module has been adapted to offer an 'expansive learning' option called a 'work-based volunteering activity' during year 2 of the programme.

'Work-based volunteering activity' module learning outcomes are:
On completion of this module, the successful student will be able to:

- apply theoretical knowledge gained through volunteering activity to own professional practice and demonstrate an appreciation of the wider context of health and well-being.

This module will call for the successful student to demonstrate:

- effective engagement and communication with relevant stakeholders.
- reflection on activity outcomes and critical evaluation of own practice to inform professional development and action plan.

(Acknowledgement to Nicky Lambert, Director of Teaching and Learning Mental Health and Social Work, Middlesex University)

This option requires students to undertake—or draw on existing—volunteer work, negotiate specific activities via a learning agreement and critically discuss the learning gained to inform their own professional development. It provides a real world opportunity for students to develop the graduate attributes now required of all Middlesex University graduates, in particular being 'ethically informed and taking social responsibility', 'being culturally competent' and 'effective team players' (Middlesex University Graduate Attributes 2018/2019).

Whereas in their formal placements students are primarily required to apply their theoretical nursing knowledge to their developing practice, in this module they are extracting learning out of their practice and applying this back to their wider, developing, professional understanding.

Many of the teaching and learning strategies developed to support professionals at work to reflect on and recognise their WBL (as in the nine key characteristic of NWBL above) are being applied to support these full-time undergraduates. In particular, critical reflection on their practice (both reflection in-action and on-action) has become key to maximising their learning. For example, asking structured questions about their own practice, both when things are not going well (*Why was that an issue? What problem-solving techniques did I use to address that issue?*) and when they are going well (*Who did I have to engage with to make that happen? How did the way I communicate facilitate that exchange?*). Although the depth and level of criticality will vary depending on the academic level required, this type of structured reflection is useful for all students undertaking practice learning.

The learning outcomes of the module are assessed through a professional portfolio requiring students to provide evidence of the activities they have engaged in as well as a critical reflection on how these activities are developing both their theoretical understanding and their broad professional skills. They are especially encouraged to consider their development within a wider social context and to provide an action plan of how they will develop these skills further. Rowe and Zegwaard (2017) stress the importance of appropriate assessment activities to support employability outcomes, and this type of portfolio assessment is flexible and relevant to students in a wide range of volunteering situations.

Other undergraduates can be encouraged to engage meaningfully in volunteering work by having their efforts recognised through such a module. Opportunities certainly exist within the University for student voice leaders (representatives) and students' union officers to develop graduate attributes and gain credit in this way.

Conclusion

This chapter has demonstrated that universities have incentives to work across perceived 'silos' and that there are clear advantages to drawing on the expertise developed through professional practice programmes of negotiated learning. This can enhance the overall learning experience for full-time undergraduate students striving for engagement that can in some ways reflect 'real world' issues, and who can then use this for professional development purposes. The challenge is often in building the type of internal culture that can enable this knowledge transfer to occur within the HE organisation. In particular, it requires academic managers and teaching staff to be receptive to 'non-traditional' forms of HE and to work openly with colleagues on this basis. This involves reappraisal very often of their own role as academics, challenging the status and practices associated with the narrow and didactic 'subject specialism' that has often been one of the hallmarks of HE.

Useful ways of enabling this in practice have included workshop sessions that have showcased the type of approaches used on WBIS at Chester and the WBL framework at Middlesex, together with opportunities for those who have only previously engaged with traditional programmes to get involved with shadowing staff who are specialists in the facilitation and assessment of NWBL (as a method rather than as a subject). These approaches are anticipated priorities for NWBL academic managers and would-be practitioners.

Our two case studies show that where such mindsets exist this can indeed be done—and with positive results for students.

References

Bennis, W., & O'Toole, J. (2005, May). How business schools lost their way. *Harvard Business Review*.

Boud, D. (2000). Sustainable assessment: Rethinking assessment for the learning society. *Studies in Continuing Education, 22*(2), 151–167. https://doi.org/10.1080/713695728

Boud, D., Keogh, R., & Walker, D. (Eds.). (1985). *Reflection: Turning experience into learning*. Oxford: Routledge.

Boud, D., & Symes, C. (2000). Learning for real: Work based education in universities. In C. Symes & J. McIntyre (Eds.), *Working knowledge: The new vocationalism and higher education*. Berkshire: SRHE/OUP.

Brodie, P., & Irving, K. (2007). Assessment in work-based learning: Investigating a pedagogical approach to enhance student learning. *Assessment*

& *Evaluation in Higher Education, 32*(1), 11–19. https://doi.org/10.1080/02602930600848218

Brookfield, S. (1991). *Developing critical thinkers: Challenging adults to explore alternative ways of thinking and acting.* San Francisco: Jossey-Bass.

Confederation of British Industry. (2009). *Future fit: Preparing graduates for the world of work.* CBI.

Department of Education. (2017). *Teaching excellence and student outcomes framework specification.* Retrieved from https://assets.publishing.service.gov.uk/government/uploads/system/uploads/attachment_data/file/658490/Teaching_Excellence_and_Student_Outcomes_Framework_Specification.pdf

Dewey, J. (1897). My pedagogic creed. *The School Journal, 54*(3), 77–80.

Edwards, M. (2014). The impact of placements on students' self-efficacy. *Higher Education, Skills and Work-Based Learning, 4*(3), 228–241. https://doi.org/10.1108/HESWBL-05-2014-0015

Eraut, M. (2010). Knowledge, working practices, and learning. In S. Billett (Ed.), *Learning Through Practice, professional and practice-based learning 1.* Dordrecht: Springer.

Garnett, J., Comerford, A., & Webb, N. (2001). Working with partners to promote intellectual capital. In D. Boud & N. Solomon (Eds.), *Work based learning: A new higher education?* Buckingham: SRHE/OUP.

Garnett, J., Costley, C., & Workman, B. (Eds.). (2009). *Work based learning: Journeys to the Core of higher education.* London: Middlesex University Press.

Gibbons, M., Limoges, C., Notwotny, H., Schwartzman, S., Scott, P., & Trow, M. (1994). *The new production of knowledge: The dynamics of science and research in contemporary societies.* London: Sage.

Helyer, R., & Lee, D. (2014). The role of work experience in the future employability of higher education graduates. *Higher Education Quarterly, 68*(3), 348–372. https://doi.org/10.1111/hequ.12055

Jackson, D. (2013). Business graduate employability—Where are we going wrong? *Higher Education Research & Development, 32*(5), 776–790. https://doi.org/10.1080/07294360.2012.709832

Jackson, D., & Chapman, E. (2012). Non-technical competencies in undergraduate business degree programs: Australian and UK perspectives. *Studies in Higher Education, 37*(5), 541–567. https://doi.org/10.1080/03075079.2010.527935

Knowles, M. (1986). *Using learning contracts: Practical approaches to Individualising and structuring learning.* San Francisco: Jossey Bass.

Little, B., & Brennan, J. (1996). *A Review of Work Based Learning in Higher Education*. Sheffield: Department for Education and Employment.

Major, D. (2016). Models of work-based learning, examples and reflections. *Journal of Work-Applied Management, 8*(1), 17–28. ISSN: 2205-2062.

Major, D., Meakin, D., & Perrin, D. (2011). Building the capacity of higher education to deliver programmes of work-based learning. *Higher Education, Skills and Work-Based Learning, 1*(2), 118–127. ISSN: 2042-3896.

Middlesex University. (2017). *Middlesex graduate attributes 2017/18*. Section 3 learning quality enhancement handbook. Retrieved from https://www.mdx.ac.uk/about-us/policies/academic-quality/handbook/lqe-handbook-section-3

Morley, D. (Ed.). (2018). *Enhancing employability in higher education through work based learning*. London: Palgrave Macmillan.

Nicolescu, B. (2002). *Manifesto of transdisciplinarity*. New York: State University of New York Press.

Paglis Dwyer, L. (2013). A review of managerial skills training in the classroom. *Journal of Management Education, 37*, 472–498. https://doi.org/10.1177/1052562912436516

Perrin, D., & Helyer, R. (2015). Make your learning count: Recognition of prior learning. In R. Helyer (Ed.), *The work based learning student handbook*. Basingstoke: Macmillan.

Perrin, D., Weston, P., Thompson, P., & Brodie, P. (2010). *Facilitating employer engagement through negotiated work based learning*. Bristol: HEFCE/DWP.

Raelin, J. (2008). *Work-based learning: Bridging knowledge and action in the workplace*. San Francisco: Jossey Bass.

Rowe, A., & Zegwaard, K. (2017). Developing graduate employability skills and attributes through work integrated learning. *Asia-Pacific Journal of Cooperative Education, 18*(2), 87–99.

Stephenson, J., & Laycock, M. (Eds.). (1993). *Using learning contracts in higher education*. London: Kogan Page.

Stephenson, J., & Saxton, J. (2005). Using the internet to gain personalized degrees from learning through work: Some experience from Ufi. *Industry and Higher Education, 19*(3), 249–258.

Talbot, J. (2017). Curriculum design for the post-industrial society: The facilitation of individually negotiated higher education in work based learning shell frameworks in the United Kingdom. In R. V. Nata (Ed.), *Progress in education* (Vol. 44, pp. 127–161). New York, NY: Nova Science Publishers.

Talbot, J., Perrin, D., & Meakin, R. (2019). What does it take for flexible learning to survive? A UK case study. In *Higher education, skills and work-based learning, 10 (1)*. https://doi.org/10.1108/HESWBL-02-2019-0022

Wall, T., & Perrin, D. (2015). *A Zizekian gaze at education*. London: Springer.

Willis, K. (2008). Framework for work-based learning. In F. Tallantyre (Ed.), *Work based learning, workforce development: Connections, frameworks and processes*. York: Higher Education Academy.

Wilson, T. (2012). *A review of business–University collaboration*. London, Department for Business, Innovation & Skills.

Workman, B., & Garnett, J. (2009). The development and implementation of work based learning at Middlesex University. In J. Garnett, C. Costley, & B. Workman (Eds.), *Work based learning: Journeys to the core of higher education*. London: Middlesex University.

3

The Role of Professional Networks in Supporting and Developing Real World Learning

Joanne Brindley and Stuart Sims

Introduction: The Changing Context of Higher Education

It is perhaps an understatement to say that the nature of UK higher education has shifted in the last decade. Not least of these changes is the transfer of the burden of funding higher education exclusively on to students and graduates. Much has been said about the dangers of marketisation and the rise of the student as consumer and potential risks this has for changing staff-student interaction (Molesworth, Scullion, & Nixon, 2010). In an environment where students' choices and expectations are shaped by an eye-watering price tag for their degree, there is an increasing requirement to ensure that they gain value for these costs (Woodall,

---

Case Studies: Joanne Brindley, Stuart Sims, Susan Noble and Amy Barlow

---

J. Brindley (✉) • S. Sims
University of Portsmouth, Portsmouth, UK
e-mail: joanne.brindley@port.ac.uk

© The Author(s) 2021
D. A. Morley, M. G. Jamil (eds.), *Applied Pedagogies for Higher Education*,
https://doi.org/10.1007/978-3-030-46951-1_3

Hiller, & Resnick, 2014). This value is often determined in a narrow, economically rationalised way which manifests itself in myriad new behaviours ranging from calculating the cost of an individual lecture to expecting to pass without reasonable engagement because they are 'paying for their degree'. In this neo-liberal model that prioritises economic exchange value, inevitably students will be looking at their job prospects and employability. Such an attitude has recently become enshrined as a representative measure of teaching quality by including employment (although importantly not employability) statistics in the Teaching Excellence Framework (TEF) (n.d.).

Expectations of Staff

While few members of academic staff in universities will be surprised by these changes, what is remarkable is the lack of substantial shifts in how, but importantly also the why of engagement with students. At the thin end of this wedge is making a case of what university is for. Many writers have addressed this extensively and exhaustively without reaching any satisfying end (Collini, 2012). Others have decried that the university is in 'ruins' (Readings, 1996) or other hyperbolic ideas which are hard to confirm without any consensus. One of the few potential ways forward out of these wide-ranging critiques comes from Barnett (2000) who argues that the (or at least a) purpose of the university is to prepare graduates for a super-complex society. Importantly, this is not restricted to 'economy' but rather recognises the importance of graduates being well rounded and adaptable to survive in a rapidly changing information-rich society. To do this effectively, Barnett argues that a move towards an ecological university is required (2017). Such an institution would reflect deeply on its whole role in society and multiple ecosystems within which it sits. Barnett suggests the following range spheres as ecologically relevant to the university: "knowledge, social institutions, persons, the economy, learning, culture and natural environment" (2017, p. 9).

For too long the economic ecosystem has dominated the shape and purpose of universities. In order to rebalance the situation towards prioritisation of the other ecological purposes of the university, there is a need to evoke a change in the way in which we engage with students and how

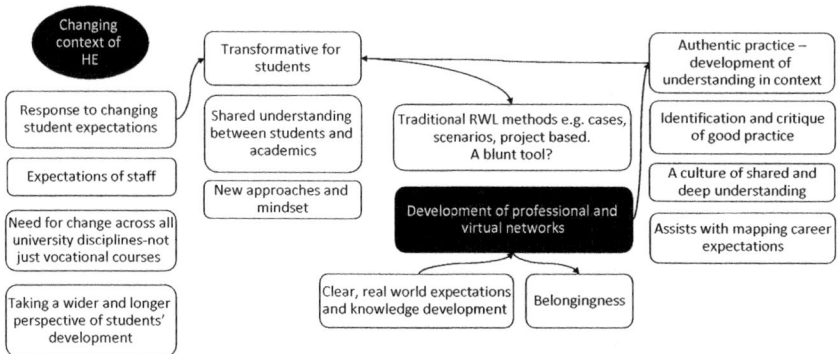

Fig. 3.1 The role of professional networks in supporting and developing real world learning

they reflect on their own priorities. Part of this must come to a necessary broadening of the concept of real world learning. All too often is this seen as synonymous with a narrow economic view, essentially that the real world is only comparable to jobs and often in a tedious and reductionist way.

This chapter seeks to explore how cooperative professional learning networks can be used as a vehicle to rebalance curriculum architecture, bringing a renewed sense of equilibrium to the learning environment, in readiness for the challenges of planning educational experiences which will prepare cohorts for the challenges of future super-complexity, using the key themes identified in concept map (Fig. 3.1).

Developing Professional and Virtuous Networks

Communities of Practice (CoP) have been identifed by Wenger and Trayner (2015, p. 1) as "groups of people who share a concern or a passion for something they do and learn how to do it better as they interact regularly"; encompassed within this definition there is an expectation that an element of learning will occur. However, as Wenger-Trayner clearly state, the occurrence of learning within a CoP cannot always be assumed.

The central tenet of a Professional CoP (PCoP), within the context of this chapter, is that all members of a structured PCoP have the expectation that the activities they undertake will be embarked upon with express intention that learning and development will be supported by all at its heart. The formation of a PCoP is to create a vehicle in which acknowledged workplace and academic masters alongside novice professionals come together to embark on a process of legitimate peripheral participation (the process of actively participating in communities of practice which facilitates the process of learning and participation, via a social context, enabling novice learners to become experts), which is embedded within a model of situated learning and facilitated via social interaction. The benefits of the coming together to cooperate as a PCoP support the deliberate construction of knowledge and the development of relational and technical skills, which are anchored within the methodised realms of the working world, opposed to a process of cognitive transmission situated exclusively within the academic environment.

Alongside the obvious benefits of a shared PCoP, there are also opportunities during real world learning activities for informal networking with future professional colleagues to occur, acting as a cornerstone which does not seek to influence future job prospects but, instead, becomes a linchpin for providing insight into future pathways via workplace supporters (e.g. mentors, coaches and supporters). This virtuous network allows students to access people who they can draw upon in the present and future to bring a sense of reality and context related to their individual experiences, which are additionally supplemented by the perceived sense of belongingness and value that a PCoP culture facilitates. Indeed, Wenger, Trayner and De Laat (2011, pp. 19–21) and Poole, Iqbal and Verwood (2018, p. 10) have identified the various forms of value which are generated from a CoP—"immediate value (for example, via activities and interactions which reveal a new perspective), potential value (which is not always apparent at first, but provides 'knowledge capital' which can be drawn upon at a later date), applied value (which has the capacity to change practice, leading to innovation), realised value (the process of reflecting on the application of knowledge), reframing value (leading to transformation of existing practices)" and "aspirational value (which may be open to the influence of others)".

Authentic Practice

Academic staff have a pivotal role in identifying ways to support the acquisition of more imaginative real world learning experiences, allowing students to acquire theoretical academic knowledge which in turn can be applied in real world settings. The meaningful application of translating theory into practice exposes students to the challenges of working in contemporary society. This does not occur solely within the act of knowledge application, but also assists in gaining a broader perspective by critically appraising the actions they have taken. Students can then consider the effect(s) their actions have had, allowing cognisance of the tacit norms and appreciations which underpin the situation and the broader organisational context. As Boyer (1990) has identified, if students are inspired to learn and discover more through independent search and inquiry, their learning experiences will become richer. By developing accountable real world experiences, students can explore their actions and beliefs on a deeper level, which will assist them in preparing for future active citizenship.

Developing a Culture of Shared and Deep Understanding

Education is a process where fledgling practitioners should be facilitated in developing the autonomy to make their own choices based on informed understanding, analysis and critical thinking. The process of being enabled to think critically invites the students to evaluate their own personal learning and create a conscious understanding of how they are making decisions and how this, in turn, is influencing their practice. Therefore, it is essential that educational providers are confident that their students are endowed with these skills, even if this may be uncomfortable to the developing cohort.

Providing an opportunity for the PCoP stakeholders to meet together on a regular basis, either formally or informally, provides a vehicle in which students are able to air and share their views and experiences in a safe space, facilitating the development of attributes required of graduates

(Cameron, Binnie, Sherriff, & Bissell, 2015). Reflective group activities are an obvious gateway mechanism to support student development with the main emphasis being placed on reflection around the *practice* aspect. It is important to remember that the act of reflection should not be perceived as a relaxed meditative process; indeed, critically reflecting on one's own behaviour is a challenging and demanding process (Osterman & Kottkamp, 1993). Davies and Kremer (2016) have described how reflection on negative or demanding events can enact an acute stress response, generating a flight or fight approach to reflective tasks (Fig. 3.2).

In order to negate using the process of reflection as a confessional or personal crusade, there should be a clear sense of purpose and balance articulated prior to this activity. The PCoP should aim to develop clear rules of engagement. If a clear and shared common language for group reflection is co-created and in place, the PCoP will be best placed to effectively support the development of a collaborative and cooperative environment, with specific focus on the acceptance and support of all

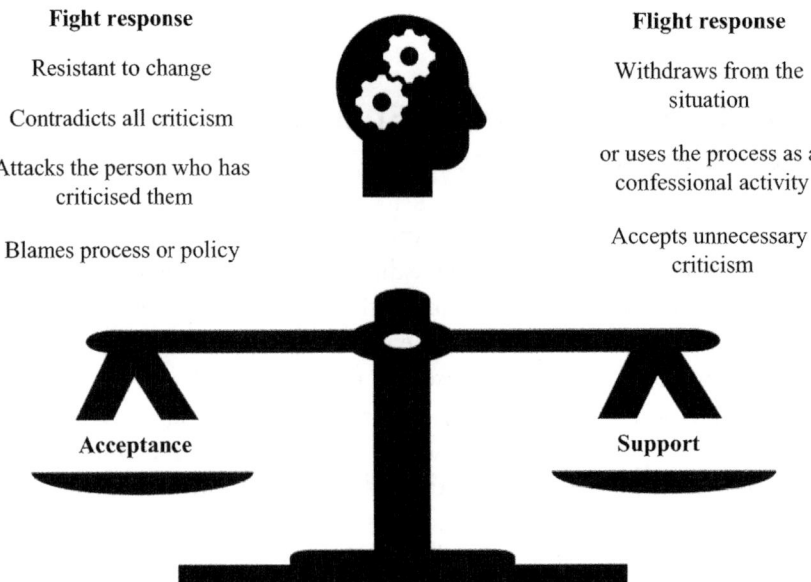

Fight response

Resistant to change

Contradicts all criticism

Attacks the person who has criticised them

Blames process or policy

Flight response

Withdraws from the situation

or uses the process as a confessional activity

Accepts unnecessary criticism

Acceptance   **Support**

Fig. 3.2 Creating a culture of shared understanding within a professional community of practice. (Adapted from Davies & Kremer, 2016)

members, driven by the opportunity to engage in critical dialogue with trusted colleagues. Explicit reflection on experiences allows learners to identify skills gaps, creating a way in which they can articulate their aspirations and learning requirements, informing their studies (Sierbert & Walsh, 2012) which in turn, allows the course teaching team to deliver bespoke activities in direct response to the cohorts individual requirements.

The exploration of individual experiences via a synergised PCoP is a necessity which enables all parties to develop a greater level of self-awareness, directly related to the nature and impact of individual performance and that of the wider group. The act of sharing is a catalyst for self-awareness which springboards opportunities for professional growth by enabling acknowledgement of both the emotional and rational dimensions of change (Osterman & Kottkamp, 1993) which are quintessential in supporting the development of a deep understanding. Taking time to verbally participate in group reflective activities can then be used to inform a written action plan or to identify professional development activities.

Knowledge Development and Real World Expectations

Learning is not an isolated occurrence but a ubiquitous coalescence of our own practices, personal perspectives and underpinning values which have arisen directly from our own prior experience. Professional learning experiences are an essential part of our development, informing what we do—underpinned by the instinctive insight we have into how we feel we should act in any given situation. As such our values and beliefs form an important part of this process. Jarvis and Watts (2012, p. 361) identify how the learning process has participation and practice "at its heart", describing how the motivation for learning is to move away from the "mundane sense of just getting through the day" and the desire to move towards the *value-laden* process of "living a worthwhile life". Taking time for professional reflective practice provides a way to step outside of our professional values and beliefs in order to critically examine how we are involved in creating social or professional structures counter to our espoused values. It enables awareness of the limits of our knowledge and how our own behaviours are complicit in our organisational practices bringing into alignment the contemporary professional practice. This can be achieved by taking the time to look back on workplace activities, both extraordinary and routine, to identify if there is any action that can be made which allows a vision of practice to be improved upon and further enhanced. Reflective activities are a key component in reviewing and achieving this change.

> ## Case Study 1
>
> **Effectiveness of Regular Practice Team Meetings to Support Reflection and Insight in Readiness for Primary Healthcare Practice with Dental Students and Staff (Joanne Brindley, Senior Lecturer in Education and Academic Lead, University of Portsmouth)**

Context

The aim of the University of Portsmouth Dental Academy (UPDA) was to develop a unique, innovative, team-based approach to dental education in a primary care setting, opposed to the more traditional secondary (hospital-based) educational delivery. The students at UPDA are in-placement students who are joined annually by a final-year cohort of out-placement dental undergraduates from King's College London Dental Institute (KCLDI).

Intervention

The introduction of the KCLDI students (which commenced in 2010, resulted in the formation of four Practice Teams, with each team having a balanced skill mix of not only students from various programmes but also academic, clinical, administration support and technical staff). Each Practice Team worked closely on the live clinical floor where they were encouraged to refer patients to one another (dependent upon individual patients' treatment requirements with a view to supporting skill acquisition) during the week. These activities were supplemented by weekly Practice Team Meetings (PTM) when individual teams' performance and progress was captured. The PTM provided an opportunity to discuss and reflect on experiences with the full range of dental team members, allowing exploration of concerns, successes and failures from a 360-degree perspective, mirroring activities which are expected to occur in the working world. The PTM provided the students with their first insight into the influence and impact that each team member elicits, effecting insight into the overall experience, supporting the identification of audit and student research project opportunities, facilitating reflective discussion about the week and identifying any shortfall or areas of good practice in relation to patient management. In order to optimise the effectiveness of the PTM, each Practice Team had three leads (clinical, academic and student). The leads were responsible for setting out a shared vision for the team identity, processes, meeting agendas and social events. The development of the PTM generated a unique opportunity for students, studying various dentistry based programmes (across differing levels of academic study) to share their thoughts, ideas and experiences, with not just their peers but also the wider dental team, in essence encompassing the three components of communities of practice (Lave and Wenger, 1991): domain, community and practice.

The regular PTM allowed members from each team time to form a professional rapport with one another on a regular basis over an extended period of time. During the meetings all team members contributed to reflective discussion about the week's events. Whilst this scenario was beneficial for the majority of students, for example, those who have good networking skills, there was a need to ensure that clear expectations and rules were set out by the PTM leads so that those students who may not perceive themselves to be 'strong students' were disadvantaged. Each team adopted a 'what is said in the team stays in the team' approach for their reflective discussions. Indeed, research conducted on their reflective activities identified that the students were positive about the benefits of discussing their experiences with one another describing how they preferred to reflect due to the 'informal' nature when 'discussed between teams'. This recognition of being part of a Practice Team underpinned the importance of a perceived safe environment in which to share individual experiences, assisted by the sense of belongingness which developed during their programme underpinned by self-actualisation (Maslow, 1943). However, there was a word of caution which was aired by one student who suggested that they wanted to be able to "discuss more freely with others what happened and what they would have done in the situation without being judged or concerned that the opinion the person has of me may change". This in all reality is difficult to facilitate as it is inevitable that people's perceptions of one another will change over time, so it is vitally important that areas for improvement are addressed by a culture of acceptance and support (Fig. 3.2) which aims to celebrate those people who have been brave enough to identify that a mistake has occurred and are willing to air and share this experience with others so that everyone can learn from them. To assist in developing a safe space, staff often took the first step by using their own personal experiences as a springboard for discussion with the students by sharing stories of their own personal successes and failures, much like village elders sitting around a campfire regaling stories of their pasts to a wide-eyed audience.

Belongingness

Another benefit of the PTM was the sense of belongingness that it generated. Belongingness is drawn from the hypothesis that humans are driven to make and maintain positive and significant interpersonal relationships (Baumeister & Leary, 1995). One of the key components to being fully engaged in lifelong learning is high levels of subjective well-being (Huppert & So, 2013); indeed, a lack of belongingness has been associated with increased stress and even suicidal thoughts (Vivekananda-Schmidt & Sandars, 2018). A culture of belongingness can be developed through the encouragement of reflective practices and the creation of social spaces and activities (Vivekananda-Schmidt & Sandars, 2018). Chiming with the research which has been conducted at UPDA by Brindley (2016) and Radford & Hellyer (2016) who have identified the perceived benefits derived from the emotional need to communicate with others, within an organisational setting—an involvement which is driven by the need to share experiences and be accepted, within the boundaries of a secure environment. Research involving students at UPDA resulted in a bespoke definition of belongingness in dental education (Radford & Hellyer, 2016) as a:

> deeply personal and contextually mediated experience in which a student becomes an essential and respected part of the dental educational environment where all are accepted and equally valued by each other and which allows each individual student to develop autonomy, self-reflection and self-actualisation as a clinician. (Radford & Hellyer, 2016, p. 543)

Conclusion

For students to be successful within their chosen profession there is a requirement to develop higher order thinking skills. The implementation of the PTM assisted with this transition by ensuring that students were no longer solely regurgitating facts or simply displaying adherence to performing set tasks at specific points within their curriculum. By taking the time to draw upon the shared experience of others student confidence increased and attention was focussed on embedding a lifelong approach to learning. The regular PTM afforded students with a space to showcase how they could modify their individual skills and knowledge and apply this to authentic situations in an agile and responsive way within the realms of the real world.

Management of Career Expectations

Studying degree courses with strong vocational links can be perceived as a fulfilling activity which acts as a vehicle to employment, whilst facilitating an opportunity for individuals to realise their career aspirations in a timely manner following graduation (HEFCE, 2018). Higher graduate employability rates and courses offering degree-level apprenticeships can attract increasing competition for places (Gov.UK, 2019). Having navigated the required hurdles in order to gain a place on a vocationally focussed course, there is an explicit expectation that these students will go onto maintaining high levels of optimism and motivation throughout their studies, especially when undertaking real world activities in outreach placements.

The downside of moving away from the safe confines of the academic facility to integrate with the future working world is that quite often difficult situations occur which do not always mirror the expected vision of professional practice. It is at this point that encounters, which are a challenge to a novice and conversely seen as routine events to experienced professionals, can in turn be viewed by the student as an aspect in which they are failing to achieve, creating tension and potential dissatisfaction within their chosen career pathway. In addition to this, a pedagogical gap can exist in the espoused prerequisite values related to professional practice and the daily reality of activities students undertake in out-placement locations (Jackson, Garcia-Zambrana, Greenlee, Aujean Lee, & Chrisinger, 2018).

This highlights the potential benefits of developing professional communities of practice, who are able to lend themselves to supporting the developing professional, by providing a safe space in which to discuss the mismatch between personal expectations and thus empowering the value of real world reality. The importance of diverse group learning (Poole et al., 2018) is that the process facilitates challenges to perceived norms. Indeed, as Eraut (2002) has identified, situated learning is not a prerequisite for local conformity but instead can lead to greater individual variation within their career context.

Putting Development into Perspective

The challenge of taking a wider and longer perspective of students' development has been met in myriad ways, many of which have their roots in the real world learning tradition. In this sense, real world learning may be highly appropriate if it can be reclaimed from some of the two-dimensional understandings of the term as drawing a spurious distinction between 'study' and 'work', and thus implying that universities are not part of the real world (James, 2015). What must be avoided is a narrow conception of real world learning which only deepens performativity and restricts student academic freedom (Macfarlane, 2016). It can be dangerous to assume that any element of pedagogy, which bears resemblance to practices found in the workplace, are inherently meaningful (e.g. the continued unpopularity of group assessments and how they are assessed). In particular, embarking on graduate-focussed activities without making it clear to students why these activities are meaningful and failing to manage these in a meaningful way feels counter to real world learning principles. While many colleagues have found success in applying the principles of real world learning, our second case study would suggest that a staff-student partnership approach which is rooted in negotiating shared expectations, purposes and responsibilities of any academic endeavour. In undertaking a staff-student partnership approach that places expectations and responsibilities on both sides of that dichotomy, a more meaningful engagement is possible.

Staff-student partnership is a concept which has gained significant traction in the UK and internationally in the last decade. The literature on staff-student partnership is a broad church; as an emerging area of practice and study, these principles have been applied in a range of contexts (see Mercer-Mapstone et al., 2017, for a review of the literature). Indeed, much of the conceptualisation encourages a focus on centralising values or principles than specific set of practices (Healey, Flint, & Harrington, 2014). Few analyses have conceptualised partnership working as a form of real world learning. Certainly, much of the evidence of the benefits of partnership focusses on the skills and employability benefits to students. Real world learning is also based on similar principles around the empowerment of students (https://www.real world learning network.org/real world learning-model/empowerment.aspx). In that sense, a partnership approach would extend this to also empower staff to be more flexible, responsive and authentic in their teaching, support and assessment. In one of the most significant conceptualisations of partnership, Healey, Flint and Harrington describe it as such:

> It is [...] about a change in mind-set and attitude to the nature of learning itself, understood as an experiential process of reflection and transformation in relation to oneself and with others. It is about cultural change in the academy, and about embracing the often-disorientating complexity of the contemporary world while maintaining the curiosity. (Healey et al., 2014, pp. 55–56)

The following case study will outline a practical way in which these principles were enacted in order to deliver a meaningful change in staff-student relationships and to rationalise the use of a real world learning approach.

Case Study 2

Negotiating a Shared Understanding and Real World Priorities Through Partnership Learning Agreements (Stuart Sims, Senior Lecturer in Higher Education, University of Portsmouth, Susan Noble, Academic Lead, University of Portsmouth, Amy Barlow, Head of Academic Development, University of Portsmouth, UK)

Context

This intervention occurred with a Year Two cohort of students in the University of Portsmouth's Fashion and Textile Design course. Lecturers as a group felt they were having difficulty in engaging the students in this year group with much of the standard expectations of the course, and this was having a natural impact upon student attainment and the culture and environment of the course. Previously this course had been highly successful in creating an effective course community, including significant casual interaction across year groups. This was a necessary element of the course as it centralises an authentic, real world learning approach with large portions of teaching and the more general experience of the course taking place in design studios. While containing a range of up-to-date and effective resources, this is naturally a finite space which usually encourages close staff-student collaboration. This Level 5 group then were somewhat of an outlier in that they had not adapted to the culture of the course and this was leading to a range of challenges for staff and students alike.

Intervention

Through concern about both student well-being and attainment, the course team reached out to the University's central Academic Development Team for support in resolving this issue. A meeting between the course team, academic developers and the Student Union occurred, and a multi-stage process was devised to co-create Staff-Student Partnership Agreements.

Particularly common in Scottish Higher Education due to the pioneering work of Sparqs (the Scottish organisation for student partnerships in quality and an affiliate of Quality Assurance Agency Scotland), partnership agreements are designed to publicly acknowledge shared responsibilities and mutual direction of travel between the university and the student body. What distinguishes such documents from similar pieces (e.g. Student Charters) is a commitment to enhancement of quality rather than minimum standards as well as an emphasis on working relationships (Williamson, 2013). Typically, these agreements are signed between a relevant senior member of university staff (e.g. Vice Chancellor and Registrar) and a member of the Student Union's Sabbatical Officer Team (e.g. President and Vice President for Education). Such documents are therefore extensions of existing frameworks of representation at the highest level and set out expectations institutionally. These tend to include value statements, link to other strategic documents and establish baseline expectations for areas such as conduct, provision and support. A critique of such agreements is that they often do not directly engage with staff or students. As such representatives are deciding what they are agreeing to. These agreements may seem opaque or distant to staff and students in their everyday lives. The principles of this particular partnership agreement was adapted in order to reflect more local-level priorities without reliance on the representation typical in institution-wide agreements.

To design a local version of a staff-student partnership agreement, a multi-stage workshop approach was undertaken. The initial workshop was conducted in the Student Union to provide a neutral environment and only included the students. While much of the initial driver was concerns around engagement and behaviour, this was not treated as remedial intervention to only target particular groups—rather a whole year group cohort approach was taken with the intent of fostering a greater sense of course community and belonging. Every student in the second year was invited and the vast majority attended. Drawing on the expertise of the Vice President, Education, a series of warm-up exercises were undertaken to get the participants actively moving and discussing before moving onto the more substantive aspects of the workshop. This then progressed to a whole group activity which asked students to reflect on their motivations and priorities around their education. The student group were then asked to stand along the back of the room at particular points to indicate the extent to which they agreed with a set of statements (almost like a living Likert Scale). Explanations of their choices were invited from the group and they were quite forthcoming about why they chose particular views, and this led to in-depth discussions about the support on the course and its links with their employability. The students were then put into groups and asked to outline what they believed their perfect course would look like. The purpose of all these activities was to encourage reflection from the students to give them a clearer idea of what they wanted from the course and beyond as well as how they could achieve this. This progressed into a second stage where members of the course team were invited in and joined a group. Drawing on the previous discussions and facilitated by the Academic Development and Student Union team, each group was invited to outline what their expectations of staff and students would be for the course. The final stage involved a separate workshop day session where students and staff brought together their priorities into a final list of responsibilities for the programme, as identified in Table 3.1:

Table 3.1 Agreed list of staff and student responsibilities

Students	Staff
• Should turn up to all sessions and recognise effort put in by tutors	• Improve communication about issues that we raise so that students understand what action is taken
• Should be considerate of space and shall share/leave space when moving between rooms	• Allow 10 minutes of feedback time for student representatives to talk to wider group
• Should be enthusiastic and positive and acknowledge what is out of control to change and good changes we've experienced	• Reward positive behaviour and attendance
• Take active steps to discuss and resolve conflicting feedback from different tutors and find the answers we need	• Be more transparent about feedback and how it links to the marking criteria
• Be on time and do not disrupt the lesson, enter quietly or wait outside—respect those that are learning	• Will start sessions on time even if students are late

Conclusion

In many ways, developing a partnership agreement is quite distinct from values and practices associated with real world learning. However, the drivers behind this intervention were around a sense of shared responsibility and collaboration which are very consistent with this tradition. Universities tend to be values-based institutions, subscribing to a particular agenda of what the purpose of education is and its role in wider society. Bridging the gap between a more liberal conception of the purpose of education and courses that adopt a more real world approach is paramount. Often the function, shape and tradition of universities are unclear to students in a massified system. This is particularly pronounced when students are attending with their future employability as their primary motivation. Engaging with principles of staff-student partnership and real world learning can surface the expectations of both groups. The work presented in this case study has yet to be evaluated fully and therefore it merely serves here as a suggestion of an approach that can address growing concerns across the sector that merges a real world learning and partnership approach. Anecdotally, the staff team reports that the benefits of the partnership agreement have mainly been felt in Staff-Student Consultative Committees where the agreed statements can be used to contextualise course issues or changes as well as holding all participants to account.

Traditional Real World Learning Versus New Approaches

Traditionally real world learning opportunities have been included within the undergraduate curriculum in specific slices, whereby students engage with a scenario, project or outplacement within a restricted timeframe, with the main focus of course content and assessment being focussed on academic tasks. With the emergence of the Fourth Industrial Revolution (4IR) future generations of students may only spend a few years using the content knowledge which they have acquired during their programmes

(Hack, 2018). As such, there is an increasingly urgent requirement to consider how we can develop authentic learning pedagogies, which move away the main focus from campus-based delivery, instead allowing a more intent focus on the development of a different skill set which consists of the adaptability, criticality and emotional intelligence which will enable students to evolve into lifelong self-directed learners. Furnishing them with the skills required for a lifetime of continually changing roles, expectations and responsibilities.

In many ways the emergence of higher-level apprenticeships could be perceived as the ultimate real world learning panacea; degree apprenticeships provide students with regular opportunities to engage with the world of work, which is underpinned by an academic base—to provide structure and tailored interstitial guidance during a student's learning journey.

As flexibility in the ways in which students access their learning increases, there is a need for the curricula to evolve to allow interdisciplinary collaboration and foster authentic learning opportunities which allow students to be endowed with the qualities required not just for lifelong learning within their disciplinary context but to enable the formation of authentic networks in preparedness for the emergence of future super complexity. Critical reflection is a key element that underpins the collaborative element of learning. In our position as educators, we have a responsibility to recreate these values attached to higher education learning. The values of liberal education are often opaque to incoming students, and a more community-orientated approach underpinned by values of partnership is a potential avenue to overcome this disparity. This is particularly pressing in a massified system where large numbers of students are entering with few preconceptions of university or are already internalising a reductionist economically minded transactional understanding of the role that universities play. The *real world* is more than just work and reducing real world learning to this is to give in to neo-liberal agendas. However, we cannot neglect the economic role that universities have, alongside the associated expectations of students, given the change in funding. As such it is incumbent on academic staff to create a community with a sense of mutually developing and evolved values to ensure that all stakeholders are fulfilled. Authentic learning is not solely about meeting the expectations or agendas of institutions, consumers or employers, but it is about creating opportunities to develop and nurture a future skill set which is able to meet the demands of our rapidly evolving society.

Partnership has often been conceptualised as a radical approach to higher education, which rethinks power-relations for the liberation of both staff and students (Wenstone, 2012). Both case study examples were very much rooted in values of reciprocity, trust and community which underpin partnership work (Healey et al., 2014). Although the second case study is situated purely within a university context, the inclusion of the shared case studies aims to acknowledge the importance of developing a collaborative and cooperative approach in supporting real world learning. Indeed, the prerequisites for effective real world learning to occur must be apparent in all stakeholders; the organisation must be keen to pursue, facilitate and support the needs of students, staff and real world stakeholders. The students must demonstrate willingness, ability and engagement with the activities which they are presented with, which must be mirrored by an overarching culture of commitment from real world stakeholders, students and staff to identify and work towards their shared goals. By creating a positive culture, within the architecture of the learning environment, there is an opportunity to share insights and multiple perspectives around learning in a real world context which becomes part of the essence in which to scaffold the foundations of positive educational experience. Failure to integrate these positive attributes into the student experience can lead to the development of a narrow view of the world, which limits the development of practical skills and suppresses empathy and creativity, which, in turn, hampers emotional resilience.

A staff-student partnership approach supported by the development of communities of practice provides all members with both responsibility for the direction of their learning community and also the skills required to engage with it.

References

Barnett, R. (2000). Super complexity and the curriculum. *Studies in Higher Education, 25*(3), 255–265. https://doi.org/10.1080/713696156

Barnett, R. (2017). *The ecological university: A feasible utopia*. Oxon: Routledge.

Baumeister, R. F., & Leary, M. R. (1995). The need to belong: Desire for interpersonal attachments as a fundamental human motivation. *Psychology Bulletin, 117*, 497–529.

Boyer, E. (1990). *Scholarship reconsidered: Priorities of the professoriate*. New York: The Carnegie Foundation for the Advancement of Teaching.

Brindley, J. (2016). The benefits of mentorship for the dental team. *British Dental Journal Team, 3*, 25–27.

Cameron, D. A., Binnie, V. I., Sherriff, A., & Bissell, V. (2015). Peer assisted learning: Teaching dental skills and enhancing graduate attributes. *British Dental Journal, 219*, 267–272. https://doi.org/10.1038/sj.bdj.2015.722

Collini, S. (2012). *What are universities for?* London: Penguin UK.

Davies, M., & Kremer, D. (2016). Reflection: How to reduce the risks. Retrieved from http://careers.bmj.com/careers/advice/Reflection%3A_how_to_reduce_the_risks

Eraut, M. (2002). Non-formal learning and tacit knowledge in professional work. *British Journal of Educational Psychology, 70*(1), 113–136. https://doi.org/10.1348/000709900158001

Gov. UK. (2019). Review of post-18 education and funding. Retrieved from https://assets.publishing.service.gov.uk/government/uploads/system/uploads/attachment_data/file/805127/Review_of_post_18_education_and_funding.pdf.

Hack, K. (2018). Brave new world—How are we preparing the Next-Generation of learners for the fourth industrial revolution? Retrieved from https://www.advance-he.ac.uk/news-and-views/how-are-we-preparing-the-next

Healey, M., Flint, A., & Harrington, K. (2014). *Students as partners in learning and teaching in higher education*. York: Higher Education Academy.

Higher Education Funding Council for England. (2018). Vocational degrees and employment outcomes. Retrieved from https://webarchive.nationalarchives.gov.uk/20180319114826/; http://www.hefce.ac.uk/pubs/year/2018/201801/

Huppert, F., & So, T. (2013). Flourishing across Europe: Application of a new conceptual framework for defining well-being. *Social Indicators Research, 110*(3), 837–861. https://doi.org/10.1007/s11205-011-9966-7

Jackson, A., Garcia-Zambrana, I., Greenlee, A. J., Aujean Lee, C., & Chrisinger, B. (2018). All talk no walk: Student perceptions on integration of diversity and practice in planning programs. *Planning Practice & Research, 33*(5), 574–595. https://doi.org/10.1080/02697459.2018.1548207

James, A. (2015). Call the world outside university anything you like, just don't call it 'real' [Blog Post]. *Times Higher Education*. Retrieved from https://www.timeshighereducation.com/blog/call-world-outside-university-anything-you-just-dont-call-it-real

Jarvis, P., & Watts, M. H. (2012). *The Routledge International Handbook of Learning*. London: Routledge.

Lave and Wenger. (1991). *Situated learning: Legitimate peripheral participation*. Cambridge: Cambridge University Press.

Macfarlane, B. (2016). *Freedom to learn: The threat to student academic freedom and why it needs to be reclaimed*. London: Routledge.

Maslow, A. H. (1943). A theory of human motivation. *Psychological Review, 50*(4), 370–396.

Mercer-Mapstone, L., Dvorakova, S. L., Matthews, K. E., Abbot, S., Cheng, B., Felten, P., … Swaim, K. (2017). A systematic literature review of students as partners in higher education. *International Journal for Students as Partners, 1*(1). https://doi.org/10.15173/ijsap.v1i1.3119

Molesworth, M., Scullion, R., & Nixon, E. (Eds.). (2010). *The marketisation of higher education*. Oxon: Routledge.

Osterman, K. F., & Kottkamp, R. B. (1993). *Reflective practice for educator: Improving schooling through professional development*. Thousand Oaks, CA: Corwin Press.

Poole, G., Iqbal, I., & Verwood, R. (2018). Small significant networks as birds of a feather. *International Journal for Academic Development, 24*(1), 61–72. https://doi.org/10.1080/1360144X.2018.1492924

Radford, D. R., & Hellyer, P. (2016, May 27) Belongingness in undergraduate dental education. *British Dental Journal. 220*(10), 539–543.

Readings, B. (1996). *The university in ruins*. USA: Estate of Bill Readings.

Sierbert, S., & Walsh, A. (2012). Reflection in work-based learning: Self-regulation or self-liberation. *Teaching in Higher Education*. https://doi.org/10.1080/13562517.2012.696539

Teaching Excellence Framework. (n.d.). Retrieved from https://www.office-forstudents.org.uk/advice-and-guidance/teaching/what-is-the-tef/

Vivekananda-Schmidt, P., & Sandars, J. (2018). Belongingness and its implication for undergraduate health professions education: A scoping review. *Education for Primary Care*. https://doi.org/10.1080/14739879.2018.1478677

Wenger, E., & Trayner, B. (2015). Introduction to communities of practice. *Communities of Practice and Social Learning Systems*. Retrieved from https://wenger-trayner.com/introduction-to-communities-of-practice/

Wenger, E., Trayner, B., & De Laat, M. (2011) *Promoting and assessing value creation in communities and networks: A conceptual framework*. Open Universiteit, Ruud de Moor Centrum. https://doi.org/10.108 0/1360144X.2018.1492924

Wenstone, R. (2012). A manifesto for partnership. *National Union of Students (NUS)*. Retrieved from https://www.nusconnect.org.uk/resources/a-manifesto-for-partnership

Williamson, M. (2013). *Guidance on the development and implementation of a student partnership agreement in universities*. Edinburgh: Sparqs. Retrieved from https://www.sparqs.ac.uk/upfiles/Student%20Partnership%20Agreement%20Guidance%20-%20final%20version.pdf

Woodall, T., Hiller, A., & Resnick, S. (2014). Making sense of higher education: Students as consumers and the value of the university experience. *Studies in Higher Education, 39*(1), 48–67. https://doi.org/10.1080/0307507 9.2011.648373

4

Real World Learning Through Civic Engagement: Principles, Pedagogies and Practices

Kristine Mason O'Connor and Lindsey McEwen

Introducing Real World Learning Through Civic Engagement

In times of unprecedented change and uncertainty, real world learning through civic engagement enables students to thrive as empowered critical thinkers and actors developing skills, confidence and capabilities for life, employment and citizenship. Real world learning through civic engagement builds university capacity to collaborate equitably with communities to strengthen and enhance social capital and address emerging societal and environmental challenges, locally and globally. This chapter presents developments in curriculum-based civic engagement and considers drivers, pedagogies, principles and examples of practice as

K. Mason O'Connor (✉)
University of Gloucestershire, Cheltenham, UK
e-mail: kmoconnor@glos.ac.uk

L. McEwen
University of the West of England, Bristol, UK

© The Author(s) 2021
D. A. Morley, M. G. Jamil (eds.), *Applied Pedagogies for Higher Education*,
https://doi.org/10.1007/978-3-030-46951-1_4

63

indicated in the concept map (Fig. 4.1). The chapter concludes with proposals to implement this transformational mode of learning.

The "definitional anarchy of civic engagement" (Sandmann, 2008, p. 91) succinctly captures the multiple diverse practices whereby universities establish real world learning opportunities with communities. Collectively such practices can be viewed through the lens of the scholarship of engagement, "connecting the rich resources of the university to our most pressing social, civic, and ethical problems ... Campuses would be viewed by both students and professors not as isolated islands, but as staging grounds for action" (Boyer, 1996, p. 20).

More than twenty years after Boyer's call to action, the nature of the 'problem contexts' to community-based learning (CBL) has shifted away from a safer core of issues towards dealing with more challenging local problems, where student engagement involves risk taking but also strong potential for Fink's 'significant learning'. For example, the 'integration' element of Fink's taxonomy of significant learning refers to connecting "ideas, people and realms of life" (2003, p. 30). "The act of making new connections gives learners a new form of *power* especially intellectual power" (ibid., p. 31).

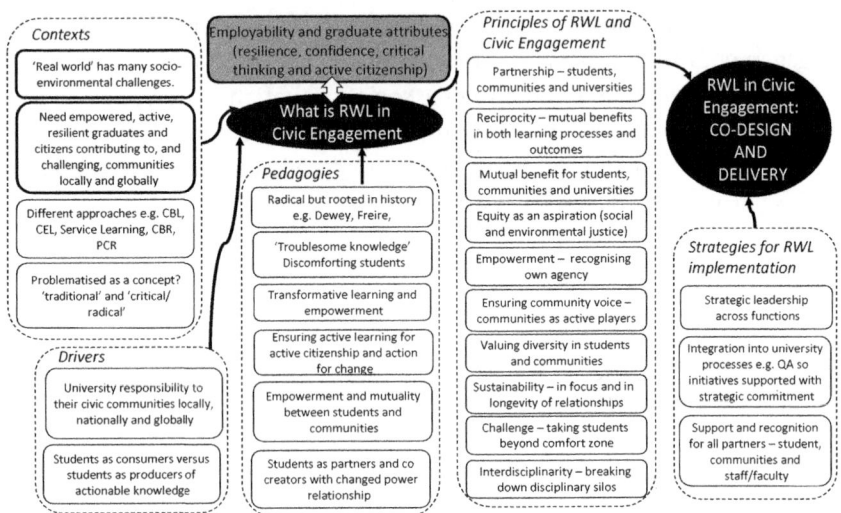

Fig. 4.1 Real world learning (RWL) through civic engagement concept map

Greater attention is now being addressed to critical parameters in community-based learning, such as how local problems are identified, the role of and benefits to students and communities, and pithy ethical issues that relate to such matters as equity, diversity and relative affluence. In the shift to this new paradigm of real world civic engagement, there is plentiful opportunity to gain insights and develop principles across a wide range of learning and experiences.

Missions, Manifestos and Declarations

Civic engagement is hardly a recent concept for universities. As Watson and others have observed, most university foundations expressed commitment to an element of service to their communities in their stated purpose and mission (Watson, Hollister, Stroud, & Babcock, 2011). This was certainly the case in the USA where service learning was rooted in the foundations of the Land Grant Colleges in the mid-nineteenth century. In differing forms, civic engagement through the curriculum has continued to thrive in the USA with over 360 "campuses with the elective [Carnegie] Community Engagement Classification" in 2018 (Brown, n.d.). In the UK, by contrast, for several decades, founders' commitments gathered dust in many a university archive whilst institutions focused on research, teaching and income-generating activities. This neglect is explained by Goddard and Kempton,

> In the UK 19th century institutions that were the predecessors of the so-called 'red brick' universities evolved to meet the needs of a rapidly evolving industrial society … These institutions depended to a large degree on local public support. During the 20th century these local links weakened with increasing central government support and influence over local government [and] the nationalisation of higher education … As a consequence many civic institutions turned their backs on their host cities. However in the 21st century some of these are seeking to reinvent themselves as civic institutions… (Goddard & Kempton, n.d.)

By 2018, over eighty UK institutions had signed up to the UK National Co-ordinating Centre for Public Engagement (NCCPE) Manifesto for Public Engagement, representing approximately half of all UK higher education institutions, and by the following year more than fifty universities had "reaffirmed their commitment to their local communities by pledging to put the economy and quality of life in their home towns and cities *at the top of their list of priorities*" (our emphasis) (Brabner, 2019).

Internationally, the past twenty years have witnessed a burgeoning of universities committing to civic engagement. In 1999, the Global University Network for Innovation (GUNI) was established. Its mission is "to strengthen the role of higher education in society contributing to the renewal of the visions and policies of higher education across the world under a vision of public service, relevance and social responsibility" (GUNI, 2013, p. 2). In 2019, it comprised 227 members across 80 countries. The Tufts Talloires Network was founded in 2005, comprising heads of universities from twenty-three countries who signed the Talloires Declaration on the civic roles and social responsibilities of higher education:

> We are dedicated to strengthening the civic role and social responsibility of our institutions … Through learning, values and commitment of faculty, staff and students, our institutions create social capital, preparing students to contribute positively to local, national and global communities. (Talloires Network, 2005)

Ten years later, over 300 university leaders from 70 countries had signed the Declaration. In 2018, Talloires' partner national and regional networks included AsiaEngage; CLAYSS: The Latin American Centre for Service Learning; Engagement Australia; and SAHECEF: South African Higher Education Community Engaged Forum.

Drivers for Change: Austerity to Posterity

Beginning with a focus on the UK, we present key drivers and imperatives for developing university civic engagement. A policy of government public austerity measures in the UK over the past decade led to funding for universities being significantly reduced. Austerity prompted calls for all publicly funded institutions, including universities, to account for themselves in terms of their societal value. Furthermore, with many being sizeable charities enjoying certain tax advantages, universities are required to be transparent in demonstrating social responsibility.

A related economic policy was the introduction of, and a hefty increase in, student fees. This, together with the annual National Student Survey rankings, promoted cultures of 'customer focus' or 'value for money'. One response has been for universities to fast-track graduate employability measures, with civic engagement activity shown to add value to the development of students' employability skills and capabilities (Mason O'Connor, Lynch, & Owen, 2011). Providing learning opportunities beyond lectures and seminars was spurred on by the introduction of the Teaching Excellence Framework (TEF) in 2017 which assesses how institutions "ensure excellent outcomes for their students in terms of graduate-level employment or further study", as well as what they are doing "*in addition*" (our emphasis) to meeting national quality standards and awards (Office for Students, 2019).

According to an NCCPE report in 2015, whilst most universities had developed an engagement strategy, it had not been fully implemented. There was "much more evidence of more traditional 'inspirational' engagement, rather than two-way exchange" (Hill, 2015, p. 6). Festivals of ideas would be an example where experts from the university enthuse and enthral audiences with presentations and demonstrations. Over the ensuing five years, universities have developed a wider range of engagement activities, from comedy clubs to supporting vulnerable community members with technical solutions. However, this growth in 'public engagement' activity is not matched by growth in strategic civic engagement through the curriculum, which remains an activity largely promoted by enthusiasts. A similar point was made in Lord Kerslake's foreword to the 2019 UPP Foundation *Civic University Independent Commission Report*; whilst there was "much enthusiasm for the civic role and many excellent individual initiatives … we found few examples of a systematic and strategic approach to the civic role based on an analysis of the needs of the place" (Kerslake, 2019, p. 5).

The international imperative for sustainable development has been another key driver for higher education, with some HEIs explicitly aligning themselves in 'whole-institution approaches' (see UNESCO, 2018, p. 45). Furthermore the United Nations Educational, Scientific and Cultural Organization (UNESCO, 2014, 2018) emphasises the importance of Education for Sustainable Development (ESD) or Learning for Sustainability (LfS), and the delivery of seventeen Sustainable Development Goals (SDGs) that aspire "to end poverty, protect the planet and ensure prosperity for all" by 2030. ESD proposes important links between local and global citizenship and the need for active citizenship, with implications for citizenship education at all educational levels. UNESCO (2018, p. 82) specifically advocates service learning as one approach "to facilitate learning about global justice and reduction of poverty" (SDG1 'No poverty') by planning and implementing "local service-learning and/or engagement opportunities for empowering poor people, reducing their vulnerability to different hazards and increasing their resilience…".

These goals apply domestically as well as internationally in relation to the roles of active citizens (see UK HM Government's 2018 *Civil Society Strategy: Building a future that works for everyone*) although the role of higher education in building social responsibility is not discussed. However, the GuildHE/NUS (2016) report *Active Citizenship: The role of higher education* and its Charter for Active Citizenship cite the UNESCO, 2009 World Conference on Higher Education (2016, p. 7):

> Higher education institutions, through their core functions (research, teaching and service to the community) carried out in the context of institutional autonomy and academic freedom, should increase their interdisciplinary focus and promote critical thinking and active citizenship. This would contribute to sustainable development, peace, well-being and the realization of human rights, including gender equity.

Pedagogies of Empowerment and Transformation

Student learning through community engagement is rooted in problem-based, reflective, 'deep learning' pedagogies of empowerment, transformation, critical thinking and social participation (Dewey, 1938; Freire, 1970; Kolb, 1984; Marton and Säljö 1976; Wenger, 1999; Mezirow, 2000, in Mason O'Connor, Lynch, & Owen, 2011, p. 106).

These pedagogies of real world learning fly in the face of students as 'customers', not only in their propensity for transformation, but in their potential to unsettle and disturb, challenging taken-for-granted beliefs about the 'real world'. The experience can be "troublesome", being conceptually difficult or "alien" (Perkins, 1999). Students may even experience "the ambivalence, anger and frustration that can accompany genuine learning" (Delucchi & Smith, 1997, p. 337). Customers certainly don't want to be troubled.

The proposition of knowledge being constructed can be traced to Dewey in the early twentieth century for whom learning necessitated acquiring and reflecting on experience; knowledge is not 'out there' to be consumed.

> The academic subjects often sort, categorize, and present lists of facts and answers in text books, but this is not how facts originally emerged. [Dewey] reminds us, instead, facts emerged from real world people trying to solve real problems. (Fallace, 2016, p. 186)

Similarly, Freire's radical pedagogy of real world learning contests the idea of the teacher depositing or 'banking' knowledge in the learner, "the more students work at storing the deposits entrusted to them, the less they develop the critical consciousness which would result from their interaction in the world as transformers of that world" (Freire, 2005, p. 73). By advocating instead 'problem-posing education', Freire opens the way for transformational knowledge to be created. Here real world learning where students engage with others in the civic sphere to address practical problems resonates with Meyer and Land's (2005) work on threshold concepts in its potential to be 'transformative', 'irreversible' and 'integrated'.

Drawing on, amongst others, the work of Dewey and Freire, Mezirow (1978, 1991, 2000, 2003) developed the concept of transformative learning, defined as "learning that transforms problematic frames of reference—sets of fixed assumptions and expectations (habits of mind, meaning perspectives, mindsets)—to make them more inclusive, discriminating, open, reflective, and emotionally able to change" (Mezirow, 2003, p. 58).

Transformative learning emphasises the role of student, teacher as facilitator and the setting for learning as being out of an individual's comfort zone and, particularly, the importance of expansion of the consciousness, change in basic world view and empowerment (McEwen, Strachan, & Lynch, 2011).

These pedagogies of real world learning connect with Gibbons' concept of Mode 2 knowledge which is

> produced in a context of application involving a much broader range of perspectives [than Mode 1]. Mode 2 is transdisciplinary not only drawing on disciplinary contributions but can set up new frameworks beyond them; it is characterised by heterogeneity of skills, by a preference for flatter hierarchies and organisational structures which are transient. It is more socially accountable and reflexive than Mode 1. (Gibbons, 2000, p. 159)

Interdisciplinarity is a key pedagogic feature of real world learning through civic engagement. Here again one is reminded of Dewey who "believed that the unity of experience artificially severed by academic subjects needed to be restored" (Fallace, 2016, p. 186); it is pertinent to note that the 2014 UK Research Excellence Framework (REF) exercise commented that "wider impacts and benefits often stem from multidisciplinary work" (UKRI, n.d.).

There is now much greater attention to wider critical national and international agendas that connect local and global, including the need for climate resilience, imperatives of learning for sustainability (UNESCO, 2018) and 'glocal' citizenship and within this, the role of citizens in such issues as place-making and local governance. This has given a new lens with which to view university civic engagement involving a 'move' from the traditional disciplines involved in service learning (e.g. education and health) to a much wider set of disciplines that span the gamut of science (STEM), social science and arts and humanities (e.g. see El-Gabry, 2018; Kramer & Fask, 2017). In his introduction to the 2017 report on the social responsibility of universities, Peter Wells, head of higher education for UNESCO, wrote:

> The role of higher education institutions in developing the critical thinking needed in young minds and researchers to find solutions to the problems facing our world can no longer be taken in isolation, but must be approached in ways that cross institutional and disciplinary boundaries. (Wells, 2017, p. 29)

Education for Sustainable Development (UNESCO, 2018) draws on pedagogies that are participatory, learner-centred, action-orientated and transformative. UNESCO cites such collaborative real world learning practices, with service-learning projects on sustainability being one learning context, in which learners take collaborative action. This links to the emergent concept of transgressive learning promoted by Lotz-Sisitka, Wals, Kronlid, and McGarry (2015)—that is, learning "to overcome the status quo and prepare the learner for disruptive thinking and the co-creation of new knowledge" (UNESCO, 2018, p. 49).

Alongside, there is increasing interest in citizenship education or pedagogies for active citizenship, and relationships between learning and action. There is longer-standing attention to citizenship education within student learning and achievement in secondary education compared with higher education (see Crick Report—Advisory Group on Citizenship, 1998; Weinberg & Flinders, 2018). Wasner (2016) explicitly identifies 'critical service learning' as a participatory pedagogical approach to global citizenship and international mindedness, while Wood, Taylor, Atkins, and Johnston (2018) emphasise the importance of learning through affective and cognitive domains for deeper democratic engagement. Although there is less *explicitly* on imperatives for active citizen participation through higher education, the Guild HE/National Union of Students (2016) report *Active Citizenship: The role of higher education* highlights service learning as one means to deliver citizen education, with emphasis on research *with* the community.

What's in a Name? Modes of Real World Learning Through Civic Engagement

In our review of approaches to university-community engagement through the curriculum, we presented a range of modes (Mason O'Connor, McEwen, Owen, Lynch, & Hill, 2011). It would be tempting to try to develop this work by constructing a continuum of practices with the emphasis on student learning at one end (e.g. service learning) and community learning the other (e.g. community-based engaged research). However, this would be disingenuous. Take for example practices named service learning. With its origins in 'volunteering', a criticism levelled at service learning is its inherent power imbalance, and whilst studies show benefit to student learning, the benefit to communities is under-researched (Blouin & Perry, 2009). Stoecker (2016) argues that too frequently service learning prioritises students' learning interests over those of the community. However, this is contested by Asghar and Rowe's (2017) work on service learning within health care: "reciprocal relationships which challenge established ideas and practices, together with engaging students in critical informed analysis are key components in ensuring service learning is socially just" (2017, p. 117).

Furthermore, Mitchell (2008) proposes that service learning is not unidimensional. She distinguishes between two forms of service learning: 'traditional service learning' and 'critical service learning' differentiated in relation to their ability to either perpetuate or change the status quo. Critical service learning also focuses on social justice with the ultimate aim being to "deconstruct systems of power so the need for service and the inequalities that create and sustain them are dismantled" (Mitchell, 2008, p. 50).

These pedagogies link to wider moves to 'radical' civic engagement in some institutions with critics of service learning arguing that the modes of engagement practice which we refer to later represent significantly more than mere changed nomenclature; rather, they represent a paradigm shift, focusing on action for change and co-production of knowledge, moving the focus from service towards equitable collaborative partnership between students, faculty and communities.

Boland portrays a defining feature of community-based learning as being:

> its explicit focus where the design and enactment of the curriculum are underpinned with a rationale which invokes—to varying extents—concepts such as active citizenship, democracy, social justice, community and civic engagement, while simultaneously advancing the goal of student learning. (Boland, 2014, p. 181)

Community-based research (CBR) expresses the growing prominence in undergraduate education to forge links between research and teaching. Engaging undergraduates as researchers enables them to "grow in confidence as they approach the demanding complexities of knowing and acting in the modern world" (Fung, 2016, p. 37). Furthermore, CBR can enable students to engage in "varying and multiple modes of generating knowledge" (Tandon, Hall, Lepore, & Singh, 2016, p. 14). "Thinking, knowing, feeling about a particular subject (manifested in the forms of arts, music, theatre, roles plays, photovoices etc.) needs to be promoted as equally effective methods as cognitive methods" (ibid.).

Community-based participatory research (CBPR) "begins with a research topic of importance to the community and has the aim of combining knowledge with action and achieving social change" (O'Mahoney, Burns, & McDonell, n.d.). Community-based *engaged* research "is conducted by, for and/or with the participation of the community members: an emergent paradigm of really useful research for the Twenty-first Century" (Hall, Lall, & Heng Chan, n.d.).

From their experience and research in the USA, Brabant and Braid (2009, p. 61) concluded, "there is no definition of civic engagement that fits all institutions, although there may be similar forces driving universities and colleges to assume a greater role in maintaining the economic, social and political health of their respective communities."

In our previous review we concluded that "this lack of definition can be considered a strength rather than a limitation, engendering local debate as to what these terms might mean in different contexts" (Mason O'Connor, McEwen, et al., 2011, p. 4).

Acting on Principles: Civic Engagement Through the Curriculum

Given there is no specific optimal mode or method of university civic engagement for universities and communities to adopt, we propose a set of key principles to serve as a lens to inform these debates; these principles are based on our exploration of literature and reflections on practice. In so doing we share the view about community-engaged research being characterised not by method or approach but by the principles which guide it. The principles we have identified are partnership, reciprocity, mutual benefit, equity (social justice), empowerment, ensuring community voice, valuing diversity, sustainability, challenge and interdisciplinarity. These are presented as axes on the spidergram in Fig. 4.2. This format was chosen, first, to emphasise that there is not a hierarchy of principles and, second, for its potential as a tool for self-evaluation and quality improvement, such as profiling development of a civic engagement project over time. It can be used to highlight which principles are being practised most powerfully, as well as those requiring further development. (Dotted line gives an example.)

These principles link to those for ESD (e.g. interdisciplinarity and empowerment) and citizenship education (e.g. valuing diversity and equity). Examples of the principles playing out in practice feature in a number of international initiatives (Table 4.1).

The four case studies (Table 4.2) presented in Chap. 5 illustrate different approaches, scales and institutional contexts to civic engagement, specific to meeting their particular objectives. As we consider below, they vividly exemplify principles of real world learning through civic engagement being put into practice.

Each of the case studies demonstrates principles of establishing effective *partnerships* for *sustainability*. In Solent University's Community

Fig. 4.2   Ten principles of real world learning through civic engagement

Innovation Programme, 'Healthy Living Project', a three-way partnership, is created, nurtured and developed between students, health practitioner and women from diverse ethnic minorities. The International Practicum Pilot, 'Limerick Inside Out', highlights, "The deliberate shift in focus from 'depth' to 'breadth' of community engaged learning … supplemented by the establishment of a strategic partnership with the Limerick City and County Council" (Gleeson, Mey and Warren-Perkinson).

Principles of *challenge* and *valuing diversity* are evident across the case studies with the 'Solent Football Leadership Programme' enabling students to "engage with a diverse range of projects and participants incorporating areas, such as working with the homeless community, women and girls, mental health and well-being, disability, youth and many more. To work with such a range of participants across a broad spectrum of projects offers students a variety of challenges and problems which are 'real world' and, as such, require real solutions" (Bourne).

Table 4.1 Real world learning through civic engagement—principles into practice

Principles	Detail	Discipline	Examples
1. Partnership	Partnerships of reciprocal exchange?	General review	Hammersley (2012)
2. Reciprocity	Reciprocity and critical reflection as the key to social justice in service learning	Health care	Asghar and Rowe (2017)
3. Mutual benefit	"Letting the village be the teacher"	Study abroad; global education	Collins (2019)
4. Equity (social justice)	"Toy design project for children in Egyptian squatter community" Creative collaborations through inclusive theatre	Engineering	El-Gabry (2018) Kramer and Fask (2017)
5. Empowerment	Improving student learning outcomes through community-based research: the poverty workshop	Sociology	Mayer, Blume, Black, and Stevens (2018)
6. Ensuring community voice	Noting absence of partner perspectives	General review	Hammersley (2012; Collins, 2019)
7. Valuing diversity	Education for citizenship: community engagement between the Global South and the Global North	Geography	Miller (2013)
8. Sustainability	Insights into the sustainability of a challenging pedagogy	Engineering, psychology, art and multidisciplinary	Boland (2014)
9. Challenge	Productive tensions—engaging geography students in participatory action research with communities	Geography	Pain, Finn, Bouveng, and Ngobe (2013)
10. Interdisciplinarity	Mapping communities "Bringing it all back home": an interdisciplinary model for CBL	Geographers collaborating Internships in large-scale urban redevelopment	Jung (2018), Schwartz (2015)

Table 4.2 Real world learning through civic engagement—four case studies

Title	Author
International Practicum Pilot: Limerick Inside Out	Tracey Gleeson, Kerstin Mey and Anne Warren-Perkinson, University of Limerick
The Solent Football Leadership Programme (SFLP)	Tracey Bourne, Solent University
The Community Innovation Programme, Healthy Living Project	Amy E. King, Solent University
Making Change Happen—Civic Engagement in Practice	Linda Cooper and Duncan Reavey, University of Chichester

The principle of *interdisciplinarity* features strongly in the case studies from the universities of Limerick and Chichester with the former stating, "Exchange, sharing and collaborations with communities in the city and the region have been developed in and across disciplines, from health and sports to law and languages, from entrepreneurship to the sciences and the creative and performing arts" (Gleeson et al.). The 'Making Change Happen—Civic Engagement in Practice' case study from the University of Chichester states, "Projects only work if students learn how to work with many different kinds of people and acknowledge that success comes from working across disciplines" (Cooper and Reavey).

The case studies illustrate how the principle of challenge can *empower* students and community stakeholders as agents of change. For example, the University of Chichester case study stresses that projects "required students to come up with a creative solution to make change happen" (ibid.). Students engaged in the International Practicum Pilot 'Limerick Inside Out' "felt that the direct interaction with community representatives and the teamwork were most empowering" (Gleeson et al.). In the Solent University 'Healthy Living Project', "Collaboration with the women was critical in shaping the project further and provided the participants and students with a feeling of shared ownership and empowerment" (King).

The principle of *ensuring community voice* features across the four case studies with the University of Chichester example emphasising "From the start, students listen to the broader community voice so they begin to understand diversity of views of stakeholders in the broadest sense—not just a head teacher or the CEO of a charity but children on the School Council, teachers in staff meetings, people in the neighbourhood" (Cooper and Reavey). The University of Limerick case study states, "By participating in the students' welcome session and the final public exhibition, various community partners with different interests came together in an informal and special setting to give voice to their work" (Gleeson et al.). The 'Solent Football Leadership Programme' highlights the local community "engaging with the project work and voicing their needs, not just for developing football itself, but also for developing communities and community cohesion via the vehicle of football" (Bourne). This illustrates the potential of community-based learning to cascade benefits beyond the direct initial focus of the initiative—important for its reach and legacy.

All of the case studies are characterised by principles of *reciprocity* and *mutual benefit*, for example, the 'Healthy Living Project' from Solent University "provides the students with a platform to put into practice classroom taught theories and skills as well as providing the community with a sustainable initiative addressing a health or social need" (King).

Collectively the case studies demonstrate diverse ways of developing and implementing real world learning through civic engagement. They express how students, faculty and community members effectively undertake challenging initiatives across a range of disciplines. They show how students forge deep connections between theories learned in lectures and seminars with the 'real world' beyond. They demonstrate how strong sustainable links are created between university and community and illustrate practical ways of promoting and inculcating principles of *equity and social justice* through real world learning. Importantly these four case studies clearly show how principles of real world learning through civic engagement can be applied in practice.

For real world learning through civic engagement initiatives to be similarly effective and sustainable, it is vital they be strategically led, encouraged and appropriately supported by their institutions; energy and commitment of students, staff and communities are necessary but insufficient. We turn our attention to this matter in the following section.

Institutions Must Do Their Own Real World Learning: Leadership and Strategy

Linking Institutional Imperatives

Writing the university civic engagement mission statement is the easy bit; the difficulty for institutions is to create a *holistic ethos* of critical reflection and open dialogue which promotes and supports real world student learning through civic partnerships. The challenge is to create learning opportunities that benefit and empower students, communities and faculty. Excellent opportunities exist to capitalise on synergies between different strategic imperatives: developing professional and personal graduate attributes—employability, learning for sustainability and active citizenship. This can be achieved by integrating agendas for critical civic engagement with those of ESD and citizenship education—linking drivers for regional, national and international development.

Implementing real world learning through civic engagement demands commitment and action on multiple fronts. Our international scoping survey showed that whilst increasing numbers of institutions had been *committing* to student learning through community engagement, there was little alignment between this commitment and institutional processes to support it (McEwen & Mason O'Connor, 2013). Other findings were the following: wide variability in recognition and reward ranging from well-established promotion processes to absence of any form of recognition; frequent lack of accounting for community engagement as part of workload allocation; few coherent processes of supportive staff and educational development, and inflexible institutional procedures which curb staff enthusiasm.

Distributed Leadership in Action

Whilst the literature on leadership of university civic engagement points almost universally to the importance of 'distributed leadership', it acknowledges there is no optimal approach; institutions need to work out for themselves how leadership is distributed, recognising that "the infrastructure for engagement does not necessarily align with the institutional hierarchy" (Liang & Sandmann, 2015, p. 37). Leadership must take place at all levels across the institution to build and support innovative creative institutional cultures. This is particularly challenging when academics are arguing that forces of marketisation generate "continuous pressures to standardize, conform, obey and duplicate in order to be 'transparent' to measurement" (Lesnik-Oberstein et al., 2015). Leaders need to challenge institutional boundaries: "entrenched interests of disciplines, academic departments, and traditional epistemology militate against the full emergence of community engaged scholarship" (Giles, 2016, p. 194). Relaxing the 'disciplinary grip' (Ivison, 2018) requires considerable leadership skill and courage. Establishing porous boundaries enables and encourages networking and innovation across and beyond the institution and "supports two-way flow of information, people and resources … which integrate and connect universities physically, digitally and intellectually to society" (Wilson, Manners, & Duncan, 2014, p. 9). It advances and fosters claims by communities within and beyond its parameters that the institution is '*our* university'.

Transformative pedagogies and key principles are the hallmarks of real world learning through civic engagement. Leading change in this direction is challenging; transformative learning, as previously indicated, can be "troublesome" (Perkins, 1999), a risky endeavour with uncertain outcomes. Leadership is required to develop courses and university quality assurance processes agile enough to foster and accredit learning that takes place in contexts where outcomes are unpredictable and where new ones might emerge. In our work on developing community engagement (Mason O'Connor & McEwen, 2012, p. 12), we devised a set of questions to assure quality of accredited community-based learning: for example, "How are 'unanticipated learning outcomes' to be recognised and assessed?"; "How is mutual benefit and reciprocity for all stakeholders maintained?"

Importantly, leadership and strategy have to ensure support and recognition for the three key stakeholders engaged in real world learning through civic engagement: students, community and faculty.

Support and Recognition for Students

Through critical community-based learning, students can acquire a variety of graduate attributes for employability, sustainable development and active citizenship. A recent publication on graduate attributes and higher education (Normand & Anderson, 2017) reinforces the view that graduate attributes sought by employers extend well beyond the possession of disciplinary knowledge. In rapidly changing social and economic contexts, a range of interpersonal skills and abilities are vital, such as self-awareness, resilience, adaptability and empathy. Real world learning through civic engagement can be a key means of developing these attributes (Mason O'Connor, Lynch, & Owen, 2011). It must be emphasised, however, that students beginning, undertaking and concluding civic engagement initiatives require appropriate support and encouragement not only for the 'academic' element of their work but, crucially, for the affective element where long-held understandings and beliefs may be challenged and the outcome of the initiative is uncertain. Importantly, students should be supported and assessed on the development of their reflective learning throughout the process of civic engagement rather than the 'success' or otherwise of the initiative.

Support and Recognition for Community

Communities are not extra-mural laboratories for university use. Community learning has to be supported and evaluated on a par with student learning. As individuals and/or groups, community members may need support for participation in civic engagement initiatives particularly those communities who are 'under-served'. This could, for example, include funds for any costs incurred engaging with university students, such as the use of reciprocal engagement spaces. As Collins (2019) proposes, communities need to be compensated justly for their work. For radical civic engagement to be facilitated, it is necessary to ensure that "equity, justice, and an appreciation of diverse value systems and perspectives are included in the development of civic actors, civic learning, and shared projects of social change in local communities" (Hicks Petersen, 2015, p. 17).

Support and Recognition for Faculty

Based on their research and work with a wide range of institutions in the UK, Manners and Duncan (2018) conclude, "without an explicit focus on developing supportive organisational cultures, staff feel discouraged from engaging externally; and the quality and effectiveness of that engagement can be compromised" (Manners & Duncan, 2018, p. 3).

In our work on building staff capacity for university-community engagement, we identified key staff attributes, skills and attitudes and dispositions which contribute to effective university-community engagement. Attitudes and dispositions include "commitment to social justice" and "willingness to engage and take risks"; skills include "design for mutual benefit" and "interdisciplinary working"; knowledge included "ethical practice" and "pedagogies of active reflective learning" (Mason O'Connor & McEwen, 2012, p. 14). Some skills needed by Faculty for CBL link well to the research skills in community-based participatory research (Durham Community Research Team, 2011). These take greater account of issues of power, rights and responsibilities and roles of all stakeholders, based on respect for, and partnership with, community members.

As well as requiring support, civic engagement has to be incentivised, recognised and valued (McEwen & Mason O'Connor, 2013). Boland's research showed engagement work was seen by academics as something they *elected* to do. "A corollary of the elective nature of this work is that civic engagement is not generally regarded as part of the academic role" (Boland, 2014, p. 190). Recruitment, promotion and appraisal systems need to recognise this work.

We conclude our discussion on leadership and strategy by referring to an international meeting of vice-chancellors in Melbourne. Acknowledging staff reluctance to be involved in civic engagement work because university rankings systems foreground research, the vice-chancellor of

Queensland University issued a challenge: "many of these global rankings are based on what we can readily measure, rather than what we have to learn to measure" (Havergal, 2017).

Conclusion

We have shown in this chapter that real world learning through civic engagement encompasses a range of rationales, pedagogies and approaches. It has developed from a paradigm of expanding learning opportunities for students through volunteering to one in which students are challenged to develop as empowered active citizens. Students are prepared for future uncertainties and opportunities, learning in partnership with others to bring about positive change. Underpinning this paradigm are key principles. Exploring, developing and applying these principles through effective leadership at all levels can enable universities to connect with communities locally and globally, providing institutional aspirational rhetoric with rich 'real world' realities.

References

Advisory Group on Citizenship. (1998). *Education for citizenship and the teaching of democracy in schools* [Crick Report]. Qualifications and Curriculum Authority. Retrieved from https://www.teachingcitizenship.org.uk/sites/teachingcitizenship.org.uk/files/6123_crick_report_1998_0.pdf

Asghar, M., & Rowe, N. (2017). Reciprocity and critical reflection as the key to social justice in service learning: A case study. *Innovations in Education and Teaching International, 54*(2), 117–125. https://doi.org/10.1080/1470329 7.2016.1273788

Blouin, D. D., & Perry, E. M. (2009). Whom does service learning really serve? Perspectives on service learning. *Teaching Sociology, 37*(2), 120–135.

Boland, J. A. (2014). Orientations to civic engagement: Insights into the sustainability of a challenging pedagogy. *Studies in Higher Education, 39*(1), 180–195. https://doi.org/10.1080/03075079.2011.648177

Boyer, E. (1996). The scholarship of engagement. *Journal of Public Service and Outreach, 1*(1), 11–20.

Brabant, M., & Braid, D. (2009). The devil is in the details: Defining civic engagement. *Journal of Higher Education Outreach and Engagement, 13*(2), 59–87.

Brabner, R. (2019). *The creation of a civic university agreement was the principle (sic) recommendation of the UPP Foundation Civic University Commission.* Retrieved from https://upp-foundation.org/over-50-universities-pledge-comchellment-to-local-communities-through-civic-university-agreement/

Brown University. Retrieved from https://www.brown.edu/swearer/carnegie

Collins, L. (2019). Letting the village be the teacher: A look at community-based learning in Northern Thailand. *Teaching in Higher Education, 24*(5), 694–708. https://doi.org/10.1080/13562517.2019.1579708

Delucchi, M., & Smith, W. L. (1997). Satisfied customers versus pedagogic responsibility: Further thoughts on student consumerism. *Teaching Sociology, 25*(4), 336–337.

Durham Community Research Team. (2011). *Community-based participatory research: Ethical challenges.* Retrieved from http://www.ahrc.ac.uk/documents/project-reports-and-reviews/connected-communities/community-based-participatory-research-ethical-challenges/

El-Gabry, L. (2018). Case study on community-based learning: Toy design project for children in Egyptian squatter community. *European Journal of Engineering Education, 43*(6), 879–894. https://doi.org/10.1080/0304379 7.2018.1451492

Fallace, T. D. (2016). John Dewey's visions(s) for interdisciplinary social studies. *Social Studies Research and Practice, 11*(1), 177–189.

Fink, L. D. (2003). *Creating significant learning experiences: An integrated approach to designing college courses.* San Francisco, CA: Jossey-Bass Higher and Adult Education.

Freire, P. (2005). *Pedagogy of the oppressed* (30th Anniversary ed., M. B. Ramos, Trans.). New York: Continuum.

Fung, D. (2016). Engaging students with research through a connected curriculum: An innovative approach. *CUR Quarterly, 7*(2), 30–35. Retrieved from http://www.cur.org/assets/1/23/win16-Article5.pdf

Gibbons, M. (2000). Mode 2 society and the emergence of context-sensitive science. *Science and Public Policy, 27*(3), 159–163.

Giles, D. E. (2016). The emergence of engaged scholarship: Seven additional years of evolution. *Journal of higher Education Outreach and Engagement, 20*(1), 193–195. ISSN: 1534-6104, eISSN: 2164-8212.

Goddard, J., & Kempton, L. (n.d.). *The civic university: Universities in the leadership of management and place.* Retrieved from https://warwick.ac.uk/research/warwickcommission/chancellorscommission/report/appendices/curds_warwick_report_final.pdf

GuildHE/National Union of Students. (2016). *Active citizenship: The role of higher education.* GuildHE. Retrieved from: https://guildhe.ac.uk/wp-content/uploads/2016/11/6710-Guild-HE-Active-Citizenship-Report-44pp.pdf

GUNI (Global University Network for Innovation). (2013). *Higher Education in the World (5). Knowledge, engagement and higher education: Contributing to social change* (B. Hall & R. Tandon, Guest Eds.). London: Palgrave Macmillan.

Hall, B., Lall, N., & Heng Chan, L. (n.d.). *Knowledge for the world we want: The emergence of the Global Alliance for Community Engaged Research (GACER).* Retrieved from: http://www.guninetwork.org/articles/knowledge-world-we-want-emergence-global-alliance-community-engaged-research-gacer

Hammersley, L. (2012). *Community-based service-learning: Partnerships of reciprocal exchange?* Special Issue: Work Integrated Learning - Investing in the Future. Papers from the Australian Collaborative Education Network Annual Conference 2012.

Havergal, C. (2017, September 24). Research focus of global rankings a 'barrier' to community engagement. *Times Higher Education.*

Hicks Petersen, T. (2015). Reviving and revising the civic mission: A radical re-imagining of "civic engagement". *Metropolitan Universities: An International Forum, 25*(3), 17–30.

Hill, F. (2015). *Taking stock: A review of university public engagement activity.* Final Report. Bristol: National Co-ordinating Centre for Public Engagement.

Ivison, D. (2018, April 12). Disciplines must relax if the big challenges are to be met. *Times Higher Education.*

Jung, J.-K. (2018). Mapping communities: Geographic and interdisciplinary community-based learning and research. *The Professional Geographer, 70*(2), 311–318. https://doi.org/10.1080/00330124.2017.1366787

Kerslake, R. W. (2019). Foreword to *Truly Civic: Strengthening the Connections Between Universities and their Place.* The Final Report of the UPP Foundation Civic University Commission, UK.

Kramer, L. A., & Fask, J. F. (2017). *Creative collaborations through inclusive theatre and community based learning: Students in transition.* Palgrave Macmillan.

Lesnik-Oberstein, K., et al. (2015, July 6). Let UK universities do what they do best – teaching and research. Letter to *The Guardian* signed by over 100 academic staff. Retrieved from: https://www.theguardian.com/education/2015/jul/06/let-uk-universities-do-what-they-do-best-teaching-and-research

Liang, J. G., & Sandmann, L. R. (2015). Leadership for community engagement: A distributed perspective. *Journal of Higher Education and Outreach and Engagement, 19*(1), 35–62. ISSN: 1534-6104.

Lotz-Sisitka, H., Wals, A. E., Kronlid, D., & McGarry, D. (2015). Transformative, transgressive social learning: Rethinking higher education pedagogy in times of systemic global dysfunction. *Current Opinion in Environmental Sustainability, 16,* 73–80. https://doi.org/10.1016/j.cosust.2015.07.018

Manners, P., & Duncan, S. (2018). *NCCPE response to UPP foundation civic university commission.* Bristol: National Co-ordinating Centre for Public Engagement. Retrieved from https://www.publicengagement.ac.uk/sites/default/files/publication/nccpe_response_to_upp_commission_300718.pdf

Mason O'Connor, K., Lynch, K., & Owen, D. (2011). Student-community engagement and the development of graduate attributes. *Education and Training, 53*(2/3), 100–115. https://doi.org/10.1108/00400911111115654

Mason O'Connor, K., & McEwen, L. J. (2012). *Developing community engagement.* SEDA Special 32. London: Staff and Educational Development Association.

Mason O'Connor, K., McEwen, L. J., Owen, D., Lynch, K., & Hill, S. (2011). *Literature review. Embedding community engagement in the curriculum: An example of university-public engagement.* Bristol: National Co-ordinating Centre for Public Engagement and University of Gloucestershire.

Mayer, B., Blume, A., Black, C., & Stevens, S. (2018). Improving student learning outcomes through community-based research: The poverty workshop. *Teaching Sociology, 47*(2), 135–147. https://doi.org/10.1177/0092055X18818251

McEwen, L. J., & Mason O'Connor, K. (2013). *Communiversity: Building staff/faculty capacity for university-public/community engagement.* Report. Retrieved from www.uwe.ac.uk/repository

McEwen, L. J., Strachan, G., & Lynch, K. (2011). "Shock and awe" or "reflection and change": How can research into transformative learning inform pedagogic practice in higher education? *Learning and Teaching in Higher Education, 5*, 34–55.

Meyer, J. H. F., & Land, R. (2005). Threshold concepts and troublesome knowledge (2): Epistemological considerations and a conceptual framework for teaching and learning. *Higher Education, 49*(3), 373–388.

Mezirow, J. (1978). Perspective transformation. *Adult Education Quarterly, 28*, 100–110.

Mezirow, J. (1991). *Transformative dimensions of adult learning.* San Francisco, CA: Jossey-Bass.

Mezirow, J. (2000). Learning to think like an adult: Core concepts of transformation theory. In J. Mezirow & Associates (Ed.), *Learning as transformation: Critical perspectives on a theory in progress* (pp. 3–34). San Francisco, CA: Jossey-Bass.

Mezirow, J. (2003). Transformative learning as discourse. *Journal of Transformative Education, 1*(1), 58–63.

Miller, G. (2013). Education for citizenship: Community engagement between the Global South and the Global North. *Journal of Geography in Higher Education, 37*(1), 44–58. https://doi.org/10.1080/03098265.2012.757299

Mitchell, T. D. (2008). Traditional versus critical service learning: Engaging the literature to differentiate two models. *Michigan Journal of Community Service-Learning, 14*(2), 50–65.

Normand, C., & Anderson, L. (Eds.). (2017). *Graduate attributes in higher education: Attitudes on attributes across the disciplines.* London: Routledge.

O'Mahoney, C., Burns, K., & McDonell, C. (n.d.). *Community-based research: An introductory guide for higher education staff.* Campus Engage. Retrieved from https://www.livingknowledge.org/fileadmin/Dateien-Living-Knowledge/Dokumente_Dateien/Toolbox/Community-Based_Research_WEB_1_.pdf

Office for Students. (2019). *What if the TEF?* Retrieved from https://www.officeforstudents.org.uk/advice-and-guidance/teaching/what-is-the-tef/

Pain, E., Finn, M., Bouveng, R., & Ngobe, G. (2013). Productive tensions—Engaging geography students in participatory action research with communities. *Journal of Geography in Higher Education, 37*(1), 28–43. https://doi.org/10.1080/03098265.2012.696594

Perkins, D. (1999). The many faces of constructivism. *Educational Leadership, 57*(3), 6–11.

Sandmann, L. R. (2008). Conceptualization of the scholarship of engagement in higher education: A strategic review 1996–2006. *Journal of Higher Education and Outreach and Engagement, 12*(1), 91–104.

Schwartz, E. (2015). "Bringing it all back home": An interdisciplinary model for community-based learning. *Journal of College & Character, 16*(1), 53–61. https://doi.org/10.1080/2194587X.2014.992910

Stoecker, R. (2016). *Liberating service learning and the rest of higher education civic engagement.* Philadelphia, PA: Temple University Press.

Talloires Network. (2005). *Talloires declaration on the civic roles and social responsibilities of higher education.* Retrieved from https://talloiresnetwork.tufts.edu/who-we-are/talloires-declaration/

Tandon, R., Hall, B., Lepore, W., & Singh, W. (2016). *Training the next generation of community based researchers: A guide for trainers.* PRIA (Society for Participatory Research in Asia), India, & University of Victoria, Canada.

UK Research Innovation. (n.d.). REF Impact. Retrieved from https://re.ukri.org/research/ref-impact/

UNESCO. (2009). *2009 World conference on higher education: The new dynamics of higher education and research for societal change.* Paris: United Nations Educational, Scientific and Cultural Organization.

UNESCO. (2014). *UNESCO roadmap for implementing the global action programme on education for sustainable development.* Paris: United Nations Educational, Scientific and Cultural Organization.

UNESCO. (2018). *Issues and trends in education for sustainable development.* Paris: United Nations Educational, Scientific and Cultural Organization.

Wasner, V. (2016). Critical service learning: A participatory pedagogical approach to global citizenship and international mindedness. *Journal of Research in International Education, 15*(3), 238–252. https://doi.org/10.1177/1475240916669026

Watson, D., Hollister, R. M., Stroud, S. E., & Babcock, E. (2011). *The engaged university: International perspectives on civic engagement.* Taylor and Francis Group: Routledge.

Weinberg, J., & Flinders, M. (2018). Learning for democracy: The politics and practice of citizenship education. *British Educational Research Journal, 44*(4), 573–592. https://doi.org/10.1002/berj.3446

Wells, P. J. (2017). *The role of higher education institutions today: Balancing the global with the local.* GUNI HEIW Report. Retrieved from http://www.guni-network.org/files/download_full_report.pdf

Wilson, C., Manners, P., & Duncan, S. (2014). *Building an engaged future for UK higher education. Full report from the engaged futures consultation.* Bristol: National Co-ordinating Centre for Public Engagement.

Wood, B. E., Taylor, R., Atkins, R., & Johnston, M. (2018). Pedagogies for active citizenship: Learning through affective and cognitive domains for deeper democratic engagement. *Teaching and Teacher Education, 75,* 259–267. https://doi.org/10.1016/j.tate.2018.07.007

5

Working and Learning Through the Local Community: Four Case Studies from Higher Education That Promote Civic Engagement

Dawn A. Morley, Tracey Gleeson, Kerstin Mey,
Anne Warren-Perkinson, Tracey Bourne, Amy E. King,
Linda Cooper, and Duncan Reavey

Introduction

Chapter 4, 'Real World Learning Through Civic Engagement: Principles, Pedagogies and Practices', discusses the rise of the civic engagement movement in higher education and the mutual benefits of connecting universities with their local communities. This seems to have increased

D. A. Morley (✉)
School of Sport, Health and Social Sciences, Solent University, Southampton, UK

T. Gleeson • K. Mey • A. Warren-Perkinson
University of Limerick, Limerick, Republic of Ireland

T. Bourne • A. E. King
Solent University, Southampton, UK

L. Cooper • D. Reavey
University of Chichester, Chichester, UK

© The Author(s) 2021   **91**
D. A. Morley, M. G. Jamil (eds.), *Applied Pedagogies for Higher Education*,
https://doi.org/10.1007/978-3-030-46951-1_5

urgency following recent concerns about the lack of citizenship educa-tion identified at primary and secondary education in the UK due to the pressures of the national curriculum (George, 2018). The UPP Foundation Civic University Commission, founded in 2018, discovered extensive civic engagement across the higher education sector but this rarely mani-fested itself as part of the university's mission (Brabner, 2019). As a result, the creation of Civic University Agreements (CUAs) has attempted to formalise a "public declaration of a university's civic properties and indi-cate how they will be delivered in partnership with ... organisations" (Brabner, 2019).

Whatever the local drivers for civic engagement, the four case studies presented within this chapter allow students an alternative route into a real world learning experience. Through 'giving back' students collabora-tively engage with different populations in diverse communities thus increasing the students' wider experience and exposure to issues often larger than their university experience. Good examples of civic engage-ment exhibit powerful ways of connecting students in their present situ-ation, whether as an international student (Case Study 1) or as part of their learning within their own universities (Case Studies 2–4), to chal-lenge and support that takes students to new depths. In fact, students experience authentic, real world situations that can stay with them for the rest of their lives; the type of immersive, innovative learning 'break(s) the script' (Heath & Heath, 2017) and is long remembered.

The case studies presented also counteract some of the emerging criti-cisms of civic engagement in higher education—universities need to work more closely with lower socioeconomic groups and diverse com-munities, form genuine partnerships where they are not the dominant party, and support quality controlled, regional change (UPP, 2019).

Although the case studies presented have their own unique history, their success is based on commonalities that have taken them all to high levels of recognition and sustainability. Their success has evolved and been built over time, indicative of the importance of a university mindset that recognises the commitment to community engagement for the long term. In Chapter 4, Mason O'Connor and McEwen comment on the importance of linking with institutional imperatives. This can take many forms—Case Study 1's initiative is founded on civic engagement princi-ples from 1972 while Case Study 4 has embedded the extension of their students' learning into community projects through their own programme ethos.

In setting up the civic engagement initiatives, university staff recognised the potential mutual benefits of extending their students learning through community groups and, in Case Study 2, this created a greater and dynamic ongoing relationship with Hampshire Football Authority and the university modules. As students worked predominantly either in new situations or with unfamiliar groups, mentorship of students was a powerful principle of all the projects. This took a variety of forms—from service level agreements under the supervision of a professional practitioner to mentorship by academics and was dependent on perceived risk and the elements of creativity and initiative that was expected of students.

Assessment within the case studies took a real world learning approach (described further in Chapter 14) where measurement went beyond the attainment of learning outcomes to "process, product, legacy and sustainability" (Case Study 4). The development of students' attributes proved the true measure of civic engagement and this success was celebrated by innovative assessment with high levels of prestige at public events or as part of internal and external award processes. Unusually for higher education, with the propensity for regular revalidation of courses, the sustainability of the civic engagement projects were a marker for longitudinal success and this experience fed back into improving the experience for the students and the communities in which they worked. The support and recognition that students attained at university extended beyond their usual experience by taking less conventional approaches and encompassed the impact on faculty and community.

Case Study 1

University of Limerick—International Practicum Pilot 'Limerick Inside Out' (Tracey Gleeson, Senior Co-ordinator, Limerick Inside Out Practicum, Kerstin Mey, University of Limerick Vice President of Academic Affairs and Student Engagement and Anne Warren-Perkinson, Implementation Advisor, Limerick Inside Out Programme, University of Limerick, Ireland)

The Values of Community Engagement

Civil and civic engagement has been at the heart of the University of Limerick (UL) and its predecessor since its inception in 1972. Exchange, sharing and collaborations with communities in the city and the region have been developed in and across disciplines, from health and sports to law and languages, from entrepreneurship to the sciences and the creative and performing arts. The interactions with communities are founded on a partnership model that seeks to foster mutuality and sustainability, co-creation and empowerment. A decade ago, the university established the President's Volunteering Award (VPA) initiative for students and an award for excellence in service to the community scheme for staff. From the beginning, the university has played a leading part in the Irish University Association's Campus Engage initiative. Campus Engage was founded in 2007 with the aim of establishing a nationwide network to foster civil and civic engagement activities across the higher education sector.

Building on recognised expertise in engaged learning and research and making fruitful existing community networks, UL first developed a *Practicum* for international students in spring 2017. This experiential learning module encompassed a range of practice-based projects co-designed with local community partners and was offered to a limited number of international students at UL as part of their credited Study Abroad programme. The planning, preparation and realisation of projects—within a 12-week teaching term—offered mutual benefits to both the students and the community partners and placed a disproportionate burden on a single academic lead. The one-off interactions created significant complexity and challenges in terms of their underlying logistics and support processes, which rendered the module unviable. In addition, the initial module concept and design was not easily replicable across different faculties and disciplines. Therefore, in response to growing interest from international students and their home institutions, it was necessary to consider alternative methods and sustainable approaches for delivering the UL *International Practicum*.

Following a period of organisational change and internal reflection, a pilot of a restructured UL International Practicum was undertaken in Spring semester 2019. The so-called Limerick Inside Out (LIO) Practicum took on 34 students. While LIO retained key concepts of the original practicum—real world experience, active learning, mutual benefit and empowerment—it tested a revised approach to aid its viability, replicability and transferability to different disciplinary and community contexts.

The pilot module promoted transdisciplinary, cross-cultural and intergenerational awareness development. Learning was facilitated off-campus within three distinct but nevertheless complementary strands: creative, political, interculturalism—which, not least, reduced the dependency on a single academic lead. Pragmatically, less emphasis was placed on singular and one-off co-created projects with community partners. Instead LIO sought to highlight the richness of Limerick City and its diverse community groups. The deliberate shift in focus from 'depth' to 'breadth' of community engaged learning in this pilot was supplemented by the establishment of a strategic partnership with the Limerick City and County Council (LCCC).

The students were welcomed into Limerick City with an opening session held in a central landmark. To support a broader experience and promote real world learning, each LIO student was issued with a travel pass for local public transport and invited to become a social media ambassador for LIO, with their contribution recognised as part of UL's VPA scheme. This served to empower students to decide for themselves how often they wanted to be in Limerick working with community partners and seeking permission to speak openly on social media about their experiences both in the module and in the wider community.

The three module strands, with distinct academic perspectives from the Faculty of Arts, Humanities and Social Sciences (AHSS), demonstrated the value of diversity in LIO as many students (such as those majoring in engineering or business) would not otherwise have had an opportunity to explore concepts of empathy, civil and civic engagement, or interculturalism in a real community setting. The LIO pilot concluded with a high-profile public exhibition of student work in a historic Limerick industrial development site, in conjunction with the premier of a local theatre production. The display was opened by the Mayor and attended by Council officials, community partners, university staff and media. It demonstrated that the students' work had covered a multitude of topics and learning experiences and served to facilitate not only a further exchange of ideas but acknowledged the evolving mutuality of the broader university-community-relationship.

Student module feedback confirmed the strong initial interest in a module that focused on real world experience as a central learning objective and highlighted ethical practice, added value and 'giving back' as central motives for them to seek out this academic offering. While the different LIO pilot strands delivered an overview of the local context and stimulated a diversity of experiences, most students felt that the direct interaction with community representatives and the teamwork were most empowering.

The students were exposed to novel methods of formative and summative assessment and feedback. The latter included the creation of posters and reflective postcards. Addressing individual challenges, students developed soft skills in support of their future employability. They also gained an understanding of the value of diversity in working with others to generate positive social change in and with their own communities.

As the community partners of the LIO pilot had not been involved in the previous UL International Practicum there were a few little preconceptions and expectations that required careful consideration. By participating in the students' welcome session and the final public exhibition, various community partners with different interests came together in an informal and special setting to give voice to their work. LIO created a unique occasion for them to explore the potential of partnerships both with UL and with each other. As several community groups became aware of further opportunities to engage with students in ways that could create additional capacity and capabilities they approached UL with new ideas for co-created and co-delivered projects.

Through the LIO pilot, community partners recognised how the different backgrounds and experience of international students can contribute to addressing local issues, and that community voices in Limerick can have global audiences augmented through social media. The LIO pilot created opportunities to involve individuals who would otherwise not have a relationship with the university. It thus catalysed a great sense of pride in both themselves and their community.

> **Case Study 2**
>
> **The Solent Football Leadership Programme (Tracey Bourne, Course Leader, BA (Hons) Football Studies, Solent University, UK)**

Course philosophy and employer feedback demonstrated the need within the football industry for 'industry ready' graduates possessing both academic knowledge and effective employability skills and a working knowledge of the industry. Whilst members of the Hampshire Football Authority (HFA) had contributed well-received guest lectures to football degree modules, the relationship was hardly reciprocal with little in return for the HFA against their involvement. Recognising the value of reciprocity, the Solent Football Development Programme (SFLP) was established in 2014 as a formalised partnership which would offer a range of benefits to students at the university, the HFA and also to a diverse range of stakeholders. The SFLP provided students with opportunities to understand the role that football can play in contributing to addressing social issues in local communities as well as investigating how the sport itself can be evolved to ensure quality of provision for all. The SFLP is a key part of each of the football modules.

The partnership has rapidly developed to incorporate County FA grassroots development projects into undergraduate modules, combining theoretical teaching, based on the County FA Football Development Strategy, with experiential learning via live football development project work. Projects were initially created and designed by HFA in alignment with the requirements of their work programme, County Plan and FA National Game Strategy, and are fully based upon analysis of community needs. The number of projects has expanded exponentially over the years, from an initial 10 in 2014 to 42 in the 2018 academic year. Students engage with a diverse range of projects and participants incorporating areas such as working with the homeless community, women and girls, mental health and well-being, disability, youth and many more. To work with such a range of participants across a broad spectrum of projects offers students a variety of challenges and problems which are 'real world' and, as such, require real solutions. Additionally, students have to be reflective and proactive in their practice to ensure that their project work continues to meet the needs of the County FA and the local community. It is also sustainable in that it provides ongoing opportunities for those communities to develop and grow their community voice through the vehicle of football. By taking the lead on the projects with community members, students are empowered to make positive change to their own knowledge, experience and employability as well as positive change to those communities with whom they are working. The ongoing nature of the support from the student workforce allows HFA to fully and sustainably support the progression and development of grassroots football in Hampshire.

A key benefit of the partnership is the impact of County FA involvement on the development and delivery of the curriculum of the modules concerned. Football Development Officers from HFA continue to guest lecture on areas of their work programme which is highly contemporary in its nature, giving both students and teaching staff contemporary knowledge and context of the football development climate. Access to changes in policy and strategy are instantaneously available, resulting in core academic content which may not be so readily available through traditional research-led teaching. In addition to delivery, HFA officers also engage on a one-to-one basis with student groups to ensure they are working proactively with their projects and participants. This allows students valuable time to engage in focused, highly individualised learning activities with a potential employer in the football industry. Moreover, it also provides the opportunity to build rapport and develop ongoing relationships with potential employers in addition to those in the local community. Conversely, HFA development officers are able to engage at a deeper level to ensure that their work programme is benefitting from the project work being undertaken, while also ensuring that students understand how the theory applies to context within their particular projects and how it can be applied in a real world setting.

Recognition for the programme' s success was seen in the 2016 nomination and award for the FA Grassroots project of the year award and subsequent nomination by the FA to UEFA for the UEFA Grassroots Football Development Project of the year award for 2016. The SFLP partnership was awarded bronze, a significant award, and European recognition for the work of the students and positive impact on the local community. An additional benefit for the local community and students is the annual Hampshire FA Grassroots Football Awards which include specific awards for the SFLP Volunteers of the year, awarded to one of the student project groups in recognition of their work on an SFLP project. The event is typically attended by over 500 stakeholders from the local community, giving further opportunity for individual students to network, share knowledge and experience with community partners, and showcase their talents and employability to potential future employers. This also allows great opportunities for knowledge transfer between communities and the academic world.

Following the initial success of the SFLP and its positive impacts on the community, the FA has adopted the programme as a model of good practice for County FAs across England, and, significantly, additional HE institutions are developing small-scale renditions of the SFLP. This development has allowed for numerous other communities to engage in similar work, thus broadening and developing the community in terms of reach, diversity, cohesion, employability and empowerment.

To date, the SFLP has reached out to and engaged with over 1500 members of the local football and non-football community, via the delivery of 42 projects delivered by over 600 students. A number of positive community impacts have been identified, with increasing numbers of participants, more stakeholders requesting to be part of the SFLP and more diverse projects such as walking football for the elderly, being incorporated in response to community needs. The local community is engaging with the project work and voicing their needs not just for developing football itself but also for developing communities and community cohesion via the vehicle of football. The SFLP offers a holistic approach to 'real world learning' and brings together the community and students to unite in opportunities that they may not have had access to had the SFLP not been in place.

Case Study 3

The Community Innovation Programme, Solent University, Healthy Living Project (Amy E. King, Health and Exercise Development Officer, Solent University, UK)

The Community Innovation Programme (CIP) at Solent University is a curriculum-based initiative which enables sport and physical activity students to work in collaboration with community members to research their needs in order to develop and deliver a project which addresses those needs. The CIP process provides students with a platform to put into practice classroom-taught theories and skills as well as providing the community with a sustainable initiative addressing a health or social need.

CIPs are developed with local practitioners to enable a gateway to the community group for the students and provide expert guidance. The students and practitioner enter into a reciprocal and mutually beneficial relationship which is governed by a service level agreement.

A CIP designed by three students in partnership with a local industry practitioner focused on health literacy and weight loss for South Asian women after a lack of women only opportunities which catered for their cultural practices was identified. The students discussed with the community-based practitioner specific needs of the participants, drawing on the partner's knowledge and experience of the demographic. These needs included injury prevention, hydration and cultural differences in regard to nutritional beliefs. Collaboration with the women was critical in shaping the project further and provided participants and students with a feeling of shared ownership and empowerment. The result was a women-only Health Literacy and Weight Loss initiative (HLWL). As the women were diverse in terms of language and ethnicity, team-building exercises were included in sessions to promote cohesion.

The students who were engaged in the HLWL CIP developed and delivered the programme under the professional guidance of the practitioner who provided the facilities, equipment and access to the community group. In return, the practitioner received a research-based sustainable programme delivered voluntarily by the students. The benefit for participants was a programme, free of charge, tailored specifically with them, which addressed their health and social needs. Although the practitioner provided guidance, the students still had overall responsibility for the CIPs content and delivery method. This encouraged the students to take ownership of the programme which also motivated and challenged them to give their best.

In order to ensure collaboration and mutual benefit among all three parties for the development of the CIP, regular meetings were held. These included focus groups and feedback sessions held with the students, practitioner and participants which also contributed to the monitoring and evaluation of the sessions. These discussions allowed the students to assess and understand the continuing and changing needs of the participants.

Providing students with real world learning experiences such as the CIP promotes processes of learning through discovery and enables the students to put into practice the skills they have been taught whilst studying for their degree. The purposeful exploration and development of these skills through the HLWL CIP was very empowering for the students involving discovery and taking ownership of their learning. When the students worked with the practitioner, they learned the importance of establishing working relationships and development of a service level agreement. They learned that to be effective, partnerships need to be reciprocal and mutually beneficial. The students developed greater understanding of diverse cultures, which led them to adapt their practice appropriately and to introduce approaches which promoted group cohesion to enable effective programme delivery.

Delivering the CIP with sustainability in mind allowed the students to both experience the concept and learn that it is fundamental to initiatives. The successful nature of the HLWL CIP encouraged one of the students to turn the CIP into a business in order to facilitate expansion and provide organisational sustainability.

The HLWL CIP had a very positive impact on the local community. Participants had somewhere safe to remove their headscarves with female only instructors taking the sessions. Coming from different backgrounds, participants were able to mix and become friends through the team-bonding exercises which brought them together. This taught the students that group cohesion is fundamental for success for both the students and the participants. Students and participants actively collaborated in the monitoring and evaluation of the project through focus groups and feedback. This promoted the participants' interest in sustainability at an individual and community level as well as ensuring their involvement with planning. To ensure individual sustainability, each woman was given a wellness pack which, importantly, included information requested by and discussed with the women, nutritional information, home-based exercise plans, injury prevention information and health promotion material related to their culture. This proved very popular with the women.

The HLWL CIP was very successful with the project still operating several years after conception. This is due to the mutually beneficial and reciprocal relationship between the students, practitioner and participants. The collaboration and involvement of participants throughout the development and delivery of the CIP, as well as considering sustainability at an individual, community and organisational level is also what made the project such a great success.

Case Study 4

Making Change Happen—Civic Engagement in Practice (Linda Cooper, Head of Education Studies and Duncan Reavey, Principal Lecturer (Learning and Teaching), University of Chichester, UK)

At the start, we were thinking only of our students—soon-to-be primary school teachers who were great at teaching but less aware how the world beyond school and university operates. We knew that schools and non-government organisations across our area were always telling us their great ideas that would never happen because they had no time or insufficient expertise themselves. It made perfect sense to challenge students to take on these visible, real world projects with local partners.

Initially we called this compulsory module 'Creativity 3'—we were giving students opportunities to develop creativity in the broadest sense. Now it is called 'Making Change Happen'. But, throughout, our pitch to the students has been the same: *You have a problem to solve. Anything goes. Solve it. This is the way the world works and what we reward. Now do it in your first job.*

Significantly, the learning and teaching decisions that led to this initiative were not based on a review of academic literature, but came from careful thinking, talk and reflection by many, including recent graduates, prospective employers and partners in the broader community (Reavey, 2013).

Over 10 years we have had around 300 projects to challenge our student teachers, each one different, and each proposed by a school or other community organisation. Here are examples of projects offered from the local community, normally by schools and NGOs: working with the Government's Department for Education to create a new National Curriculum for first aid; restoring a school pond and generating innovative teaching resources; community sleepovers at a museum; creating new primary school resources to understand the Mayan civilisation; bringing non-English-speaking parents into the school community; making phonics resources for early years children; effective use of 'green screen' technology in school; using historical artefacts and digital resources to bring a museum to life; fire awareness games for the fire service to use with repeat fire starters.

Each project has required students to come up with a creative solution to make change happen. Students address the challenges in self-selected teams of 3–4 students over realistic timescales—typically 6 months—to provide authentic, meaningful end products for and with the external clients. Our aim is that students learn to communicate and act in a professional manner with a variety of stakeholders by working in partnership with them. They learn to negotiate the peaks and troughs of managing a project from conception to conclusion and beyond. They do all the physical work required. They gain marks for process, product, legacy and sustainability of their project.

At the start, students find the tasks daunting and question their ability to succeed. However, they are given the time and support to progress at whatever pace feels right. Lecturers mentor the students; the right level of facilitation (less rather than more) coupled with belief in the abilities of our students gives outcomes that are usually more than students (and lecturers, and external clients) ever think possible. By successfully completing difficult projects, the students are empowered to act as agents of change, a key aim for this learning experience.

Immediately after completing their projects, students enthuse about success in taking risks, solving problems and seeing a difference. However, we find it more helpful to judge success based on their longer-term reflections after they have been teaching for several years. For example, Emily, now a Deputy Head, was part of a project that changed the nature of lunchtimes for an infant school: "More than anything else, it showed us that even with very little experience as new teachers working in a new school, change can be brought about if you have a clear vision. It also showed us the power of teamwork in school, and with different stakeholders on board you really can make a difference … the teamwork values it taught me are in my thoughts and within my practice every day."

Nearly all of the 300 projects have led to a distinctive end product which continues to be used. For example, one group worked with the Sussex Snowdrop Trust to produce a resource pack for schools on bereavement and how teachers can address challenges that arise in school if a child in school is diagnosed with a life-threatening or terminal illness. This is frequently accessed online and, according to the charity, is 'brilliant'. We have many reports like this.

However, some impacts are sometimes harder to quantify. Schools and organisations mostly envision an outcome that is tangible. Initially so do the students—after all, contrasting 'Before' and 'after' photos will surely generate good marks. However, with some projects it soon becomes clear that change goes beyond this. Projects change people—not just students but also those they work with in the wider community.

Applying Principles of Real World Learning

The model for our approach is simple. No funding, no contracts, simply university and community working as honest, open partners to benefit student learning through doing something useful together. Clearly there is reciprocity as community partners benefit too—there are always more project proposals than we need and, while they are pleased to be able to give opportunities to our students, they certainly see significant benefits for themselves. This is founded on mutual benefit and a clear understanding of each partner's responsibilities from the start. Our students are empowered in ways they would not expect on a teacher education course, but so too are some of the stakeholders who became significant players even though not in senior roles (e.g. school caretaker, teaching assistant). From the start, students listen to the broader community voice so they begin to understand diversity of views of stakeholders in the broadest sense—not just a head teacher or the chief executive of a charity but children on the School Council, teachers in staff meetings, people in the neighbourhood. Students will insist on this even when some stakeholders suggest shortcuts. Students are rewarded in their grades for legacy and sustainability of the project into the future—therefore have every incentive to plan a careful hand over—but given their commitment to the project, they would want to do this anyway. Projects only work if students learn how to work in partnership with many different kinds of people and acknowledge that success comes from working across disciplines. Across all of this, perhaps our strongest plea to those designing university courses is to give students the space, support and belief to take on a real challenge so that they can succeed beyond their (and our) expectations.

References

Brabner, R. (2019). How to be a better civic university. *Times Higher Education*. Retrieved from https://www.timeshighereducation.com/opinion/how-be-better-civic-university

George, M. (2018). Citizenship education in 'parlous' state. *Times Education Supplement*. Retrieved from https://www.tes.com/news/citizenship-education-parlous-state

Heath, C., & Heath, D. (2017). *The power of moments: Why certain experiences have extraordinary impact*. London/Toronto/Sydney/Auckland/Johannesburg: Bantam Press.

Reavey, D. (2013). Wanted! Agents of change: Enabling students to make change happen in their professional world. In T. Bilham (Ed.), *For the love of learning. Innovations from outstanding university teachers* (pp. 191–197). Palgrave.

UPP foundation. (2019). *A guide to preparing civic university agreements*. Retrieved from https://upp-foundation.org/wp-content/uploads/2019/07/2202-UPP-Foundation-A-Guide-to-preparing-Civic-University-Agreements-Booklet-A4-digital.pdf

6

Real World Learning and the Internationalisation of Higher Education: Approaches to Making Learning Real for Global Communities

Md Golam Jamil, Nazmul Alam, Natascha Radclyffe-Thomas, Mohammad Aminul Islam, A. K. M. Moniruzzaman Mollah, and Annajiat Alim Rasel

Real World Learning in the Changing Landscape of Higher Education

Nineteenth-century American educational reformer Horace Mann's proclamation of education as the 'great equaliser of the conditions of men' has a wider meaning in contemporary educational policies and practices (Mann, 1957). The dramatic expansion of knowledge domains in present-day academic disciplines, and enhanced explanations of the

M. G. Jamil (✉)
Bristol Institute for Learning and Teaching, University of Bristol, Bristol, UK
e-mail: golam.jamil@bristol.ac.uk

N. Alam • A. K. M. Moniruzzaman Mollah
Asian University for Women, Chattogram, Bangladesh

© The Author(s) 2021
D. A. Morley, M. G. Jamil (eds.), *Applied Pedagogies for Higher Education*,
https://doi.org/10.1007/978-3-030-46951-1_6

107

connection between learning and its applications, show strengths of formal education in every sphere of human life. The importance of higher education is significant as it is often associated with people's earning, living standards and roles in sociopolitical actions. Because of the strong focus on subject specialisation and employability, higher education is goal-oriented in terms of the meanings and applications of the learning it delivers to students and other stakeholders.

Applications of the learning gained from higher education can be diverse, for example, in areas of research, employment, further education, cultural networking, and political negotiation. Hence, ensuring versatility in the learning and teaching activities, or in the overall term curriculum, is often challenging because it requires geographically relevant and culturally acceptable educational practices. For this reason, higher education academic programmes are generally expected to address both local and international sources of information, their transferability to different sociocultural constructs, and practical considerations regarding potential implications of the knowledge and skills transfer across borders. The expression 'real world learning', with its literal meaning, echoes these requirements indicating learning as a context-bound, culture-oriented, and applied practice.

Real world learning is relatively a new lingo increasingly being used in the education literature referring to students' authentic and positive learning experiences. Researchers, for example, Rau, Griffith, and Dieguez (2019); Sharma, Charity, Robson, and Lillystone (2018); and Marriott, Tan, and Marriott (2015) have used other terms like experiential learning, applications of learning for individual development, discipline-led experience, and concrete experience to mean real world learning. The approach is partly comparable with some traditional academic models,

N. Radclyffe-Thomas
Glasgow Caledonian University, London, UK

M. A. Islam • A. A. Rasel
BRAC University, Dhaka, Bangladesh

for example, problem-based learning, service learning, and project-based learning (Boss, 2015; Brundiers, Wiek, & Redman, 2010). Real world learning has not yet become a distinguishable pedagogic paradigm, but its various unique features are developing, which offer insights into its principles and power in higher education.

Real world learning is a fresher attention at tertiary-level education compared to its sustained presence in primary and secondary school curricula for long time (Maxwell, Stobaugh, & Tassell, 2015). While there has been a continuous emphasis on critical, reflective and practice-based learning at universities in the past five decades, currently there is an increasing focus on various applied forms of education to facilitate real world learning experiences. The term 'applied' is self-explanatory, which generally indicates the practical use or applications of learning (Ovenden-Hope & Blandford, 2017). However, the educational policies and academics may consider the applications of learning from two standpoints: (1) learning by doing or facilitating teaching/learning through 'incorporating applications' of specific learning points (2) and preparing students with the knowledge and skills for 'future applications' of learning. On the one hand, 'incorporating applications' refers to applied pedagogic actions, for example hands-on practice or student-learning activities based on authentic educational content. On the other, 'future applications' highlight the knowledge and skills that students gain through educational experiences and for the purpose of application in defined areas, mainly in professions and work.

Conceptualising Real World Learning in Internationalised Curricula

There are many examples of international academic mobility in higher education during the early years of the very old universities. Nalanda Mahavihara, a monastic university founded in the fifth century in India, attracted thousands of foreign students from distant Buddhist world, such as China, Korea and Japan (Barua, 2016). Historical records, for example the travelogue of a Chinese visitor called Xuanzang, describe the exclusive lifestyle and academic culture of the foreign students who travelled across many countries to study theology, languages and medicine at this ancient university (Pinkney, 2015). There are also instances of policy-level consideration for international students at such academic institutions. For example, Emperor Frederik Barbarossa in his 'Authentica Habita' document, published in 1158, discussed the aspects of freedom for foreign students studying at the University of Bologna in Italy (Otterspeer, 2008). Although various international elements have been prevalent in higher education since the beginning of universities, specific discussions on the internationalisation of academic programmes started to become popular only in 1980s with enhanced awareness and deliberations on global cultures, quality of education, and options for employment. Presently, many universities are placing an emphasis on international collaboration for strengthening teaching, research and the recruitment of international students to generate revenue. According to the forth Global Survey Report of the International Association of Universities, about 75% of 1300 institutions in 131 countries have internationalisation agenda in their core strategies (Egron-Polak & Hudson, 2014). This indicates a worldwide recognition about developing curricula that match academic and professional requirements of both local and international stakeholders.

Internationalisation in higher education is broadly the amalgamation of "intercultural and international dimensions into the curriculum" (OECD, 2004, p. 7). It connects local and global cultures together and have impacts on major curricular areas, such as teaching methods, academic support, assessment, and learning gain (Leask, 2015). The key aim of the internationalisation is to enable "knowledge of self, and of self in relation to others, and seeing personal change as a necessary precursor to social change" (Clifford & Montgomery, 2015, p. 48). Because of these demands, internationalised academic programmes need to be external-facing, or linked to the real world, where students are treated as cultural agents and learning is a context-bound process. That is why an international curriculum targeted for real world learning is expected to enable students to become global citizens who learn and apply their knowledge and skills with considerations of diverse social, academic and

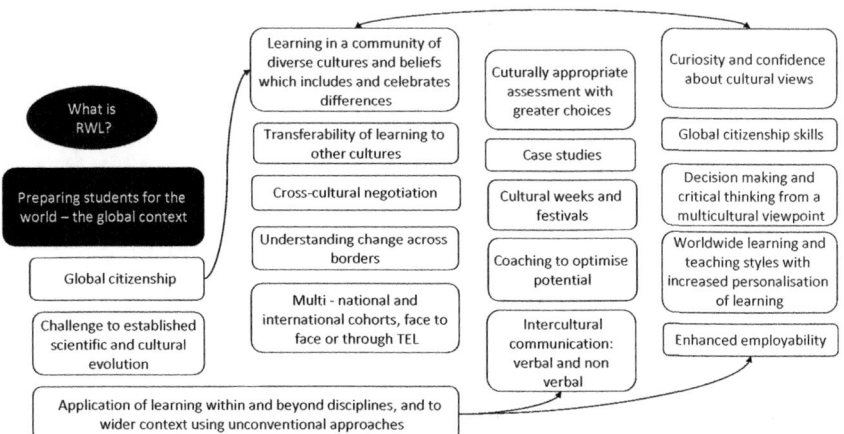

Fig. 6.1 Concept map on real world learning and internationalised academic programmes

employment contexts. The concept map (Fig. 6.1) illustrates some fundamental objectives of real world learning, such as enhanced awareness of global cultures, efficient intercultural communication skills, and strong capacity to think critically in the perspective of international academic programmes. The concepts drawn in the map emerged while we, the authors of this chapter, were reflecting on our personal teaching and educational research experiences linking with the value of real world experiences and external-facing curricula (see the conclusion chapter for the procedure we followed). Although the concept map is based on our personal experiences and professional beliefs, it widely denotes two contemporary and overarching focuses of the internationalised curricula: roles and impacts of globalisation, and the effects of teaching and learning on such global curricular features (Vishwanath & Mummery, 2019).

The educational notions depicted in the concept map offer the following four thematic areas associated with real world learning in the context of internationalised curricula, or more precisely international academic programmes.

Ethos: students are global citizens and work-ready with essential employability skills

Purposes: to build awareness of cultural diversity, help students
                transfer learning across borders and to different
                professions
Methods: culture-rich and applied pedagogies, coaching, collabo-
                ration, communication
Learning gain: curiosity and confidence, critical thinking and decision-
                making skills, employment skills, global citizenship
                skills, ability to incorporate different learning styles

We must acknowledge that the integration of these academic elements in higher education for improved learning experiences is not a brand-new idea. Rather, there is ample evidence suggesting their full or partial implementation. In the following section, we discuss three features of real world learning in international academic programmes. With reference to original case studies, we explore if the associated teaching and learning practices provide any pedagogic guidelines suitable for greater higher education sector.

Real World Learning in Action: An Evidence-based Discussion

The relationship between real world learning and global citizenship is crucial in international curricula. From a philosophical standpoint, true global citizens do not confine knowledge within conservative and nationalistic ideologies; rather they tend to see the validity of the knowledge from disparate social, economic, and cultural angles of vision. For example, while conducting a scientific experiment, students with the spirit of global citizenship are expected to acknowledge its wider impacts in different locations. They also try to contextualise foreign events, examples, and methodological approaches, for instance a teaching or learning strategy, in their learning. This feature in the curricula and pedagogies supplies them the opportunity to reflect and think critically and, at the same time, encourages them to relate learning to professional practices. Presently, the greater availability of technological resources has opened the door for students and academics to compare and contest individual views with divergent cultural entities within and beyond local contexts. Therefore, it is now less difficult to materialise external-facing curricula which are adequately inclusive, particularly through their connections with different locations, cultures, and people's views.

The following sections contain three case studies, collected from UK and Bangladeshi universities, which evidence how students develop themselves to be global citizens through some carefully designed academic interventions. The UK and Bangladesh are two geographically and economically dissimilar countries, but it is interesting to notice their uniformity in terms of educational aims towards real world learning and internalisation of academic programmes.

Accommodating Diversity and 'Wider' Application of Learning

Curriculum is an umbrella term covering almost every philosophical and practical aspect of formal education, including teaching methods, learning approaches, educational resources, and academic development strategies. Different higher educational institutions may consider their respective curriculum unique because of individual viewpoints and emphasis, but the overall expectations have a common ground. For example, contemporary universities generally want their curricula to facilitate critical and reflective practices and prepare students to deal with local and global challenges. Additionally, students are expected to gain specialised academic and professional competencies, contributing to the creation of educated workforce needed for a healthy economy and knowledge-based society.

International elements in higher education can potentially offer enhanced learning outcomes, including better language skills, and intercultural communication and networks (Jibeen & Khan, 2015). The approach has strengths to improve one's career prospects, especially if the required knowledge and skills are needed in target socio-economic and employment situations. Besides, from the higher educational institution point of view, internationalised learning culture can bring reputation and improve quality of academic programmes through increased global competitions and financial sustainability with the help of external sources of funding. Because of these multifaceted features, internationalised curricula in higher education can address the following two academic expectations:

1. the teaching and learning are accessible and suitable for international audiences, such as students, faculty members, and researchers; and
2. the educational outcomes can accommodate and be transferred to diverse global settings, for example the economic activities and job market in a particular country or region

Apart from preparing local students as global citizens, universities are also supposed to be welcoming to international students with different cultural backgrounds and economic classes. They should try creating inclusive educational environment and practical support systems to enable learning for all. In an international academic environment, providing language support is a prerequisite if the medium of instruction is different from students' first language. Similarly, essential training on academic conventions and standards need to be facilitated for those coming from different learning cultures. In addition to helping students to attune in new educational environment, the curricula need to have the provision for building capacity to transfer knowledge and skills to various social and economic circumstances. University graduates are generally expected to contribute to the national development programmes, which may vary in countries and regions. Therefore, higher education curricula should be able to help students become strategic while designing and implementing initiatives that fit in local cultural expectations. The following case study taken from a Bangladeshi university describes two academic programmes designed for international students and their future involvement in national and regional development initiatives.

Case Study 1

Pathways for Promise and Access Academy (Nazmul Alam, Associate Professor and Head of Public Health, Asian University for Women, Bangladesh, and AKM Moniruzzaman Mollah, Professor of Biological Sciences and the Head of Science and Math Programmes, Asian University for Women, Bangladesh)

The Asian University for Women (AUW), a regional university based in Chattogram, Bangladesh, is dedicated to nurture the next generation of leaders for Asia and the Middle East. AUW offers academic programmes to promising young women from various cultural, religious, ethnic, and socio-economic backgrounds. It follows a liberal arts curriculum at pre-collegiate and undergraduate levels in social science and science disciplines. The education programmes combine leadership training, professional development and mentoring, and footing in critical thinking and problem-solving skills. Two pre-undergraduate programmes, namely Pathways for Promise and Access Academy, prepare students in English, Mathematics, and critical reasoning skills in the liberal arts tradition. All academic programmes taught in English and the academic environment are supportive to enable multiculturalism in the campus and residential life. In 2019, the university had students from 17 Asian countries representing many ethnic backgrounds.

A major challenge at AUW has been to ease the transition for international students coming from different education systems, languages of instruction and curriculum patterns. This challenge is even critical given AUW's noble mission to teach young women from the underprivileged communities where English and quantitative skills at admission are a major issue. To address the problem, in 2008, AUW started 'Access Academy', a one-year programme to standardise English, mathematics, and critical reasoning skills before students start their undergraduate studies (AUW, n.d.). In 2016, the university introduced a flagship programme called 'Pathways for Promise', which offers an English-language intensive course for preparing students to study in the Access Academy programme. As a result of this spanning course, it has been possible for the Pathways programme to recruit young women from the ready-made garment (RMG) factories in Bangladesh (Jahangir, 2016), from the Rohingya refugee communities in Bangladesh and Myanmar, and from Afghanistan, Palestine, and Yemen for tertiary-level education.

International academic programmes in higher education generally aim to improve students' awareness of other cultures and values. However, the risk of this objective is that the students may not have adequate opportunities to deal with their own contexts and cultures (Leask, 2015). Pathways for Promise and Access Academy programmes have created the space for combining students' own social and cultural contexts, such as their country-specific economic development needs, in the teaching and learning. Yet, the pedagogic approaches involved in these programmes follow internationally recognised educational methods where English, an international language, is used as the medium of instruction. The Pathways programme primarily focuses on developing students' English-language skills in an approach that equips them with linguistic and communicative competencies, enabling them to become effective communicators in both academic and social environments. The students go through a competency-based learning approach in which language is treated as a medium of interaction and communication among people from different cultures aiming to achieve common goals and purposes. This helps them fulfil the expectations of any international curricula which are to develop cross-cultural and intercultural awareness (Clifford & Montgomery, 2017). Another important aim is to develop students' teamwork and leadership skills. These behavioural competencies are achieved through core curricular and extracurricular activities, such as project work and community engagement. Enabling students to take responsibility for their own learning is also an integral aspect. So far, the outcomes of the programme have been very encouraging as the students have demonstrated excellent perseverance to work for their own and for the betterment of their home countries.

The Access Academy is contributing with great novelty by recruiting female students from several fragile and conflict-affected countries where female education has become virtually elusive. For example, through an agreement between AUW and Daughters for Life Foundation (http://daughtersforlife.com), many disadvantaged young women from the Middle East have received scholarships for undergraduate education. AUW and the Daughters for Life Foundation have supported vulnerable students from Palestine and Syria in tuition waivers and awards to cover all costs of their undergraduate studies including learning at the Access Academy. Besides, the university has successfully mobilised international collaboration with Afghanistan, a country where most systematic and destructive abuses against women have been executed through the denial of education. In recent years, more than 100 students from various disadvantaged and ethnic groups in Afghanistan have been recruited. These women, who once feared to even dream, now actually stand with their heads held high.

With the unique educational interventions by Pathways for Promise and Access Academy programmes, AUW has been reaching more students in Asia and the Middle East (in 2019, there were enrolments from Yemen and Senegal for the first time). The university has graduated over 700 exceptional young women to become leaders in their communities. Ninety percent of them have received employment or enrolled in higher education programmes within one year of their graduation. Among the employed graduates, around 85% work in their home countries. Twenty five per cent of graduates are enrolled in further studies, with some completing programmes at world-renowned higher educational institutions, such as Stanford, Columbia, Johns Hopkins, Oxford, Edinburgh, and Yonsei. In addition to the academic support from Pathways for Promise and Access Academy, the students have also been benefited from the AUW's extensive international networks with educational institutions, industries, and employers. These links have eventually helped them obtain places in internship and study abroad programmes, and in securing employments internationally. At the same time, AUW has been able to develop its curriculum and engage many visiting faculty members, resulting in a stronger academic profile and achievements.

The performativity and impacts of a university are reflected through the way its academic programmes are devised and delivered. The curriculum of the Pathways for Promise and Access Academy programmes at the Asian University for Women demonstrates strengths of rigorous academic coaching to optimise potentials of exceptional and struggling students. One of the challenges in such an educational approach is fostering curiosity and confidence among the students to deal with different social, cultural, and religious views (Cameron, 2019). It is also plausible that the students face challenges while practising critical thinking and communication from multicultural viewpoints. Yet, this type of bridging or preparatory programmes facilitate "borderless, capitalist, civic, collaborative, cosmopolitan, disciplinary, marketised" characters which are the defining elements of modern higher education curricula (Barnett, 2013, p. 51). Moreover, the value of such programmes is widespread as the students' learning gains are developed through and connected with real world circumstances.

Creating Cross-cultural Learning Space

A very small number of university students get a chance to study abroad, and the number is much lower in developing countries (de Wit, Gacel-Avila, Jones, & Jooste, 2017). However, the blessings of modern technology offer the provision for being connected with international academic stakeholders and share cross-cultural views while studying in the home country. This kind of knowledge sharing is essential in some academic disciplines; for example, business students need to understand consumer behaviours, marketing cultures, and business policies in different places. Technology-enabled and internationally connected curricula can help them attain useful competencies to become engaged in diverse cultural, economic, and political perspectives.

Research findings show higher student motivation and participation in international academic programmes (Trinh & Conner, 2019). However, we know very little about how students engage and behave in similar programmes when they are based in the home countries, and the teaching and learning are conducted using technology. Research findings on technology-enhanced learning provide indications of several challenges, for example gaps between technological designs and pedagogic actions (Davey, Elliott, & Bora, 2019), and participants' lack of understanding of the cultural and intellectual backgrounds of their peers (Jamil, 2018). On the contrary, there is ample evidence of successful learning delivered by technology-enhanced activities, for example improved self-awareness and reflective practice through blogging (Barrett, Hayes, & Hollinshead, 2019), and rich academic discussion through Facebook-generated tasks (Manca & Ranieri, 2013). The next case study describes how an online classroom enables positive learning experiences for students studying in their home countries in Europe and Asia.

Case Study 2

Collaborative online international learning (Natascha Radclyffe-Thomas, Professor of Marketing and Sustainable Business at the British School of Fashion, Glasgow Caledonian University, UK)

Collaborative online international learning (COIL) is an award-winning project launched in 2013 to deliver authentic education through formal and informal collaboration between higher educational institutions in the UK and Asia. The International Fashion Panel (IFP), a global classroom in the form of a private Facebook group and part of the COIL project, has been facilitating collaborative work practices between students at four universities studying in areas of fashion design, business, marketing, media and communications. Students in the IFP are undergraduates, and the global classroom provides blended learning integrated into specific modules, for example, Fashion Branding or Media Communications. The initial partner institutions were the London College of Fashion and City University Hong Kong. Subsequently, the collaboration has extended to LASALLE College of the Arts, Singapore, and RMIT's satellite campus in Ho Chi Minh City, Vietnam.

Developed to support internationalisation in its widest sense, the IFP had the following motivations behind its formation :

1. to facilitate international research in the area of fashion branding and marketing
2. to support a peer network in order that students recognise not just others' but also their own social and cultural capital
3. to stimulate cultural exchange and promote intercultural communication competences
4. to introduce internationally situated project briefs focusing on non-homogenous markets
5. to support international students, especially those with English as a second/foreign language, in group work and class discussions
6. to simulate industry work practices with peer collaboration via asynchronous and digitally enabled communication

The IFP is primarily being used in the first year of studies. The teaching teams at each partner institution have conducted curriculum-mapping exercises which help them identify synergies in modules across content and assessment design. The students have been introduced to the global classroom, with an emphasis on its functions and benefits as a platform for collaborative research, in project briefings.

Due to the global nature of the creative industries, and the risks of cultural appropriation and/or cross-cultural communication crises, an agreement has been established among institutions regarding the necessity of examining the local-global nexus, and how it manifests in products and marketing communications.

The name 'International Fashion Panel' was chosen to minimise real and perceived teacher-student hierarchies and the cultural distance between home and international students. The programme encourages students to recognise and develop their own expertise and the value of their knowledge and opinions. The objectives are achieved through a series of introductory activities designed to foster a community of learners and to demonstrate the shared interests and references between peer learners in each location—an example being asking students to create a post stating three companies they want to work for and three places they would like to live. Most students are familiar with presenting themselves via social media platforms; thus the exercise was fairly low-risk and they could reveal information as much or little as they wished. The activity highlighted the global nature of the fashion industry and offered students a chance to situate their (geographic) place within that. By sharing aspirations, they discovered the shared interests and preferences denoting a community of practice. It also served to foreground internationalisation in a positive way through recognising students' diverse backgrounds as they discussed each other's posts. In a similar manner, the positive integration of a non-homogenous and international lens on the practice of marketing communications was further integrated by a brand identity activity which uses a series of tutor-created brand mood boards representing a range of international fashion brands. Students were asked to discuss their interpretations and post comments on the perceptions of each brand's identity and strategy using the 4Ps framework (product-place-price-promotion). The activity served to familiarise them with the global classroom format before moving into deeper engagement in the form of peer collaboration and review. The examples of such activities include cross-cultural seminar discussions and debates. Having posted a question such as 'to what extent do you think there is global fashion?' tutors facilitated in-class small group discussions, the summaries of which were captured as comments on the tutors' original post. As the course in London has a large cohort, the global classroom has run several concurrent seminars and provided students an opportunity to contribute to a live cross-campus conversation. Students in the partner colleges have joined the discussion sessions or used the results to prompt their own, although these have been conducted asynchronously due to the time difference.

Graduates who aspire to work in the creative industries are increasingly required to work in virtual teams, often with culturally diverse colleagues. Additionally, the strategy and content they create are required to reflect the international nature of contemporary industry. Most approaches to internationalisation of curriculum attempt to expose students to alternate cultural artefacts and practices. While designing separate but aligned project briefs that explicitly reference the global classroom as a source of primary research, tutors of such curricular methodology require students to propose internationally viable strategies for selected fashion brands. To address this need, recent project briefs of the global classroom have asked students in Hong Kong to select a local Chinese brand to launch in London. Students in London were given an Asian city to research and either bring a local brand to London or launch a British brand there. To help students do useful research prior to seminars, global classroom tutors posted relevant articles and sources for further information.

The International Fashion Panel has so far connected over 750 students, tutors, and industry experts in exploring common interests and co-creating knowledge. Experiences of the students have been studied through exploratory investigations using questionnaires, focus groups, students' reflective writing, as well as analyses of the group's metrics and tutors' observations. The findings indicate positive outcomes, particularly in facilitating geographically dispersed individuals to connect, share, and create content and ideas. The global classroom is only one aspect of the teaching delivery, but its ability to research and sense-check with peers living in the target markets has emerged as an invaluable source of qualitative data and feedback which ultimately enhance students' work. Students have been found supporting their peers by preparing local fashion intelligence reports and providing feedback on work in progress. Overall, based on a model of communities of practice, it has created a successful network of learners for whom the classroom has been extended beyond the walls of their institutions, and their social and cultural capital has been enhanced and recognised. The following comment of a participant represents positive impacts of the IFP and the global classroom:

> It's like being a part of this creative learning community and people from different cultural backgrounds coming together to talk about the same topic. … it helped understand the perspective of people from the countries we based our project on. I also learnt so much about what people from other countries thought about my own culture. It was a very helpful learning experience. (London-based student)

(A detailed description of the collaborative online international learning project is available in Radclyffe-Thomas, Peirson-Smith, Roncha, Lacouture, and Huang, 2018).

The IFP and global classroom are an international and technology-enhanced curriculum environment which addresses two major educational challenges. First, many students and faculty members often fail to recognise the purposes and goals of international programmes (Green & Whitsed, 2015); therefore the global classroom provides appropriate briefings to its students on the procedures and benefits of their participation. Second, managing learning experiences of diverse student cohorts based in different countries is problematic (Irvine, Molyneux, & Gillman, 2015), so the global classroom sets small and controlled activities in the beginning to prepare students to partake in deeper and more complex tasks in later stages. The collaborative and dialogic nature of the learning activities, and the profession-focused content, also help them become part of wider communities of practice (Wenger, 1998). Overall, the virtual learning environment creates a cross-cultural space enabling self-reflection and openness to other cultures, and curiosity about non-homogenous industries situated in different geographic locations.

Linking Contexts with Inquiry and Analysis

International curricula demand contextual multiplicity in the learning and teaching. The requirement is compatible with emerging real world learning concepts which have a primary focus on the continuation and application of learning beyond formal education. Embedding inquiry and 'linking knowledge to action' in education can facilitate continuing and applied features (Brundiers et al., 2010). They can also supply pedagogic options for collaboration and deep learning, and equip students with utilisable lifelong skills (Tong, Standen, & Sotiriou, 2018). However, the success of inquiry-based education depends on students' prior knowledge and cultural capital in the forms of critical thinking, interdisciplinary knowledge, and communication skills. Besides, many students struggle with dissimilar educational approaches, for example collaboration and questioning, especially if they are contradictory and different from their previous learning experiences (Rienties, Nanclares, Jindal-Snape, & Alcott, 2013). Consequently, some students find the learning experiences unconventional, inconsistent, and time and resource demanding (Bak & Kim, 2015). It is plausible that many students cannot participate equally and struggle academically in international academic programmes which involve culturally variant stakeholders and unique learning goals.

Inquiry-based learning is an intellectually stimulating academic approach which has recently gained ground in contemporary higher education. The approach has potentials to connect research and employment skills in education, and help students embrace twenty-first-century workplace challenges through innovative and creative measures (Acar & Tuncdogan, 2019; Campbell & Groundwater-Smith, 2013). The following case study, taken from BRAC University in Bangladesh, shows a developmental approach to strengthen traditional curriculum for supporting students to participate in inquiry-based learning with enhanced awareness of global perspectives and future professions.

Case Study 3

Outcome-based programme design (Mohammad Aminul Islam, Senior Lecturer at the Institute of Languages, BRAC University, Bangladesh, and Annajiat Alim Rasel, Undergraduate Programme Coordinator at the Department of Computer Science and Engineering, BRAC University, Bangladesh)

BRAC University in Bangladesh follows broad-based or holistic approaches to learning and teaching. Since 2007, its academic programmes have been receiving outcome-based educational interventions on a regular basis to improve students' awareness of global perspectives. In addition to continuous quality improvement, in 2016, the university placed an emphasis on General Education (GenEd). Consequently, since 2018, Outcome-Based Education (OBE) has become a key driver of the university's overall curriculum. While implementing these programmes, the university took measures to ensure that the taught courses are academically relevant and globally competitive. As part of the process, the design of each academic course starts with a broad and general curriculum framework emphasising communication, critical thinking, quantitative skills, technological skills, and global thinking skills. All these components are interlinked in such a way that the students can align their learning with various real-life international challenges, starting from the orientation of a topic to the assessment of learning through concept-building activities. The curriculum has been further developed through recommendations from various accreditation bodies, resulting in a clearer focus on mapping its every component in granular details, from Programme Educational Objectives (PEO), Programme Learning Outcomes (PLO), down to Course Learning Outcomes (CLO), and how they are addressed in each learning and assessment activity. The curriculum and faculty members have been prepared with the help of BRAC University's Institutional Quality Assurance Cell (IQAC) and Professional Development Centre (PDC). PDC offers courses like Theory and Practice of Learner-centred Teaching (TPLT). TPLT is a professional development programme for BRAC University faculty members which includes teaching-learning methods, feedback rubric, technology-enhanced learning, collaboration, inquiry, practice, and production of articulations.

The text and reference materials as well as the 'project challenges' used in the taught units for the students are brought directly from international examples. For instance, books are chosen such that they are written by persons who are considered to have contemporary authority on the subjects, and the contents are complemented with authentic examples chosen from international locations. In 'project challenge' tasks, students are asked to analyse their proposed solutions in terms of different time zones and cultural variations (including values, languages, and preferences). As books tend to get outdated relatively quickly, students are encouraged to interact with professionals for exposure of fresh perspectives and industry challenges, and mimic what they would be doing in their job or during postgraduate education.

To instil research and development practices in the learning, students are introduced to challenges and are assessed on how their solutions take global contexts into account. The tasks are facilitated in collaborative, interactive, and sometimes flipped environment where the role of the instructors is mainly as facilitators and co-learners. Students are challenged with worklets based on professions or postgraduate life preceded by bridge materials. This helps them make a smooth connection between the topics covered with some anticipated profession-related challenges that they may face in future. The teaching also uses evidence-driven and interactive peer-instruction method (Mazur & Somers, 1999). Classes generally start with a review of past topic, content for the day along with pre-assessment and post-assessment, and a preview of upcoming topics. In the case of a course involving communication skills, global awareness is emphasised using examples like 'thumbs up', which is a positive feedback in many cultures, but the same gesture is treated very negatively in the cultures of some Asian countries. In courses having technical components, students are made aware of different languages and colours, accessibility issues for users with disabilities, scalability of solutions, robustness, and account for the increasing global security concerns, such as data leaks and data breaches. Students are exposed to a wide range of tools and resources, such as VuFind for knowledge discovery, Moodle LMS, KJS ThinkBoard (a Japan International Cooperation Agency pilot project for e-learning in Bangladesh), Mentimeter, and various simulation tools in their learning. Additionally, they deal with technical instruments and frameworks which are applied in relevant industries. Students also attend tutorial sessions where they can discuss academic confusions and receive further challenging tasks.

While accomplishing the coursework, students are required to interact with professionals and academics on global forums, such as Stack Overflow, Stack Exchange, Quora, newsgroups, Facebook/Google groups, Piazza, and MOOC platforms. They are made familiar with examples of what they may expect in their jobs or postgraduate studies at local or international institutions. They are also exposed to strategic thinking on how to handle unseen, complex, and hard-to-tackle problems, trade-offs and compromises, the importance of looking at the same problem from different angles, breaking down a problem into subproblems, and collaborative approaches to problem solving. The course contents include various local and international compliance issues, for example international industrial certifications and international competitions. As academic disciplines are often different in terms of their learning goals and teaching approaches (Shulman, 2005), the nature, content, and features of these courses vary in different academic disciplines. Besides, regular modification and adjustment take place for all the courses in every semester to stay relevant to the needs of the future, to improve student engagement, and to support their sustainable active learning.

Outcome-based academic interventions at BRAC University have delivered some significant success. The students are receiving internship, industrial mentorship, and job offers from local and international organisations. Many have joined research-based programmes just after completing their degrees. Many batches of the students have initiated their own start-up companies. Students are regularly participating in national and international competitions and winning prizes. The academic changes and their outcomes have already contributed to boosting the ranking of BRAC University.

Internationalisation of academic programmes prioritises cross-cultural competencies and intercultural awareness (Knight, 2013). Enabling inquiry and analysis in global-facing programmes requires students' cultural and academic readiness. Faculty members' positive attitudes and perceptions towards internationalisation are also pivotal in the process (Childress, 2010). BRAC University's outcome-based curriculum development initiative demonstrates a structured approach to embedding inquiry and analysis in international academic programmes. Yet, it is plausible that students' capacities to partake in such educational environment vary because they bring different types and levels of learning cultures and critical thinking abilities in the class.

In higher education literature, various guidelines regarding effective teaching and student participation in inquiry-based learning are available

(Coffman, 2017; Mieg, 2019; Pedaste et al., 2015). However, discussions on how these approaches are relevant and linked to student learning in international academic programmes and life-long learning contexts are inadequate; thus it requires further exploration. It is also important to gauge the roles and impacts of academic and social support in students' learning journeys.

Conclusions

The discussion in this chapter sheds light on some pertinent curricular features delineating real world learning in internationalised academic programmes. Real world learning emerges as a context-rich and applied educational approach having potentials to enable engagement, critical thinking, cooperation, and knowledge transfer beyond formal educational settings. The main objective of the approach is to transform students into global citizens who are ready to learn through cross-cultural exploration and collaboration, and are equipped with essential competencies to apply learning to real-life actions. The external-facing educational environment is a key driver in the internationalisation process and real world learning pedagogies, although both encourage students to apply critical thinking and analysis in understanding their own cultures too.

The notions and practical examples detailed in the three case studies signpost effective approaches to designing and implementing authentic learning activities in international academic programmes. The discussion provides at least three guiding principles: (1) inclusion of wider communities and their views as well as academic and professional needs in the teaching and learning practice, (2) creating opportunities to expand collaboration and communication across geographic borders, and (3) amalgamation of local and global views in learning activities, such as inquiry, reflection, and analysis. Philosophically, all these elements can supply opportunities to practise real world learning with enhanced global thinking skills, but it is likely that they may not always lead to high student satisfaction. One of the reasons is that many students face difficulties while studying in international learning environments as they go through distinct cultural adaptation and academic assimilation processes. Therefore, the quality and quantity of students' learning gain may exceptionally vary in international academic programmes. This may also pose a challenge for faculty members, particularly in managing disparate levels of student achievement and satisfaction. To overcome the problems, the case studies, along with the learning and teaching concepts, suggest some curricular strategies, such as delivering preparatory academic programmes to enhance students' communication skills and cultural awareness; providing exposures of international social, economic, and political events to enhance students' motivation and engagement; and using modern technology to reach diverse people and cultures situated in different geographic locations. It is possible that these suggested actions will face resistance, or they may require to include alternative curricular strategies for successful teaching and learning in specific higher educational institutions. However, the discussed real world learning concepts and the real examples can be a starting point to explore evidence-based and sustainable academic approaches suitable for the internationalisation of higher education.

References

Acar, O. A., & Tuncdogan, A. (2019). Using the inquiry-based learning approach to enhance student innovativeness: A conceptual model. *Teaching in Higher Education, 24*(7), 895–909. https://doi.org/10.1080/1356251 7.2018.1516636

Asian University for Women (AUW). (n.d.). History. Retrieved May 5, 2019, from https://asian-university.org/who-we-are/history/.

Bak, H., & Kim, D. H. (2015). Too much emphasis on research? An empirical examination of the relationship between research and teaching in multitasking environments. *Research in Higher Education, 56*(8), 843–860. https://doi.org/10.1007/s11162-015-9372-0

Barnett, R. (2013). *Imagining the university*. London: Routledge.

Barrett, G. A., Hayes, A., & Hollinshead, J. (2019). Study abroad and developing reflective research practice through blogs: A preliminary study from the United Kingdom. *Journal of Criminal Justice Education, 30*, 463–474. https://doi.org/10.1080/10511253.2019.1580757

Barua, J. B. (2016). *Ancient Buddhist universities in Indian sub-continent.* Meadville: Fulton Books.

Boss, S. (2015). *Real-world projects: How do I design relevant and engaging learning experiences.* Alexandria: ASCD.

Brundiers, K., Wiek, A., & Redman, C. L. (2010). Real-world learning opportunities in sustainability: From classroom into the real world. *International Journal of Sustainability in Higher Education, 11*(4), 308–324.

Cameron, A. (2019). Cultural and religious barriers to learning science in South Africa. In B. Billingsley, K. Chappell, & M. J. Reiss (Eds.), *Science and religion in education* (pp. 189–202). Cham. Retrieved from: Springer. https://doi.org/10.1007/978-3-030-17234-3_15

Campbell, A., & Groundwater-Smith, S. (Eds.). (2013). *Connecting inquiry and professional learning in education: International perspectives and practical solutions.* London: Routledge.

Childress, L. K. (2010). *The twenty-first century university: Developing faculty engagement in internationalization* (Vol. 32). New York: Peter Lang.

Clifford, V., & Montgomery, C. (2015). Transformative learning through internationalization of the curriculum in higher education. *Journal of Transformative Education, 13*(1), 46–64. https://doi.org/10.1177/1541344614560909

Clifford, V., & Montgomery, C. (2017). Designing an internationalised curriculum for higher education: Embracing the local and the global citizen. *Higher Education Research & Development, 36*(6), 1138–1151. https://doi.org/10.1080/07294360.2017.1296413

Coffman, T. (2017). *Inquiry-based learning: Designing instruction to promote higher level thinking.* Maryland: Rowman & Littlefield.

Davey, B., Elliott, K., & Bora, M. (2019). Negotiating pedagogical challenges in the shift from face-to-face to fully online learning: A case study of collaborative design solutions by learning designers and subject matter experts. *Journal of University Teaching and Learning Practice, 16*(1), 3.

Egron-Polak, E., & Hudson, R. (2014). *Internationalization of higher education: Growing expectations, essential values.* IAU 4rd Global Survey Report. Paris: IAU.

Green, W., & Whitsed, C. (Eds.). (2015). *Critical perspectives on internationalising the curriculum in disciplines: Reflective narrative accounts from business, education and health* (Vol. 28). Rotterdam: Sense Publishers.

Irvine, J., Molyneux, J., & Gillman, M. (2015). 'Providing a link with the real world': Learning from the student experience of service user and carer

130   M. G. Jamil et al.

involvement in social work education. *Social Work Education, 34*(2), 138–150. https://doi.org/10.1080/02615479.2014.957178

Jahangir, A. (2016, November 4). The Workers' Revolution. *The Daily Star.* Retrieved November 25, 2019, from https://www.thedailystar.net/star-week-end/spotlight/the-workers-revolution-1308979

Jamil, M. G. (2018). Technology-enhanced teacher development in rural Bangladesh: A critical realist evaluation of the context. *Evaluation and Program Planning, 69,* 1–9. https://doi.org/10.1016/j.evalprogplan.2018.04.002

Jibeen, T., & Khan, M. A. (2015). Internationalization of higher education: Potential benefits and costs. *International Journal of Evaluation and Research in Education, 4*(4), 196–199.

Knight, J. (2013). The changing landscape of higher education internationalisation–for better or worse? *Perspectives: Policy and Practice in Higher Education, 17*(3), 84–90. https://doi.org/10.1080/13603108.2012.753957

Leask, B. (2015). *Internationalizing the curriculum.* London: Routledge.

Manca, S., & Ranieri, M. (2013). Is it a tool suitable for learning? A critical review of the literature on Facebook as a technology-enhanced learning environment. *Journal of Computer Assisted Learning, 29*(6), 487–504. https://doi.org/10.1111/jcal.12007

Mann, H. (1957). *The Republic and the School: Horace Mann on the Education of Free Men.* 12th Annual Report to the Massachusetts Board of Education–1848. New York: Teacher's College, Columbia University.

Marriott, P., Tan, S. M., & Marriott, N. (2015). Experiential learning—A case study of the use of computerised stock market trading simulation in finance education. *Accounting Education, 24*(6), 480–497. https://doi.org/10.1080/09639284.2015.1072728

Maxwell, M., Stobaugh, R., & Tassell, J. L. (2015). *Real-world learning framework for secondary schools: Digital tools and practical strategies for successful implementation.* Bloomington: Solutions Tree Press.

Mazur, E., & Somers, M. D. (1999). Book reviews-peer instruction: A user's manual. *American Journal of Physics, 67*(4), 359–359.

Mieg, H. A. (2019). *Inquiry-based learning–undergraduate research.* Berlin: Springer. Retrieved from. https://doi.org/10.1007/978-3-030-14223-0

OECD. (2004). *Internationalisation and trade in higher education: Opportunities and challenges.* OECD Publishing. https://doi.org/10.1787/9789264015067-en

Otterspeer, W. (2008). *The bastion of liberty: Leiden University today and yesterday*. Leiden: Leiden University Press.

Ovenden-Hope, T., & Blandford, S. (2017). *Understanding applied learning: Developing effective practice to support all learners*. London: Routledge.

Pedaste, M., Maeots, M., Siiman, L. A., De Jong, T., Van Riesen, S. A., Kamp, E. T., ... Tsourlidaki, E. (2015). Phases of inquiry-based learning: Definitions and the inquiry cycle. *Educational Research Review, 14*, 47–61. https://doi.org/10.1016/j.edurev.2015.02.003

Pinkney, A. M. (2015). Looking west to India: Asian education, intra-Asian renaissance, and the Nalanda revival. *Modern Asian Studies, 49*(1), 111–149. https://doi.org/10.1017/S0026749X13000310

Radclyffe-Thomas, N., Peirson-Smith, A., Roncha, A., Lacouture, A., & Huang, A. (2018). Developing global citizenship: Co-creating employability attributes in an international community of practice. In D. Morley (Ed.), *Enhancing employability in higher education through work based learning* (pp. 255–275). Cham: Palgrave Macmillan. https://doi.org/10.1007/978-3-319-75166-5_14

Rau, K., Griffith, R. L., & Dieguez, T. A. (2019). Out of the classroom and into the deep end: Real world learning at ICCM. In M. A. Gonzalez-Perez, K. Linded, & V. Taras (Eds.), *The Palgrave handbook of learning and teaching international business and management* (pp. 159–184). Cham: Palgrave Macmillan. Retrieved from. https://doi.org/10.1007/978-3-030-20415-0

Rienties, B., Nanclares, N. H., Jindal-Snape, D., & Alcott, P. (2013). The role of cultural background and team divisions in developing social learning relations in the classroom. *Journal of Studies in International Education, 17*(4), 332–353. https://doi.org/10.1177/1028315312463826

Sharma, S., Charity, I., Robson, A., & Lillystone, S. (2018). How do students conceptualise a "real world" learning environment: An empirical study of a financial trading room? *The International Journal of Management Education, 16*(3), 541–557. https://doi.org/10.1016/j.ijme.2017.09.001

Shulman, L. S. (2005). Signature pedagogies in the professions. *Daedalus, 134*(3), 52–59. https://doi.org/10.1162/0011526054622015

Tong, V. C., Standen, A., & Sotiriou, M. (Eds.). (2018). *Shaping higher education with students: Ways to connect research and teaching*. London: UCL Press.

Trinh, A. N., & Conner, L. (2019). Student engagement in internationalization of the curriculum: Vietnamese domestic students' perspectives. *Journal of Studies in International Education, 23*(1), 154–170. https://doi.org/10.1177/1028315318814065

Vishwanath, T. P., & Mummery, J. (2019). Reflecting critically on the critical disposition within internationalisation of the curriculum (IoC): The developmental journey of a curriculum design team. *Higher Education Research & Development,* *38*(2), 354–368. https://doi.org/10.1080/0729436 0.2018.1515181

Wenger, E. (1998). *Communities of practice: Learning, meaning, and identity.* Cambridge: Cambridge University Press.

de Wit, H., Gacel-Avila, J., Jones, E., & Jooste, N. (Eds.). (2017). *The globalization of internationalization: Emerging voices and perspectives.* London: Taylor & Francis.

Part II

Moving Learning into Real World Practice: Extending Student Opportunities in Higher Education

7

Designing and Supporting Extraordinary Work Experience

Dawn A. Morley, Paul Marchbank, Tony Steyger, Lesley Taylor, Anita Diaz, and Pauline Calleja

Introduction

A definition of work-based learning would posit that it situates the application of what students have learnt in the classroom, both academic and 'theoretical' learning, with practical skills within the real world environment of work.

Traditionally, it's an ancient way of learning whereby an apprentice works with a master and dates back, in Europe, to Hellenic Greece and the writings of Plato in the fifth century. Work-based learning (WBL) gained its current propensity in the Middle Ages through medieval craft guilds where apprenticeships were viewed as an appropriate training (More, 1980).

D. A. Morley (✉)
School of Sport, Health and Social Sciences, Solent University, Southampton, UK

P. Marchbank • T. Steyger • L. Taylor • A. Diaz
Solent University, Southampton, UK

P. Calleja
Griffith University, Brisbane, QLD, Australia

© The Author(s) 2021
D. A. Morley, M. G. Jamil (eds.), *Applied Pedagogies for Higher Education*,
https://doi.org/10.1007/978-3-030-46951-1_7

The apprenticeship system allowed for artisans to learn their craft in a similar fashion and facilitated their own 'personal epistemologies' by learning through practice (Billett, 2012). This latter aspect is key to understanding the, often tense, relationship between traditional university education supporting a didactic, behaviourist tradition, against the vocational or apprenticeship model transferred through mimesis which relies on observing, copying and mimicking (Billett, 2012).

Subsequently, with the notable exception of medicine and law which have long established histories of workplace training in conjunction with university education, the vast majority of modern subjects and occupations have seen a paradigm shift towards utilising work-based learning—through the sandwich year, practicum, work experience, placement or degree apprenticeship—in order to facilitate the 'personal epistemology' (Billett, 2012) afforded through unique engagements in real world settings and tasks with key industry partners. This has highlighted the disparity between the cultural value of an occupation versus a vocation; the former is associated with the professions and, ergo, has more 'worth' to society, while the latter simply provides paid employment (Billett, 2009). This may also be a factor in the denigration of certain subjects, such as media and the arts, which form some of the case studies within this chapter and strive to make explicit their academic validity and adherence to higher-level learning in the context of non-traditional industries.

Central to work-based learning is that both the university and the industry should enjoy mutual benefit from the arrangement. The student gains through exposure to work and furthers skills, attributes and identities useful to their future employability, whilst giving a future employer reassurance that the student has already been 'tested' within the workplace.

Importantly for the university, as the operation of work-based learning is resource intensive, it contributes significantly to measurable outcomes and impacts important in a sector where metrics have gained greater significance. Within the UK, the Destination of Leavers from Higher Education (DLHE), the National Student Survey (NSS), the Teaching Excellence Framework (TEF) and the forthcoming Knowledge Exchange Framework (KEF) provide examples of this trend. These statistics are all influenced, directly or indirectly, by the operation of a WBL strategy that speaks to and fulfils the needs of students and industry alike. However, the success of designing and supporting extraordinary work experience lies not with just adding a placement to theoretical learning but a deep integration of the two so that students are able to connect their learning and evolving identities across the different contexts of university and work. For the purposes of this chapter, the authors argue that WBL is an integral part of real world learning as its very success depends on its connectiveness with a wider and more integrated approach to student learning.

With courses that are more occupationally focused, there is an expectation that graduates will have a smoother transition to their chosen careers (Billett, 2009). This is gained in greater part through work-based experiences which are considered 'authentic' and allow students opportunities to engage in real world situations which simulate or provide professional practice. In many ways this replicates the master and apprentice scheme of old but with new challenges such as applying the course theory and assessment in a non-traditional higher learning environment with different expectations and support networks.

Before writing this chapter, three authors participated in a facilitated concept mapping activity in order to envision how a WBL experience could transcend the ordinary and become extraordinary (Fig. 7.1).

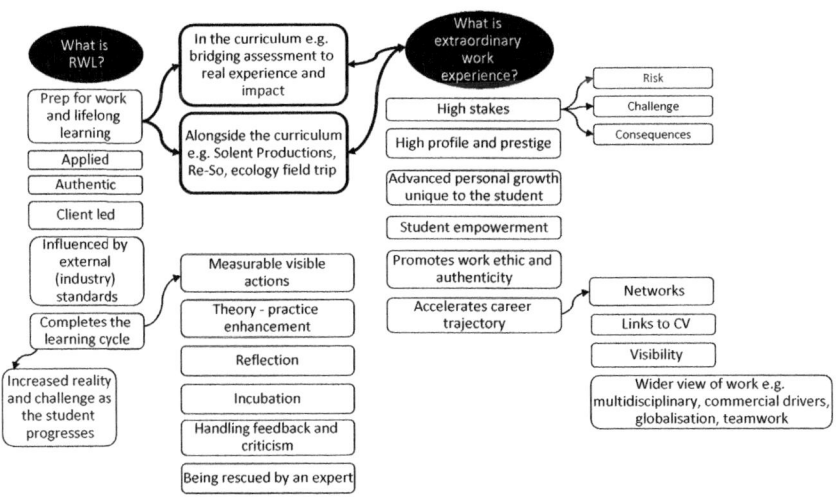

Fig. 7.1 Concept map from the authors

For a work experience to be extraordinary it needs to extend the students' practice learning beyond the commonplace. Generally, extraordinary work experiences provide 'high stakes' learning that add to the piquancy and stretch of students' work experience by, for example, increasing the perceived risk or immediacy of the learning. Fuller interactions between the student, university and external agent can also take the students beyond standard 'occupational knowledge' (Billett, 2009) to one where they were more likely to adopt increased agency and graduate skills pertinent to the workplace. As such the students' interactions and engagement with their experience would come with a level of autonomy and empowerment so there is a potential to make their own judgements—the case studies within the chapter demonstrate this in the increased creatively for the filmmaker and the product choice for the retailer and designer. In turn this allows advanced personal growth unique to the student and accelerates their own personalised career trajectory (Billett, 2009). Where work-based experiences in all their forms have become relatively ubiquitous, the four case studies included within the chapter have taken the student's position within that experience and extended the student's own autonomy and control within its operation.

The concept map also identified an extraordinary work experience as not only authentic but carrying high profile and prestige. Three case studies, included in the chapter, have a visual presence—in broadcasting, as a high street retailer and on an ecology field trip—where all give the students high cultural exchange value. This allows students to work within the ultimate authentic real world environments as they have real and very measurable consequences. In all examples, and especially that of an assessment brief on a nursing module, the higher education institutions have faced the challenge of bridging the theory to practice gap in their own unique ways.

In order for courses to provide work experiences such as these, it is recognised that academics may have to work flexibly and unconventionally in order to circumnavigate the restrictions of traditional university structures and processes. Two case studies provide work experience as an extracurricular opportunity to catch the timeframes of real world learning that sit outside of university semesters. Students may also have to be supported through a spiral curriculum (Bruner, 1960) to support an evolution of their real world learning from a 'safe' environment, of an incubator or simulator situation, to one where there is an increasing element of student mistakability and possibility of failure. Here the importance of preparation, research and planning becomes invaluable and integral to the gaining of the quantity and quality of placement hours. In the example of Case Study 1, media students are working with real clients broadcasting from the Glastonbury music festival; ultimately for the BBC, it is imperative that their work is exemplary and comes at the pinnacle of their learning trajectory. Courses may explicitly build on the skills recognised for their own students' professional trajectory and mitigate against the established difficulties of placement learning—the theory-practice divide and inappropriate assessment.

Four case studies have been integrated into the three overarching themes of extraordinary work experience: **accelerating professional confidence through immersive, high stakes learning, adding high value to aspects of practice pedagogy** and **recognising the negative aspects of practice learning and promoting the interdependence of theory and practice.** The case studies are not exclusive to their sections but provide best practice examples under their themes.

Accelerating Professional Confidence Through Immersive, High Stakes Learning

An extraordinary work experience not only builds professional confidence but accelerates it to such an extent that it is obvious to both internal and external parties as well as to the student themselves (Morley et al., 2017). This confidence goes beyond the sole attainment of technical competencies (Kinsella, 2009, 2010) but is a presentation of a greater, actionable knowledge within the work setting. Aristotle (trans 2009) developed the twin concepts of praxis and phronesis whereby the apprentice developed a reasoning influential to reflexive and informed action as well as a moral responsibility for what they did. Kemmis (2012) believes that these attributes are still pertinent to the development of a well-rounded professional even today.

Polanyi's demonstration of professional knowledge, through what he termed 'the tacit dimension' (1966), was traditionally learnt through the intimate learning relationship between the master and apprentice. The quandary exists today as to how students in higher education can experience an immersive and high stakes learning experience which is scalable and appropriate to contemporary expectations of study and employment. One of the many challenges of work experience is when the work is so immersive that students are unable to extricate their learning from what they are doing (Eraut, 2000, 2004).

Klein (1998) believes that the focus of learning should deliberately identify what can be used for future use. Experts "engage in deliberate practice, so that each opportunity for practice has a goal and evaluation criteria, they compile an extensive experience bank, they obtain feedback that is accurate, diagnostic and reasonably timely, they enrich their experiences by reviewing prior experiences to derive new insights and lessons from mistakes" (Klein, 1998, p. 104). Strategies, such as reflection, discussed in Chapter 13, are other possible learning mechanisms to achieve this.

Schön (1983) argued that the complexity of professional decision making also needed to accommodate for the unplanned circumstances of practice. A restriction to taught theory does not allow students to arrive at unconventional solutions which are often required in the realities of complex, real world practice.

Adding to new knowledge proves empowering for students (Bradbury-Jones, Sambrook, & Irvine, 2011) and students learnt best through an appropriate mix of challenge and support (Grealish & Ranse, 2009). Eraut (2000) found that a significant triangular relationship existed between challenge, support and confidence of students. The consequence of one of the points of the triangle being missed was a loss in student confidence and the motivation to learn. Based on several research studies that examined workplace learning, Eraut (2004) found that novices' work needed to be challenging enough for their level of expertise without it becoming daunting or students developed ineffective coping mechanisms. Appropriate allocation of work and supervision was crucial to promoting students' confidence so they could gain exposure to learning opportunities while simultaneously being supported through the negative aspects of learning in real life settings. Wenger (2012) recommended that students gained a deep insight into their future professions if they were immersed, even for a short period of time, into their full future roles. Morley (2015) found that first-year student nurses were incentivised after their unplanned participation in a cardiac resuscitation for they not only had performed successfully in highly regarded, high stakes learning but had participated and been supported well above their expected stage of education.

The structuring of practice learning was influential to students' progress (Eraut, 2004). Allocation to activities removed from practice, rather than peripheral to it, eroded the potential for situated learning to occur (Lave & Wenger, 1991). Gherardi, Nicolini and Odella (1998) introduced the concept of 'situated curriculum' in an ethnographic study of Italian construction site managers and the importance of context and design to realise learners' potential. Case Study 1 provides a novel example of how work experience on an undergraduate media course was developed to provide greater authenticity and certainty to the student work experience with subsequent deep impact on learning and the university's reputation within the media sector.

> ### Case Study 1
>
> **Launching a Successful In-house Company to Deliver Real World Clients (Tony Steyger, Associate Professor, Television and Media Production, Solent University, UK)**

When Southampton Institute became Southampton Solent University in 2005, there was a strategic commitment to grow its small but relatively successful undergraduate media provision, particularly in television production. A new programme of courses was validated, teaching staff from industry were recruited and investment was secured to build a TV studio and fully equipped outside broadcast vehicle and buy sufficient high-definition video equipment and editing software.

Media education at the time was becoming a crowded marketplace. The south coast was already well served by HE providers, including Bournemouth and Portsmouth, whilst Brighton and Chichester were entering the tussle for new students with their own infrastructure investment.

One tactic for Solent to compete in the sector for new students was to secure valuable curriculum accreditation for the programme of courses from Skillset, the industry-led skills body, thus providing a Kitemark of quality. A significant pre-requisite for Skillset accreditation was for undergraduate courses to embed into the curriculum 120 hours of guaranteed work experience for each student on professional projects. This was a particular challenge for Solent as the television industry in Southampton was tiny and the majority of broadcast companies were based in and around London, some 75 miles away. The challenge was how the Television Production programme at Solent could guarantee work experience to its expanding cohorts and provide the 'industry-ready' graduates Skillset demanded.

In 2007 a solution to this dilemma emerged as the university decided to pledge financial support for an in-house media production company, Solent Productions, designed as a mechanism to develop professional experience for students on a range of projects. This institutional commitment took into account the rapid maturing of the internet's video capabilities, exemplified by YouTube's recent launch and exponential growth. It seemed that everyone at the time wanted video content for their company or organisation and Solent's media staff were inundated with requests, many coming with budgets to match.

In addition to this unsolicited demand for content that helped kickstart Solent Productions, academic staff and others tapped into their own external networks to lever interesting production projects. One of these was to provide high-definition video content at the Glastonbury Festival from performance areas not covered by the BBC. In these early years, other partnerships were also forged with the National Health Service (NHS), Philips, Sony, Cowes Week, British University and Colleges Sports and Bestival, amongst others.

In 2008 the first application for Skillset accreditation was not successful, but in the following year the Television Production programme secured the coveted 'Tick'. Skillset acknowledged that a key part of the bid documentation had been the innovation of launching Solent Productions and its role in professionalising the students. In particular, the work experience engine created had impressed the assessors with its tally of 5000+ hours of professional student work per year.

Nicole Hay was the Senior Accreditation Manager at Skillset at the time. "Solent Productions played a healthy role during accreditation—replication of professional practice within HE is crucial to giving students that experience of work-readiness. You've got real-life external clients. Actually, it's not replicating industry practice, it is industry practice."

Since then, work experience opportunities for students have grown threefold. The impressive scale of these opportunities is helped by the fact that many projects involve longer events, outside broadcasting operations and consequently significant crewing numbers.

To coordinate these ongoing production activities, especially during the summer months, involves dedicated staffing. Solent Productions is subsidised by the University and is able to hire recent graduates on fixed-term contracts, providing them with a staging post between education and industry. These graduate staff organise a deepening pool of students eager for paid work. Commissioned work that comes with funding offsets the level of subsidy required and varies year on year.

The core pedagogy underpinning Solent Productions is 'learning by doing' (Savin-Baden, 2000), creating 'real world learning' experiences alongside the curriculum. For students, the career advantages and personal gains are multiple. There are higher than average graduate employment numbers (DLHE) for TV graduates. The list of the alumni working in industry is remarkable and countless student testimonials cite the value of working with professionals on live projects, experiencing the real pressures of delivery, clients and briefs.

For many students, there is a real appetite to put themselves under these pressures, whether or not they are mandatory as part of a degree programme. Recruitment of students by the Solent Productions team involves a formal application process, shortlisting and interviews. Students often become fully immersed in the projects, working and camping together for days at a time during the summer months at festivals and events. Confidence and self-belief are often increased and students realise they are working in the world they aspire to. They are notching up first-hand experience of effective teamwork and responsible communication, taking feedback and responding to constructive critiques. They form strong relationships with others and their professionalism off-site bleeds into their education.

It's often noted by staff that students working off-site often return transformed. Others seem ready for deeper engagement once the next semester starts. And the effect on career aspiration is clear to see. Jake Atkins, now a successful videographer, reflected recently on his time as a final year student in 2011. He says, "One of the best experiences of my career so far was going to the Glastonbury Festival with Solent Uni, the perfect start to my career in the TV and Video Industry!"

Many teaching and technical staff are also keen to stay abreast of new technologies and workflows offered as part of professional real world projects. Solent Productions is able to offer these individuals continuing professional development opportunities, on-site, on projects that are prestigious and reputation-building, testing and stretching whole production teams. More recently there have also been some direct broadcast commissions from the BBC and Showcase Cinemas that have added to the collective *cache* of working with Solent Productions.

But it has not all been plain sailing. The promise to clients by Solent Productions is to produce professional, and even broadcast standard output, created largely by students under supervision in a not-for-profit environment. This subsidised business model clearly would not survive outside HE, but there has been a concern that Solent Productions might be competing unfairly with local media start-ups, perhaps even those set up by Solent graduates.

To obviate this, the company collaborates where possible with graduates and fledgling operations, contributing to a wider economic development. Furthermore, many of the projects are large scale and simply wouldn't otherwise happen. If an outside broadcast project or live-stream event was tendered for at commercial rates, the costs would be so prohibitive that the opportunity would probably evaporate.

Another difficulty Solent Productions has is delivering quality content, on time, whilst meeting the client brief and expectations. To overcome the obvious risks involved, Solent's in-house teaching and technical staff are vital in providing quality assurance and delivery guarantees. Students alone are not enough as they are still learning professional practice and are not contracted employees. There is much encouragement by management for staff to take important supervisory roles with student crews, graduate staff and professional alumni, in order to minimise the risk. Staff involvement usually creates a complete and robust 'skills chain' dedicated to delivering the required media content to a professional standard.

In a teaching university such as Solent where currently only limited academic research takes place amongst the staff, the reframing by management of these supervisory roles as scholarly or enterprise activity, and perhaps as a precursor to more traditional research outputs, is the way in which the 'skills chain' can remain strong and for Solent Productions to continue to innovate for the benefit of staff and students alike.

Over a decade later, Solent Productions is an established model for best practice in media education amongst academics and industry alike. It has won awards, gained national recognition and features in institutional submissions for the Teaching Excellence Framework. It has levered valuable civic partnerships across the city and plays a key role in selling the university to prospective applicants and their parents. And at its heart is the essence of 'learning by doing', providing students with personal and professional experiences for life.

Adding High Value to Aspects of Practice Pedagogy

Ellstrom (2011) explains that a learning environment can be categorised as enabling or constraining dependent on how smoothly a student can transition between adaptive (the acquisition of skills or the aforementioned, technical competencies) and developmental (professional critique or the aforementioned actionable knowledge) learning. The difference can be viewed as the nuances that exist between students undertaking training, where they may be competent to a high level, and education where students are, from the outset, encouraged to think more broadly, alternatively and with an in-built sense of critique and reasoning.

Case Study 1, already presented, showcases developmental learning where students' immersion into high stakes learning through authentic TV production gives students an edge to their work experience—thus making it extraordinary—that would not have the same impact if the learning was not contributing to a commercial product.

Although students often experience a balance of adaptive or developmental learning through their work experience, developmental learning can be augmented if learning, as argued by Klein (1998), is given due attention and this can be achieved in the curriculum design, the practice pedagogy or both. Holbery, Morley and Mitchell (2019, p. 56), in their examination of the coaching of student nurses on placement, found ways students were best supported to expansive learning (Fuller & Unwin, 2003) that "encouraged a supportive environment for students to learn higher level skills such as dialogue, problem solving and reflexive forms of expertise". This was achieved through three distinct phases of students connecting with their colleagues, establishing their prior knowledge and expanding this expertise through a social model of learning where students worked with a diversity of staff.

An extraordinary work experience may further isolate skills, or work conditions, that are deemed particularly important to professional development within a discipline. Peer learning, as a means of encouraging collaboration and team building at both university and the workplace, is gaining traction in higher education (Hilsdon, 2014; Keenan, 2014). In practice, peer learning can enhance belonging, promote cooperation and support enhanced employability skills (Wilson, Cooper, & Baron, 2019) when due attention is given to the stage and application of learning. Case Study 2, like Case Study 1, creates an innovative situated context for learning yet explicitly enhances learning through the promotion of peer

Case Study 2

Employability Benefits from Embracing Challenge as Teams: The Purbeck Wildlife Student Environment Research Team Placement (Dr Anita Diaz, Professor in Conservation Ecology, Bournemouth University, UK)

learning and support in the authentic real world context of research on an ecology field trip.

Student Environment Research Teams (SERTs) http://www.cocreate4science.org/serts/ are a Bournemouth University initiative founded on the principle of creating team-learning opportunities for students that also simultaneously create new knowledge in partnership with academics and professional practitioners. The Purbeck Wildlife SERT is funded and mentored as a close collaboration between Bournemouth University and the National Trust and also involves a range of other conservation organisations. It was founded in 2016 and runs annually. It is based around a two-week camp-based residential project where students and staff work together to conduct wildlife surveys that address conservation ecology science questions. Students also help with planning before the SERT and outreach communication of the work afterwards. Mentoring from staff scaffolds students' learning and fosters a strong work ethic. It also encourages students to find ways of demonstrating their skills and competencies so that they can communicate these to future employers.

Through SERTs students gain key employability skills in wildlife conservation and environmental science. Successful careers in these areas demand self-responsibility, resilience, commitment and communication skills as well as strong subject-specific skills. These 'soft' employability skills are often forged in crucibles of challenge where people are stretched beyond their comfort zones. However, challenging placements are risky, particularly in a HE climate dominated by student satisfaction, as their full value may not become apparent to the students until after they graduate. Consequently, such placements are rare and yet much needed to support student development into effective graduate citizens for the twenty-first century.

The Purbeck Wildlife SERT work placement aims to address this need by providing students with an authentically challenging work placement environment in which they can both gain subject-specific skills in ecology and advance their personal growth of soft employability skills. The authenticity of challenge opportunities provided by the Purbeck Wildlife SERT is achieved by students entering as partners into communities of practice (CoP) of researchers and practitioners committed to conserving species (Morley et al., 2018). This means that the work the students do has practical consequences for conservation. This fosters engagement and enhances the overall learning experience. The placement is advertised together with other placements on the internal university system 'Careerhub' and students apply in the same way as they do for other work placements by sending a curriculum vitae and covering letter. Students are then interviewed informally to discuss if the placement is right for them. Up to 15 students have been accepted on the placement per year to date. All placements are technically co-curricular on the degree course, that is, they must be passed but are not credit bearing. This gives students and placement hosts scope to try something innovative which may not work without risking it impacting on a student's marks.

During the placement students also analyse their data in the evenings so they can present their findings to the National Trust. The presentation is a formal PowerPoint session delivered by the students on the last day of fieldwork. This puts the students under real world pressures of time and exposure. Furthermore, students are immersed in a field camp context for the two weeks of fieldwork and are expected to also lead the management of their team camp needs such as cooking rotas. Students hone their abilities to communicate constructively with other members of the CoP through their roles as both student leader and team members. All of this combines to create a high stakes environment that purposefully place students in exposed positions of accountability as team leaders.

Key subject-specific skills gained on the placement include species identification, fieldwork management and data analysis. Wider competencies include communication, resilience, problem-solving and being able to demonstrate sustained responsibility. These skills and competencies are highly applicable to a range of careers as well as specifically to the very competitive careers in wildlife conservation. They map strongly onto the degree programme learning outcomes: "have critical understanding of the scientific, technical, and regulatory bases of conservation ecology and wider environmental issues" and "apply these skills to specific environmental problems, and also communicate effectively". Students can tailor the balance of skills and competencies they develop depending on which leadership roles they select. Consequently, the aspiration is that this placement empowers all students to accelerate their individual career trajectories.

The most profound growth in student learning is around their gaining of an integrated sense of empowerment and responsibility as a result of being part of a team. This fosters strong engagement with learning new skills and a willingness to overcome barriers. Fieldwork conditions and the very rustic field camp arrangements are new challenges for many of the students as is the reality of long working days and expectations of consistently accurate work. The duality of support and expectation arising from students being accountable members of the team promotes a strong work ethic. This directly drives students to work hard to develop and share their subject-specific skills in, for example, species identification or data analysis, so that they contribute to the success of the team. Students also develop a strong appreciation of the need for give-and-take flexibility, personal responsibility and peer support. There have been occasions where staff provided mentoring support at specifically intense moments of conflict and challenge. However, the focus for mentors has remained on supporting students to take the opportunity to practice and demonstrate their emotional intelligence rather than on stepping in as arbitrators.

The Purbeck Wildlife SERT has wider impacts beyond benefits to the individual students involved. Fundamentally, it has cemented a strong partnership between Bournemouth University and the National Trust which is building forward to create new research and knowledge exchange opportunities. This will support the co-creation of an innovative monitoring programme for conservation management of the Purbeck Heaths National Nature Reserve that aims to provide a model for landscape-scale monitoring that can be adopted across other landscapes that are important for wildlife and people's well-being. Becoming thought leaders in this field will benefit wider society and raise the profile and prestige of both the university and National Trust.

Overall the student experience on the Purbeck Wildlife SERT embodies the core purpose of Bournemouth University which is "to inspire learning, advance knowledge and enrich society". Student learning is inspired through co-creating new research knowledge in partnership with academics and practitioners which has special value because it enriches society by benefiting nature. An extraordinary work experience arises from authentic fused engagement by all stakeholders; the core fuel for that fusion is trust.

Recognising the Negative Aspects of Practice Learning and Promoting the Interdependence of Theory and Practice

Reoccurring areas in practice pedagogy have the potential to undermine student learning and dilute the ability of work experience to reach an extraordinary level. Factors such as poor induction (Quinlaven, Sookraj-Bahal, Moody, Levington, & Taylor, 2019), the use of exclusive professional language (Gherardi et al., 1998; Wenger, 1998), poorly designed assessment and lack of support systems (Morley, 2015) were all found to have an effect. From an institutional point of view, the number of students seeking work placements as part of their programmes of study puts a strain on any ambition for students to only be exposed to exceptional learning situations. In the drive to find an increasing number of placements for an increasing number of students, universities enter a numbers game, often against other institutions of higher education, to address the programme requirements.

Although new higher degree apprenticeship schemes, explored in Chapter 11, meticulously address many of the recognised negativities of practice learning in their curriculum design, other innovative examples exist where universities create their own extraordinary work experience. Case Study 3, from Solent University, provides an example of a work experience hub where many of the university programmes capitalise on an externally facing retail space created by the university itself by its integration into its curriculum design.

Case Study 3

The Student Led Retail Store: Flexible and Creative Embedded Learning (Lesley Taylor, Senior Lecturer—Academic Lead Re:So, Solent University, UK)

Re:So (The Retail Solent Initiative) was founded as a pop up in 2012 by the Solent University's Head of Faculty of Creative Industries to give students a showcase to test and sell their own products, on a commission basis, in a real retail environment. Equally it was designed with work-based learning in mind, allowing students to take responsibility for running an off-campus retail store whilst accruing a large amount of work placement hours. Typically, Re:So provides 2000–3000 hours per year across its associated programmes.

The products range from fashion and accessories to art, homewares and publications and are promoted by the store team as part of their job roles. The store also trades at external events such as the student Fresher's Fair, music festivals and themed daytime events in a local nightclub.

The store model does not have a traditional product supply chain so the student team must work to promote and refresh the product offer and presentations as part of their learning. Re:So's upstairs location is also a challenge and those working on social media placement have this as their focus to make the store visible online to as many potential customers as possible.

Twenty-five taught modules from two Schools (i.e. Art, Design and Fashion, and Business, Law and Communication) are linked to the store. Outcomes vary from products to events, analytical business reports, marketing proposals and instore spatial and decorative designs. This gives the brief a live client and the outcomes from a real world perspective. Students can apply for roles at the store or submit their own proposals.

Not all students can afford to take a placement in London so Re:So provides accessible, local and high impact work experience where the store provides work similar to retail head offices and design studios, just on a smaller scale. Social media input, marketing plans and event organisation would be unusual in a larger retailer's store, so this gives a point of difference.

Placement students are able to come to the store to discuss what they wish to learn, and a job can be drawn up in a bespoke fashion to suit these requirements. The hours are flexible, the staff rota being drawn up according to their availability. Hence a placement can be three full weeks or spread across a few months if they prefer and allows the student to continue with paid work they may already have.

One course, BA (Hons) Product Design, runs a module entitled 'Design for Manufacture' whereby the student must understand the store and its customer profile, interview the staff and the Academic Lead proposes a product that can retail under £15. Two are selected by the Academic Lead and Course Leader and the production process involves a small budget from the School to allow for purchase of materials. The products are created in the University's workshop. They are promoted by the course and the store on social media with the student receiving a portion of the sale price, after commission.

The Product Design students are briefed in the store by their Course Leader and the Academic Lead is introduced, who gives an overview of the store. They see how the store operates and have the opportunity to ask questions as they examine the store themselves. The two staff members are then both present to give feedback at approximately a six-week (mid-module) presentation whereby the students show their designs and thought processes to that point. The feedback enables them to edit or to rethink at this stage so that they stay close to the brief and to ensure they are aiming for a commercially viable product. The final selection is made at that hand-in point where prototypes and product proposals are again reviewed by the two staff members. Two items are nominated, and the students go into a production process with the Course Leader to create 5–10 of their design for pre-Christmas launch in the store.

Mostly the links between placement and academia occur as the result of a 2000-word reflective, theory-based assignment. Those that undertake the work-based learning unit are asked to reflect upon what they learned about themselves, rather than the skills they learned. They apply reflective theory and include diary extracts to support their findings.

When working on linked modules, students also learn from the student staff at the store as they are often the point of contact for when a student visits to ask questions about the business. Internally a work placement student will learn from a more established paid member of the team, most of whom have come through that system themselves. Training and day-to-day running of the store is student-led and is advertised as such to make Re:So unique.

The highest paid student role of sales manager is one that works closely with the Academic Lead and stays in post for up to 2.5 years and can really make the role their own. They grow in confidence in this time and become quite autonomous in their working style, which prepares students for industry. Each year there has been a paid graduate intern role giving them the responsibility of being the store manager on a 12-month contract. The interns can 'model' the store procedures as they see fit and streamline ways the team are recruited, trained and work.

The graduate interns have mostly gone into management roles straight from their contracts, hence fast-tracking their employability.

In particular, the interdependency between the theory and practice in a students' programme of study is significant to the curriculum design and pedagogy of an extraordinary work experience. Bjorck and Johansson (2018), in their investigation of the terminology used by students, found that the traditional polarised view of the dualism of theory and practice was unhelpful to a more seamless view of theory and practice conjoined and as "harmonious points of departure for learning" (p. 9). The often-geographical divide between the academic course component at university and practice on work experience can underlie further micro divisions in delivery, assessment and the support that students receive. This can create opposing forces within the same course that only students are aware of as they move between the different learning environments of their programmes of study.

The fragmentation of learning that can occur between university and work is a well-recognised phenomenon in many professional courses and the resultant schism leads to deep-seated problems for students' immediate and long-term development. Theory is embedded in and is inseparable from practice (Schön, 1983), yet students often fail to make the connection between their academic learning and how this can be translated into the world of work (Dibben & Morley, 2019). Real world learning replicates, or as closely as is reasonably possible, the authentic world of work where practice and theory are rarely separated, and one constantly stimulates the other. The theory-practice divide is often positioned as extremes on an education-training continuum which is counter-intuitive to a continual and explicit articulation of applied pedagogy to the students' learning.

Trede and McEwen (2012) found that critical awareness is a graduate skill of a developing professional and one where awareness of the source of knowledge is essential to differentiate between that which is objective and that based on professional socialisation and tradition (Eraut, 2000). Roberts (2006) argues that this lack of awareness can impede the absorption and sharing of new skills and risks socialisation to one way of thinking.

Argyris and Schön (1974) and Smith (2012) identify a difference between practitioners' intentions in practice and ideal course of action: *espoused theories* against a privileging of what is already used in practice—*theories in use*. Allen (2009, p. 653) found that this was the case with prospective teachers who articulated their "in-field experience as practical, real and immediate and on-campus work as theoretical and remote".

Furthermore, acquiescence by the student, and an inability to exercise their voice due to political and power structures on work experience, can distort students' ability to question, connect and critique the learning they are experiencing (Bradbury-Jones et al., 2011). Working in a supported environment can ease this process (Bradbury-Jones et al., 2011) as well as encouraging students' engagement with this powerful para curriculum as part of their development (Allan, Smith, & O'Driscoll, 2011).

Awareness and strategies to explicitly integrate theory and practice vary according to programmes of study. Provision, through recalibrating the curriculum, is one such strategy where the use of authentic assessment can assess the application of theory to practice, another is attending to the redesign of the balance and integration between academic study and work experience as showcased in a nursing module in Case Study 4. In particular, the case study explicitly demonstrates the mutual benefit of knowledge exchange between the theoretical and practical elements of a course.

Case Study 4

Assessment That Has Helped Bridge the Theory to Practice Gap (Dr Pauline Calleja, Senior Lecturer, School of Nursing and Midwifery, Griffith University, Australia)

At master's level 'Emerging issues in disaster and pandemic planning, response and management' in the School of Nursing and Midwifery, students experience a scaffolded series of assessment items that has helped bridge theory to practice.

Students report wide-scale changes to existing health service policy. In some cases, there was no policy in place or only work guidelines existed and students' recommendations provided an impetus for change. Mostly students were involved in working parties or became clinician stakeholders in the portfolios that related to disaster or pandemic preparedness in their hospital or health service. This then created opportunities for applied leadership that was in addition to their clinical work with patients.

The online course deliberately requires students to directly apply legislation, theory and best practice guidelines to their local context to influence practice. Assessment, learning outcomes, threshold concepts and learning activities were explicitly linked for students in this course. For each learning activity the student was explicitly told how it helped them prepare for assessment or challenge practice or perceptions.

Assessment 1 2000 w, 35% weighted, critical analysis essay

Students critically evaluate how well prepared the student's local workplace is to respond to a disaster or pandemic activation using legislation and literature. Students choose an event type and review the local policy or guidelines and make recommendations to improve local policy/guidelines. Students often engage with managers in their workplace in order to identify which policy or guidelines to evaluate and are often encouraged to discuss possible recommendations with their line managers once they have evaluated the strengths and gaps to ensure recommendations are practicable and not just theoretical. Students are required to make an argument for priority of recommendations as well, and they often find that their clinical supports can assist them to make this argument by debating the pros and cons of their recommendations. Students can include workplace feedback about their recommendations to lend credibility to their recommendation's prioritisation.

Assessment 2 Twelve-minute presentation, and discussion board management, response to other students' discussion board, 40% weighting (20% presentation, 10% discussion management, 10% response to other students' presentations).

Students choose real world events that have publications about them (e.g. 9/11 in 2001, Ebola virus disease breakout and London train bombing). Students research the management and outcomes of the event and apply lessons learned from this to their local context to create and deliver a recorded presentation on an online discussion board thread. Students then manage their discussion thread related to their presentation and participate in online discussion boards about three other students' presentations. This approach also exposes students to both disaster and pandemic events and policy variations that they would not be able to achieve in traditional essay-only assessments.

This assessment leverages knowledge students gain about their local policies in assessment 1 and then, using critical evaluation skills, apply a real event to their local workplace and policy and make recommendations for improvement of preparedness and management. Students also gain other skills such as managing an online asynchronous conversation through clear guidelines on what students should comment on when watching others' presentations which has increased the depth and quality of the discussion. The context of the authentic event engages students deeply in the assessment, and this is one of the most highly evaluated aspects of the course. Most students also share this presentation with their colleagues and managers before submitting for feedback and in this way directly influences policy and awareness in their own workplace.

Assessment 3 Reflective assessment, weighting 25%, 1000–1500 w.

Students review their presentation and the discussion board. They reflect on the presentation and the peer feedback and responses in the discussion thread. Students share their presentation's strengths and shortfalls and the quality of the peer discussion before proposing refinements or give a defence of the recommendations made in the presentation for local management of the chosen topic with reference to the literature and feedback.

This final assessment focuses on students' ability to reflect on and critically review discussion, their recommendations and the quality of their presentation. This is an essential skill for healthcare professionals when selecting interventions and evidence to support practice. We are currently redeveloping this final assessment to encompass an evaluation of students' learning across the whole course and therefore close the loop on their learning and intention to apply their learnings to practice.

Student feedback outlines the incidental impact that the first two assessments have on their wider development. Most students report that this has given them confidence to develop educational resources for asynchronous learning with colleagues who work across shifts and off-site. Students also report that as a result of their recommendations being locally applicable, they were invited onto more committees or into leadership roles because their managers saw their potential to continue to improve practice in other areas of need.

For some students this change in how they were seen as leaders was profound; one student reported that her work on these assessments led to her ability to present her recommendations for improvement of a work practice very well in an interview and attributes this to her successful promotion.

Evans, Guile, and Harris (2009) and Evans, Guile, Harris, and Allan (2010) highlight how theoretical knowledge acquired at university needs to be carefully 're-contextualised' to make it available to students, first, in their university learning and then to enable them to transfer their learning to a practice context. Thus, the theory of academic learning (content re-contextualisation) needs to 'travel and alter' through the curriculum development of the simulation (pedagogic re-contextualisation), be applied to clinical practice within the work-based setting (workplace re-contextualisation) and then made accessible and usable by the student whilst in practice (learner re-contextualisation).

Using Evan's theory of re-contextualisation, Morley, Bettles and Derham (2019) found that assumptions that certain pedagogies, such as simulation, naturally carried learning into the practice context were often incorrect. Multiple barriers, such as the students' confidence to admit to their learning needs with their new practice supervisor, were highlighted and demonstrated the importance that attention was given to theoretical connections and university learning in the different context of practice.

This can be achieved through a variety of routes and the theory-practice divide can be bridged by students working with specialists who naturally broker the academic and practice elements by their wide-reaching professional experience (Morley, 2018) or particular roles that focus on ensuring the university experience continues to be supported on placement (Eccles & Renaud, 2018) through the coaching of graduate skills.

Conclusion

The case studies that provide the applied examples within this chapter showcase the attributes of an extraordinary work experience originally mapped by the authors. The case study authors' creative pedagogies, with their ability to work imaginatively with university structures and processes, have provided students with immediate and longitudinal opportunity to accelerate both their learning and work readiness. This all takes place in an environment different in every way to the traditional university setting and the extraordinary work experience will use this authenticity to its advantage by providing learning that is accelerated and connects powerfully with students' affective engagement. Each case study role models an attention to the detail of learning, so students' work experience is reinforced, and it's worth made explicit to them. Once complete, students have the opportunity to tap into ongoing professional networks—acknowledged by the number of alumni who support the university initiatives long after they have graduated.

Collectively, the case studies have become market leaders outside of their universities as their work experience has extended the students' impact into wider industry and community involvement, thus building the university reputation as a result. Innovative and well thought through work experience has an impact not only on students' learning but also on the motivation of staff, their pride in their pedagogy and product which feeds back into the student experience. In an extraordinary work experience, immersion is mutual for both academic and student.

Increasingly, however, due in greater part to the growing numbers of students on vocational degrees with an expectation on an integral placement experience, universities are having to source these opportunities in an ever-increasingly crowded marketplace. Subsequently, many establishments have had to form a new paradigm and find new and imaginative methods by which to concurrently give the student what they want and the industry what they need. As such, universities have had to 'think outside the box' and find ways in which to manage large cohorts, and their expectations, with the resource limitations of, often, local businesses or services.

References

Allan, H. T., Smith, P., & O'Driscoll, M. (2011). Experiences of supernumerary status and the hidden curriculum in nursing: A new twist in the theory-practice gap? *Journal of Clinical Nursing, 20*(5–6), 847. https://doi.org/10.1111/j.1365-2702.2010.03570.x

Allen, J. (2009). Valuing practice over theory: How beginning teachers re-orient their practice in the transition from the university to the workplace. *Teaching and Teacher Education, 25*, 647–653. https://doi.org/10.1016/j.tate.2008.11.011

Argyris, C., & Schön, D. (1974). *Theory in practice: Increasing professional effectiveness.* San Francisco: Jossey Bass.

Billett, S. (2009). Realising the educational worth of integrating work experiences in higher education. *Studies in Higher Education, 34*(7), 827–843. https://doi.org/10.1080/03075070802706561

Billett, S. (2012). *Towards an account of learning through practice: Traditions, practices and potentials.* Paderborn: University of Paderborn.

Bjorck, V., & Johansson, K. (2018). Problematising the theory-practice terminology: A discourse analysis of students' statements on work-integrated learning. *Journal of Further and Higher Education., 43*(10), 1363–1375. https://doi.org/10.1080/0309877X.2018.1483016

Bradbury-Jones, C., Sambrook, S., & Irvine, F. (2011). Nursing students and the issue of voice: A qualitative study. *Nurse Education Today, 31*, 628–632. https://doi.org/10.1016/j.nedt.2010.10.030

Bruner, J. (1960). *The process of education.* Cambridge, MA: The President and Fellows of Harvard College.

Dibben, L., & Morley, D. A. (2019). Using the living CV to help students to take ownership of their learning gain. In A. Diver (Ed.), *Employability via higher education: Sustainability as scholarship.* Springer.

Eccles, S., & Renaud, V. (2018). Building students' emotional resilience through placement coaching and mentoring. In D. A. Morley (Ed.), *Enhancing employability in higher education through work based learning.* Palgrave Macmillan.

Ellstrom, P.-E. (2011). Informal learning at work: Conditions, processes and logics. In M. Malloch, L. Cairns, K. Evans, & B. O'Connor (Eds.), *The sage handbook of workplace learning* (pp. 105–119). London/California/New Delhi/Singapore: Sage.

Eraut, M. (2000). Non-formal learning and tacit knowledge in professional work. *British Journal of Educational Psychology, 70*, 113–136. https://doi.org/10.1348/000709900158001

Eraut, M. (2004). Informal learning in the workplace. *Studies in Continuing Education, 26*(2), 247–273. https://doi.org/10.1080/158037042000225245

Evans, K., Guile, D., & Harris, J. (2009). *Putting knowledge to work: integrating work-based and subject-based knowledge in intermediate level qualifications and workforce up skilling.* Retrieved from https://thecet.org/wp-content/uploads/2018/10/Book-of-Exemplars.pdf

Evans, K., Guile, D., Harris, J., & Allan, H. (2010). Putting knowledge to work: A new approach. *Nurse Education Today, 30*, 245–251. https://doi.org/10.1016/j.nedt.2009.10.014

Fuller, A., & Unwin, L. (2003). Learning as apprentices in the contemporary UK workplace: Creating and managing expansive and restrictive participation. *Journal of Education & Work, 16*(4), 407–426. https://doi.org/10.1080/1363908032000093012

Gherardi, S., Nicolini, D., & Odella, F. (1998). Toward a social understanding of how people learn in organizations: The notion of situated curriculum. *Management Learning, 29*, 273–297.

Grealish, L., & Ranse, K. (2009). An exploratory study of first year nursing students' learning in the clinical workplace. *Contemporary Nurse, 33*(1), 80–92.

Hilsdon, J. (2014). Peer learning for change in higher education. *Innovations in Education and Teaching International, 51*(3), 244–254. https://doi.org/10.1080/14703297.2013.796709

Holbery, N., Morley, D. A., & Mitchell, J. (2019). Expansive learning. In D. A. Morley (Ed.), *Facilitating learning in practice. A research-based approach to challenges and solutions* (pp. 56–71). London/New York: Routledge.

Keenan, C. (2014). *Mapping student-led peer learning in the UK.* HEA. Retrieved from https://www.heacademy.ac.uk/system/files/resources/peer_led_learning_keenan_nov_14-final.pdf

Kemmis, S. (2012). Pedagogy, praxis and practice based higher education. In J. Higgs, R. Barnett, S. Billett, M. Hutchings, & F. Trede (Eds.), *Practice-based education. Perspectives and strategies* (pp. 81–100). Rotterdam/Boston/Taipei: Sense Publishers.

Kinsella, E. A. (2009). Professional knowledge and the epistemology of reflective practice. *Nursing Philosophy: An International Journal for Healthcare Professionals,* *11*(1), 3–14. https://doi.org/10.1111/j.1466-769X. 2009.00428.x

Kinsella, E. A. (2010). The art of reflective practice in health and social care: Reflections on the legacy of Donald Schön. *Reflective Practice,* *11*(4), 565–575. https://doi.org/10.1080/14623943.2010.506260

Klein, G. (1998). *Sources of power. How people make decisions.* Cambridge/London: The MIT Press.

Lave, J., & Wenger, E. (1991). *Situated learning. Legitimate peripheral participation.* New York: Cambridge University Press.

More, C. (1980). *Skills and the English working class.* Croom Helm.

Morley, D. A. (2015). *A grounded theory study exploring first year student nurses' learning in practice.* (Doctor in Professional Practice). Bournemouth: Bournemouth University.

Morley, D. A. (2018). The "ebb and flow" of student learning on placement. In D. A. Morley (Ed.), *Enhancing employability in higher education through work based learning.* Palgrave Macmillan.

Morley, D. A., Archer, L., Burgess, M., Curran, D., Milligan, V., & Williams, D. (2017). *A panel discussion - the impact of the university student placement experience on both students and academics.* Paper presented at the ExCiTes Teaching and Learning conference, 5th January 2017, University of Surrey, Guildford, UK.

Morley, D., Diaz, A., Blake, D., Burger, G., Dando, T., Gibbon, S., & Rickard, K. (2018). Student experience of real time management of peer working groups during field trips. In D. A. Morley (Ed.), *Enhancing employability in higher education through work based learning.* London/New York: Palgrave Macmillan.

Morley, D., Bettles, S., & Derham, C. (2019). The exploration of students' learning gain following immersive simulation – The impact of feedback. *Higher Education Pedagogies,* *4*(1), 368–384. https://doi.org/10.108 0/23752696.2019.1642123

Polanyi, M. (1966). *The tacit dimension.* London: Routledge and Kegan Paul.

Quinlaven, L., Sookraj-Bahal, S., Moody, J., Levington, A., & Taylor, C. (2019). Comprehensive orientation and socialisation. In D. A. Morley (Ed.), *Facilitating learning in practice. A research-based approach to challenges and solutions* (pp. 6–17). London/New York: Routledge.

Roberts, J. (2006). Limits to communities of practice. *Journal of Management Studies, 43*(3), 623–639. https://doi.org/10.1111/j.1467-6486.2006.00618.x

Savin-Baden, M. (2000). *Problem-based learning in higher education: Untold stories*. Buckingham: The Society for Research into Higher Education and Open University Press.

Schön, D. (1983). *The reflective practitioner. How professionals think in action*. Aldershot: Ashgate Publishing Limited.

Smith, M. K. (2012). Chris Argyris: Theories of action, double-loop learning and organizational learning. *The encyclopedia of informal education*. Retrieved from http://www.infed.org/thinkers/argyris.htm

Trede, F., & McEwen, C. (2012). Developing a critical professional identity: Engaging self in practice. In J. Higgs, R. Barnett, S. Billett, M. Hutchings, & F. Trede (Eds.), *Practice-based education. Perspectives and strategies* (pp. 27–40). Rotterdam: Sense Publishers.

Wenger, E. (1998). *Communities of practice. Learning, meaning and identity*. New York: Cambridge University Press.

Wenger, E. (2012). *Social learning theory and healthcare education*. Paper presented at the Contemporary Issues in Clinical Education, Institute of Education, London.

Wilson, K., Cooper, N., & Baron, M. (2019). Student peer support and learning. In D. A. Morley (Ed.), *Facilitating learning in practice. A research-based approach to challenges and solutions* (pp. 32–43). London/New York: Routledge.

8

Making Projects Real in a Higher Education Context

Roy Hanney

Introduction

A reconceptualisation of projects, away from projects as a model of management towards projects as a model of practice (Hodgson & Cicmil, 2006), offers an opportunity to see project-based learning (PjBL) as a social practice (Fig. 8.1). Given the desirability of the use of live projects as a means of drawing real world learning into the curriculum, this approach offers a new perspective that begins to address a number of problems with project working within a higher education context. It takes as a founding principle the notion that real world learning occurs within a community of practice (Wenger, 1998) and argues that, for real world learning to occur, educators within HEI's need to foster communities of practice (Wenger, 1998) within which students can participate as productive members.

Case studies: Rhiannon Jones, Ana Gaio and Lada T. Price

R. Hanney (✉)
Solent University, Southampton, UK
e-mail: roy.hanney@solent.ac.uk

© The Author(s) 2021
D. A. Morley, M. G. Jamil (eds.), *Applied Pedagogies for Higher Education*,
https://doi.org/10.1007/978-3-030-46951-1_8

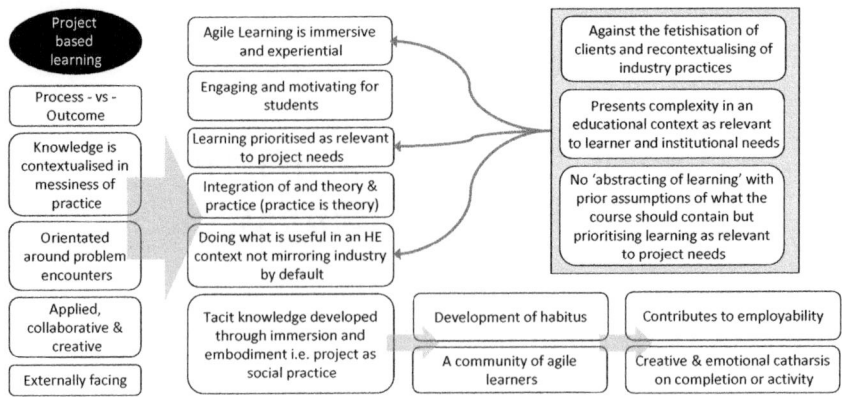

Fig. 8.1 Agile learning through PjBL concept map

A community of practice (Wenger, 1998) requires novices to learn more than just technical competences and entry level practical skills. They are socialised into a community of practice through the experience of socially situated signifying practices. Students are therefore exposed not only to what can be seen to be done but also to that which is hidden through tacit understanding, transmission of meaning, contextualisation of tools and techniques, all of which render the experience more meaningful. The chapter addresses how we as educators build into the learning process the kind of experience that enables students, as novice practitioners, develop the kind of tacit sensibilities found among expert practitioners.

A shift from executability to learnability of projects foregrounds the ontological characteristics of a 'becoming mode' of project working (Hanney, 2018). It is one that offers opportunities for exploring the ways in which educators can transition communities of learners into communities of practice and thereby lead to a process of socialisation into real world working. Case studies drawn from examples of project-based learning on a range of practice-based course at UK HEI's will illustrate how such a reconceptualisation of projects (Bredillet, 2010) might aid educators in making projects real in an HE context.

Rethinking Project Management

Many of the classical texts on project management begin with the assumption that projects are a historical phenomenon, citing examples such as the pyramids (cf. Nicholas, 2004; Shenhar & Dvir, 2007), the Great Wall of China, the Tower of Babel, or even the act of Creation itself (cf. Morris, 1994) as evidence of the historicity of this concept. There is though, no historical evidence to support such claims and it is unlikely that these ancient peoples employed the kinds of models of organisational control that would today be recognised as project management. In fact, the term is believed to have first originated in an article in the *Harvard Business Review* in 1959 (Winter, Smith, Cooke-Davies, & Cicmil, 2006) reflecting a then emerging sub-discipline of organisational studies which concerned itself with the adoption of newly formulated tools for the optimisation of organisational process (Bredillet, 2010). The classical view of a *project as a temporary endeavour undertaken to create a unique product, service or result* (Project Management Institute) is further codified through the development of professional bodies and institutionalised frameworks during the 1960s. During this period, we also see the arrival of large-scale project methodologies such as the *Project Management Body of Knowledge* which is developed by the Association of Project Managers, along with *Projects in a Controlled Environment* 2 which is developed by the UK government. The main focus of these approaches was to provide a normative framework for managing task-orientated activities within a directed command and control hierarchy (Winter et al., 2006) for delivering organisational benefit. A project is formulated by these systems approaches as an instrumental tool for managing project process and the metaphor for this methodology is that of a "machine that requires optimisation" (Svejvig & Andersen, 2015, p. 280), the main focus for which is the execution of a task.

Around the turn of the millennium, a number of researchers in the field of project studies began to re-evaluate the way in which projects were conceptualised in order to "better account for project phenomena" (Floricel, Bonneau, Aubry, & Sergi, 2014, p. 1091). By redirecting their accounts away from the instrumental towards the social, they aimed to develop a deeper understanding of the nature of projects and project organisations. This became known as the Scandinavian School within the literature on the subject (cf. Lundin & Söderholm, 1995; Packendorff, 1995; Sahlin-Andersson & Söderholm, 2002). Instead of orientating themselves towards a positivist or functionalist conception of projects aimed at the optimisation of performance, they begin to present projects as a "lived experience" (Floricel et al., 2014, p. 1094). Thus, scholars in the field begin to reflect on the lived reality of what it is to do projects leading to a recognition of a project as *a temporary organisation established by its base organisation to carry out an assignment on its behalf* (Packendorff, 1995), the main focus for which is value creation, that is, to create a desirable development in another organisation (Winter et al., 2006). Table 8.1 sets out some key contrasts between the two views of a project. Of interest here, given the context of the study, is the shift away from *executability* towards *learnability* as a philosophical framework: a key distinction that informed the theoretical perspective of the research undertaken into project-based learning.

This is important because it begins to offer a way of thinking about how the siting or location of a project (i.e. in industry or in education) might impact on the use of projects. Particularly, in a pedagogic context, it might be beneficial to think about the nature of projects as a concept. However, while the rethinking projects view "reflects a broader and more holistic perspective in which projects might be conceptualised as temporary organisations" (Svejvig & Andersen, 2015, p. 280). It is important to recognise that this new concept builds in a pluralistic way on what has gone before and sees the classical tradition as embedded within the rethinking approach. That is to say, while there are of course benefits to those doing projects in the adoption of the instruments, tools and

Table 8.1 Contrasting views of a project adapted from Svejvig and Andersen (2015, p. 280)

Classical project management	-vs-	Rethinking project management
Executability, simplicity, temporarity, linearity, controllability and instrumentality.		Learnability, multiplicity, temporarity, non-linearity, complexity, uncertainty and sociability.

concepts drawn from the classical approach, to do so uncritically renders only a partial theorising of what it is to do a project (Hodgson & Cicmil, 2006).

The Critical Projects Movement

The launch of an ongoing series of symposiums entitled *Making Projects Critical* in 2003 heralds the arrival of a platform for divergent critical perspectives that offer alternative viewpoints on projects. The symposium led to the publication of a key text in the literature and, in 2009, to the publication of a special issue of *Ephemera* (Cicmil, Hodgson, Lindgren, & Packendorff, 2009), further developing this school of socio-political critique and the re-imagining of projects. Thus, the *Critical Projects Movement* emerged as a response to the need to draw upon ever more interdisciplinary resources in order to counter what is conceived as the techno-rationalism of the positivist view of projects (Cicmil et al., 2009). The movement critiques traditional assumptions made about project methods including the idea that they are "compelling and essentially sound" (Hodgson & Cicmil, 2008, p. 145), suggesting instead that there is an increasing body of evidence to suggest that these are anything but sound. They argue that the focus on tools and techniques doesn't allow for a critique of politics, power and the historically embedded nature of projects (Cicmil et al., 2009).

Instead the *Critical Projects Movement* sets a new agenda that draws upon a "wider and more critical intellectual resources than the instrumental rationality, quantitative and positivist methodologies and technicist solutions which have been traditionally brought to bear in attempts to understand and control the project form of organising" (Cicmil et al., 2009, p. 86). For example, Winter et al. (2006) questions a dominant assumption in project management studies that the model of project life cycle should be the primary object of study. Such an assumption results in an emphasis on the creation of a *product* rather than creation of *value* (Winter et al., 2006) and the benefit of a project to the different groups of project stakeholders (including the participants). This shifting of attention away from product to value is of key interest for educators since, it is argued, in project-based learning, the final output (i.e. product) is a consequence of the doing (i.e. value) of a project. In other words: it is the experience of doing a project not the final artefact that drives learning. Winter et al. (2006) goes on to argue that our theories are only ever partial, and that the complexity of a project is such that often our models and theories fail to acknowledge this. It is the acknowledgement of this complexity and the need to theorise it adequately that has led to the rethinking and reconceptualising of projects presented here.

Projects as Practice

This re-imagining of projects as a *lived experience* gives primacy to an *interpretivist* or *relativist* ontological account (Lewis, 2013, p. 14) of projects over those with a concern for codified, normative models of management. The rejection of what might be thought of as an *empirical realist ontology* (Lewis, 2013, p. 14) allows for the investigation to recognise the situated nature of projects as a form of social practice that is subject to continual change. Following Linehan and Kavanagh (2006, p. 55) it might be possible to begin to think of a project as an emergent or "becoming ontology". A *becoming ontology* embraces the *Heraclitean* notion of the world as chaotic and ever unfolding and stands in contrast to a *Parmenidean, being ontology*, which embodies instrumental, regulatory principles for structuring experience (cf. Hanney, 2018, p. 11). Again, a differentiation is posited between the metaphorisation of a project as a *machine* to a project as a *practice* (Gauthier & Ika, 2012, p. 15), in other words, a shift between models of organisation and models of practice. What is seen here is that the *Critical Projects Movement* challenges our understanding of projects and project management by highlighting alternative perspectives. Linehan and Kavanagh argue that rather than take a singular point of view about projects it is "better to think of a project first as a language and second as a practice" (Linehan & Kavanagh, 2006, p. 55). Thus, the shift from a *realist* to a *relativist* ontological account of projects mirrors the "practice turn" in sociology (Blomquist, Hällgren, Nilsson, & Söderholm, 2010, p. 9) and offers a view of projects as a socially constructed enterprise that places human agency at the heart of any meaningful enquiry into the subject.

It is argued that the relationship between structure and agency is a dialectical one and both Giddens (1984) and Bourdieu (1988) identify the mutually constitutive relationship between structure and agency (Seo & Creed, 2002), suggesting that tensions between structural elements within social relations (contradictions) have the effect of empowering social actors to become "change agents" (Seo & Creed, 2002, p. 223). In fact, Bloomquist goes further (Blomquist et al., 2010, p. 7) and, following Bourdieu (1990), argues the relationship between structure and agency is a causal one. For these scholars, agency is understood as a form of praxis or, in other words, as any "action embedded in a historical system" (Seo & Creed, 2002, p. 223) that comes about as a result of the "ruptures and inconsistencies within social relations" (Seo & Creed, 2002, p. 225) and enables social actors to engage in a restructuring of social relations within which they are embedded. For Bourdieu (1984) an investigation of praxis includes a study of what is done as well as the situatedness of action within a social milieu. What is then presented here, a *becoming* ontology, is one in which the social actor is engaged in an unfolding act of transformation. It is this act of transformation, as the results within the articles will argue, that should be at the heart of any theoretical underpinning of project-based learning.

From the position of a *becoming* or relativist ontology, it should be possible to formulate a series of key principles for researching *projects-as-practice*. Blomquist et al. (2010, p. 13) presents just such a set of principles suggesting that the research should focus on the following:

- What is done and from there develop an understanding of wider contexts, that is, research is practitioner focused and moves from interior to exterior.
- The practice rather than on models of management such that the reasons for taking actions are made central, for example, how do people actually solve problems.
- The dynamics of communities of practitioners within organisations and the ways these overlap with other organisational communities.

- The interaction between local and global and exterior and interior factors in order to understand how these factors influence practice.
- The entanglement and intertwining of communities and practices in order to understand the situatedness of practice.

Taking these principles as a starting point, it is understood that "that to develop a sound theoretical basis for project management, the very nature of projects needs to be examined" (Bredillet, 2010, p. 6). This can be undertaken through a synthesis of the reconceptualising of projects that has occurred within organisational studies, with theories of learning and educational development. In doing so it is argued that educators would be better placed to re-imagine project-based learning as an agile pedagogy for 'social learning' (Wenger-Trayner & Wenger-Trayner, 2015) not as a model for the management of learning.

Case Studies

This chapter asks if it is possible to enhance real world learning experiences through the use of live projects in Higher Education. It proposes that in order to better understand how real world learning occurs within an HEI setting, our understanding of the nature of live projects, and by inference project-based learning, needs to be reformulated. The chapter proposes a shift from projects as models of management and rethinking of projects as forms of social practice. It suggests that if educators wish to enhance the use of live projects within the curriculum, then it might be helpful to think of projects as a social domain rather than an administrative tool. To do so allows for the shift from the short-term interiority of task-based learning in which teams coalesce around tasks and disperse upon completion as typified by the use of fully or partially simulated live projects within individual modules or units of learning. Towards an approach in which students begin the process of socialisation into the community of practice they will encounter on their transition from education into employment.

The chapter presents three case studies which to varying degrees attempt to address this need to ease students across the boundary between employment and education. Case Study 1 outlines a project undertaken by Interior Design students at Derby University who were challenged to design a mobile public art space. Case Study 2 sketches out a project undertaken by postgraduate Culture, Policy and Management students at City University that engaged with small cultural enterprises to provide marketing support, while Case Study 3 saw Journalism students at Sheffield University participate in a live 'Newsday' style event supported by professional data journalists. In each case the use of a live project aims to introduce students to the application of theory to practice, provide for an engagement with industry, structuring activity around the principle of learning by doing. In each case the project sought to generate an encounter with the real world for students that would ease their transition from education to employment.

To what extent the cases presented here achieve these goals can be evaluated against the degree to which the students begin the process of socialisation into their respective communities of practice. This can be characterised further by analysing the occurrence of 'social learning' (Wenger-Trayner & Wenger-Trayner, 2015) in each of the cases. For Wenger-Trayner and Wenger-Trayner (2015) 'social learning' occurs within communities of practice. It is the process of acquiring membership of a community that has ongoing 'continuity and purpose', infers the adoption of a 'shared identity' and a 'collective intention' towards a sustained contribution to a shared domain of disciplinary knowledge.

Case Study 1 perhaps exemplifies this ethos best with its focus on 'conversations' between industry professionals and students as novice practitioners. The partnership appears to have established behavioural norms and sets out a collective sense of a work ethos. It is assumed, this would have been further enforced by the participation of industry professionals who would have modelled these kinds of behaviours for students. Siting much of the activity for the project off-campus also provided for a deepened real world context. While the public launch of the project frames the project as having a real world output, a live project of this kind requires a real world client with a real business need to achieve the situatedness that brings liveness to a project (Hanney, 2013). This project achieves this goal while also offering a civic context thereby situating professional practice within the context of a public space. This gives the project a real sense of value and places the students practice firmly within the context of a creative industries business model. The key element of the project that meets the requirement for social learning is the modelling of practice by industry professionals in partnership with the students. While there is always likely to be an element of simulation in any educationally contrived project, the partnership model offered here must surely offer the most beneficial experience for the students.

The biggest challenge for all of the case studies presented here is the allocation of resources. Setting up live projects can be extremely time consuming and risky (e.g. the author's own experience of a live project, the client for which was declared bankrupt mid project, is an example of the kind of risk that might be encountered). The investment in time for staff, students and industry professionals can be high. Industry partners can be asked to work with inexperienced students to deliver high-quality outputs to clients under tight deadlines. Timelines for real world projects rarely fit within narrow academic scheduling. Projects are often transdisciplinary and may require additional academic and/or practical support to deliver project outputs. Case Study 2 attempts to negotiate some of these challenges by shifting some of the work of setting up the project onto the students. In this case study the students are required to self-select a client and to manage that relationship themselves. Given the nature of the organisations with which the students engage there are clearly opportunities for students to bring real world value to the projects they undertake for these organisations. The students are required to negotiate with their self-selected clients, identify problems and present solutions. There is certainly a strong sense of the situatedness of the project as a real world learning experience. However, the students are asked to think of themselves as a sub-department within the organisation for whom they are undertaking the project, or to consider themselves as a team of external consultants. In both cases the students conceptualise themselves as exterior to the organisation whose sole role is to function as a client for the project. This is perhaps the most common formulation of a live project, for example, students work as a team to deliver a project for an external client. The main issue with this approach is that the social learning is limited to encounters with the client, intra-team collaboration and academic input. There is little if any modelling by industry professionals (in this case marketing professionals), mentoring is undertaken by the academics supporting the project and while students undoubtedly gain confidence and expertise, there is little if any prospect of their socialisation into a community of practice.

Case Study 3 meets these challenges halfway by bringing professionals on campus to work with students to deliver project outputs. This works in this particular context as the students are familiar with the 'Newsday' as a simulated classroom-based activity. The inclusion of practicing journalists into the environment added a liveness to the event that enabled the course team to introduce a new and challenging topic of study. There is a strong emphasis on 'learning by doing' and again we see students working in partnership with industry professionals. Here there is going to be a significant amount of modelling of practice, a sharing of tacit knowledge of social norms, community etiquette and a deepening of disciplinary knowledge through applied learning strategies. The use of peer feedback to further embed ownership of learning is significant here as is the sense that 'social learning' is not always hierarchical. Of course, one of the aspects of a 'Newsday' style of activity is that there is an additional kind of deadline-related liveness present within the activity. This is akin to the kinds of time-constrained challenges offered by hackathons or 48-hour film challenges. Time becomes a key driving factor in the delivery of the project outputs.

The main issue that this final case presents concerns the simulated nature of the project. The activity aims to mimic, mirror or transfer the newsroom experience to the classroom. While there is nothing wrong with simulated experiences as a mode of learning by doing it begs a question as to whether or not the activity is actually project-based learning at all. Perhaps it would be more appropriate to think of this case study as an example of task-based learning. The lack of a real-value output to an external client is key here and while the involvement of industry professionals is indicative of a potential for social learning a live project must surely include some kind of deliverable output for a real client who gains some business value from the interaction (Hanney, 2013). It would seem that Case Studies 2 and 3 present two halves of the equation: Case Study 2 lacks the mentoring of industry professionals, while Case Study 3 lacks the real-value project output for a client.

Nevertheless, both of these case studies evidence real value for students who gain better understanding of the subject they are studying. In all three case studies there is a clear sense of learning by doing, of mirroring of industry practice, and, to a differing degree, all three include some forms of social learning. However, if the purpose of the projects in each case study is to ease the transition between the education and the world of work it is arguable that there are limitations at play. These may well be in part down to the constraints around resources (time and cost) as well as issue of quality (of the experience and of the project outputs). It is clear from all of the case studies that live projects are challenging to set up and deliver. No doubt this presents difficulties for educators wishing to develop a real world learning approach within their own curriculum. The benefits to the students though are vividly captured by the three case studies. Students develop more advanced skills, acquire disciplinary vocabulary, and foster industry contacts and awareness of professional practice. All of the case studies to one degree or another begin the process of socialising students as novices into their destination community of practice.

Case Study 1

Acting Locally, Thinking Globally: Design Within Out Walls (Dr Rhiannon Jones, Post-Doctoral Researcher, Digital Material Artistic Research Centre, College of Arts, Humanities and Education, School of Arts, University of Derby, UK)

A cohort of Interior Design students undertook a live project to develop a conceptual idea for a mobile touring art space in partnership with a 'creative industry client'. Entitled S.H.E.D. the brief asked students to design a reconfigurable touring space that would facilitate community dialogue, thereby framing students' understanding of industry-facing relationships and project management through the simulation of a real world business encounters. The S.H.E.D live project encouraged students to explore and develop their own voice and design identity, creating inspiring solutions for spatial environments including residential, commercial and historical spaces. The degree programme facilitates learning in dedicated professional design studios and acquiring a range of skills in the design and development of spaces as well as being involved in live projects, where students have collaborative opportunities with local and international partners. The live project aimed to take a project off-the-page, from classroom to workshop—and then straight to market. The brief asked students to investigate possibilities for converting a garden shed into a mobile touring structure to operate as a public art space with multiple configurations (from intimate space to festival stage). It needed to be robust and movable; retain its DIY, upcycled aesthetic; consider the ongoing touring costs and material maintenance; be suitable for both indoor and outdoor use, day and night. Learning outcomes considered client's needs, construction, materials and finishes, services, zoning, furniture, and ergonomics.

Students were encouraged to think as experts and equals. Industry colleagues engaged with the students as knowledgeable co-creatives, not as novices or student learners. Students were equal creative partners and treated as colleagues. Everyone attended meetings, presentations and workshops contributing equally to creative decision-making. Due to the tight deadline for delivery, the project was reliant on the student's active participation and working ethos in order to make this possible. The brief was discussed weekly and tailored sessions nurtured ideas as a group and responded to the students' design processes. Meetings took place off-campus: they were taken out of the classroom to the art studio. Working in a real world setting enhanced the dedication and care given to the brief. Conversations were essential to building a collective, rather than a competitive ethos. Media students documented the project, and this enabled peer-to-peer interdisciplinary learning.

An industry launch served as a means for further situating the student's participation in a real world context which placed the students centre stage at this public event. A panel discussion, with industry feedback on the design, gave students a sense of pride and ownership. Students saw their design concepts realised as a pragmatic artefact. They made professional industry connections and became more civic minded through the design process, which required them to answer questions about how to design dialogic spaces. They developed skills in new areas through participatory engagement with industry professionals rather than just with tutors. A community of practice emerged, enabled through a multifaceted framework for learning, where students, in partnership with industry professionals, balanced pressure and responsibility to deliver an industry-ready product. Real world learning was not simulated here; it was actualised, embedded and industry-facilitated through constant open and creative dialogue. The whole degree course is dynamic and co-creative in that it welcomes students' own voices/cultures and values risk-taking and experimentation. It further aims to equip students with all the relevant skills and knowledge ready for the 'real' world upon graduation. Live projects provide exposure to the wide field, that is, interior design, exploring various spatial typologies such as residential interiors, commercial interiors, that is, retail, corporate, set-stage and exhibition design and hospitality, as well as exploring adaptive reuse/regenerative design to name but a few, with a focus on employment opportunities open to an interior design graduate.

This live project challenged preconceptions around applied learning and creative industry partnerships can achieve within an educational context. Students 'shed' preconceived ideas about where pedagogy takes place and increased their personal and professional confidence. They continue to have ongoing involvement in a project that otherwise would not exist without participation in the project. However, live projects of this kind require an investment of time that is difficult to negotiate within the highly scheduled world of academia. Furthermore, the educational context is not ideally placed to deliver to industry deadlines or time scales. There is also a need for industry professionals to devote extended amounts of time to a project of this nature which may conflict with commercial needs.

Case Study 2

Connecting Theory with Practice in Arts Marketing (Dr Ana Gaio, Programme Director, MA Global Creative Industries, School of Arts and Social Sciences, Department of Sociology, City University, UK)

A group of postgraduate Culture, Policy and Management (CPM) students undertook a live project with a self-selected London-based arts/

cultural organisation. The project was undertaken as part of an Audiences and Marketing (module) which sought to re-problematise concepts learned in other (core) Managing Organisations and Culture modules. The module aims to explore the claims made by practitioners and academics that the specificity of arts/cultural marketing derives from the interrelationships between culture, policy and management. It requires students to approach the topic strategically and applies theory to practice. It also enables students to look at the arts marketing paradigm from a Cultural Policy (core module) perspective although links can be found with most other modules. Ultimately, the project reflects and articulates the MA CPM's bias towards the state sponsored cultural sector as well as its cross-disciplinary nature. The brief required students to devise a marketing strategy for their chosen client. Students are supported but ultimately each team is expected to converge around their project to mobilise and manage its mix of marketing knowledge, experience and talent. The organisations selected by the students are normally small cultural organisations (any art/cultural form) which are either known to a student/s or found through networking. Once groups identify their organisations, they negotiate access to it, research it and develop a full marketing strategy for the client organisation. Learning outcomes included application of theory to practice, facilitation of interaction with marketing professionals, evaluation of the specificity of arts/cultural marketing to encourage the formation of communities of learning.

Students are given freedom to decide how they organise themselves and their work. No specific direction is given in terms of project management. It is assumed that as students will have taken a core management module in a previous semester, they already have a grounding in organisational strategy and management. Gathering information involves engaging with relevant organisation staff, identifying problems, attending events, audience observation and demographic research. Students will typically evaluate relevant organisational documentation and review its existing marketing strategies (although in small organisations, especially, marketing activity is often reactive or tactical). Students know that the marketing strategy is the group's and not the organisation's but understand the need to explain their choices in their final assessment submission. Developing the marketing strategy will normally entail dialogue with the organisation in order to generate cogent, realistic and supported claims. Whilst a debrief between students and organisation is not required, this often happens as students test their findings with the organisation in the project's final stages.

The self-selected client organisation is not involved in the assessment and the project is clearly framed as a student-led educational activity that sits within a course module. Through immersion, situated learning, students gain experience of the day-to-day reality of arts marketing practice in cultural organisations and combine 'theoretical knowing' with 'application to practice'. Their engagement with the staff at the selected organisation introduces the students to the community's ways, culture and jargon thereby contributing to the beginning of the student's socialisation into a community of practice, a 'peripheral participation' of sorts. The students also benefit from the development of intra-group social capital through meaningful participation. By the end of the experience students display a comprehensive and in-depth knowledge and understanding of marketing and its key concepts, their relevance or application (or not) to arts marketing. They talk about and use marketing language meaningfully and comfortably and display a newfound confidence. Many students add this project to their CVs which evidences the significance that participation in the project has for them individually. The applied nature (partly, at least) of CPM as a field of studies inherently calls for engagement with the sector and the arts marketing project effects the MA CPM's aims to develop the student as an independent and critical individual; produce competent professionals ready to enter the cultural sector and to engage with the sector. Preparing students for employment and enhancing their employability are key to this agenda—the arts marketing project is instrumental in connecting students, especially those interested in a marketing career, with the sector and its arts marketing community, day-to-day practice and realities.

While this live project aims to replicate the kind of learning that occurs in everyday work and the membership of a community of practice there are constraints around the project's ability to achieve these aims. Students are encouraged to work closely with the client organisation, and this often includes close collaboration. However, the experience of student groups is highly variable and dependant of a wide range of factors. The ideal is for students to work in partnership with the selected organisation as if they were a department within the organisation (e.g. marketing team) or as a team of external consultants. Negotiating relations with the selected organisation is complex and success often depends on factors such as group cohesion, work ethic and application of disciplinary knowledge. Furthermore, the commitment of the client organisation is also subject to variability of conditions since the project doesn't always have a real world benefit for the selected organisation and this can impact positively or negatively on the experience.

> ## Case Study 3
>
> **Data Hounds—Learning to Research, Analyse and Visualise (Dr Lada T. Price, Course Leader, MA Journalism, Department of Media Arts and Communications, Sheffield Hallam University, UK)**

The live project began when we invited two experts from the Press Association (PA) to assist us in designing and running workshops for beginner data journalists on the BA and MA Journalism courses. Both are professionally accredited by the National Council for the Training of Journalists (NCTJ) and aims to prepare students for work in digital newsrooms. Students have to excel at traditional newswriting as well as being able to work with new digital formats and show they can work with data accurately and efficiently. Most news organisations now expect their employees to have these skills and this project aimed to provide Journalism students with sufficient insights and techniques to help them in their future employment. The aim of the project was to teach future journalists how to gather, process and present quantitative data. The possession of data skills opens up new possibilities for students to tell a compelling story in traditional and digital formats and is applicable in all stages of the journalistic process. We organised interactive workshops with the experts from the PA creating learning experiences that simulate the real world of journalism practice. The majority of our 34 undergraduate and postgraduate Journalism students described their skills and experience of working with data prior to the workshops as 'none' or 'basic'.

The workshops were structured in a way that ensures students' active involvement and contribution. The plan was based entirely on daily real-life news practice at the PA in order to 'transfer' the newsroom into the classroom. Apart from a brief explanation of what 'data journalism' is and what it entails in daily journalism practice, the rest of the workshops were very hands-on and focused on a 'learning by doing' experience. Organised in small teams the students worked together with the journalists. They were very eager to get input and tips from practicing data journalists and apply this to their learning. The participants were particularly interested in how journalists put together stories at the PA step by step and mirror this process in their own work. While several students experienced difficulties during an exercise on obtaining and structuring data accurately, guidance from the experts helped to successfully complete the task. Students were most engaged with the content during the final part of the workshop, which mimicked live 'breaking news' event. This was seen an opportunity to put everything they had learned in practice. There was a 'buzz' of activity and conversation with the PA journalists (as editors) as students organised themselves in a pattern they were already familiar with due to regular intensive 'newsdays' held throughout their courses of study.

The most valuable aspect of the workshop was working together with journalists and receiving one-to-one guidance during tasks that were perceived as complex and unfamiliar. During the workshops, students received expert feedback but were also assessing and generating their own feedback. We learned that students who had very little knowledge or experience of data journalism can be encouraged and inspired through practical and fun tasks that they perceived as 'very useful' and 'valuable' for their future journalism practice. The feedback showed that being taught and working alongside experienced professionals in data journalism was praised by all participants as it allowed them to actively participate in a real-life newsroom experience. The journalists noted that they enjoyed sharing their professional tips with the students and treated all participants as equals. The project participants developed skills in sourcing and structuring of data in order to present it in an optimal manner for analysis; how to go about extracting stories from data using the analytical techniques most commonly employed by the PA; outlining and communicating analytical findings in a way that others can use through storyboarding and briefing; learning key principles of data visualisation and the use of graphics to illustrate information.

While the planning and delivery of the project went smoothly, we found that on the days of the workshops several students who had signed up did not attend. It's possible that they were anxious or nervous about the prospect of working with highly experienced professionals. Previous research suggests that journalists sometimes openly admit that they chose a career in journalism to escape numeracy. Working with data is a challenge for young and aspiring journalists who sometimes lack basic mathematic skills and they could feel they were not up to the task. If we were to do this again, we would invite the journalists to speak to students in a very informal Q&A session before they came to conduct the workshops. This of course would be difficult as our 'teachers' were working journalists who cannot take time off work regularly to do this. Our project concluded that introducing modules on working with data in the journalism curriculum, where students become accustomed to basic and more advanced skills, can be significantly enhanced by inviting data journalists to share their everyday practical experience and work alongside learners.

Conclusion

It is argued above that a 'becoming mode' (Hanney, 2018) of project-based learning (PjBL) foregrounds the learnability of the experience of undertaking project work. This ontological shift away from models of management towards a reconceptualisation of projects as a practice places the pedagogic imperative at the heart of project working. Importantly, it provides a philosophical underpinning for thinking about projects as a fundamentally social practice. The fetishisation of 'industry practices' is subsumed to the needs of the educational context, while assessment focuses less on 'connoisseur' evaluation of project outputs in favour of reflection on experience and lessons learned. In its ideal form students will undertake live projects situated in a real world context with a real client, who has a real business need. Furthermore, there is an expectation that the output of a project should at least have the potential for real business value for the client.

As has been shown above there are variations on this formulation that move between the ideal and innumerable other approaches that are more or less simulated. The client may be more or less real, be external/internal to the educational context, be imagined, be self-selected, or otherwise provided. What is argued here is that the role of the client is less important than the coaching role of industry professionals since the client really only serves to provide a real world context. What is crucial to the experience and what is missing from most live projects to one degree or another is the integration of mentoring, modelling and coaching from industry professionals. It is this factor that is most likely to drive student's engagement, motivation and participation. It is the beginning of their initiation into a community of practice that is of most pedagogic value, not their interactions with a proposed fictional/real client. That is not to say that these interactions are not of value. But let's be real about this, in the real world, novices don't get to lead client negotiations as this is often a mission critical to the business concerned.

If the transition between the educational context and employment is an important factor for students, then their awareness of the kinds of social behaviours that would be expected of them by their chosen community of practice must be paramount. Novices are socialised through participation in the community and over time gain tacit knowledge of the social norms, etiquette and deepen disciplinary knowledge through applied learning strategies. Members provide support for each other, form relationships based around mutual learning, engage in reputation building and crucially interact regularly and learn together. Importantly, members of the community are practitioners who share a repertoire of tools, techniques, strategies that are commonly recognised as a domain of practical activity. One of the ways that the community bonds is around shared repertoire of stories, cases and mythologies which inform their practice, stories the students will only encounter through interaction with other members of a community of practice.

All three of the case studies presented in this chapter offer a means for students to begin this transition and start their initiation into a chosen community of practice. In each case study, educators have developed a methodology for live projects that to one degree or another support that process. There are clearly challenges though. Foremost among these are the constraints around the kinds of resources required to support the administrative burden that comes with live projects. The inflexibility of timetables and the academic lifecycle also poses problems. Engagement with potential clients, industry professionals and the kind of relationship building this requires also poses a challenge for educators. Nonetheless, it is important to recognise that if real world learning is to be adopted as a primary pedagogic discourse then the use of live projects with high-quality mentoring/modelling/coaching from industry professionals is the gold standard for project-based learning.

References

Blomquist, T., Hällgren, M., Nilsson, A., & Söderholm, A. (2010). Project-as-practice: In search of project management research that matters. *Project Management Journal, 41*(1), 5–16. https://doi.org/10.1002/pmj

Bourdieu, P. (1984). *Distinction: A social critique of the judgement of taste.* London: Routledge & Kegan Paul.

Bourdieu, P. (1988). Vive la Crise!: For heterodoxy in social science. *Theory and Society, 17*(5), 773–787.

Bourdieu, P. (1990). *The logic of practice.* Cambridge: Polity.

Bredillet, C. (2010). Blowing hot and cold on project management. *Project Management Journal, 41*(3), 4–20. https://doi.org/10.1002/pmj.20179

Cicmil, S., Hodgson, D., Lindgren, M., & Packendorff, J. (2009). Project management behind the facade. *Ephermera theory & politics in organization, 9*(2), 78–92.

Floricel, S., Bonneau, C., Aubry, M., & Sergi, V. (2014). Extending project management research: Insights from social theories. *International Journal of Project Management, 32*(7), 1091–1107. https://doi.org/10.1016/j.ijproman.2014.02.008

Gauthier, J.-B., & Ika, L. A. (2012). Foundations of Project Management research: An explicit and six-facet ontological framework. *Project Management Journal, 43*(5), 5–23. https://doi.org/10.1002/pmj.21288

Giddens, A. (1984). *The constitution of society: Introduction of the theory of structuration.* Berkeley: University of California Press.

Hanney, R. (2013). Towards a situated media practice: Reflections on the implementation of project-led problem-based learning. *Journal of Media Practice, 14*(1), 43–59. https://doi.org/10.1386/jmpr.14.1.43_1

Hanney, R. (2018). Doing, being, becoming: A historical appraisal of the modalities of project-based learning. *Teaching in Higher Education, 23*(6), 769–783. https://doi.org/10.1080/13562517.2017.1421628

Hodgson, D., & Cicmil, S. (2008). The other side of projects: The case for critical project studies. *International Journal of Managing Projects in Business, 1*(1), 142–152. https://doi.org/10.1108/17538370810846487

Hodgson, D. E., & Cicmil, S. (2006). Are projects real? The PMBOK and the legitimisation of project management knowledge. In D. E. Hodgson & S. Cicmil (Eds.), *Making project critical* (pp. 29–50). Basingstoke: Palgrave Macmillan.

Lewis, B. (2013). *What is a project? Towards a new ontology for projects and project management.* Paper presented at the Critical Management Studies Conference, University of Bristol.

Linehan, C., & Kavanagh, D. (2006). From project ontologies to communities of virtue. In D. E. Hodgson & S. Cicmil (Eds.), *Making projects critical* (pp. 51–67). Basingstoke: Palgrave Macmillan.

Lundin, R. A., & Söderholm, A. (1995). A theory of the temporary organization. *Scandinavian Journal of Management, 11*(4), 437–455. https://doi.org/10.1016/0956-5221(95)00036-U

Morris, P. W. G. (1994). *The management of projects.* London: Thomas Telford.

Nicholas, J. M. (2004). *Project management for business and engineering: Principles and practice* (2nd ed.). London: Elsevier.

Packendorff, J. (1995). Inquiring into the temporary organization: New directions for project management research. *Scandinavian Journal of Management, 11*(4), 319–333. https://doi.org/10.1016/0956-5221(95)00018-Q

Sahlin-Andersson, K., & Söderholm, A. (2002). *Beyond project management: New perspectives on the temporary-permanent dilemma.* Abingdon: Marston Book Services.

Seo, M.-G., & Creed, W. E. D. (2002). Institutional contradictions, praxis, and institutional change: A dialectical perspective. *The Academy of Management Review, 2*, 222.

Shenhar, A., & Dvir, D. (2007). *Reinventing project management: The diamond approach to successful growth and innovation.* Boston, MA: Harvard Business School Press.

Svejvig, P., & Andersen, P. (2015). Rethinking project management: A structured literature review with a critical look at the brave new world. *International Journal of Project Management, 33*(2), 278–290.

Wenger, E. (1998). *Communities of practice: Learning, meaning, and identity.* Cambridge: Cambridge University Press.

Wenger-Trayner, E., & Wenger-Trayner, B. (2015). Introduction to communities of practice: A brief overview of the concept and its uses. Retrieved from https://wenger-trayner.com/introduction-to-communities-of-practice/

Winter, M., Smith, C., Cooke-Davies, T., & Cicmil, S. (2006). The importance of 'process' in rethinking project management: The story of a UK government-funded research network. *International Journal of Project Management, 24*(8), 650–662.

9

Real World Learning: Simulation and Gaming

Jonathan Lean, Jonathan Moizer, Cathrine Derham, Lesley Strachan, and Zakirul Bhuiyan

Introduction

Simulations and games have become increasingly popular methods of teaching and learning within the Higher Education sector over recent years (Lean, Moizer, & Warren, 2015; Moizer & Lean, 2010). They have been used in subject areas as diverse as entrepreneurship (Newbery, Lean, Moizer, & Haddoud, 2018), history (McCall, 2016) and nursing (Koivisto et al., 2018). Simulations and games enable the learner to gain

J. Lean (✉) • J. Moizer
University of Plymouth, Plymouth, UK
e-mail: jonathan.lean@plymouth.ac.uk

C. Derham
University of Surrey, Guildford, UK

L. Strachan
SimVenture, York, UK

Z. Bhuiyan
Solent University, Southampton, UK

© The Author(s) 2021
D. A. Morley, M. G. Jamil (eds.), *Applied Pedagogies for Higher Education*,
https://doi.org/10.1007/978-3-030-46951-1_9

insight into real world situations in an authentic and engaging way without the need to leave the classroom. They allow students to experiment and see the impact of their decisions and actions within a safe environment and without any real world consequences. Hence, they offer valuable insights into contexts that may be difficult for students to experience directly in the real world due to the level of risk, the cost or the timescale involved.

This chapter aims to review the role of simulations and games as proxies for real world learning. The structure and focus of the chapter draws on a concept-mapping exercise undertaken with the book editors as part of the development of this publication (see Fig. 9.1). In the sections that follow, the nature of simulations and games is first discussed with reference to examples in higher education. Next, the position of simulations and games within the field of real world learning is explored, emphasising their potential to contribute to and extend the learning experience of higher education students. Their learning benefits are then evaluated along with some of the challenges associated with their use. Three case studies illustrating the use and value of simulations and games in a range of subject disciplines are presented. The chapter concludes by considering

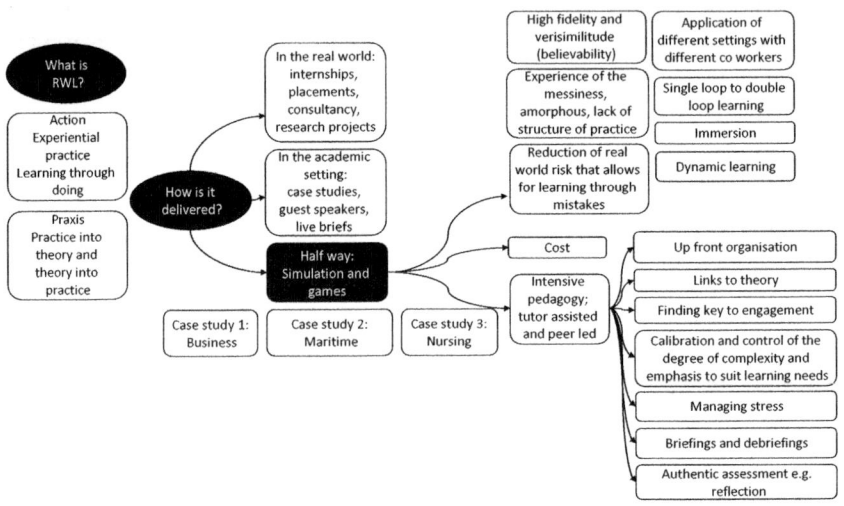

Fig. 9.1 Concept map from the authors

key implications for educational practice and areas for future research and pedagogical development.

The Nature of Simulation and Gaming and Its Role in Real World Learning

The use of simulations and games in higher education has gained increasing attention in recent years as such learning techniques have increasingly become normal features of academic programmes across a range of subject disciplines (Baptista & Oliveira, 2018; Hainey, Connolly, Stansfield, & Boyle, 2011; Ibrahim, Masrom, Yusoff, Zainuddin, & Rizman, 2017; Moizer & Lean, 2010; Subhash & Cudney, 2018; Wouters & van Oostendorp, 2017). Whilst much current attention has been on the growth in the use of computer-based 'serious games' (Boyle et al., 2016), the nature and variety of simulation and gaming approaches continue to become richer and more diverse. Techniques range from highly sophisticated online serious games that allow students to immerse themselves in a computer-generated world to more traditional approaches such as role-plays where students play characters within a classroom setting. Lean, Moizer, Towler, and Abbey (2006) demonstrate the diversity of approaches available to educators by developing a typology of simulations and games that distinguishes between those that are *computer-based* (including gaming simulations, training simulations and modelling simulations) and *non-computer-based* (including role-plays and educational games, such as board games and paper-based games). Hence, simulations and games can take many varied forms, providing a very wide range of options to support student learning.

Whatever the exact nature of the simulations or games used by educators, what they share in common is that they attempt to imitate or represent some form of real world phenomenon, process or entity. In the context of real world learning, simulations and games therefore hold a unique position and play a very particular role. By definition, simulations and games *do not* involve direct engagement in real world situations; rather they imitate aspects of the real world to facilitate learning. For instance, a computer-based business simulation game may allow students to go through the process of making decisions on aspects of marketing, finance and production for a 'virtual' company to compete with other virtual companies and to see the results of these decisions without any engagement at all with real companies or industrial settings. Similarly, a legal role-play may allow law students to experience legal processes and develop client representation skills without setting foot in a courtroom. Therefore, from a pedagogical perspective, simulations and games occupy a space that sits between the classroom and the real world.

Given that simulations and games may be considered a 'half way house' between traditional classroom learning and real world learning, it could be argued that they are in some ways less valuable or effective than learning that is fully embedded in real world activity. However, simulations and games typically seek to imitate real world phenomena and processes that, for various reasons, are difficult for students to experience in an actual real world setting. Therefore, they can be considered an important link between theories espoused in the lecture hall and the real world.

Most commonly, the reasons for employing a simulation or game instead of a learning experience set fully in the real world relate to issues of *risk*, *cost* or *timescale* or a combination of two or more of these factors. In the real world, some activities may be judged to present too much of a *risk* to be suitable as a learning approach. Such risks may be to the students themselves, other people or property/resources. For example, Human Patient Simulators are sophisticated software-facilitated manikins that are used in medical education to enable medical students to undertake procedures without the risk of harming real patients (Al-Elq, 2010; Hogg et al., 2019). The *cost* of undertaking certain real world activities with students may be considered prohibitive, meaning that simulation-based approaches are attractive and useful. For instance, the 'Bridge Simulation' used at Solent University in the UK to train students in the field of maritime navigation is cost effective compared to using real ships to develop the required knowledge and skills (see Case Study 1). Finally, the *timescale* required to undertake some activities in the real world is impractical in the context of educational programmes where modules of study may only run for a period of 10–15 weeks. A particular advantage of simulations is that time can be compressed. For example, in a computer-based business simulation, decisions and financial result cycles that may stretch out over several years in the real world can be played out by students over a few days or weeks. The ability to operate in simulated time rather than real world time opens up possibilities for learning that may not otherwise be possible.

Case Study 1

Bridge Simulation—Changing Behaviours for Enhanced Actions (Zakirul Bhuiyan, Senior Lecturer in Ship Simulation, Southampton Solent University, UK)

Shipping is the key to the global economy with the majority of maritime transport operations being carried out by seafarers. Seafarers need to be competent, experienced, skilled and knowledgeable as shipping is a highly technical and professional discipline. Many of the operational mistakes, emergencies and critical situations that have occurred on board ships have been attributed to human error, usually as a result of incompetence and lack of training and education (Barnett, 2004). Bridge simulation is a system commonly used in marine navigational training to enable ship navigating officers to develop their knowledge and experience of operational skills such as ship navigation, collision avoidance and ship handling skills, both in open seas and confined waters. It involves virtual representations of real ships as well as surrounding environmental conditions and geographical areas. Its versatile and realistic functionalities have expanded the scope of maritime training to encompass both operational seafaring skills and behavioural skills such as leadership and management.

Bridge simulation enables the creation of dynamic, real-life situations in a controlled classroom environment where navigating officers can practice new techniques and skills and obtain insights from instructors and peers. Students transfer their theories to real world situations in a risk-free operating environment. They deal with multiple problems and learn to prioritise multiple tasks under similar high stress, changing conditions (including environmental conditions such as weather) to those in actual ship-board operations. Each ship officer's performance is evaluated holistically to make a formal assessment of competence in a variety of simulation scenarios. This training can be described through three major theoretical paradigms of learning. Firstly, the competence-based and training-focused professional learning activities which can be defined as a behaviourist approach (Pavlov, 2010; Skinner, 2011). Secondly, the maritime profession and associated education involve various critical thinking, problem-solving, decision-making and situation analysis activities which refer to the theories of the cognitive domain (Hollon & Beck, 1994). Thirdly, the discussion-based, shared and professional community-driven working environment is where the application of constructive approaches to learning is made (Vygotsky, 1978).

The most important part of a training session is the debriefing, which is conducted at the end of each simulation exercise when the saved exercise is replayed for the reflections of both the seafarers and instructors. Debriefing is the key to the entire learning process, during which trainees' knowledge and attitudes are applied, evaluated and synthesised (Ellman, 1977) and this process integrates the simulation experience into the learning environment (Gatfield, 2006). During the debriefing session, trainees, peers and instructors critically examine and comment on what went wrong, what could be learned and improved and so forth. Trainees have the freedom to express themselves and they need to justify their actions. Furthermore, the relationship between students and instructors replicates the real-life relationship between professionals. Learning is all about change—change brought about by the development of skills, understanding something new and/or changing an attitude. Therefore, feedback in the form of debriefing can be a powerful motivator to learning.

During the simulation training, lecturers suggest that the seafarers follow the upper stages of Bloom's taxonomy (problem solving, critical thinking, analysis, evaluation) in the reflection and development of their active learning (Bloom, 1956). The reflection processes involve questioning from the learner, collaborative activities and application of learning in the practical field. Because of the process-driven and applied features of the reflections, the assessment is predominantly subjective for this type of activity, against a range of competency-based objectives. Learners compare their current progress against desired goals, resulting in changes to their motivation and self-perception of ability (Nicol &

Macfarlane-Dick, 2006) and it narrows the gap between their current and desired levels of achievement and having a positive effect on behaviours, emotions and beliefs.

Although simulation courses are offered at many higher educational institutions, their educational features are under-researched (Pallis & Ng, 2011). The nature and procedures of simulation training activities are similar to traditional professional training programmes as they predominantly involve skills-based repetitive actions. Therefore, the question may arise of whether simulation programmes can fit into traditional higher education curricula which greatly emphasise progression-driven and research-integrated educational approaches for deep and meaningful learning (Stern, 2016). The query is largely unanswered as the pedagogical aspects of simulation training are still under-researched. This knowledge gap creates scope for exploring the pedagogical aspects of training, for example, its instructional strategies, learning outcomes and student engagement. Maritime simulation training programmes are required to fit traditional and typical higher education curricula; there is a need for lecturers to link professionalism, research and interpersonal skills to develop excellence in their teaching practices. Moreover, this promotes an enthusiasm for learning and encourages the maritime community to set its sights higher with a view to translating maritime education practices for the wider higher education community. Bridge simulation training is tightly regulated (nationally and internationally) and also competence based. How these factors fit into higher education frameworks is a topic requiring further research if bridge simulation training is to work successfully in a multidimensional education environment.

It is evident that simulations and games address many of the key limitations of some forms of real world learning by overcoming the issues of risk, cost and timescale. In doing so, simulations and games considerably extend the scope of real world learning by facilitating learning experiences that may not otherwise be accessible to students. Simulations and games may not offer the same level of insight into the real world as some other forms of learning that are fully embedded in actual professional practice settings. However, due to their particular strengths and characteristics, they provide educators with valuable options for engaging students in impactful experiential learning activities. In the next section, further benefits of simulation and gaming are explored, alongside some of the challenges associated with their use.

Benefits of Simulations and Games for Real World Learning

A feature of real world learning is that it allows students to experience the complex, amorphous and sometimes messy nature of practice within professional or work-related settings (McGrath, Harris, & Whitelaw, 2016; Tai, Canny, Haines, & Molloy, 2017). Simulations and games aim to mirror such contexts by enabling students to learn about the realities of practice but within a more controlled environment. Learners are able to develop highly relevant work-related skills and 'pre-experience' different forms of activity before real world engagement (Goi, 2019; Strachan, 2016). Thus, simulations and games support employability whilst also promoting deeper learning (Marda, Economou, & Bouki, 2018; Narayanan & Turner, 2019; Scholtz & Hughes, 2019). Case Study 2 reports on research relating to the impact of a business simulation on the self-perceived employability skills of students.

Case Study 2

Can a Business Simulation Game Develop Students' Employability Skills? (Lesley Strachan, Learning and Development Manager, SimVenture)

This case study evaluates the use of a serious business simulation game (SimVenture Evolution) to develop employability skills. Business simulation games have been engaged as a pedagogic tool for over 50 years to create effective experiential learning opportunities (Keys & Wolfe, 1990). Simulation games also have the potential to encourage employability skills (Gopinath & Sawyer, 1999). Clarke (2009) identified a wide range of hard and soft skills that enhance the student learning experience because students can collaborate by testing 'what if' business scenarios.

Furthermore, it is reported that simulation games allow students to experience a valid representation of real world business issues (Faria, 2006) and that students' enthusiasm for simulation games is very positive (Vos & Brennan, 2010) leading to increased student engagement (Strachan, 2011). Students themselves perceive that simulations are an effective learning method (Jennings, 2002) because they bridge the gap between theory and practice (Avramenko, 2012). However, it is unclear whether undergraduate students are aware of the employability skills they could potentially develop via a simulation.

Any attempt at defining 'employability skills' is clouded by the difficulty in collating a strict list of attributes that employers will agree on (Iuliana, Dragos, & Mitran, 2014). The findings reported in this case study utilise the Confederation of British Industry (CBI, 2009) definition of employability skills because they are widely discussed by employers across the industries into which graduates seek employment. These skills include self-management, team working, business and customer awareness, problem solving, communication and literacy, application of numeracy, and the application of information technology. Underpinning these skills is a positive attitude: a 'can-do' approach, a readiness to take part and contribute openness to new ideas and a drive to make these happen. Whilst businesses often lament the perceived lack of graduate skills (Leitch, 2006; Wingrove, 2014), this may in part result from students being unable to identify and articulate what skills they have developed. This case study demonstrates that students can become more aware of and develop their employability skills through a business simulation game.

The aim of the study was to test whether an online business simulation game (SimVenture Evolution) could improve students' self-perceived employability skills. A mixed interpretative approach used two structured questionnaires—one before the simulation game began and one upon completion. The sample included undergraduate students from Southampton Solent University, London South Bank University and the University of Southampton from business and marketing subject areas.

Figure 9.2 presents the results collated from all the three universities, showing the change in self-perceived employability skills.

The most significant outcome was the awareness and development of students' problem-solving skills, followed by teamwork, business

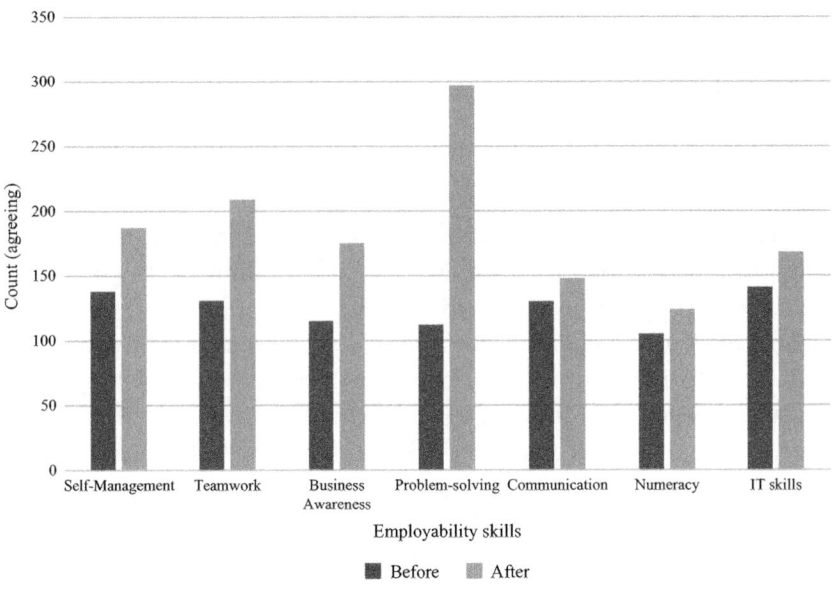

Fig. 9.2 Change in self-perceived employability skills

awareness and self-management. Qualitative feedback indicated that students were able to make an increased connection between theory and real-life contexts with comments such as 'I have been able to apply business theories to a real-life situation'. Importantly, students reported an increased awareness and development of all their employability skills. Since operating a business is not generally straight forward, students needed to develop a problem-solving approach to deal with the situations that evolved during the simulation, so the awareness and development of this skill is encouraging to see. The developments in teamwork skills were particularly interesting outcomes and may be as a result of students taking on Director roles as they work together to run their simulated company. This was something they found engaging and realistic and it was noticed by tutors that on many occasions, student teams would stay in-role after class to continue working on the simulation together. Other positive outcomes included attendance levels at 94% because students were 'actively involved', 77% of students reported a positive experience and assessment submission rates were 97%. Tutors were also freed up to spend valuable time giving formative feedback to students.

Despite these positive outcomes, academic staff at the case universities did face some barriers to adoption: particularly institutional re-structuring and cost cutting, academic scepticism, and the difficulty of finding unbiased advice about suitable simulation games. The sharing of good practice and evidence which demonstrates that business simulations add value to the student learning experience and support the development of employability skills is likely to be a key factor in the continued adoption of such technology-based learning.

The benefits that simulations and games bring to learning result from a number of important and distinctive features. These features are discussed in turn below.

Fidelity

The level of fidelity achieved in a simulation or game concerns how closely it corresponds to the real world (Moizer et al., 2019). High-fidelity can be important to a simulation where transfer of knowledge learnt within the game to real world situations is required (Jones & Bursens, 2015; Petridis et al., 2012), such as in the case of medical procedures. Some authors though contend that high levels of fidelity can distract students from learning, particularly in the context of computer-based serious games (Dankbaar et al., 2016). Some studies conclude that simplified games that strip out some of the aspects of complexity that exist in the real world can support more effective learning (Wright-Maley, 2015). By isolating and bringing to the fore the effect of key variables or drivers, simple simulations can benefit student understanding of processes or real world phenomena. Resultantly, links to theory taught in the classroom can be drawn out more readily (Avramenko, 2012) in a way that supports praxis (Ruggiero & Watson, 2014). Perhaps counter-intuitively, it can be argued that simulations and games bring benefits to the field of real world learning because their ability to, in effect, simplify the real world can strengthen learning. By combining high levels of verisimilitude (i.e., how real a game or simulation 'feels') with a more tailored level of fidelity, student engagement can be sustained allowing such approaches to achieve impactful learning (Devine, 2016).

Educator Control

A notable feature of simulations and games is that, from an educator perspective, they bring benefits in terms of learning design and control (see, e.g., Arnab et al., 2015; Carvalho et al., 2015). For instance, in a role-play, educators are able to develop particular characters, settings and scenarios that best support the learning objectives of a particular module of study. Such a level of control may not be possible in real world situations. Furthermore, key aspects of the dynamics within a simulation or game can often be controlled by educators. For example, within a business simulation game, it is possible to introduce critical incidents such as a change in interest rates or exchange rates or even a global recession. Critical incidents such as these can have a powerful impact on learning, as they force students to reconfigure their thinking and behaviour as normal assumptions and routines are disrupted (Cope, 2003). Events of this nature may only occur infrequently in the real world or may not occur at times convenient for learning during the course of a particular module or programme (Lean, Moizer, & Newbery, 2014). Through a simulation or game, students are able to experience an occurrence that they would be unlikely to encounter through other forms of real world learning. For instance, in the context of a business simulation game, they could see the impact of an exchange rate change on levels of demand for a product and implement responses accordingly, or in a computerised environmental management simulation, a natural disaster could be simulated to allow students to evaluate and implement appropriate responses.

A further aspect of educator control relates to feedback and reflection. Within a simulation or game, it is normally possible to 'pause' time and to design-in periods for debriefing, feedback or reflection (Crookall, 2010). In many real world situations, it can be challenging to include such interventions. Stepping out of a real world situation to reflect or receive feedback may simply not be practical. In addition, many computer-based simulations provide ongoing in-game feedback on performance. Such capabilities provide educators with multiple opportunities to harness the benefits of reflective learning (Bilgin, Baek, & Park, 2015; Van der Meij, Leemkuil, & Li, 2013). Case Study 3 highlights the importance of debriefing within a non-computerised simulation, focusing on the role that debriefing plays in supporting the feedforward of learning from a simulated setting to real world practice.

Case Study 3

Real-Time Immersive Simulation to Evaluate Students' Ability to Feed-forward Their Learning from Simulation into Real-Life Practice (Cathrine Derham, Associate Dean (Education), School of Health Sciences, University of Surrey, UK)

Simulation enables students to safely practise skills and develop knowledge in a learning environment that closely replicates clinical practice (Cook, 2014). Real-time immersive simulation is a pedagogic approach which immerses students in real-life situations that require them to act, behave and think as if in clinical practice (Lopreiato et al., 2016). In response to students' requests for additional preparation prior to final clinical placements, a real-time immersive simulation event was introduced into a BSc Nursing Studies programme at the University of Surrey. Students from three fields of nursing took part in the learning experience. Three clinical settings were developed: ward settings for adult and child, field nursing students, and a drop-in environment for people experiencing mental health issues. These environments enabled students to experience scenarios relevant to their own area of practice.

The simulation event lasted one and a half hours and consisted of approximately 15 parallel scenarios which enabled the inclusion of the different nursing subspecialties. Students were asked to act as newly qualified nurses whilst caring for their patients and managing the clinical environments. If students wanted additional clinical support, they could phone switchboard to make this request. Patients, relatives, carers, doctors and outreach teams were played by academic staff, practice partners and actors. Students cared for patients and managed the situations they found themselves in, as if they were working in real world practice. The simulation was followed by a debriefing session which was facilitated by an experienced practitioner. The facilitator used open-ended statements to encourage discussion and used observational data taken during the simulation to prompt and guide feedback. The debriefing process is a vital component of learning via simulated practice. Facilitated discussion and reflection helps students to recontextualise their experiences (Evans, Guile, Harris, & Allan, 2010) and apply their learning to the real world setting. The overall aim of this immersive simulated experience was to enable learning which would inform future practice in the real world setting and would therefore represent learning gain. Learning gain was defined as an improvement in knowledge, skills, work-readiness and personal development (Office for Students, n.d.) which resulted from the students' own unique and individual involvement in the immersive simulation.

To ascertain whether learning gain had been achieved, research using a mixed-methods approach was carried out (Morley, Bettles, & Derham, 2019). Students recognised the immersive simulation event as a valuable learning opportunity and considered it had informed their professional development and preparation for practice. However, some students experienced difficulties in transferring learning from the simulated practice setting into the clinical environment. They identified barriers to the recontextualisation process (Evans et al., 2010), which impacted upon learning gain and the ability to feedforward learning. Barriers included a lack of individualised and personalised feedback during the group debriefing session and cautious and selective sharing of identified learning needs with mentors in the practice setting. Both impacted upon students' ability to further develop knowledge and skills and resulted in a disconnect between the two learning environments. Students who achieved successful workplace recontextualisation (Evans et al., 2010) were in a better position to achieve learning gain. These students tended to be proactive in their use of feedback and demonstrated self-regulatory behaviours, entering into a collaborative relationship with mentors, setting goals and plans for ongoing learning which was informed by their experiences during simulated practice.

It is important to recognise barriers and enablers which impact upon learning gain and this assists educators in the development of this approach and allows students to engage with and benefit from simulation pedagogy more successfully.

Learning Through Mistakes

Linked to the challenges of risk associated with many forms of real world learning, a key strength of simulations and games is that they allow students to learn through the process of making mistakes. Within simulations and games, learners typically make decisions or enact behaviours and are then able to see the outcomes of their actions. In contexts such as medicine, business and law the impacts of poor decisions or ill-conceived actions can be serious and, in the case of medicine, potentially life threatening. Yet, from a learning perspective, the lessons gained from mistakes are very powerful. Therefore, simulations and games provide learners with a 'safety net', allowing them to make decisions without fear of the potential negative outcomes. Such a safe environment enables students to experiment and try out ideas in a way that might not be possible in the real world. If things go wrong, nobody is hurt and the outcomes can be an important focus for reflective learning (Koivisto, Haavisto, Niemi, Katajisto, & Multisilta, 2016; Kriz & Manahl, 2016; Pariafsai, 2016).

Double-Loop Learning

A characteristic of simulations and games is that activities can be repeated such that students are able to experience a phenomenon on more than one occasion (Ebner & Holzinger, 2007; Fortmüller, 2009; Pesare, Roselli, Corriero, & Rossano, 2016). This brings particular benefits in terms of the depth of learning, with the potential for students to move from *single-loop* learning to *double-loop* learning. Argyris and Schön (1974, 1996) contend that single-loop learning occurs where learners operate within existing goals, plans and decision rules and do not question the governing variables that may affect a particular phenomenon. In contrast, double-loop learning occurs when experience leads to a shift in understanding, such that assumptions and goals change and mental models are adjusted. The ability to repeat simulations and games, such that learners see how their actions and decisions affect outcomes or performance through numerous cycles, enables students to learn from extended experience and recognise the limitations in their existing mental models (Moizer, Lean, Towler, & Smith, 2006). Resultantly, they may change their approach to goal setting and planning (Kiili, 2007; Tao, Yeh, & Hung, 2015). Hence, such learning benefits may be readily attainable in a simulated environment but may be more challenging to achieve in other real world learning contexts.

Challenges of Using Simulations and Games

The advantages of using simulations and games for learning across a range of higher education disciplines are numerous and the capacity of such techniques to extend the reach of real world learning is clear. However, employing simulations and games is not without challenges. Whilst their use has become significantly more widespread in recent years, there are a variety of reasons why some educators may remain reluctant to employ simulations and games.

Lean et al. (2006) draw on previous literature to identify three key categories of potential barrier that represent challenges to the use of simulations and games by educators within Higher Education. The first relates to the *risk of the unknown*: that is, a reluctance amongst instructors to try new teaching approaches and a lack of awareness regarding the range of simulation and game options available. Educators may naturally be concerned about things going wrong when using new approaches, particularly where there is a perceived risk of technical problems that might affect the student learning experience. In an educational environment where student evaluation of instructors has become increasingly important, some educators may be inclined to stay with tried and tested learning approaches. Nevertheless, it remains the case that simulations and games provide a relatively safe environment for learning; a technical problem with an online business game may have an impact upon students' classroom experience, but this may be considered manageable compared to a significant financial loss which might be incurred if students were tasked to run a comparable business in the real world. A further consideration relating to this category of barrier concerns awareness. Despite the growing range of simulations and games that have been developed across a variety of subject areas, with many available 'off-the-shelf' and ready to use, a simple lack of awareness amongst educators about the options available may inhibit their use (Diehl, de Souza, Gordan, Esteves, & Coelho, 2014; Pei Rui Chan & Zary, 2019).

The second category of barrier identified by Lean et al. (2006) concerns *resource*. For example, the need for time to develop simulations and games, or to become proficient in using them, is an important consideration. Using simulations and games is not an easy option; even the most advanced computer-based games are not self-teaching. Even though they are often pre-designed by others, preparing to use a particular simulation or game typically requires a considerable time commitment on the part of instructors for front-end planning and familiarisation (Egenfeldt-Nielsen, 2004). Additional resource considerations might include the availability of technical support and any costs associated with the purchase of materials, online access or physical resources such as computer hardware (McGrath et al., 2018; Usherwood, 2015). Whilst such costs may be only a fraction of those that may be incurred if students undertook activities for real, they can still be significant in some cases and may represent an obstacle to implementation (Bhagat, Liou, & Chang, 2016).

A third barrier category discussed by Lean et al. (2006) relates to *suitability*. Modules and programmes of study in higher education are centred around the attainment of specified learning outcomes. Any learning activity within a given module or programme must be aligned with learning outcomes and, where appropriate, formative or summative assessment. Therefore, a key challenge for educators is to identify, or develop, simulations and games that are appropriate to achieving the learning outcomes of their module (Biagi & Loi, 2013; Terras & Boyle, 2019). Whilst many of the more generic modules on popular study programmes are increasingly well served by simulations and games that are available commercially or for free, for some subject areas, it may simply be that case that suitable learning resources are not available or are not sufficiently tailored to the specific requirements of a module. In addition to considering learning outcomes, educators make judgements about suitability in terms of how students may react to a given approach to learning. In the case of simulations and games, these techniques may be novel to some students and evidence suggests that learner perceptions of them are not homogenous. Whilst many students embrace them, some have been shown to exhibit more negative responses particularly around how the IT aspects of a game operate (Burdon & Munro, 2017; Mayrath, Traphagan, Heikes, & Trivedi, 2011).

Interestingly, survey evidence collected from instructors from a UK university indicates that factors associated with suitability, alongside concerns related to risk, represent the most significant issues in the use of simulations and games (Lean et al., 2006). This suggests that whilst challenges linked to the availability of time and other resources exist, they can often be overcome. Thus, the major considerations for educators are, perhaps as they should be, associated with academic judgements linked to the learning experience of students. That is, are available techniques suitable in relation to the aims of a given module and will the learning activity run smoothly and effectively from a student perspective?

In the concluding section of this chapter, the implications of simulations and games for pedagogical practice in the field of real world learning are explored alongside some recommendations for further research.

Conclusion: Implications for Practice and Research

Simulations and games, in all their various forms, offer Higher Education educators considerable scope to enrich the learning experience of students. As demonstrated by the case studies presented in this chapter, they can be applied across a wide range of subjects and in a variety of diverse learning contexts. They provide a solution to some of the key barriers to real world learning, namely risk, cost and timescale. Further, simulations and games bring advantages associated with levels of fidelity and educator control and their capacity to support learning through allowing mistakes to be made by students. They also allow double-loop learning to occur as students' mental models of the world develop. As a bridge between traditional learning and real world learning, they enable educators to facilitate realistic insights into practice whilst maintaining many of the benefits of class-based activity.

Nevertheless, as with any pedagogical approach, there are challenges associated with using simulations and games. These need to be understood and managed by educators to ensure effective learning. A key issue for educational practice is the importance of initial assessment of techniques in terms of their suitability for addressing learning outcomes and providing an engaging experience for students within a given subject or learning context. Gaining an awareness of the range of existing options is an important first step, and given the disparate nature of information available, the time required to research and try out alternative techniques is not to be underestimated. Further, it may be that, where suitable options are limited, customisation or bespoke development may be required. Even where this is not required, significant up-front familiarisation and planning is typically needed ahead of implementation. As is common with other forms of real world learning, the need for careful pre-planning takes a significant investment in time and energy; and this doesn't stop once the simulation or gaming activity begins. Such techniques are not self-teaching but require ongoing engagement by educators. This may involve progress monitoring, various learning interventions, in-activity feedback and post-activity debriefing and reflection.

Despite the significant efforts required in using simulations and games, the learning benefits can be substantial. Still, it is also true to say that empirical evidence on the impacts of simulations and games in Higher Education is currently limited. Whilst there is a growing body of research (see, e.g., the 2015 Special Issue of the *International Journal of Management Education*—Lean et al., 2015), a need exists to understand how such approaches affect learning and other desirable outcomes relevant to different fields of practice. For example, these may include employability skills, entrepreneurial intent and subject-specific technical skills. In addition, very little current research examines how the benefits of simulations and games might be enhanced to support even more effective learning. For instance, how does assessment design affect learning through simulations? What is the role of reflective debriefing and how can this be leveraged to best effect? How can the learning benefits of simulation be enhanced through the use of critical incidents? How do group dynamics influence learning in a team game? Such questions ensure that there are rich opportunities for further important pedagogical research contributions in this field. As the range of applications of simulations and games grows and further empirical evidence is accumulated, our understanding of the role of such techniques within the realm of real world learning will undoubtedly increase, enabling the development of more effective learning.

References

Al-Elq, A. H. (2010). Simulation-based medical teaching and learning. *Journal of Family & Community Medicine, 17*(1), 35–40. https://doi.org/10.4103/1319-1683.68787

Argyris, C., & Schön, D. (1974). *Theory in practice: Increasing professional effectiveness*. San Francisco, CA: Jossey-Bass.

Argyris, C., & Schön, D. (1996). *Organisational learning II*. New York: Addison-Wesley.

Arnab, S., Lim, T., Carvalho, M. B., Bellotti, F., De Freitas, S., Louchart, S., … De Gloria, A. (2015). Mapping learning and game mechanics for serious games analysis. *British Journal of Educational Technology, 46*(2), 391–411. https://doi.org/10.1111/bjet.12113

Avramenko, A. (2012). Enhancing students' employability through business simulation. *Education+Training, 54*(5), 355–367. https://doi.org/10.1108/00400911211244669

Baptista, G., & Oliveira, T. (2018). Gamification and serious games: A literature meta-analysis and integrative model. *Computers in Human Behavior, 92*, 306–315. https://doi.org/10.1016/j.chb.2018.11.030

Barnett, M. (2004). Risk Management training: The development of simulator-based scenarios from the analysis of recent maritime accidents. In *Proceedings of the Advances in International Maritime Research Conference*. Tasmania: IAMU Tasmania.

Bhagat, K. K., Liou, W. K., & Chang, C. Y. (2016). A cost-effective interactive 3D virtual reality system applied to military live firing training. *Virtual Reality, 20*(2), 127–140. https://doi.org/10.1007/s10055-016-0284-x

Biagi, F., & Loi, M. (2013). Measuring ICT use and learning outcomes: Evidence from recent econometric studies. *European Journal of Education, 48*(1), 28–42. https://doi.org/10.1111/ejed.12016

Bilgin, C. U., Baek, Y., & Park, H. (2015). How debriefing strategies can improve student motivation and self-efficacy in game-based learning. *Journal of Educational Computing Research, 53*(2), 155–182. https://doi.org/10.1177/0735633115598496

Bloom, B. S. (Ed.). (1956). *Taxonomy of educational objectives. Vol. 1: Cognitive domain.* New York: McKay.

Boyle, E. A., Hainey, T., Connolly, T. M., Gray, G., Earp, J., Ott, M., ... Pereira, J. (2016). An update to the systematic literature review of empirical evidence of the impacts and outcomes of computer games and serious games. *Computers & Education, 94*, 178–192. https://doi.org/10.1016/j.compedu.2015.11.003

Burdon, W. M., & Munro, K. (2017). Simulation–is it all worth it? The impact of simulation from the perspective of accounting students. *The International Journal of Management Education, 15*(3), 429–448. https://doi.org/10.1016/j.ijme.2017.07.001

Carvalho, M. B., Bellotti, F., Berta, R., De Gloria, A., Sedano, C. I., Hauge, J. B., ... Rauterberg, M. (2015). An activity theory-based model for serious games analysis and conceptual design. *Computers & Education, 87*, 166–181. https://doi.org/10.1016/j.compedu.2015.03.023

CBI. (2009, March 26). *Future fit – Preparing graduates for the world of work.* Retrieved from https://www.universitiesuk.ac.uk/policy-and-analysis/reports/Documents/2009/future-fit-preparing-graduates-for-the-world-of-work.PDF

Clarke, E. (2009). Learning outcomes from business simulation exercises. *Education & Training, 51*(5/6), 448–459. https://doi.org/10.1108/00400910910987246

Cook, D. A. (2014). How much evidence does it take? A cumulative meta-analysis of outcomes of simulation-based education. *Medical Education, 48*(8), 750–760. https://doi.org/10.1111/medu.12473

Cope, J. (2003). Entrepreneurship learning and critical reflection: Discontinuous events as triggers for 'higher-level' learning. *Management Learning, 34*(4), 429–450. https://doi.org/10.1177/1350507603039067

Crookall, D. (2010). Serious games, debriefing, and simulation/gaming as a discipline. *Simulation & Gaming, 41*(6), 898–920. https://doi.org/10.1177/1046878110390784

Dankbaar, M. E., Alsma, J., Jansen, E. E., van Merrienboer, J. J., van Saase, J. L., & Schuit, S. C. (2016). An experimental study on the effects of a simulation game on students' clinical cognitive skills and motivation. *Advances in Health Sciences Education, 21*(3), 505–521. https://doi.org/10.1007/s10459-015-9641-x

Devine, J. (2016). Real enough? Realism and simulation design in the political science classroom. In L. Wasylkiw & J. L. Tomes (Eds.), *Mount A Teaches* (pp. 121–134). Canada, BC: Friesen Press.

Diehl, L. A., de Souza, R. M., Gordan, P. A., Esteves, R. Z., & Coelho, I. C. M. (2014). Gaming habits and opinions of Brazilian medical school faculty and students: What's Next? *Games for Health Journal: Research, Development, and Clinical Applications, 3*(2), 79–85. https://doi.org/10.1089/g4h.2013.0069

Ebner, M., & Holzinger, A. (2007). Successful implementation of user-centered game based learning in higher education: An example from civil engineering. *Computers & Education, 49*(3), 873–890. https://doi.org/10.1016/j.compedu.2005.11.026

Egenfeldt-Nielsen, S. (2004). Practical barriers in using educational computer games. *On The Horizon, 12*(1), 18–21. https://doi.org/10.1108/10748120410540454

Ellman, N. (1977). Before the simulation fails: Avoiding potential pitfalls. *Social Studies, 68*(6), 251–253.

Evans, K., Guile, D., Harris, J., & Allan, H. (2010). Putting knowledge to work: A new approach. *Nurse Education Today, 30*(3), 245–251. https://doi.org/10.1016/j.nedt.2009.10.014

Faria, A. J. (2006). History, current usage, and learning from marketing simulation games: A detailed literature review. *Proceedings of the Marketing Management Association*, 138–139.

Fortmüller, R. (2009). Learning through business games: Acquiring competences within virtual realities. *Simulation & Gaming, 40*(1), 68–83. https://doi.org/10.1177/1046878107308075

Gatfield, D. (2006). *Engine room simulator instructor course, Session 10/2. Carrying out a simulator exercise: Debriefing.* METNET.

Goi, C. L. (2019). The use of business simulation games in teaching and learning. *Journal of Education for Business, 94*(5), 342–349. https://doi.org/10.1080/08832323.2018.1536028

Gopinath, C., & Sawyer, J. E. (1999). Exploring the learning from an enterprise simulation. *Journal of Management Development, 18*(5), 477–489.

Hainey, T., Connolly, T. M., Stansfield, M., & Boyle, E. A. (2011). Evaluation of a game to teach requirements collection and analysis in software engineering at tertiary education level. *Computers & Education, 56*, 21–35. https://doi.org/10.1016/j.compedu.2010.09.008

Hogg, E. S., Kinshuck, A. J., Littley, N., Lau, A., Tandon, S., & Lancaster, J. (2019). A high-fidelity, fully immersive simulation course to replicate ENT and head and neck emergencies. *The Journal of Laryngology & Otology, 133*(2), 115–118. https://doi.org/10.1017/S0022215118002347

Hollon, S. D., & Beck, A. T. (1994). Cognitive and cognitive-behavioral therapies. In A. E. Bergin & S. L. Garfield (Eds.), *Handbook of psychotherapy and behavior change* (pp. 428–466). New York: Wiley.

Ibrahim, R., Masrom, S., Yusoff, R. C. M., Zainuddin, N. M. M., & Rizman, Z. I. (2017). Student acceptance of educational games in higher education. *Journal of Fundamental and Applied Sciences, 9*(3S), 809–829. https://doi.org/10.4314/jfas.v9i3s.62

Iuliana, P., Dragos, M. I., & Mitran, P. C. (2014). Identification of employability skills – Starting point for the curriculum design process. *Economics, Management & Financial Markets, 9*(1), 237–246.

Jennings, D. (2002). Strategic management: An evaluation of the use of three learning methods. *The Journal of Management Development, 21*(9), 655–665. https://doi.org/10.1108/02621710210441658

Jones, R., & Bursens, P. (2015). The effects of active learning environments: How simulations trigger affective learning. *European Political Science, 14*, 254–265. https://doi.org/10.1057/eps.2015.22

Keys, B., & Wolfe, J. (1990). The role of management games and simulations in education and research. *Journal of Management, 16*(2), 307–336. https://doi.org/10.1177/014920639001600205

Kiili, K. (2007). Foundation for problem-based gaming. *British Journal of Educational Technology, 38*(3), 394–404. https://doi.org/10.1111/j.1467-8535.2007.00704.x

Koivisto, J. M., Haavisto, E., Niemi, H., Haho, P., Nylund, S., & Multisilta, J. (2018). Design principles for simulation games for learning clinical reasoning: A design-based research approach. *Nurse Education Today, 60*, 114–120. https://doi.org/10.1016/j.nedt.2017.10.002

Koivisto, J. M., Haavisto, E., Niemi, H., Katajisto, J., & Multisilta, J. (2016). Elements explaining learning clinical reasoning using simulation games. *International Journal of Serious Games, 3*(4), 29–43. https://doi.org/10.17083/ijsg.v3i4.136

Kriz, W. C., & Manahl, W. (2016). Understanding and changing systems through hybrid simulation game design methods in educational contexts. In T. Kaneda, H. Kanegae, P. Rizzi, & Y. Toyoda (Eds.), *Simulation and Gaming in the Network Society. Translational Systems Sciences* (Vol. 9, pp. 79–93). Singapore: Springer. https://doi.org/10.1007/978-981-10-0575-6_7

Lean, J., Moizer, J., & Newbery, R. (2014). Enhancing the impact of online simulations through blended learning: A critical incident approach. *Education & Training, 56*(2/3), 208–218. https://doi.org/10.1108/ET-01-2013-0007

Lean, J., Moizer, J., Towler, M., & Abbey, C. (2006). Simulations and games: Use and barriers in higher education. *Active Learning in Higher Education, 7*(3), 227–242. https://doi.org/10.1177/1469787406069056

Lean, J., Moizer, J., & Warren, M. (2015). The use and impact of simulations in management education. *International Journal of Management Education, 13*(3), 349. https://doi.org/10.1016/j.ijme.2015.11.001

Leitch, S. (2006, December). *Prosperity for all in the global economy: World class skills: Final report.* TSO (The Stationery Office). Retrieved from http://www.official-documents.gov.uk/document/other/0118404792/0118404792.pdf

Lopreiato, J. O., Downing, D., Gammon, W., Lioce, L., Sittner, B., Slot, V., & Spain, A. E. (2016, June). *Healthcare Simulation Dictionary.* Society for Simulation in Healthcare. Retrieved from http://www.ssih.org/dictionary

Marda, M., Economou, D., & Bouki, V. (2018). Enhancing deeper learning using empathy and creativity in serious games role-play simulations. In *European Conference on Games Based Learning* (pp. 785–791). Brighton: Academic Conferences International Limited.

Mayrath, M. C., Traphagan, T., Heikes, E. J., & Trivedi, A. (2011). Instructional design best practices for Second Life: A case study from a college-level English course. *Interactive Learning Environments, 19*(2), 125–142. https://doi.org/10.1080/10494820802602568

McCall, J. (2016). Teaching history with digital historical games: An introduction to the field and best practices. *Simulation & Gaming, 47*(4), 517–542. https://doi.org/10.1177/1046878116646693

McGrath, J. L., Taekman, J. M., Dev, P., Danforth, D. R., Mohan, D., Kman, N., … Talbot, T. B. (2018). Using virtual reality simulation environments to assess competence for emergency medicine learners. *Academic Emergency Medicine, 25*(2), 186–195. https://doi.org/10.1111/acem.13308

McGrath, M., Harris, A., & Whitelaw, P. A. (2016). Scaffolding a destination simulation into an undergraduate hospitality and tourism program. In M. Scerri & L. K. Hui (Eds.), *CAUTHE 2016: The Changing Landscape of*

Tourism and Hospitality: The Impact of Emerging Markets and Emerging Destinations (pp. 1133–1139). Sydney: Blue Mountains International Hotel Management School.

Moizer, J., & Lean, J. (2010). Toward endemic deployment of educational simulation games: A review of progress and future recommendations. *Simulation & Gaming, 41*(1), 116–131. https://doi.org/10.1177/1046878109359052

Moizer, J., Lean, J., Dell'Aquila, E., Walsh, P., Keary, A. A., O'Byrne, D., … Friedrich, R. (2019). An approach to evaluating the user experience of serious games. *Computers and Education, 136*, 141–151. https://doi.org/10.1016/j.compedu.2019.04.006

Moizer, J., Lean, J., Towler, M., & Smith, G. (2006). Modes of learning in the use of a computer-based business simulation game. *International Journal of Learning Technology, 2*(1), 49–61. https://doi.org/10.1504/IJLT.2006.008692

Morley, D., Bettles, S., & Derham, C. (2019). The exploration of students' learning gain following immersive simulation – The impact of feedback. *Higher Education Pedagogies, 4*(1), 368–384. https://doi.org/10.1080/23752696.2019.1642123

Narayanan, E., & Turner, J. J. (2019). Perceptions of simulation games and the role they play in creating an enterprising and employable graduate. *International Journal of Education, Psychology and Counseling, 4*(30), 179–196.

Newbery, R., Lean, J., Moizer, J., & Haddoud, M. (2018). Entrepreneurial identity formation during the initial entrepreneurial experience: The influence of simulation feedback and existing identity. *Journal of Business Research, 85*, 51–59. https://doi.org/10.1016/j.jbusres.2017.12.013

Nicol, D. J., & Macfarlane-Dick, D. (2006). Formative assessment and self-regulated learning: A model and seven principles of good feedback practice. *Studies in Higher Education, 31*(2), 199–218. https://doi.org/10.1080/03075070600572090

Office for Students. (n.d.). *Learning Gain*. Retrieved from https://www.office-forstudents.org.uk/advice-and-guidance/teaching/learning-gain/

Pallis, A. A., & Ng, A. K. (2011). Pursuing maritime education: An empirical study of students' profiles, motivations and expectations. *Maritime Policy & Management, 38*(4), 369–393. https://doi.org/10.1080/0308883 9.2011.588258

Pariafsai, F. (2016). Effectiveness of a virtual project-based simulation game in construction education. *International Journal of Scientific Research in Science, Engineering and Technology, 2*(5), 377–393.

Pavlov, P. I. (2010). Conditioned reflexes: An investigation of the physiological activity of the cerebral cortex. *Annals of Neurosciences, 17*(3), 136–141. https://doi.org/10.5214/ans.0972-7531.1017309

Pei Rui Chan, K., & Zary, N. (2019). Knowledge, use and barriers to Serious Games in undergraduate medical education. https://doi.org/10.31219/osf.io/2f7rw

Pesare, E., Roselli, T., Corriero, N., & Rossano, V. (2016). Game-based learning and gamification to promote engagement and motivation in medical learning contexts. *Smart Learn Environments, 3*(5). https://doi.org/10.1186/s40561-016-0028-0

Petridis, P., Dunwell, I., Arnab, S., Protopsaltis, A., Hendrix, M., & de Freitas, S. (2012). Game engines selection framework for high-fidelity serious applications. *International Journal of Interactive Worlds, 2012*, 1–19. https://doi.org/10.5171/2012.418638

Ruggiero, D., & Watson, W. R. (2014). Engagement through praxis in educational game design common threads. *Simulation & Gaming, 45*(4–5), 471–490. https://doi.org/10.1177/1046878114553570

Scholtz, F., & Hughes, S. (2019). A systematic review of educator interventions in facilitating simulation based learning. *Journal of Applied Research in Higher Education.* https://doi.org/10.1108/JARHE-02-2018-0019

Skinner, B. F. (2011). *About behaviorism.* New York: Knopf Doubleday.

Stern, N. (2016). *Building on success and learning from experience: An independent review of the research excellence framework.* London: Department for Business, Energy and Industrial Strategy.

Strachan, L. (2011). Do business simulation games improve a graduate's employability? *Graduates with Impact: Through Excellence in Business Education Conference.* 10th March 2011. Bournemouth.

Strachan, L. (2016). Teaching employability skills through simulation games. *Journal of Pedagogic Development, 6*(2), 8–17.

Subhash, S., & Cudney, E. A. (2018). Gamified learning in higher education: A systematic review of the literature. *Computers in Human Behavior, 87*, 192–206. https://doi.org/10.1016/j.chb.2018.05.028

Tai, J. H. M., Canny, B. J., Haines, T. P., & Molloy, E. K. (2017). Implementing peer learning in clinical education: A framework to address challenges in the "real world". *Teaching and Learning in Medicine, 29*(2), 162–172. https://doi.org/10.1080/10401334.2016.1247000

Tao, Y. H., Yeh, C. C. R., & Hung, K. C. (2015). Validating the learning cycle models of business simulation games via student perceived gains in skills and knowledge. *Educational Technology & Society, 18*(1), 77–90.

Terras, M. M., & Boyle, E. A. (2019). Integrating games as a means to develop e-learning: Insights from a psychological perspective. *British Journal of Educational Technology, 50*(3), 1049–1059. https://doi.org/10.1111/bjet.12784

Usherwood, S. (2015). Building resources for simulations: Challenges and opportunities. *European Political Science, 14*, 218–227. https://doi.org/10.1057/eps.2015.19

Van der Meij, H., Leemkuil, H., & Li, J.-L. (2013). Does individual or collaborative self-debriefing better enhance learning from games? *Computers in Human Behavior, 29*(6), 2471–2479. https://doi.org/10.1016/j.chb.2013.06.001

Vos, L., & Brennan, R. (2010). Marketing simulation games: Student and lecturer perspectives. *Marketing Intelligence & Planning, 28*(7), 882–897. https://doi.org/10.1108/02634501011086472

Vygotsky, L. (1978). Interaction between learning and development. *Readings on the Development of Children, 23*(3), 34–41.

Wingrove, L. (2014, December 10). Are graduates lacking the skills that employers need? Retrieved from https://www.trainingjournal.com/blog/are-graduates-lacking-skills-employers-need

Wouters, P., & van Oostendorp, H. (2017). Overview of instructional techniques to facilitate learning and motivation of serious games. In P. Wouters & H. van Oostendorp (Eds.), *Instructional techniques to facilitate learning and motivation of serious games* (pp. 1–16). New York: Springer. https://doi.org/10.1007/978-3-319-39298-1_1

Wright-Maley, C. (2015). Beyond the "Babel problem": Defining simulations for the social studies. *The Journal of Social Studies Research, 39*(2), 63–77. https://doi.org/10.1016/j.jssr.2014.10.001

10

Learning Enterprise and Entrepreneurship Through Real Business Projects

Lucy Hatt

Introduction

Global and European economic and employment policies increasingly emphasise the importance of enterprise and entrepreneurship. Entrepreneurship is the "key to job creation and growth in modern society" (Nielsen, Klyver, Evald, & Bager, 2012, p. xv), and entrepreneurial competencies are highly sought after by policy-makers and practitioners (Hofer et al., 2010).

The Finnish 'Tiimiakatemia' which started in 1993 at JAMK University of Applied Sciences in Jyväskylä, Finland (Team Academy Worldwide, n.d.), was developed in response to this demand for more entrepreneurial graduates and the changing nature of the job market. Students on such undergraduate degree programmes learn in coached teams by starting and running real businesses.

Case studies: Lucy Hatt and Lauren Davies

L. Hatt (✉)
Newcastle University, Newcastle upon Tyne, UK
e-mail: lucy.hatt@newcastle.ac.uk

© The Author(s) 2021
D. A. Morley, M. G. Jamil (eds.), *Applied Pedagogies for Higher Education*,
https://doi.org/10.1007/978-3-030-46951-1_10

This chapter introduces entrepreneurship in education and offers a critique of the experiential real world nature of the Team Academy approach, suggesting a complementary conceptual grounding using the threshold concepts framework (Meyer & Land, 2003, 2005) to identify what is distinctive about entrepreneurship to enable curricular development and the integration of entrepreneurship with diverse academic subjects beyond business.

The chapter includes four case studies from two UK universities using a Team Academy informed approach: Northumbria University and the University of the West of England.

Entrepreneurship and Entrepreneurship Education

Entrepreneurship is important as it is a significant factor in driving economic growth (Entrepreneurship Policy Framework and Implementation Guidance, 2012). Enterprise and entrepreneurship education have been identified as potential enablers of positive social, economic and political change, increasing the likelihood of successful graduate employment across all subject areas, and positively contributing to the likelihood of graduates leading "rewarding and self-determined" professional lives (Entrepreneurship Policy Framework and Implementation Guidance, 2012; Matlay & Carey, 2007; QAA, 2018). Higher education is generally regarded as an appropriate place for the development of entrepreneurship (QAA, 2012).

According to the QAA (2018, p. 7), enterprise is "the generation and application of ideas, which are set within practical situations during a project or undertaking". They define entrepreneurship as "the application of enterprise behaviours, attributes and competencies into the creation of cultural, social or economic value". There is, however, a general lack of consensus regarding what entrepreneurship education in higher education really means (Pittaway & Cope, 2007), what needs to be learnt, whether it can be learnt, where it is best learnt, how to learn it and how to measure if it has been learnt. There remain unanswered questions concerning how (and if) the higher education sector can contribute to entrepreneurship (Davey, Hannon, & Penaluna, 2016). There is no stable canon of knowledge that represents entrepreneurship and no established methodology for entrepreneurship education (Michels, Beresford, Beresford, & Handley, 2018). A general lack of research-grounded discussion on the quality of entrepreneurship education initiatives has been highlighted (Béchard & Grégoire, 2007), particularly in relation to what makes pedagogical innovations effective. There is a concern that the emergence and growth in entrepreneurship education has been faster than educators' understanding of what should be taught, and how outcomes might be assessed (Neck & Corbett, 2018).

Providing academic content to potential entrepreneurs offers some benefits, but merely treating entrepreneurship as just another subject is not likely to be effective. According to the Economist Intelligence Unit (Helping entrepreneurs flourish: Rethinking the drivers of entrepreneurship, 2014), entrepreneurs have clear opinions regarding what would make more effective entrepreneurship education. They hold that education needs to go beyond imparting a specific body of knowledge, believing this approach to be largely obsolete given the growing accessibility of data. Education needs to be more experience driven and personalised, where students can learn how to apply information together with skills of creativity and problem solving. Educators need to create learning environments where risk taking is encouraged so students realise that failure is a normal part of development. Networking is also of primary importance, learning the skills necessary to network successfully and the role of networking in enabling better contact with the professional world both for employment and for mentoring purposes.

Existing approaches to entrepreneurship education can be broadly grouped into three (Hannon, 2005; Heinonen & Hytti, 2010; O'Connor, 2013) or, with the addition of 'embedded', four (Gibb, 2002; Lackéus, 2015a; Morselli, 2019; Pittaway & Edwards, 2012):

1. 'Teaching about': a theoretical approach to gain an understanding of the phenomenon of entrepreneurship. 'About' approaches are theoretical and guided by content.

2. 'Teaching for': a vocational approach to learn the skills, knowledge and attitude needed to become an entrepreneur. 'For' approaches are orientated to occupation.
3. 'Teaching through': an experiential approach to develop an understanding of entrepreneurship through experiencing entrepreneurial processes, the aim being to go through a real entrepreneurial learning process in 'safe' conditions.
4. In embedded approaches entrepreneurship is delivered within other non-business subjects, the aim being to give learners entrepreneurial experience and awareness relevant to their field of study (Pittaway & Edwards, 2012).

Whilst 'teaching for' and 'teaching through' have gained in popularity, some regard 'teaching about' as indispensable because, they argue, only by understanding theoretical frameworks can students adapt and flourish in an uncertain future (Fiet, 2001). Others argue that 'for' and 'about' approaches are the most relevant to students wishing to become entrepreneurs, whilst the 'through' and 'embedded' approaches are useful to any student (Lackéus, 2015a). There is a tension between what is easy to deliver in the existing educational context and what is most effective.

Despite continuing debate about whether entrepreneurship can be taught and, if so, how best to teach it and whether university is the right place to learn it, the prevailing neo-liberal ideology has led to a huge increase in the provision of entrepreneurship education in higher education. This fragmented and disparate educational landscape has resulted from differing assumptions about the purpose of entrepreneurship education at university.

The three main themes evident when identifying the purpose and impact of entrepreneurship education, namely increasing the number and success of new ventures; enhancing the employability of graduates and increasing their value in the job market; and preparing students for an uncertain future, are equally important but difficult to measure and connect directly with any specific educational intervention. This lack of clarity concerning an overarching purpose is also evident in the sector as a whole and not just in entrepreneurship. As Rothblatt (2006) notes, there is a general lack of clarity around what a university is, or what one is for. Moreover, disparate purposes of entrepreneurship education inhibit effective curricula development. A more conceptual approach is called for. This chapter proposes that the objective of entrepreneurship education is to further knowledge and understanding of entrepreneurship and to enable students to understand how an entrepreneur thinks and practises in the world.

Team Academy

The Team Academy approach undoubtedly produces some very desirable outcomes. Graduate employment levels and number of student start-ups are claimed to be significantly higher than those of other more traditional programmes (Tosey, Dhaliwal, & Hassinen, 2015). Increased self-awareness is the most commonly reported and most highly valued participant outcome (Ruuska & Krawczyk, 2013), and visitors are typically impressed by the confidence, capability and energy of team entrepreneurs (students), and their ability to take initiative and responsibility (Tosey et al., 2015). Students emerge with excellent soft-skills and a highly developed network of potential customers, employers, mentors and investors (Davey, 2016).

The Team Academy approach represents a very new way of structuring and delivering an undergraduate programme, and it has little defined knowledge content. In the original Finnish version of the approach, nothing is taught didactically and there is no set curriculum. Students have to acclimatise to a learning environment where there is minimal direction and instruction regarding what to learn or how to learn it. The Team Academy approach deliberately positions itself as radically different to traditional forms of higher education typically organised by academic discipline and shifts the focus from teaching to learning, but not learning according to what is determined by the educator. Team Academy does not give its students grounding in the typical range of business disciplines and justifies this by arguing that the students' own reading is led by the business needs and development of the individual. It is also based on a premise that specialist expertise, when needed, can be sourced externally.

Team Academy is described as a "radical form of socio-constructivism" or "radical constructivism", it is based on a "constructive-humanistic learning concept" (see Akatemia—working to learn, 2019; Davey, 2018; Halttunen, 2006; Leinonen, Partanen, & Palviainen, 2004; Lizartza, 2012). It is representative of programmes where constructivist views have become ideologically and epistemologically opposed to the presentation and explanation of knowledge (Kirschner, Sweller, & Clark, 2006).

Teams of students create and operate real business projects supported by coaches in a conscious and deliberate contrast to traditional business programmes that might offer a form of experiential learning through the use of simulations. The students own their businesses outright and the universities have no stake in them. This level of authentic investment in the success or failure of their business projects increases the students' levels of psychological and emotional engagement in their enterprises (Tosey et al., 2015). Students are organised to work in teams and tasked with making money, pooling their experience to become more personally effective and to develop effective team working skills.

The experience is centred on regular sessions with a coach, typically called training or coaching sessions or action learning sets once or twice a week, where the coach encourages dialogue to facilitate peer learning and knowledge creation. In these sessions, students sit with their coach in a circle. They discuss their business projects, what they have learned, report on finances and plan. The coach may be an academic member of staff or an external business-person with relevant business start-up experience, depending on the institution.

Northumbria University at Newcastle and the University of the West of England were the first two UK universities to introduce a Team Academy style programme in 2013. Some six years later, the programmes retain some but not all of the original Team Academy features. Re-applying the Team Academy approach wholesale in other countries has many challenges, indeed Tosey et al. (2015) argue that the Team Academy model worked integrally as a coherent whole and queried whether it could be transferred successfully outside the host nation with any modifications at all, however rational or necessary they appeared. This view is not shared by all and Davey's case study (2016, p. 14) calls the Team Academy model "highly transferrable" owing to "its well-structured and documented approach, which can be adapted to the needs of the host institution".

For example, in the Northumbria version of Team Academy, students cannot hire and fire each other as they all pay fees, neither can progression on the programme be dependent on any other criteria than satisfactory performance in summative assessments. The university cannot charge students for 'office rental', and there are no equivalent preferential tax arrangements for business co-operatives. The institutional requirements regarding quality assurance dictate a modular format for the degree, making non-module specific sessions challenging to timetable and workload, and this impacts on the design of assignments. As the programme has developed at Northumbria University, taught knowledge content has been introduced, although there is considerably less content than on other mainstream Business Management programmes. The description of the course given by a 2019 graduate sums up the student experience.

> We did not generally have lectures or seminars. On the course we had a variety of business and academic coaches with very different backgrounds stretching from Venture Capitalism, Serial and Portfolio Entrepreneurship to Careers and the Psychology of the Entrepreneurial Mind-set. Although this system was hard to adopt initially in first year, I honestly think it was for the best. We had coaches with real experience in business that could provide us with contacts, help grow our business networks and teach us how to get through business struggles, all of which were extremely important for our own personal development as business students and potential entrepreneurs. I feel we are extremely well prepared for the workplace due to the way that the course was designed. We had coaching sessions twice a week where we could choose what to learn and we had to take ownership of our own learning. I must admit this was hard at first when we didn't have businesses, but as soon as we started doing real business activity, each and every one of us came to a coaching session passionate about teaching something that we had learnt and eager to listen to see if we could apply others' lessons to our own business projects. It was like a positive multiplier effect. Our assignments' objectives were to integrate the academic literature of business with the practical application of our businesses in context. This was a great way to make our assignments very interesting and also a good

way to force us to do the parts of business that most people tend not to enjoy such as accounting and planning, etc. I also loved how the feedback received was always based on our business activity as well as the assignment criteria.

The current programme design addresses aspects of 'learning through' and 'learning for' entrepreneurship, but important aspects of 'learning about' can be further strengthened through application of the threshold concept framework. Candidate threshold concepts in entrepreneurship are proposed here as particular types of knowledge that are central to entrepreneurship that will enable educators to teach entrepreneurship better and to improve the learning experience of students (Barradell & Kennedy-Jones, 2015).

Candidate Threshold Concepts in Entrepreneurship

The threshold concept framework posits that in any academic discipline there are concepts that have a particularly transformative effect on student learning. Termed threshold concepts, they represent a transformed way of understanding something, without which the learner cannot progress (Meyer & Land, 2005). In transforming the learner, threshold concepts change the learner's perceptions, subjectivity and worldview. There is a repositioning of the self (Meyer & Land, 2005) where the learners' understanding of the nature of their own existence and their conception of reality adjusts; an ontological as well as a conceptual shift. This can often be uncomfortable and is therefore sometimes resisted. Mastery of a threshold concept simultaneously changes an individual's idea of what they know and who they are (Cousin, 2009). Such conceptual understanding is likely to be irreversible and is unlikely to be forgotten or unlearned. Threshold concepts are also characterised by their integrative nature in that they expose how other things can be related to each other.

Defining the threshold concepts in any subject discipline is likely to inform the development of the curriculum in order that it might be optimised. Threshold concepts are concepts that bind a subject together, being fundamental to ways of thinking and practising in that discipline

(Meyer & Land, 2003, 2005). The concepts that are critical to thinking as an entrepreneur, and consequently to entrepreneurship, may be termed entrepreneurship threshold concepts (Meyer & Land, 2003, 2005). Using the threshold concept framework (Meyer & Land, 2003) to define entrepreneurship presents an important opportunity in terms of both the credibility of the subject area and the design and delivery of enterprise and entrepreneurship curricula in higher education. The use of the term 'candidate threshold concept' (CTC) started to appear from 2008 (Osmond, Turner, & Land, 2008; Shanahan, Foster, & Meyer, 2008; Zander et al., 2008) and has been used here to communicate a sense of fluidity and openness to the potential evolution of these concepts in entrepreneurship. CTCs in entrepreneurship are being offered as starting points for discussion, selection and further consideration, not as absolute fixed definitions.

The Promise of Threshold Concepts in Entrepreneurship

Identifying threshold concepts in entrepreneurship could be useful for entrepreneurship educators in a number of respects: to avoid an over-stuffed curriculum, to unblock student learning and facilitate curriculum development and to demarcate the discipline.

Identifying some concepts as 'threshold' offers a way of differentiating between core learning goals which enable the learner to see things in a different way and other learning goals which, though important, do not have the same significantly enabling and transformative effect. This allows the educator to focus on the conceptual understandings that enable a fuller understanding of the subject, and foster integration of knowledge, avoiding an over-crowded curriculum. The burgeoning interest in entrepreneurship education, as perhaps typical of any subject seeking to establish itself as an academic discipline, has led to a proliferation of learning outcomes and competencies that risk overwhelming an entrepreneurship educator wishing to address the subject comprehensively. That said, there are methodological challenges in distinguishing between 'key', 'core' and 'threshold' concepts (Barradell, 2013).

Failure to understand, view or interpret a threshold concept will stop the progression of learning. The threshold concept framework addresses the kind of complicated learner transitions learners undergo (Cousin, 2008). Recognising threshold concepts and the different ways individual learners approach them will enable educators to make the curriculum more effective and efficient and to unlock learner progress.

> The significance of the framework provided by threshold concepts lies, we feel, in its explanatory potential to locate troublesome aspects of disciplinary knowledge within transitions across conceptual thresholds, and hence to assist teachers in identifying appropriate ways of modifying or redesigning curricula to enable their students to negotiate such transitions more successfully. (Land, Cousin, Meyer, & Davies, 2006, p. 205)

Osmond et al. (2008, p. 244) used the threshold concept framework as lens to identify the "underlying agenda of things students need to have" in the context of a transport and product design course. By clarifying the "knowledge practices" (p. 244) students needed to acquire, Osmond et al. (2008) sought to identify pedagogic strategies to enhance the student learning experience. This potential benefit is of particular interest in entrepreneurship, which has not evolved from an academic context, but is a product of the market. The threshold concept framework offers a way of seeing and understanding disciplinary ways of thinking (Donald, 2002) and 'ways of thinking and practising' (McCune & Hounsell, 2005) in the discipline. An understanding of the threshold concepts of a discipline supports a person in becoming part of the 'disciplinary tribe' (Becher & Trowler, 2001) and helps reveal a discipline's underlying episteme (Timmermans & Meyer, 2017).

The Six Candidate Threshold Concepts in Entrepreneurship

A staged stakeholder curriculum inquiry involving semi-structured interviews, a Delphi survey and concept mapping workshops was conducted with entrepreneurs, entrepreneurship educators and entrepreneurship students in a doctoral research study (Hatt, 2020).

Six CTCs in entrepreneurship were developed from the combined entrepreneur and entrepreneurship educator data sets. These CTCs can be used to explain what is distinctive about thinking like an entrepreneur and offer a complementary conceptual grounding to identify what is distinctive about entrepreneurship to enable curricular development and the integration of entrepreneurship with diverse academic subjects beyond business.

1. **Entrepreneurial Agency**

    The entrepreneur practises value creation as a self-organising, proactive and self-regulating individual who reflects on and learns from their behaviour in order to contribute to their life circumstances.

2. **Context Is Opportunity**

    The entrepreneur realises that all contexts can be contexts for value creation, and as such are rich in opportunity, even those that others might not regard as such.

3. **Context Is Resource**

    The entrepreneur realises that all contexts present the means to enable value creation through the exploitation of the opportunities that have been or are yet to be recognised. All contexts not only are the source of opportunity for the creation of value but also present the means with which to bring it to fruition.

4. **Risk Is Missed Opportunity**

    The entrepreneur associates risk with opportunities for value creation that are not pursued as well as those that are, in terms of opportunity cost. Risk is more likely to be associated with actions not taken, rather than actions taken. There is a bias towards action and away from caution and inaction. Negative consequences are perceived to be more likely associated with actions not taken, rather than with actions taken.

5. **Value Is Determined by the Customer**

    The entrepreneur understands the subjective nature of value creation and recognises that only the prospective customer may perceive value. The customer plays a superordinate role in valuing the offer, and the entrepreneur relegates their own perceptions of value.

6. **Entrepreneurship Is a Practice**

The entrepreneur practices value creation iteratively and not as a singular event. Value creation is not a 'one off' and entrepreneurs are always thinking of the next opportunity.

How to Educate Students in Entrepreneurship

Having identified the CTCs in entrepreneurship above, the pedagogical design must also be taken into consideration. Operating best within a framework for engagement, a pedagogical approach was developed from educator data, to create both a desire and an enabling context for experiential entrepreneurship education. Students need to understand the relevance of the knowledge to them and why and when it could prove useful.

Integrated experiential learning opportunities are important, and practical, real-life activities need to form significant parts of the curriculum. Time for reflection needs to be designed in and students need to be given the opportunity to understand failure as a valuable learning experience, although this is particularly challenging in an educational context with an increasingly diverse student cohort. Theoretical knowledge content needs to be integrated with practical experiences and teamwork was critical in encouraging students to develop independence from tutors. Teams can be used as a resource for both knowledge and emotional support and can be pivotal in the development of student engagement, and improved student outcomes. Teaching entrepreneurship knowledge content is important, supporting the argument that theory is the most practical thing that students can be taught (Kuhn, 1962). Use of theory ensures that students are able to act when they encounter new or unfamiliar situations.

The case studies in this chapter illustrate aspects of the pedagogical design of the UK Team Academy style programmes and associate the development of understanding of some of the CTCs in entrepreneurship with them.

Conclusion

This chapter sets out some of the challenges in enterprise and entrepreneurship education, presenting the Team Academy approach as a partial answer. Candidate threshold concepts are offered as way to address the lack of conceptual entrepreneurship knowledge taught in the current form of such programmes. If entrepreneurship is regarded not only as an instrumental good (valuable because of what it enables students to do) but also as an intrinsic good (valuable as an end in itself), a more conceptual approach is called for.

Education, according to Collini (2012), encourages students to recognise the ways in which particular bits of knowledge are not fixed, eternal, universal or self-sufficient, by exposing them to the experience of enquiry into those things. Almost any subject matter may be the subject of such enquiry, but there has to be engagement with a 'particular' subject matter. It cannot be done by ingesting a set of abstract propositions about the contingency of knowledge.

Establishing a clearer subject identity for entrepreneurship using threshold concepts allows it to defend itself from the perils of genericism. As it is a product of the market, entrepreneurship shares a kind of emptiness with generic skill sets, which can be explained by its previous lack of intrinsic theoretical and conceptual content. Collini (2012) argues that generic skills are effectively becoming abstract propositions when incorporated into the curriculum without the requirement of the students to engage in a particular subject matter. The skills agenda is "rather like training people in tricks for improving their memory but without their having any past to recall" (Collini, 2012, p. 145).

A well-functioning university delivers many positive indirect outcomes resulting from the primary outcomes of education, advanced scholarship and research. In as much as the purpose of a university course in entrepreneurship may be regarded as the 'means', the direct outcomes may be regarded as the 'ends'. There are many other indirect outcomes of a university, but they should not be confused with its overarching purpose. The reason for the existence of a university is not to produce the indirect outcomes it does. A course in entrepreneurship does not exist in order to maximise the employability of its graduates or to generate student start-up businesses although again these outcomes might well result as indirect by-products. Likewise, in the course of furthering advanced scholarship and research it is likely that graduates will be well prepared for the future, being highly employable and possibly starting their own businesses thus making a valuable contribution to economic growth.

> We constantly fall into the trap of justifying an activity—one initially (and perhaps for long thereafter) undertaken because of its intrinsic interest and worth—as something we do because it yields incidental benefits which are popular with those not in a position to appreciate the activity's intrinsic interest and worth. If we find ourselves saying that what is valuable about learning to play the violin is that it helps develop the manual dexterity that will be useful for typing, then we are stuck in a traffic-jam of carts in front of horses. (Collini, 2012, p. 91)

Four case studies follow this chapter, each illustrating an aspect of the Team Academy approach to entrepreneurship education in more detail and drawing out how each attempts to teach 'about', 'through' and 'for' entrepreneurship, linking to specific CTCs in entrepreneurship.

Case Study 1

Letting Students Learn by Creating Value for a Third Party (Lucy Hatt, in a previous role of Senior Lecturer, Northumbria University, Newcastle, UK)

'Effective Team Working' is a level four (first year) module running as part of the Team Academy style programme at Northumbria University. It was informed by the work of Lackéus (2015b) who suggests value creation as an educational philosophy. This can be summarised as letting students learn by applying their competencies to create something of value for an external stakeholder. In doing this, the entrepreneurial competencies of self-efficacy, tolerance of uncertainty and ambiguity, and interpersonal skills are developed. These competencies are also highly attractive to employers. Lackéus found strong links between interacting with the outside world and the development of entrepreneurial self-efficacy. Hence this assignment requires students to deliver a workshop to pupils in their old school or college around the topic of effective team working in an enterprising context, of their own design. The task develops an increased tolerance for uncertainty and ambiguity, as arrangements and rearrangements have to be made and the schools' or colleges' needs identified and met. By completing this task in teams, interpersonal skills are developed along with greater levels of self-awareness. This task not only develops the enterprising skills of both the university students and the pupils of the schools and colleges they visit, but also promotes the university, the programme and the experiential learning approach to our target audience, driving recruitment. Summative assessment is in the form of an individual reflective report on the experience of undertaking this challenge.

The course requirement for students to start their own business means that the restrictions on visas for international students prevent them from taking it. The timing of the assessments is fixed to allow for students to deliver the workshops from their home addresses if necessary. The team approach permits students who are unable to return to their own school or college for whatever reason to join with others who are.

The successful completion of this assignment builds an understanding in the students of two of the candidate threshold concepts in entrepreneurship set out in the preceding chapter: **entrepreneurial agency** and **value is determined by the customer**.

The task at first appears to be very challenging; however, the risk exposure and perceived vulnerability of individuals is limited by team membership. The students usually form a very robust support network for each other. The students are required to regulate and organise themselves into teams and to be proactive in approaching the schools and colleges. They are also required to gather feedback from their team members and the workshop participants and reflect on it, in order to fully realise their learning from the experience and be able to apply it in other circumstances. This experience allows them to develop a greater understanding of **entrepreneurial agency**.

As the value created in the form of the workshop is authentic, and the workshops are not artefacts created solely for the purposes of assessment, the task is meaningful and motivates the students to deliver their best work. As the 'customers' or workshop participants are real, and give real feedback, it is their perspective that has the greatest weight in the perception of the value of what the students have created. This experience allows them to develop a greater understanding of **value is determined by the customer.**

Several students stated in their assignments that this task had been one of the most valuable on the programme. One student noted:

> In terms of my personal growth and the bond I have created with my team, I feel that this workshop has been far more influential than any of the other tasks I have been part of this year. … the whole assignment was down to the team and myself, and what effort we put in we would get out. For example, we had to find somewhere to conduct the workshop, arrange what we wanted to do and I believe this freedom has increased my commitment for wanting success. I feel the lack of restriction allowed me to use my creative side and explore this when coming up with the workshop. … this has opened my eyes to a new set of potential skills that I may hold, and I look forward to exploring these in the future.

Case Study 2

Collaboration Between Students of Law and Entrepreneurship (Lucy Hatt, in a previous role of Senior Lecturer, Northumbria University, Newcastle, UK)

Some of the information in this case study was prepared by Victoria Roper, Senior Lecturer, Northumbria School of Law, Northumbria University, and used with her permission.

An ongoing cross-disciplinary teaching and learning project at Northumbria University involves law students and entrepreneurship students on a Team Academy style programme working collaboratively to share and build upon their knowledge. The law students are participating, as part of their studies, in the Student Law Office in the Faculty of Business and Law at Northumbria University which offers a free legal advice and representation service to the public to those who cannot afford it, through clinical practice. Final-year Business Law students and students from the Team Academy style programme work together in teams to help each other identify legal issues and solve business problems. They meet regularly over the course of the academic year. The project was designed with constructivist principles in mind and a philosophy that "teaching is not a matter of transmitting but of engaging students in active learning, building their knowledge in terms of what they already understand" (Biggs & Tang, 2011, p. 22). Unusually, the project immerses students in the roles of both learner and teacher, whilst exposing them to students from another discipline.

The constructivist ideology underpinning the teaching project suggests students learn best when they are given the opportunity to build their own understanding, knowledge and learning, instead of "acquiring it pre-packaged and ready-made" (Exley & Dennick, 2004, p. 5). The project was designed to bridge the gap between theory and practice through experiential learning. In particular, it allows students to appreciate the complexity of 'real life'.

The business students have no legal background are often ignorant of the legal factors that should be taken into consideration when starting a business. They are commonly faced with legal problems relating to their start-up business projects which they are unsure how to resolve. The law students have been studying law for a number of years and are given the opportunity, through the project, to apply their knowledge to real-life businesses. The project is designed to bridge the gap between theory and practice through experiential learning. In particular, it allows students to appreciate the complexity of 'real life'.

Wider lessons for collaborative learning and teaching more generally have been extrapolated from the project and findings have been used to inform practice in other parts of the Faculty, through a staff development workshop, the university, and the wider higher educational community. The project has general relevance to any disciplines considering working together. The project has also been a transformational experience for staff of two disciplines that, although in the same faculty, are based in different locations and rarely come into contact. The project has made an outstanding contribution to the professional development of colleagues, in particular early career teachers, by affording them exposure to experiential teaching with multiple students from different disciplines, in sharp contrast to more traditional didactic approaches where the teacher teaches and the student listens.

The project builds an understanding in the entrepreneurship students of one of the candidate threshold concepts in entrepreneurship set out in the preceding chapter: **Context is Resource**. Through participating in this project, the students realise that their current educational context presents the means to enable value creation through the exploitation of the opportunities that have been or are yet to be recognised. They learn that they have access to knowledge from multiple sources, including students on other programmes, not just their course lecturers. Students come to understand that all contexts not only are the source of opportunity for the creation of value but also present the means with which to bring it to fruition.

Case Study 3

A Self-Managed Learning Contract (Lauren Davies, Team Coach/Lecturer in Enterprise and Entrepreneurship, University of the West of England, UK)

A core aspect of the Team Entrepreneurship programme (another example of a Team Academy style programme) at the University of the West of England (UWE Bristol) is self-managed learning. It is argued that the absence of a manager to dictate development goals requires entrepreneurs to develop a high level of self-awareness to set their own goals and measure progress towards them. Irrespective of whether students go on to run their own venture after graduating, developing skills in self-reflection and the ability to manage one's own learning and development can be considered core enterprising competencies and thus attractive to a wide range of employers, as well as being key for those pursuing entrepreneurial career paths. The QAA, 2018 Guidance in Enterprise and Entrepreneurship Education, for instance, lists 'action and reflection' as a core entrepreneurial competency for entrepreneurs and intrapreneurs alike. It is argued that "individuals successful in enterprise or entrepreneurship often have heightened levels of self-awareness developed through reflecting upon, and continually learning from, their actions; they use failure to inform progress" (QAA, 2018, p. 24).

The ability to manage one's own learning through critical self-reflection is considered a core entrepreneurial competency. However, since working effectively in a team is a core component of the programme, students also need to develop the ability to agree their individual development goals with their team company. This mirrors the reality of professional development within organisations in which personal goals must align to organisational goals. Furthermore, by agreeing personal goals with their team members, students learn to hold each other accountable and to develop coaching skills by ensuring their peers have set appropriate goals and are making adequate progress towards them.

This approach is underpinned by the Learning Contract, a written assessment that focuses on self-reflection and the setting and monitoring of personal development goals. The Learning Contract is created by all students on the programme at the start of each academic year and reviewed at regular intervals throughout the year. The Learning Contract seeks to answer the following key questions:

- Where have I been?
- Where am I now?
- Where do I want to get to?
- How will I get there?
- How will I know when I have arrived?

Students draw on reflections of their learning prior to joining Team Entrepreneurship and/or from the past year(s) on the programme to further understand their strengths, development areas, interests and motivations and utilise these insights to establish clear goals for the year ahead. The Learning Contract is reviewed and agreed by their team members, and to achieve good marks they should reflect upon the feedback they have received from peers and how this has informed the development of their Learning Contract.

Students update their Learning Contract on a regular basis, discussing changes and updates with their Team Company and writing blog posts to summarise key updates and progress. They then submit a final Learning Contract towards the end of the academic year in which they reflect on their progress towards the goals established at the start of the year and discuss whether their goals have changed and what they have learned about themselves over the past academic year. The Learning Contract is marked by the student's Team Coach who provides feedback on the appropriateness of their goals, plans and commitments and on the effectiveness of their self-reflection and insights gained from team feedback. While the Learning Contract is marked by the Team Coach, it is the student and their peers that establish and agree their personal development goals, thus offering a high degree of personal autonomy over their learning.

This self-managed, iterative approach to learning aligns with the recommendation of Robinson, Neergaard, Tanggaard, and Krueger (2016) for a need to move away from teacher-led entrepreneurship education to more student-centred learning and a focus on lifelong learning practices. By allowing students to set their own goals and take responsibility for monitoring their progress against them, a greater sense of personal ownership is achieved amongst the cohort. This approach encapsulates the CTC of **entrepreneurial agency** discussed earlier in this chapter in which entrepreneurs are viewed as self-organising, proactive, self-regulating individuals with the ability to reflect on and learn from their current and past experiences.

In summary, the Learning Contract encapsulates the self-managed approach to learning that is core to Team Academy and utilises an iterative, self-reflective assessment to facilitate students' approach to managing their own learning. The process of reviewing and agreeing their Learning Contract with their Team Company provides students with experience of giving and receiving constructive feedback, and they are assessed on how effectively they reflect on and utilise this feedback. The Learning Contract draws together key learnings from the students' entrepreneurial practices as well as their reflections on their individual goals, strengths, development areas and motivations, thus enabling them to develop high levels of self-awareness and strengths in critical self-reflection.

Case Study 4

The Client Project (Lauren Davies, Team Coach/Lecturer in Enterprise and Entrepreneurship, University of the West of England, UK)

The Client Project is a practical, team-based assignment that runs in parallel across all three-year groups within the Team Entrepreneurship programme at the University of the West of England (UWE Bristol). Students work in teams comprised of a sub-group of members within their Team Company and sub-groups of members from Team Companies in the other year groups. This is a fairly unique example of students working collaboratively on an assessment across different levels of study, and this innovative approach helps to build a strong sense of cohort identity.

The approach also requires students to adopt specific roles, with final-year students acting as consultants to the second-year students, second-year students taking on a team leadership role and first-year students executing the project under the guidance of their second-year team leaders. This allows students to develop different roles over the course of the programme and to draw on their experiences from the previous year. The second-year students can learn a lot about effective team leadership skills from reflecting on those that were (or were not) demonstrated by their team leaders the previous year.

The Client Project exemplifies the CTC of **value is determined by the customer** as described previously in this chapter. Students are required to complete a specific project for an external client and to produce a report and presentation outlining the work they have completed and their recommendations for the future growth and development of the external organisation. The brief is outlined by the client, and they are assessed by how effectively they have met the brief with the client's feedback on their report and presentation informing their final grade for the assessment. This requires students to listen and understand the needs of their client and to ensure that they are delivering value as defined by the external organisation. Students must also consider the value that they bring to the project as defined by their other team members, since they are assessed for their individual contribution by their peers with the option to deduct or increase individual marks according to each team member's contribution.

The Client Project also provides opportunity for students to build connections with external stakeholders and to develop experience of working in a business-to-business environment. For students with smaller-scale business-to-consumer ventures or those that have experienced difficulty in establishing a new venture, the Client Project can provide a transformative learning experience. Within the National Student Survey students have described it as "the best experience that I use for interview examples" and regarded it as a "fantastic opportunity" for solving real problems for real businesses.

For some students the client project has helped to achieve the CTC of **context is opportunity**, as described previously in this chapter. Those that have maximised the opportunity of the Client Project have realised that it offers much greater value than simply achieving a good grade in the assessment, providing opportunity for meaningful connections to be established with external organisations that can lead to further opportunities. For example, a final-year student that took part in the Client Project in his second year has continued to work with his client on a consultancy basis. In their final year of study on Team Entrepreneurship students at UWE Bristol have four options for their final-year Creative Enquiry Project (equivalent to a dissertation on a more traditional programme). One of the options is a consultancy project for an external client, and this student has taken this option, continuing to create and gain value from the client relationship established during his second year.

Reflecting on his experience of working with the client, this final-year student said:

> The first time I came into contact with (the client) was January 2019, in my second year of Team Entrepreneurship at UWE whilst undertaking the mandatory marked client project. They had recently created a business that sells a small, rocket-shaped accessory that is sold internationally. They gave us a challenging six-part assignment, including a big competitor analysis task, research into their international distributors and developing some tools for them to use to contact their distributors. We managed to carry out the assignment to a high standard, got great feedback from the clients and achieved a high 2:1 for the assignment. Fast forward a year, and I am currently working with them again as part of a consultancy style dissertation.

I currently act for them as a marketing strategy consultant, carrying out an audit on their digital marketing presence and recommending changes to their digital marketing strategy.

The Client Project is also a prime example of the UWE Bristol Team Entrepreneurship approach to curriculum design which mirrors the iterative nature of entrepreneurial practice that is expected of students. The programme team utilises feedback from students to make changes to modules and assessments each year, thus building on learnings from previous years and ensuring that student feedback is acted upon where applicable. Based on feedback from last year's students regarding low levels of engagement from final-year students, the programme team has made a key change to the client project for 2019–2020. Previously, the clients were selected for the students using the contacts of the Team Coaches and wider programme team. In some instances, this resulted in final-year students having little understanding of the needs of the clients and thus limited scope to offer effective consultancy to their second-year sub-team. It also meant the students were less invested in the project overall since the clients were selected for them. To overcome these issues for 2019–2020 the programme team have introduced a new aspect to the Client Project in which the final-year students have to source the clients for their second- and first-year teams. The impact of this change is explained further by another final-year student:

> Last year the clients were given to us, and the final-year students didn't really know much about the clients so they couldn't really help us as second-year students to help the client. This shows that if you are given something and you didn't put any effort into it, you will be less motivated and will not understand how best to complete the task. However, this year we have the opportunity to get to know the clients by sourcing them ourselves, and we will be of greater support to our second-year teams as we will understand the problems the client has.

The student also discussed the skills he is developing through having to source clients directly, including the confidence and ability to speak to potential clients over the phone, adapting the message each time and learning from each failure and success.

In summary, the Client Project is an innovative example of experiential learning via a live project. The project requires a strong understanding of **value is determined by the customer**, as well as by peers. The project offers a unique opportunity for students to collaborate across the three levels of study and utilise insights gained from previous engagements in the project to inform their approach as their roles adapt at each level. The newly added component of final-year students sourcing clients adds a new dimension to the project with final-year students displaying greater levels of commitment and motivation and developing key skills in communicating effectively with external stakeholders.

References

Akatemia – working to learn. (2019). Retrieved from http://www.akatemia.org.uk/

Barradell, S. (2013). The identification of threshold concepts: A review of theoretical complexities and methodological challenges. *Higher Education, 65*(2), 265–276.

Barradell, S., & Kennedy-Jones, M. (2015). Threshold concepts, student learning and curriculum: Making connections between theory and practice. *Innovations in Education and Teaching International, 52*(5), 536–545. https://doi.org/10.1007/s10734-012-9542-3

Béchard, J.-P., & Grégoire, D. (2007). Archetypes of pedagogical innovation for entrepreneurship in higher education: Model and illustrations. In *Handbook of research in entrepreneurship education: A general perspective* (Vol. 1, pp. 261–284). Cheltenham & Northampton, MA: Edward Elgar.

Becher, T., & Trowler, P. R. (2001). *Academic tribes and territories: Intellectual enquiry and the cultures of disciplines* (2nd ed.). Buckingham: SRHE/ Open University Press.

Biggs, J. B., & Tang, C. (2011). *Teaching for quality learning at university: What the student does* (4th ed.). Maidenhead: McGraw-Hill Education (UK).

Collini, S. (2012). *What are Universities for?* London: Penguin Books Ltd..

Cousin, G. (2008). Old wine in new bottles or a new form of transactional curriculum inquiry? In R. Land, J. Meyer, & J. Smith (Eds.), *Threshold concepts within the disciplines* (pp. 261–272). Rotterdam: Sense Publishers.

Cousin, G. (2009). *Researching learning in higher education*. New York: Routledge.

Davey, T. (2016). Team learning through starting a business at Tiimiakatemia. Retrieved from University-Business Cooperation in Europe website: https://ub-cooperation.eu/index/casestudies

Davey, T. (2018, February 26). TIIMIAKATEMIA Finland (TEAM ACADEMY) – Earn A Degree By Building A Successful Business! – UIIN Blog. Retrieved from https://blog.uiin.org/2018/02/tiimiakatemia-finland-team-academy-earn-degree-building-successful-business/

Davey, T., Hannon, P., & Penaluna, A. (2016). *Entrepreneurship education and the role of universities in entrepreneurship: Introduction to the special issue*. London, England: SAGE Publications.

Donald, J. G. (2002). *Learning to think: Disciplinary perspectives. The Jossey-Bass Higher and Adult Education Series*: ERIC.

Entrepreneurship Policy Framework and Implementation Guidance. (2012). Retrieved from New York and Geneva: http://unctad.org/en/PublicationsLibrary/diaeed2012d1_en.pdf

Exley, K., & Dennick, R. (2004). *Small group teaching: Tutorials, seminars and beyond*. London: RoutledgeFalmer.

Fiet, J. O. (2001). The theoretical side of teaching entrepreneurship. *Journal of Business Venturing, 16*(1), 1–24. https://doi.org/10.1016/S0883-9026(99)00041-5

Gibb, A. (2002). In pursuit of a new 'enterprise' and 'entrepreneurship' paradigm for learning: Creative destruction, new values, new ways of doing things and new combinations of knowledge. *International Journal of Management Reviews, 4*(3), 233–269. https://doi.org/10.1111/1468-2370.00086

Halttunen, J. (Producer). (2006, 28/01/2019). Team Academy – Award winning entrepreneurship education from Jyvaskyla, Finland. Presentation given at OECD/IMHE Conference, Copenhagen, Denmark.

Hannon, P. (2005). Philosophies of enterprise and entrepreneurship education and challenges for higher education in the UK. *Entrepreneurship and Innovation, 6*(2), 105–114. https://doi.org/10.5367/0000000053966876

Hatt, L. (2020). *Using the threshold concept framework to enhance entrepreneurship curricula in higher education*. (PhD), University of Durham, Durham.

Heinonen, J., & Hytti, U. (2010). Back to basics: The role of teaching in developing the entrepreneurial university. *The International Journal of Entrepreneurship and Innovation, 11*(4), 283–292.

Helping entrepreneurs flourish: Rethinking the drivers of entrepreneurship. (2014). The Economist Intelligence Unit Retrieved from https://perspectives.eiu.com/talent-education/helping-entrepreneurs-flourish/white-paper/helping-entrepreneurs-flourish?redirect=TRUE

Hofer, A., Potter, J., Fayolle, A., Gulbrandsen, M., Hannon, P., Harding, R., … Phan, P. H. (2010). From strategy to practice in university entrepreneurship support.

Kirschner, P. A., Sweller, J., & Clark, R. E. (2006). Why minimal guidance during instruction does not work: An analysis of the failure of constructivist, discovery, problem-based, experiential, and inquiry-based teaching. *Educational Psychologist,* *41*(2), 75–86. https://doi.org/10.1207/s15326985ep4102_1

Kuhn, T. S. (1962). *The structure of scientific revolutions* (2nd ed.). Chicago, IL: University of Chicago Press.

Lackéus, M. (2015a). Entrepreneurship in education: What why, when how. Entrepreneurship360 background paper. Paris: OECD. Retrieved from https://www.oecd.org/cfe/leed/BGP_Entrepreneurship-in-Education.pdf

Lackéus, M. (2015b). *Value creation as educational philosophy. (Doctor of Engineering)*. Gothenburg, Sweden: Chalmers University of Technology.

Land, R., Cousin, G., Meyer, J. H. F., & Davies, P. (2006). Conclusion: Implications of threshold concepts for course design and evaluation. In J. Meyer & R. Land (Eds.), *Overcoming barriers to student understanding: Threshold concepts and troublesome knowledge* (pp. 195–206). London, New York: Routledge.

Leinonen, N., Partanen, J., & Palviainen, P. (2004). *The team academy: A true story of a community that learns by doing.* Jyväskylä: PS-kustannus.

Lizartza, A. (2012). Introducing Team Academy Finland. Retrieved from https://www.slideshare.net/alizartza/introducing-team-academy-finland

Matlay, H., & Carey, C. (2007). Entrepreneurship education in the UK: A longitudinal perspective. *Journal of Small Business and Enterprise Development,* *14*(2), 252–263.

McCune, V., & Hounsell, D. (2005). The development of students' ways of thinking and practising in three final-year biology courses. *Higher Education,* *49*(3), 255–289. https://doi.org/10.1007/s10734-004-6666-0

Meyer, J. H. F., & Land, R. (2003). Threshold concepts and troublesome knowledge (1) linkages to ways of thinking and practising within the disciplines. In *Improving student learning theory and practice – 10 years on* (pp. 412–424). Oxford: OCSLD.

Meyer, J. H. F., & Land, R. (2005). Threshold concepts and troublesome knowledge (2): Epistemological considerations and a conceptual framework for teaching and learning. *Higher Education,* *49*(3), 373–388. https://doi.org/10.1007/s10734-004-6779-5

Michels, N., Beresford, R., Beresford, K., & Handley, K. (2018). From fluctuation and fragility to innovation and sustainability: The role of a member network in UK enterprise education. *Industry and Higher Education, 32*(6), 438–450.

Morselli, D. (2019). The assessment of entrepreneurial education. In *The Change Laboratory for Teacher Training in Entrepreneurship Education* (pp. 17–36). London: Springer.

Neck, H. M., & Corbett, A. C. (2018). The scholarship of teaching and learning entrepreneurship. *Entrepreneurship Education and Pedagogy, 1*(1), 8–41. https://doi.org/10.1177/2515127417737286

Nielsen, S. L., Klyver, K., Evald, M. R., & Bager, T. (2012). *Entrepreneurship in theory and practice: Paradoxes in Play*. Cheltenham: Edward Elgar Publishing.

O'Connor, A. (2013). A conceptual framework for entrepreneurship education policy: Meeting government and economic purposes. *Journal of Business Venturing, 28*(4), 546–563. https://doi.org/10.1016/j.jbusvent.2012.07.003

Osmond, J., Turner, A., & Land, R. (2008). Threshold Concepts and spatial awareness in transport and product design. In R. Land, J. Meyer, & J. Smith (Eds.), *Threshold Concepts within the disciplines* (pp. 243–258). Rotterdam: Sense Publishers.

Pittaway, L., & Cope, J. (2007). Entrepreneurship education: A systematic review of the evidence. *International Small Business Journal, 25*(5), 479–510.

Pittaway, L., & Edwards, C. (2012). Assessment: Examining practice in entrepreneurship education. *Education + Training, 54*, 778–800.

QAA. (2012). *Enterprise and Entrepreneurship Education. Guidance for UK Higher Education Providers*. Retrieved from http://www.qaa.ac.uk/docs/qaas/enhancement-and-development/enterprise-and-entrepreneurship-education-2018.pdf?sfvrsn=15f1f981_8

QAA. (2018). *Enterprise and Entrepreneurship Education: Guidance for UK Higher Education Providers*. Retrieved from https://www.qaa.ac.uk/docs/qaas/enhancement-and-development/enterprise-and-entrpreneurship-education-2018.pdf?sfvrsn=15f1f981_8

Robinson, S., Neergaard, H., Tanggaard, L., & Krueger, N. F. (2016). New horizons in entrepreneurship education: From teacher-led to student-centered learning. *Education + Training, 58*(7/8), 661–683.

Rothblatt, S. (2006). *The modern university and its discontents: The fate of Newman's legacies in Britain and America*. Cambridge: Cambridge University Press.

Ruuska, J., & Krawczyk, P. (2013). *Team academy as learning living lab.* Paper presented at the European Phenomena of Entrepreneurship Education and Development. University Industry Conference, Amsterdam.

Shanahan, M., Foster, G., & Meyer, J. H. F. (2008). Associations among prior acquisition of Threshold Concepts, learning dimensions, and examination performance in first year economics. In R. Land, J. H. F. Meyer, & J. Smith (Eds.), *Threshold Concepts within the disciplines* (pp. 155–172). Rotterdam: Sense Publishers.

Team Academy Worldwide. (n.d.). Retrieved from www.akatemia.org.uk/what-is-team-academy/team-academy-worldwide/

Timmermans, J. A., & Meyer, J. H. F. (2017). A framework for working with university teachers to create and embed 'Integrated Threshold Concept Knowledge' (ITCK) in their practice. *International Journal for Academic Development, 20,* 1–15. https://doi.org/10.1080/1360144X.2017.1388241

Tosey, P., Dhaliwal, S., & Hassinen, J. (2015). The finnish team academy model: Implications for management education. *Management Learning, 46*(2), 175–194. https://doi.org/10.1177/1350507613498334

Zander, C., Boustedt, J., Eckerdal, A., McCartney, R., Moström, J. E., Ratcliffe, M., & Sanders, K. (2008). Threshold concepts in computer science: A multi-national empirical investigation. In *Threshold concepts within the disciplines* (pp. 105–118). Leiden: Brill Sense.

11

The Journey of Higher Degree Apprenticeships

Claire Hughes and Gillian Saieva

Introduction

Real world learning (RWL) is becoming a vital component for curriculum enhancement, due to the realisation that "real-world rigour is required to increase the adaptability of higher education graduates in a fast-changing business environment" (Woodside, 2018, p. 2). This chapter will explore how RWL pedagogies are at the centre of the Higher and Degree Apprenticeships (HDAs) outlining the history and rationale for the introduction of HDAs and the benefits for all stakeholders undertaking HDAs. The added value that RWL brings to HDAs highlights the career and personal gains that this pedagogy brings to both apprentice and organisations alike. In addition, discussion and case studies will

Case studies: Lisa Rowe, University in the North of England, Claire Hughes and Gillian Saieva

C. Hughes (✉) • G. Saieva
Solent University, Southampton, UK
e-mail: claire.hughes@solent.ac.uk

© The Author(s) 2021
D. A. Morley, M. G. Jamil (eds.), *Applied Pedagogies for Higher Education*,
https://doi.org/10.1007/978-3-030-46951-1_11

identify the journey map for the design, development and implementation of this type of pedagogy, along with discussion around the challenges.

To set the scene, it should be remembered that the very essence of building and developing higher-level skills was a vital component of HDAs, which neatly dovetails into RWL pedagogies. To quality assure the HDAs, each apprenticeship had a set standard, developed across the trailblazer group, made up of training providers, employers and professional bodies. In addition, the Quality Assurance Agency introduced apprenticeship characteristics:

> Apprenticeships incorporating higher education are constituted as first and foremost a job which requires work-integrated learning ... the workplace becomes a site for the development and generation of knowledge, understanding, skills and professional behaviours rather than just a site for their application. (QAA, 2019)

The definition means that there is a direction and set of requirements for curriculum design, which gives a direction to training providers to enable adherence and illustration of learning gain for each individual and organisation. However, these requirements do underline the need for innovation into the curriculum design, delivery and partnership working with the employer to ensure all these requirements were met.

It is acknowledged that this chapter does not seek to provide a full-range solution, but a reflection on the lessons learnt so far and seeks to cover some of the main areas for consideration. To assist this a concept map was developed to frame the insights for this chapter and can be seen in full in Fig. 11.1.

What Are Higher Degree Apprenticeships?

The government's role to ensure the UK is not caught in a 'low skills equilibrium' has long held a view that vocational training and apprenticeship policies are key to moving production up the value-added chain, enhancing productivity and economic growth across a wider range of sectors (Wilson et al., 2003).

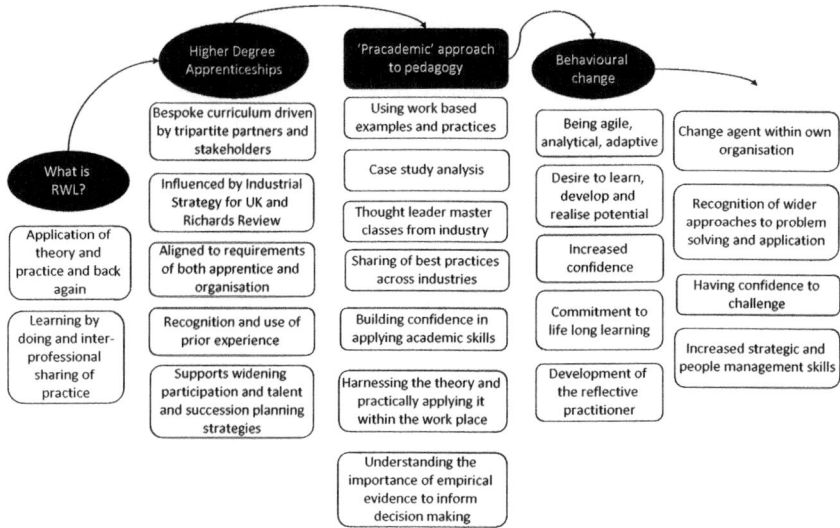

Fig. 11.1 Concept map from the authors

Higher level and degree apprenticeships have brought together different cultures and methods of designing, delivering and assessing knowledge, skills and behaviours, funding learners and learning providers, data reporting, quality management and its review or inspection. (Felce, 2019)

HDAs are a recent addition to the learning and development circuit of apprenticeships, and while this chapter seeks to give an understanding of their reason for being, it is important to know their origins. Apprenticeships in England have had a long history, from the first national apprenticeship system of training in 1563 with the medieval craft guilds, to the professions and newer industries of engineering, shipbuilding, plumbing and electrical work during the 1900s (House of Commons Library: Mirza-Davies, 2015). The last three decades have seen the highest rate of reform with schemes such as 'Modern Apprentices' announced in 1993, 'Advanced Apprenticeships' in 2004 and after the general election of 2010, 'Higher Apprenticeships' followed (House of Commons Library: Mirza-Davies, 2015). This was further shaped by new minimum standards introduced in 2012, developed by Trailblazer groups, consisting of employers, professional bodies and training providers to develop apprenticeship standards against professions. In 2017 the apprenticeship levy was introduced, where organisations with an annual salary bill of more than £3 million incurred a levy payable at 0.5% directly into a sub-HMRC account; this could then be claimed back by organisations for drawdown of the monies to training providers as payment for apprenticeships (ESFA, 2019). This also allowed non-levy payers to be supported against these unclaimed funds with incentives to pay only 5% of the training cost, with the balance drawn from the unspent pot of money held by the government. The policy drivers for the introduction of the apprenticeship levy are still considered by many to fund young people into employment; however, as argued by Anderson (2019), productivity is the overarching reason. This change further saw the development of HDAs in 2016 and the university sector entering the apprenticeships market. Higher apprenticeships can span from level 4 to level 7, while Degree apprenticeships are at level 6–7 to include bachelors and masters degree programmes.

This was a significant new policy direction for the UK, and much of this recent change was a result of the government in 2012 launching the Richard Review of Apprenticeships to answer questions about their future direction and understand further their purpose for employers, individuals and their impact on the economy (HM Government, 2012). They were interested in the quality of the current provision and what 'good' might look like at a time when the focus was towards economic recovery, with an anticipation of growth; this presented key questions around how best to invest towards a knowledge economy, changing demands against technology, scientific knowledge and career changes, particularly at the latter stages of individuals' careers and multi-age workforces. It was also anticipated that a call for investment in new and higher-level skills would put an increased premium on knowledge work as a direct result of the sustained rise of international markets such as China and India who were competing in the upstream part of the value chain and contributing to the innovation landscape (Lund et al., 2019). Predications around this shift towards knowledge-intensive activities, with a focus on cognitive and non-cognitive skills, identified that a re-balancing of skills needed to take place, where people needed to be able to innovate, learn and develop against a broader range of skills (Joynes et al., 2019). There has been a renewed focus for apprenticeships to deliver on design, commercial and communications skills and not solely technical skills as previously, leading to the need for a real world approach to learning and teaching.

The Richard Review (HM Government, 2012) received much scrutiny; however, its alignment to the government's approach at the time of launch evoked the below statement from the then Business Secretary—Vince Cable (2012):

> The Richard Review echoes the Government's current thinking on putting employers in the driving seat of our apprenticeship programme. This will be vital to ensure the skills of our workforce fit with employer needs ... His recommendations will help us to build on the current successes of our apprenticeships programme and tailor a programme which is sustainable, high-quality and meets the changing needs of our economy in the decades to come.

The essence of upskilling the UK was also evidenced in the Industrial Strategy which blueprinted the vision of Theresa May's Conservative Government, launched in 2016 after the EU Referendum, which aligned to industries of the future and sought to set out to improve the lives of people and the pathway to productivity for the UK (HM Government, 2017). With a focus on the 'Grand Challenges' this aligned to the changing needs of the economy with a firm vision to put the UK at the forefront of tackling major global changes which will transform the future, such as artificial intelligence, the ageing society, clean growth and future of mobility (HM Government, 2017). With these challenges in mind, HDAs sought to deliver against key areas of knowledge and skills development, to support both young and existing employees retain highly skilled jobs in an ever-changing global economy through both theoretical and RWL pedagogic practices.

RWL is at the core of the HDAs, along with social mobility and widening participation, as it allows study towards a qualification not always initially accessible to a greater range of apprentices. It could be suggested that this new-found confidence is because it is based around work and that financial constraints of study are relieved as the employer is the sponsor (Parrett, 2018). There has been much discussion across this area as to who and what level should be accessing the funding to be able to apply for an HDA (UVAC, 2019); however, it could be argued that by the very nature of the ethos and underpinning rationale for introducing the HDAs, these should remain open to all, especially as the UK Industrial Strategy clearly outlines that upskilling and filling in skills gaps is still an imperative focus:

> Higher education plays a significant role in bringing benefits for the UK economy, particularly in the provision of higher-level skills that are needed by employers both nationally and within local areas. (HM Government, 2017)

HDAs may also enable organisations to attract and retain potentially untapped talent and perhaps reduce the growing trend of employers struggling to fill posts (CIPD, 2019); which will be ever important in these current complex economic, political and social landscapes.

In addition to the 'upskilling' that is observed, there are also a range of benefits for social change too. Many employers have embraced HDAs as an opportunity to reflect diversity and widening participation. An example of the potential impact is evident in the work between the police service in Nottinghamshire with the University of Derby, where they have claimed HDAs have resulted in a 20% increase in female recruits, a 9% increase in recruitment from Black, Asian and minority ethnic (BAME) groups and overall 50% of recruits being the first in their family to enter Higher Education (UUK, 2019). The case study below highlights further the success that HDAs are having in driving change and opportunity, including social mobility, gender equality and closing the skills gap in leadership.

Case Study 1

HDAs are drivers for social change and opportunity (Lisa Rowe, Director of Business Engagement and Partnerships, University of Chester Business School, UK)

The Centre for Work Related Studies (CWRS) at University of Chester launched the Chartered Manager Degree Apprenticeship (CMDA) in Autumn 2016, followed by the Senior Leaders Master's Degree Apprenticeship (SLMDA) in Spring 2018. The CMDA comprises a BA (Hons) Business Management and Leadership, operating with 6 cohorts and 91 apprentices. The SLMDA facilitates two pathways—the MA/MSc Business and Management for Senior Leaders or the Master of Business Administration, currently comprising 8 cohorts and 164 apprentices. Data to inform this case study has been collected from a sample of these apprentices, their employers and academic tutors as part of a doctoral thesis. The research took place through unstructured and semistructured interviews and questionnaires and was followed by systematic analysis to identify themes and patterns in the data. The profile of apprentices is diverse and indicates a distinct shift at undergraduate in terms of both gender and age, complementing both the full-time provision and CWRS's traditional suite of work-based learning programmes (Table 11.1). The data also suggest that management degree apprenticeships may be an effective intervention to improve gender equality in senior roles, with a significant majority of female management apprentices.

As Wilton (2018) points out, 47% of UK Chartered Manager Degree Apprentices are from some of the UK's most economically deprived regions; therefore, the benefits of increased social mobility are becoming apparent. Yet, the latent effects of social-economic status in formative years is also an important consideration, evidenced by stories of low income and limited parental aspirations as early barriers to HE: "We were

Table 11.1 Profile of degree and master's level apprentices at University of Chester

Programme	Enrolments	Male	Female	Average age	Consultancy projects
CMDA	91	21 (23%)	70 (77%)	32	273
SLMDA	164	54 (33%)	110 (67%)	40	164
Combined	255	75	180	36	437

all (six siblings) made to work from when we were thirteen so we didn't have those opportunities" (Business Impact Manager, NHS). The majority of CMDA respondents have previously been unable to access HE because of their background, whereas SLMDA respondents have been restricted by their individual financial and family responsibilities, illustrated by the comment: "I have two children under the age of three and both my wife and I work full time, so we don't receive supported childcare yet. Coupled with the fact I am still paying off my undergraduate debt meant I couldn't justify the costs of an MA or MBA" (Facilities Manager, NHS).

As such, HLAs provide an overwhelming opportunity for mid-career advancement at work. Educational aspirations and goal setting for career progression are widely evident, but whilst mature apprentices might appear to have significant workplace experience at programme entry, it is apparent that this does not necessarily translate to the vital high-level leadership and management skills, behaviours and competencies, valued as essential components of career development by both employers and employees. Data from a number of employer interviews confirm the difficulty in recruiting individuals equipped with these skills, specifically 'capable', 'motivated', 'person-centred leaders' who can 'influence', 'problem-solve' and 'create impact'.

Here, there is increasing evidence that both programmes can develop critical leadership skills to meet industry demand:

> Having a masters will provide the level of qualifications expected for this type of role. This course has given me insight into a broad range of tools and techniques that have helped me develop my leadership style, but also give me skills in financial management, research and managing organisational change, which are key aspects to the roles I will be looking to in the future. (HR Manager, Manufacturing)

This endorsement of leadership development through work-based learning is further evidenced by the growing numbers of apprentices who have already received significant promotions whilst on-programme, in itself providing motivation to other apprentices within the organisation and cohort: "Being an NHS Manager with a clinical background, I realised I would benefit from completing a management course to gain business knowledge and skills. I have been able to quickly apply many of the theories I have learnt to my job role. During a tender presentation to commissioners I used critical success factors to demonstrate our unique selling points in comparison to private provider competitors. In addition, I have utilised the Marketing module in preparation for writing the Trust bid to continue to deliver the service. These are just a couple of many examples of how I have put what I have learnt into practice to gain promotion" (Director, NHS).

There is also extensive evidence of enhanced engagement and workplace performance from undertaking these courses; "He's just stepped up to the mark, he's grown overnight" (Team Supervisor, Manufacturing); "I've not seen that that motivation in her and I think this coursework has given her the stamina to be able to do that" (Team Leader, PR & Marketing Agency); "In terms of achievements in this last 6 to 8 months she's probably already advanced beyond what some people achieve in most of their careers" (Office Administrator, Engineering Sector).

Indeed, the success of the two programmes has brought numerous other tangible benefits. The department's close links with employers enable the academic team to maintain their own practitioner knowledge and more effectively support individuals, organisations and the wider local economy with critical skills development needs. The current cohorts alone will deliver more than 400 individually negotiated consultancy projects, creating a wealth of research and knowledge transfer opportunities, significant leadership skills development outcomes and unprecedented talent sourcing and retention for the region.

The Benefits for the Apprentice, Employer and Training Providers of Higher Degree Apprenticeships

Having reviewed the macro benefits of apprenticeships, the next section seeks to explain in greater detail the perceived benefits across all three parties: apprentice, employer and training provider. The essence of the tripartite relationship would be key to the success of this approach with all parties responsible for the outcome.

Key to the apprenticeship approach is the employer being at the heart of the process. Unlike traditional education learning, HDAs are driven by employer demand in the first instance; therefore, the issue around employability and designing courses to fit with what industry demands is part of the development process. The formerly known Institute for Apprenticeships was created in 2016, now known as The Institute for Apprenticeships and Technical Education (IfATE), to oversee the development, approval and publication of apprenticeship standards and assessment plans and latterly the occupational maps for T levels and apprenticeships. They work with the Trailblazer groups and have a further External Quality Assurance role and are accountable for the quality of apprenticeships. The Department of Education (DfE) hold accountability for the England Apprenticeship Programme, while the Education and Skills Funding Agency (ESFA) is responsible for policy and funding of apprenticeships and ensuring effective delivery of programmes across training providers. All training providers must be on the Register of Approved Training Providers (RoATP) in order to be able to engage with apprenticeships.

The Future of Degree Apprenticeships Report (Universities UK, 2019) provides a summary of the overarching key benefits that HDAs deliver across the three parties:

- Apprentices are positive about the opportunities that degree apprenticeships provide for gaining a degree, and often a professional qualification as well, while they are learning and earning in the workplace.
- Employers are positive about the contribution apprentices make to their organisations and the opportunity it gives to address key skills shortages, enhance opportunities for their own employees and widen the talent pool of their recruits.
- Universities are positive about the stronger relationships they have been able to build with employers, the enhanced opportunities for success and progression they can provide for their apprentices, and the innovation they have promoted in learning and teaching.

In order to deliver against the 'knowledge-led economy' (HM Government, 2017) and support higher economic growth with higher-level skills development, HDAs provide the opportunity for universities and education providers to get closer to employers to support talent development within organisations by upskilling existing and new staff and further address talent shortages, particularly in public services, which incorporates RWL.

To firstly consider the perceived benefits for the apprentice, students of any age can now consider a funded route to higher education and skills development. The dilemma for the school leaver to go to university with the assumed debt, or to try and find a job, has the additional option to be employed directly with an organisation that has engaged with the upskilling benefits of using the apprenticeship route for talent development. This provides the apprentice with both job security and career prospects, alongside the benefits of RWL in learning on the job, focused mentoring from their line manager and experiencing higher education and professional pedagogy, such as reflective practice to support life-long learning. The 'earn while you learn' caption is of key attraction to both the potential apprentice and parents. However, research suggests a 'second-class' stigma is still held towards apprenticeships and HDAs, when compared with conventional university degrees, with the ongoing perception that HDAs require fewer academic skills (Universities UK, 2019).

While more needs to be done to showcase the impact and quality of apprenticeships to date, the process to gain an HDA contains additional rigour over and above a traditional degree, and in non-integrated apprenticeship degree cases, to include an end point assessment (EPA), carried out by an external organisation (EPAO). This assesses the apprentice's knowledge, skills and behaviours against the apprenticeship standard and requires reflection against key skills, knowledge and behaviour learning areas. This often includes a work-based learning project and viva. The apprentice emerges from the process having evidenced a wide range of RWL attributes and subsequently is more employable moving forwards due to the nature of the applied real world learning that has taken place throughout their programme of learning as an apprentice. These 'upskilling' benefits are then observed not just by the individual but within the organisation too.

The Synergies Between HDAs and RWL Pedagogy

For any HDA there is a requirement to prove that learning gain has taken place over and above skills that the apprentice had already, prior to starting; funding relies on this (ESFA, 2019). Initially, it can be difficult to understand how this may happen, given the large number of experienced senior managers undertaking HDAs, as opposed to the 16–21-year-old grouping who normally start from a lower-level skill base, where returns may be more easily observed. To overcome this a skills mapping and analysis system can be introduced, which illustrates that learning gain is actually very tangible and impactful, as highlighted by the feedback from experienced professional apprentices: "I now have knowledge and a pool of resources to draw down upon and fills that previous skills gaps" and "I like that the course gives extra value in the networking opportunities and identifying how organisations approach different challenges."

Given that the apprentices are required by the apprenticeship standard to not only learn the academic knowledge, but to evidence use of it within the workplace, they quickly become reflective practitioners to identify how this has developed their skills across their job roles; this gives RWL the perfect platform. Therefore, it could be suggested that the very essence of HDAs marrying the workplace and academia, making it practically academic, is why the RWL pedagogy is a natural mode of delivering the provision.

Challenges for Curriculum Design, Delivery and Partnership Working

Whilst the HDAs new starters are still missing the high targets that the government set, there are still a large number of apprentices starting programmes, with more having been at the mature and post-graduate level than perhaps was initially anticipated (Moules, 2019). With most training providers working with multiple partners, across both open and closed cohorts, design can be complex in order to meet the requirements of illustrating learning gain across the different aims of multiple partners, all of which have different development objectives. Therefore, it is important to cover all the design bases and work in partnership together on this (QAA, 2019). The very first steps should be to design and develop the course against the standard with a careful match to ensure that both the theory and RWL can be incorporated into each unit. Once this mapping and curriculum design has taken place flexibility also needs to be developed, to meet the wide range of individual and organisational experience, to ensure they build the core topic knowledge, whilst then being able to apply this to their own job role and institutions. This can be achieved from the outset in the tripartite relationship building where understanding of what development needs to take place from an individual point of view can then lead to holistic enhancement of the wider team and organisational development too. This was evidenced in the feedback received from apprentices: "It is also helping the wider team as she is able to use her knowledge and bring in practices that perhaps weren't done, and by sharing this across the team it widens the knowledge", and "He came back and explained what he had done and is now implementing this approach to the Board of Directors for our latest project."

The curricula can be designed to cover as many bases as possible at the design and development stages, without having prior knowledge of the specific requirements and then further developed after discussion across the tripartite partnership. Universities may also be in the position of co-designing a course with a specific employer, which brings both benefits in that the curriculum can be tailored specifically to their combined needs, but can also lead to challenges too. Case study 2 gives an example of how the curriculum can have a bespoke design when solely working with one large employer. This also outlines the benefits of the sole partnership, allowing for experts to co-deliver some of the knowledge input with a strong real world learning output. However, whilst this reduces some challenges, the case study also outlines some of the observed difficulties of working with a single organisation and reflects on advice for peers on how to proceed on a similar journey, including cross stakeholder working.

The year 2017 was the start of our Chartered Manager Degree Apprenticeship (CMDA) journey. A feasibility study was followed by submission of a successful business case and finally acceptance of the programme by the University Programme Approval Group. The year 2018 saw us with a viable programme offering and seeking students.

Conversations with a local public sector organisation led to our engaging with and being successful in a tendering process. We had secured a large employer with a significant local presence who believed they would be sending at least 60 students per year over the next 5 years to our CMDA programme. This exceeded our initial expectations, and focus shifted away from engaging with new employers.

Working with one employer has obvious advantages. Discussions around contracts were more straightforward and the admissions process (significantly different to typical university admissions) was facilitated by receiving documentation through just one channel. Managing the tripartite meetings was also significantly easier, with colleagues able to condense student/mentor appointments into one day cutting down on administration and travel time.

When it came to planning and delivering the teaching, tutors were able to design sessions specific to the particular workplace, a real advantage for such a practical course. Indeed, the organisation provided guest speakers who were able to contextualise some of the learning for the accounting and Human Resource Managment (HRM) modules. Student feedback on this was extremely positive. They commented, both informally and through tutorials, how they felt they were able to apply the learning to the workplace almost from the start. Indeed, to meet the CMDA standards it was important that students were able to see how the knowledge could be applied in the workplace. The knowledge delivery in the classroom was supported by discussions around how this could support the development of the learner and the success of the organisation. Assessments required students to take this new knowledge into the workplace, reflecting on how effectively management thinking could be applied in the real world.

However, despite the advantages of working with one large employer, care needs to be taken. It soon became apparent that the numbers of students joining the course would be significantly lower than projected. The number was lower again for the next cohort a year later. Whilst we were assured this was in no way related to the quality of the programme, this was little consolation. Teaching staff had been recruited in anticipation of the projected students, and the actual numbers had very real implications for the sustainability of the programme. The phrase 'all our eggs in one basket' was all too apt.

Whilst the confirmation of the contract was tremendous news, the employer requested a course start date 6 weeks hence. The programme had been designed; however, the short lead in time presented us with resourcing issues. Keen to establish a good rapport with the employer, we agreed a start date in 10 weeks, a real challenge.

The administrative procedures proved to be a major hurdle to clear. Highly experienced, our admissions team were used to processing courses with traditional 2 × 11-week semesters. Assessment deadlines, re-sit periods and exam boards were all scheduled and resourced in line with the established academic year. The CMDA proved to be something of a 'culture shock' and required some sensitive negotiations between two organisations with long-established procedures. However, there was again an advantage to having only one employer. Planning meetings included administrative staff from both sides, something which may not have been practical with a dozen smaller employers. This helped to develop a positive working relationship from the outset.

The employer invited us to showcase our offering at a number of in-house apprenticeship recruitment events. These were to encourage applications for both the Level 6 CMDA and the Level 3 and Level 5 programmes which were being delivered by the employer. Interest was strong, but the majority of prospective applicants were in roles more suited to levels 3 and 5, depleting the potential Level 6 numbers.

As numbers for the second CMDA intake were again lower than hoped, the employer agreed that the next cohort could be opened up to allow applications from other sectors and employers. Maintaining a course with just one employer had become unsustainable.

Lessons learned:

In such a competitive environment, securing a contract with a large employer is a real bonus. However, these are some of the lessons we have taken away from our experience:

1. Clarify the numbers: It is worthwhile establishing how the employer has arrived at their projections, and the impact of factors such as alternative training provision which may divert potential students. This may seem like common sense, however, when there is only one employer this is so very important.
2. Keep an eye on the market: Whilst the programme numbers are increasing with more employers joining, the concerns could have been addressed sooner if conversations and plans had been made earlier.
3. Level of understanding of the qualification/process: Do not assume that the employer has a full understanding of how things work. Misunderstandings/misconceptions can have quite significant impacts.
4. Student understanding and awareness of the commitment: Get involved in the recruitment and internal induction processes. It is possible that the students are unaware of what is involved, having quickly jumped at the chance of a free course/CPD with limited information.
5. Staff involvement: There were real advantages gained by including support staff in conversations with the employer. This helped to gain internal support for this new programme as well as speeding up the planning process.

Putting RWL holistically at the core of an HDA curriculum enables a strong pedagogic approach, but it needs more than just pedagogic drivers to ensure success. It is vital to create strong tripartite relationships and solutions between all parties: training provider, employer and apprentice as all have significant roles to play to ensure success (UVAC, 2016).

The employer and apprentice are the key players in really identifying where these learning gains are required to create the most developmental impact. This also enables identification of the most appropriate HDA that will bring the most learning gain. At the application stage, a skills scan of the apprentice's current and future skills can be reviewed with other application documents, such as a personal reflective statement, to outline the apprentice's commitment and fit to professional development with their long-term individual and organisational strategic objectives.

The training provider then starts the development of the apprentice and work-based mentor in building knowledge of the HDA standard and evidence collection. This can take place in many forms, but an initial in-depth interview can be useful here. The starting point for this can be discussing the skills scan and then objective setting for outputs that the individual and organisation are ideally requiring. In this way the individual and organisational drivers are incorporated even at this initial stage leading the way for a work-based development plan for the learning gain, set in the ethos of RWL, to be identified even before starting the HDA. This is still based on generic course learning outcomes but by working in this tripartite partnership, bespoke design can be incorporated. In addition, this also acts as a valuable relationship builder between the tripartite parties and aids an early understanding for the training provider of any extra support or specific organisational learning outcomes that the employer ideally requires. These specific requirements can then be mapped and supported, for example, case studies, mentor matching, network building, guest speakers and workshops.

It has been outlined that developing the correct curriculum, working closely in the tripartite relationship and ensuring an RWL learning and teaching experience are key elements to drive success, yet another element of pastoral support is vital too. Case study 3 outlines the experiences to date around delivering apprenticeship provision to groups of apprentices who are working whilst studying. Support needs to be embedded to ensure that both the academic and work-based learning outcomes can be achieved, whilst maintaining the apprentices' well-being.

Case Study 3

Understanding the apprentices' health and well-being challenges within the learning experience across the Solent University CMDA, SLMDA and Operations and Departmental Manager apprenticeship programmes (Claire Hughes, Apprenticeship Programme Manager and Course Leader - Business and Gillian Saieva, Head of Subject, Business, Finance and Accountancy, Solent University, UK)

Undertaking an HDA, whilst working a significant job position, alongside other personal commitments, can be challenging for students. Added to this, apprentices are normally experienced and successful in their job roles, so are used to being experts within their knowledge and/or comfort zones, yet find themselves entering into an HDA, which can push them outside of those zones. The HDA is academically demanding, given they may have limited experience of higher education, whilst having to continue working significant jobs and managing other personal commitments, this can stretch apprentices' well-being and lead to severe doubts of confidence about whether they should or can study at this level. This is not a new phenomenon (Norman & Hyland, 2003) and is still prevalent. The most confident of person may need to be brought back on track, and this brings many challenges both for pedagogic and pastoral practices. To ensure that the apprentice is supported a number of innovations can be applied, which includes having a personal professional development unit as a core part of the curriculum, which supports their own personal journey in self-awareness, their drivers, managing teams, their leadership styles and their future goals. Giving apprentices time to reflect in this way is a luxury not often taken within the traditional work-based setting. It heightens self-awareness and encourages openness and is assisted by the tripartite relationship that is designed to support this development. This also enables permission for apprentices to openly discuss their strengths and identify a plan for their future personal and career development. This self-awareness improves working and personal professional development practices in the workplace alongside increasing confidence and resilience.

The feedback from both apprentices and employers below illustrates the power that correctly designed support can bring. When asked about how the HDA had benefitted them, apprentices fed back 'life-changing' and 'changed them as a manager, for the better'. The same question for employers brought up the themes that the apprentices had more confidence and positive changes were observed within their behaviours and the apprentice's scope to see the 'bigger strategic' picture. Assigning a mentor can also be beneficial especially when an apprentice is having doubts or struggling to juggle all their commitments and can be a powerful tripartite relationship builder as exemplified below:

> a massive thank you to you for all your help support and guidance. You have boosted my confidence when needed and was much appreciated.
> Thank you for all your support and encouragement, it would not have been possible to complete and achieve my qualification without this.

Assisted by an established tripartite relationship, it is important to keep the employer aware of students' challenges and become the intermediary when necessary. This is valued by all parties, especially when a difficult conversation is needed about the apprentice's well-being or lack of achievements, alongside the inevitable conversations about the 20% off-the-job training elements where issues from either side are reported.

In addition to other support, the apprenticeship progress reviews are vital. By going out to the workplace to build relationships with employers and apprentices, this allows complex or difficult situations to be solution driven and is a powerful way to remind all parties just how much RWL in work and learning can be achieved. All of this combined, works to build up not only confidence of the apprentice and manager in their apprentice, but the confidence to learn and take this knowledge back into the workplace and apply it for the benefit of the teams and organisation: "it's professionalised the work that I do" and "it is that they are getting credited for doing their jobs professionally and from a cultural prospective I think it is showing that there is a buy in to staff development and career progression…it's a long-term investment."

It should be impressed upon both the apprentice and organisation that studying for an HDA is not the easiest route to take due to all the challenges outlined above; it does mean that apprentices have to draw on their resilience and time management skills. Therefore, it is vital to ensure that strong pastoral processes are in place to ensure the apprentices' well-being and to convey any concerns with the organisation, as this is part of the tripartite relationship role and responsibilities.

The Challenges for External Organisations in Supporting Real World Learning for HDAs

When creating an RWL learning pedagogy there is the need for the internal organisational infrastructure to be carefully constructed. This comes with the discussions about the onboarding and during the induction processes; both the apprentice and the employer need to be clear about the requirements as the apprentice needs to be able to work within the scope of the standard and draw the evidence down from their own working practices. For example, the finance role in many organisations is often devolved from individual job roles; this has created challenges in collecting this evidence base and solutions having to be identified between the tri-partite parties.

These are the areas that when undertaking the skills scan need to be agreed at an early stage, with regular review points, so as to avoid setting an apprentice up to fail. Work-based mentors and line managers need to be just as supported in what the standard requires, as it is imperative the line manager buys-into and gives full support. Without either of these it would limit the positive RWL impact across the whole team and would be detrimental to the learning gain of the apprentice and potentially lead to failure to meet the End Point Assessment requirements for the apprenticeship.

A further infrastructure challenge that has been observed is how the employer approaches the minimum of 20% off the job training element. All parties normally understand the need to give this time and sign learning agreements which outline how this will be delivered upon. In some cases, organisations don't pro-actively acknowledge or plan for the apprentice's need to be able to delegate some responsibilities, to allow for the 20% time. This can lead to the apprentice's well-being challenged by having 20% less time to do the 'day job'. Some organisations may face challenges in the resource re-allocation that is required and the messaging here is vital from the outset. Although short-term operational issues may ensue, the apprentice's learning gain has the potential to being in an excellent return in both the short and longer term. Many employers have fed back that they were able to delegate their own work to their apprentice team member due to their expanding knowledge and confidence, which then left them more time for the top-line strategy work:

> [talking about benefits of knowledge built up]…to support my manager, I have taken some of the higher-level work load from her and taking it and running with it and just being more confident to get on with it.

The Challenges of Implementation of HDAs Within Higher Education

In higher education non-standard courses have faced difficulties aligning to the infrastructures of traditional course management (JISC, 2013) when, for example, IT systems are not aligned to a non-standard format, assessment regulations need amendments and courses do not fit the traditional year for academic exam boards. There is a need for more flexibility in how higher education is taught to increase access (Higher Education Commission, 2017), especially as HDAs will continue to grow in popularity and these 'non-standard' courses increasingly become 'the norm'. It is important to recognise these challenges and to have processes in place through careful planning and work groups made up from the full range of stakeholders to align these practices. Best practices have seen cross-university working groups set up, with all the key academic and professional service stakeholders meeting regularly to identify and resolve working practices challenges to create a streamlined and uniformed approach to the internal management of the HDAs, along with partnership contract meetings where challenges and best practice are discussed.

Conclusion

Those working in the area of higher degree apprenticeships already know how life changing these courses can be for apprentices, not only in their working and leaderships practices, or in their outputs that benefit their teams and organisations, but to their personal development and increase in confidence too. HDAs reflect the essence of real world learning that develops students for employability and learning, and, in this instance, is done very explicitly through the immediate course and pedagogy itself.

The HDAs provide a valuable contribution to management and leadership skills across UK organisations, which could contribute to the UK productivity issues "management skills could account for a quarter of the productivity gap between the UK and the US" (HM Government, 2017). Given those challenges, it is vital that RWL stays as the core narrative of the HDAs as without, the individual and organisational learning gains would just be a download of topic knowledge, defeating the very reason that the HDAs were introduced.

The journey when developing, implementing and delivering HDAs can at times be a hard and winding one, but as with every long journey, the satisfaction at the end of completing it depletes the painful parts of the journey. HDAs are at the cutting edge of changing practice in higher education, and by using careful mapping, sharing best practice, cross-university working and learning to work in tripartite partnerships, the learning journey for all parties can be successful. HDA complexity within traditional higher education supports the need for more research to better understand how to make an excellent apprenticeship experience for all.

References

Anderson, A., 2019. Keynote: Exploring the Future Challenges and Priorities of Higher and Degree Apprenticeships Provision, UVAC Higher Apprenticeships Conference

Commons Library: UK Parliament: Mirza-Davies, J. (2015). *A short history of apprenticeships in England: From medieval craft guilds to the twenty-first century.* Retrieved from https://commonslibrary.parliament.uk/economy-business/work-incomes/a-short-history-of-apprenticeships-in-england-from-medieval-craft-guilds-to-the-twenty-first-century/

CIPD 2019 Labour Market outlook view from employers Autun. (2019). Accessed 4 January 2020. Available: https://www.cipd.co.uk/Images/labour-market-outlook-autumn-2019_tcm18-67336.pdf

Education and Skills Funding Agency. (2019). *Apprenticeship funding rules for main providers.* Retrieved from https://assets.publishing.service.gov.uk/government/uploads/system/uploads/attachment_data/file/821581/1920_Provider_Rules_Version_1.0_FINAL.pdf

Felce, A. (2019). Managing the quality of higher education in apprenticeships. Higher Education, Skills and Work-Based Learning. 9.10.1108/HESWBL-10-2018-0106.

Higher Education Commission. (2017). *One size won't fit all.* Retrieved from https://www.policyconnect.org.uk/sites/site_pc/files/report/1005/fieldreportdownload/hec-web.pdf

HM Government. (2012). The Richard review of apprenticeships. Retrieved from https://www.gov.uk/government/news/the-richard-review-of-apprenticeships

HM Government. (2017). *Industrial strategy building a Britain fit for the future.* Retrieved from https://assets.publishing.service.gov.uk/government/uploads/system/uploads/attachment_data/file/730048/industrial-strategy-white-paper-web-ready-a4-version.pdf

Joynes, C., Rossignoli, S., & Fenyiwa Amonoo-Kuofi, E. (2019). *21st Century Skills: Evidence of issues in definition, demand and delivery for development contexts (K4D Helpdesk Report).* Brighton, UK: Institute of Development Studies.

JISC. (2013). *Non standard courses.* Retrieved from https://www.jisc.ac.uk/guides/managing-course-information/non-standard-courses

Lund, S., Manyika, J., Woetzel, J., Bughin, J., Krishnan, M., Seong, J., & Muir, M. (2019). *Globalisation in transition: The future of trade and value chains.* McKinsey Global Institute. Retrieved from https://www.mckinsey.com/featured-insights/innovation-and-growth/globalization-in-transition-the-future-of-trade-and-value-chains

Moules, J. (2019). Apprenticeship numbers rise in England for the first time since levy reforms. Retrieved from https://www.ft.com/content/a3000176-5144-11e9-b401-8d9ef1626294

Norman, M., & Hyland, T. (2003) The role of confidence in lifelong learning. Retrieved from http://sprite.bolton.ac.uk/201/1/ed_journals-7.pdf

Parrett, S. (2018). A degree of confusion over apprenticeships. *TES.* Retrieved from https://www.tes.com/news/degree-confusion-over-apprenticeships

Quality Assurance Agency. (2019). Higher education in apprenticeships characteristics Statement A. Retrieved from https://www.qaa.ac.uk/news-events/news/supporting-higher-education-in-apprenticeships-qaa-publishes-new-guidance

Universities UK. (2019). *The future of degree apprenticeships #Earnandlearn.* Retrieved from https://www.universitiesuk.ac.uk/policy-and-analysis/ reports/Documents/2019/future-degree-apprenticeships.pdf

University Vocational Awards Council. (2016). The future growth of degree apprenticeships. Retrieved from https://www.universitiesuk.ac.uk/policy-and-analysis/reports/downloads/FutureGrowthDegreeApprenticeships.pdf

UVAC. (2019). *Review of Post-18 education and funding June 2019.* Retrieved from https://uvac.ac.uk/augar-and-apprenticeships-uvacs-initial-response/

Wilson, R., Hogarth, T., Bosworth, D., Dickerson, A., Green, A., Jacobs, C., ... Watson, S. (2003). *Tackling the low skills equilibrium: A review of issues and some new evidence, A report for the DTI.* Coventry: IER, University of Warwick.

Wilton, P. (2018, April 26). *Management degree apprenticeships: The UK's engine room where overalls are not required.* Universities UK. Retrieved from https:// www.universitiesuk.ac.uk/blog/Pages/management-degree-apprenticeships-UK-engine-room.aspx

Woodside, J. (2018, July 9). Real-world rigour: An integrative learning approach for industry and higher education. *Sage Journal.* https://doi. org/10.1177/0950422218784535

Part III

**Future Higher Education Direction:
Engaging Real World Learning
Through Innovative Pedagogies**

12

Making Inspiration Mainstream: Innovative Pedagogies for the Real World

Carina Buckley and Maria Kukhareva

Introduction

Innovative pedagogies are those which represent a move away from 'established institutional practices' towards a more flexible, student-centred approach to learning and the learning space (Jamieson, Dane, & Lippman, 2005), often born of a vision for what could be and dissatisfaction with what is (Lock, Kim, Koh, & Wilcox, 2018). While an improvement in student engagement is often a driver for innovation and research (e.g. Haggis, 2009), that same drive can inhibit innovation through fear of unfavourable student feedback, reducing a willingness to take risks in delivery (Lock et al., 2018). Instead, we contend that a learning

---

Case studies: Christie Pritchard, Maria Kukhareva and Carina Buckley

---

C. Buckley (✉)
Solent Learning and Teaching Institute, Solent University, Southampton, UK
e-mail: carina.buckley@solent.ac.uk

M. Kukhareva
Organisational Development, University of Bedfordshire, Luton, UK

D. A. Morley, M. G. Jamil (eds.), *Applied Pedagogies for Higher Education*,
https://doi.org/10.1007/978-3-030-46951-1_12

269

development stance can support innovative pedagogies through its focus on student-centred working and embedding within the disciplines. Although innovation by definition ceases to be so when it becomes mainstream, we argue that innovation itself can be a mainstream activity, aligning the micro-, meso- and macro-environment of the university (Lock et al., 2018).

Learning development is an approach to higher education predicated on emancipatory practice and partnership working (ALDinHE, n.d.). In the context of an increasingly competitive higher education environment, it serves to enable the building of relationships with students, by helping them make sense of and get the most out of their learning (ALDinHE, n.d.). As such it has a central role to play in student engagement, since active student involvement in academic tasks and events is held to be vital for the success of their overall learning experience (Xerri, Radford, & Shacklock, 2018).

Within a social constructivist pedagogy, engagement tends to be defined as active, interactive and observable behaviours, the performance of which will contribute towards the individual student's achievement in their learning (Gourlay, 2015). From this viewpoint, engagement, understood as the 'time, effort and commitment' given by students (Xerri et al., 2018, p. 592), is restricted to classrooms, where interventions planned by teachers are experienced by students (Zepke, 2015).

However, learning development's emancipatory standpoint requires that engagement be taken more broadly, to encompass the networks of social relations that bind students with staff, and peers with each other, and the resultant institutional culture (Xerri et al., 2018). In addition, as well as broadening out the theoretical approach to engagement from the individual, it must also go beyond the curriculum and beyond the classroom (Gourlay, 2015; Zepke, 2015) for reframing as a holistic and experiential approach to learning that promotes student transformation.

Innovative pedagogies that embrace ideas around real world learning support this reframing by focusing on authentic tasks that are situated and contextualised and which help to bridge the gap between theory and practice (Fig. 12.1). Where real world learning might more usually be taken to refer to live briefs, simulations and so on, in this framing the emphasis is more on a learning ethos of partnership working in

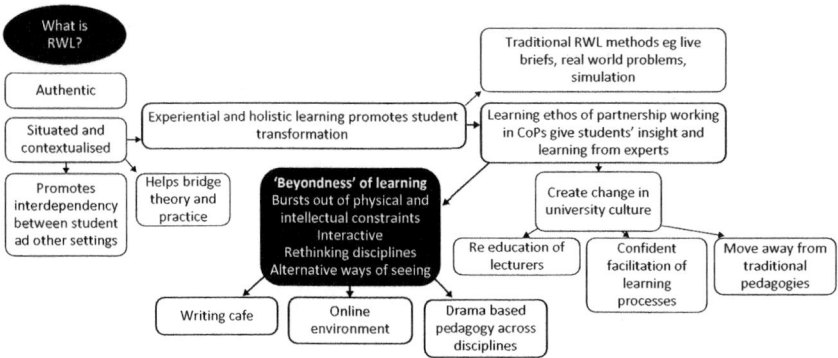

Fig. 12.1 Concept map from the authors

communities of practice, providing students with insights from the experts they work alongside.

This chapter presents three case studies of innovative pedagogies for real world learning that burst out of the physical and intellectual constraints that traditional pedagogies reproduce, however inadvertently. This 'beyondness' of learning allows for alternative ways of seeing through the cross-pollination of disciplinary approaches, interactivity outside the subject group and flexibility in teaching spaces. We introduce a three-tiered model for innovative practice based on different conceptions of the teaching space through which flow three waves of innovation, in the physical space, the subject and the technology. The teaching space can be physical or digital, individual or institutional; in each case it is a space for roles and responsibilities to be negotiated and knowledge to be actively constructed.

These case studies reframe innovation as a mainstream activity for engagement, highlighting practices that while in themselves might be innovative in their approach or formulation, nevertheless are presented as standard and integral to the learning experience, thus keeping them real, achievable and effective.

Case study 1. How the University of Plymouth (UK) helps students learn beyond the classroom through an innovative Writing Café. Students can explore the discourse of academic writing from their own disciplines and experiences, breaking down conceptions of what it means to write at university.

Case study 2. How the University of Bedfordshire (UK) facilitates student learning beyond the subject through drama-based pedagogies. Students can connect more deeply with their discipline through dialogic meaning-making and by drawing on affective and aesthetic learning domains.

Case study 3. How Solent University's (UK) SOL Baseline enables learning beyond the technology through a standardised, narrative-based approach to the virtual learning environment (VLE). Students can explore a rich, curated online environment that invites collaboration and interaction with peers and experts.

What Do We Mean by Real World Learning?

Real world learning has tended to be defined as an opportunity for students to work on projects or problems that have originated in the community or with a particular business or industry partner, such that students get to apply the theoretical knowledge they have learned to an authentic situation (Brundiers, Wiek, & Redman, 2010). The benefit to the learning experience lies in the conjunction between the applied and the immersive aspects, whereby the students feel part of the (non-university) working environment whilst undertaking the (non-university) industry-related tasks. Engagement is improved by locating learning activities within a social and experiential context, thus allowing richer opportunities for sense-making (Jennings, Cater, Hales, Kensbock, & Hornby, 2015) that may be more complex and unstructured than the classroom environment would normally allow, often with the guidance of industry professionals (Theodosiou, Rennard, & Amir-Aslani, 2012), and often with a significant affective component (Molderez & Fonseca, 2017).

While this is what is most commonly understood by real world learning, this chapter expands it by including any types of learning spaces and environments that allow for more complex, non-linear engagement with the subject, discipline or topic, and which do not necessarily imply the involvement of industry professionals. We look for ways for real world learning to provide space for emotional and physical engagement with the discipline or topic, as well as intellectual.

Gardener (2008) proposes an idea of a "synthesising mind", as one of the "five minds" that will be "urgently needed" (p. 7) by our graduates in the near future, whose task will be, more than ever, to be able to work with a diverse range of information in a dynamic and rapidly evolving world. Howard also makes it clear, however, that the synthesising mind will be complementing rather than diminishing the value of the 'disciplined mind', which is associated with the narrower discipline-specific mastery.

We describe this process as the 'beyondness' of learning: going beyond the classroom learning, whether that is through the use of an extended learning space (Case studies 1 and 3), or beyond the discipline (Case study 2); or focusing on the physical space (Case study 1), the emotional space (Case study 2) or the collaborative space (Case study 3). These examples of real world learning are immersive and authentic, without being bounded by the requirements of specific industries. For example, Case study 2 uses theatre, imagination and play to help students deepen their learning, simulating real world contexts without the involvement of industry/subject professionals. The simulation goes beyond the subject and into the heart of the learner.

Emotional engagement is known to predict learning, which in turn supports academic achievement (Sagayadevan & Jeyaraj, 2012), but for real world learning to be successful it must also be authentic, in that it must draw on and develop the same thought processes that a professional would use (Kreber, 2013), in activities that are socially framed and situated (Quigley, 2014).

Every individual is part of a community, and authenticity emerges when an individual engages in what Heidegger calls "public life" through discourse, which simultaneously interprets, constructs and constrains (McDonald & Wearing, 2013, pp. 50–51). Authenticity in this context is not about "a deeper inner self" (Guignon, 2004, p. 125, cited in McDonald & Wearing, 2013, p. 50) but instead is about finding meaning through the critical questioning of "the world outside ourselves" (Kreber, 2013, p. 26). Our tendency is to see ourselves as separate from the community—"the they"—rather than also being one of the constituents of that community, so that the focus remains on individuality rather than the "collective formation of social roles" (Stroh, 2015, p. 254). Ironically, it is through the distance created by this individuality that we come to understand our "being-a-community". This is the key to authentic living (Stroh, 2015, p. 256).

Using Heidegger's ideas around Being and 'the they', Kreber (2013) suggests that authenticity in a teaching situation relates to experiencing what feels most true or real. By extension, those learning in an authentic real world situation could therefore expect to be able to examine their own values and ideals, more than simply the content of that learning. Being able to do so, and indeed demonstrate their values and ideals to others, is a central component of an increased sense of authenticity in oneself. Therefore, teaching students how to interpret and construct meaning, rather than delivering content, supports authenticity by helping them recognise that they have an active role to play in the community. When we as educators impose learning upon them, we have failed to realise that the students have a part to play in determining the nature of that learning.

Authentic real world learning, therefore, contributes to and supports individual authenticity through the opportunities it provides for social contact and positive affect (Lenten, Slabu, Sedikides, & Power, 2013).

Transformation in Student Learning: The 'Beyondness' of Learning

As mentioned in the introduction, we are presenting our take on innovation through a three-tiered multidimensional model, which captures the cross-sectional and cross-disciplinary nature of pedagogical activity in our case studies. The model (Fig. 12.2) draws attention to the way innovation is perceived: it suggests how traditional boundaries can be crossed

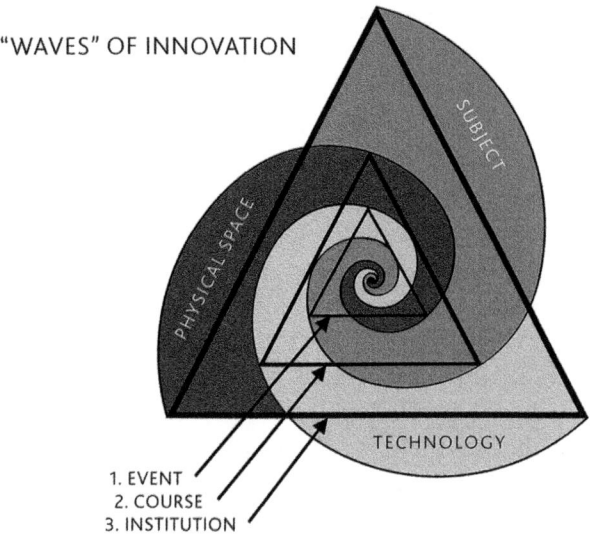

Fig. 12.2   Model for the dynamic interdependence of learning spaces and sites of innovation

and blurred, and how knowledge and practice can be shared, while maintaining the existing structures.

In Fig. 12.2, the triangles represent the 'levels' across which innovation takes place or, in other words, the scale of innovative activity. The innovative practice can occur at a single/multiple event level (small triangle in the centre) or at a course level (larger triangle) or at the level of the whole institution (largest, external triangle).

The spirals in the model can be viewed as 'waves' of innovation, the domain in which (or perhaps, beyond which) innovative activity occurs. In our case, it is the domain of subject (mid-grey spiral), the physical space (dark spiral) and the technological space (pale spiral).

The model also allows the capture of various 'shapes and sizes' in which innovative activity can occur. The visual illustrates that although innovation may start at any level and be taken forward by different teams across a range of areas of learning, there is potential to continue crossing the boundaries further, expanding and embedding innovative approaches into teaching and learning development. We would like to propose that a partnership cross-team approach is key to first seeing innovation as a mainstream activity and then making it happen.

Thus, our first case study proposes a way to enhance student learning by taking them physically outside the classroom and into a stimulating learning environment in a Writing Café, for the whole course cohort. This is represented by the dark 'physical space' spiral and the second largest triangle on the diagram.

The second case study focuses on an interdisciplinary collaboration, which takes the students temporarily outside their subject, and invites them to engage with their discipline through drama-based learning methods and techniques, through a series of workshops, designed by a cross-disciplinary team of professionals. In the diagram, this case study is represented by the mid-grey spiral (subject), taking place at the level of an event (central, smallest triangle).

The third case study in this chapter details the process of developing and implementing an innovative technological approach to student learning (the pale spiral) across the whole university (the largest, external triangle).

The 'beyondness' of learning is a tool for authenticity. The interplay between the site and the medium of innovation serves to expand and make explicit a learning community that exists beyond the immediate experience of the student. All three case studies present a different way in which the alienation of the individual from the community is overcome, creating a means by which the student can negotiate their role and construct knowledge alongside others. Each case study presents a different strategy but with the same goal: complex, dynamic and situated learning environments that value student-centred, emancipatory practices.

Situated Learning: Beyond the Classroom

Situated learning arose as an instructional method that would enact the link Lave and Wenger (1991) had originally observed between cognition and the environment, in a process that they termed 'legitimate peripheral participation'. In this model, those new to a field learn it by taking part in it in the presence of more experienced others. They are exposed to the discourses, resources and practices of the community not as an observer but as a participant, negotiating their engagement through the building of relations between themselves and other practitioners, and themselves and the field. In this relation-based understanding of learning, the student comes to understand themselves as a practitioner and a member of the community through having themselves recognised as such by others. Identity is essentially social in nature, and the successful adoption of a new identity such as 'student' means to adopt the socially negotiated goals, behaviours, values and ways of thinking and feeling of that identity (Ashforth, 2012).

To learn therefore means to participate in a social community of other learners, interactions with whom allow for the development of one's identity. Hwang, Chang, Chen, and Chen (2018) emphasise the value of situated learning for problem-solving, in that the context itself becomes a participant, framing and reflecting the issues and perspectives that the students bring. In this way, simply being a part of the community is a valuable contribution to learning in that the more it is experienced, the more richness there is in how it is experienced (Callary, Werthner, & Trudel, 2012).

In Case study 1, the Writing Café at the University of Plymouth is a space that frames and supports the development of students' academic literacies in a real world, authentic way. It does so through its valuing of community and collaboration, with students learning from each other and the tutor providing 'cognitive apprenticeship through modelling, coaching and prompting for further reflection' (Hwang et al., 2018, p. 1201). Students spend time with others engaged in writing and taking part in salient and authentic activities and discussions, and in doing so learn to develop the identity of 'writer'. The learning space is student-centred and experiential, removed from the bounds of both course and subject.

Case Study 1

The Writing Café as an innovative space (Christie Pritchard, Student Learning Manager, University of Plymouth, UK)

A large slate globe sits on the edge of the worn desk, piles of old books are scattered all around and the Penguin book cover wallpaper is illuminated by a large floor lamp. The furniture is old; each piece has had a former life, perhaps in someone's home, the marks of their stories still present. The aroma of coffee and toasted teacakes fills the air and there is a sense of purpose in the atmosphere. This isn't the scene you would usually find in a post-1992 university, but it is what greets you when you enter the Writing Café at the University of Plymouth. The physical space can be considered as a performative space, where interactions between the tutor and student occur (Barnett, 2011; Bennett, 2006). The spatial 'norms' of these areas continue to be influenced by the pedagogic principles of the 1960s and 1970s and are still dominant with building planners today (Bennett, 2006). As such they privilege some learning activities over others (Temple, 2008), therefore making the practice of student and staff partnerships challenging. Traditional institutional architecture provides an optimum environment for teacher-centred practices, and the delivery of content to students, but the Writing Café was founded on the belief that much learning takes place between places, in social areas, cafes, corridors, walks across campus and residential areas. In this sense the Writing Café is a real world environment where the physical space underpins the intended pedagogy and disrupts the privileged positioning of the 'expert'. Much like its historical predecessor, the coffeehouse, the space forces dialogue, collaboration and debate.

The concept of the Writing Café was to move away from individual one-to-one support provided by a Learning Developer with a student to creating a multidisciplinary environment for discussing ideas and sharing drafts of writing. By having Learning Developers, trained Writing Mentors and students sit around a table, disciplines and levels of study collide and the boundaries between the expert and the novice are shifted as each can explore the discourse of academic writing from their own disciplines and experiences. Along with serving great coffee and locally sourced food, conversations and activity in the Writing Café have ensured that both novices and more experienced writers are able to learn about writing together (Carnell, MacDonald, McCallum, & Scott, 2008). This is because any 'stumblings and violations' incurred are not just characteristic of novice writers, but are features of writing itself and they may be obscured if there is no discussion of writing-in-progress (Wenger, 1998 cited in Murray & Newton, 2009, p. 550). In this sense, the Writing Café contributes to the demystification of writing, where social experience, openness and dialogue encourage people to explore techniques to improve their own approach to writing, and their understanding of knowledge production.

The Writing Café is considered as a purposeful space that can provide an opportunity for all involved to 'overcome the challenges and obstacles in their efforts to write effectively and productively' (Moore, 2003, p. 333). It was an attempt to disrupt the status quo of supporting the development of academic writing within higher education in an instrumental way and in a sense provide a different space that legitimised an academic literacies approach (Lea & Street, 1998). Over the last 30 years, the growing body of research that examined the notion of academic literacies (Barton & Hamilton, 1998; Lea & Stierer, 2000; Lea & Street, 2000; Street, 1984) problematised the belief that literacy, including academic writing, is a set of skills that can be taught and acquired by students and therefore applied in numerous contexts outside of their studies (Lea, 2004). Since its initial conception the debate has evolved and has demonstrated how literacies cannot be reduced to a set of cognitive skills as they have different identities and 'literacy practices are what people do with literacy', thus 'practices are not observable units of behaviour since they also involve values, attitudes, feelings and social relationships' (Street, 1993, p. 12). Whilst our theoretical understanding of academic writing may have progressed, many of our university campus spaces, practices and services have not. If we consider academic writing in this manner, then we also need to explore and uncover these complexities of social processes and practices being culturally and spatially bound and varying in different environments, disciplines and contexts (Lea, 2004). The Writing Café is a place dedicated to doing just that. Rather than solely focusing on 'good and bad' educational judgements about a student's writing, like a bolt-on study skills model, our practice takes into account the complex and intertwined discourses and power relationships at play within the institution and in student learning.

All members of the community are working together to interpret meaning and co-construct knowledge and whilst this does not take place with every student we meet, the Writing Café aims to support students and staff to consider both the implicit and explicit practices of higher education and encourages individuals to value their own position. It contributes to the demystification of writing, where social experience, openness and dialogue encourage people to explore techniques to improve their own approach to writing, and crucially their understanding of knowledge production. The space supports these discussions and interactions, emphasising the pedagogic approach and providing a real world environment in which this learning can take place.

Imagination and Emotion: Beyond the Subject

The proposed 'waves' of innovation model also allow for capturing innovative practice that can go beyond the discipline (in our case, the pedagogy of the discipline) at the level of an event (in our case, a timetabled workshop). In other words, we point to ways in which educators can create opportunities for "beyondness of learning", which invites the students to draw on their contextual thinking, defined by Repko et al. (2017, p. 7) as the "ability to view a subject from a broad perspective by placing it in the fabric of time, culture, or personal experience". Connections can also be made here with the authors' reference to 'integrative thinking', whereby students are asked to integrate their subject knowledge and their personal experience, in order to respond to the task presented by the facilitator.

With this in mind, Case study 2 illustrates how drama-based methods have the potential to help the students to connect with their discipline of choice, through creating deeper and more personalised, and therefore meaningful and even transformative, learning experiences. In this respect, Davis (2015) states that transformative learning can occur through activities, through which participants "come to see aspects of the world or themselves in new ways, and where the meaning making may lead to changes in consciousness, in beliefs and actions". Davis's work draws on Vygotsky's concept of perezhivanie (see Fleer, Rey, & Veresov, 2016; Rey, 2016), a term that can be translated as 'living through', or 'reliving' an experience, which is described as the second most authentic state after the real experience itself. Drama-based methods are designed to activate the state of perezhivanie, which draws on the affective and relational domains, thus creating "affirmative injunctions" (Allan, 2013, p. 37), which then affect students' intrinsic motivation and results in deeper learning (Fleer et al., 2016; Rey, 2016).

Case Study 2

Facilitating student learning beyond the subject through drama-based pedagogies (Maria Kukhareva, Head of Organisational Development, University of Bedfordshire, UK)

This case study presents an example of real world learning whereby students were invited to engage with the subject knowledge through the method of drama-based pedagogy, which would traditionally 'sit' outside the subject domain. The approach that was developed would not have been possible without a partnership approach to student learning and development, as it drew on expertise from three distinct parties: the teaching and learning team, the disciplinarians from the Business school and an artist (theatre director). The aim of this collaboration was an initial exploration, followed by the design of an innovative pedagogical activity that goes beyond the traditional realms of a single discipline (presented as the mid-grey triangle in Fig. 12.2) and thus promotes transformational learning through creating authentic, engaging and possibly surprising experiences. The resulting teaching methods were applied within scheduled workshops (the 'event' level in the model) across several subjects in the institution's Business school, which invited experimentation within the established boundaries of the curricula and the unit. This case study offers an insight into the design that underpinned the 'beyond the discipline' innovative approach in the classroom, and invited students to expand their own expectations and understandings of their approach to learning 'in the discipline'.

The drama-based pedagogy approach can be presented as a set of cross-disciplinary teaching tools. These tools—for example, image work, role work and metaphor—allow educators to draw effectively on the students' affective and aesthetic learning domains; this leads to deeper engagement with the topic through dialogic meaning-making (see Dawson & Lee, 2018). While this method can be highly enriching and complementary across the curriculum, it also has potential to challenge the students' expectation of the scope of their discipline and the associated teaching methods. In other words, drama as pedagogy can act as a catalyst for learning development, which encourages the students to go beyond the subject—with the view to later return to the subject, with a broadened and deepened knowledge and understanding of the latter.

For these new approaches to be effective, all educators in the cross-disciplinary partnership went through a process of intensive, iterative and reflective learning from each other. A shared value of students' learning development supported the partnership ethos. This open collaboration led to the necessary method transfer between the three expert groups: from teaching drama (artistic theatre director) to drama pedagogy (teaching and learning) and to 'teaching in the discipline' (subject specialists in law, marketing, tourism management). The resulting approach, therefore, possessed certain interdisciplinary features—as it emerged as an amalgamation of drama-based pedagogy and 'teaching in the discipline'.

As part of this reiterative dialogue, aspects of curricula were explored through the lens of enhancement through the 'infusion' of drama-based pedagogy, with a view to increasing student engagement and interactivity. The lecturers' teaching disposition and facilitation style were also considered, as this would affect the delivery and impact students' engagement and learning. Overall, seven new workshops were designed and delivered across the three subjects. Figure 12.3 captures the iterative method design process.

The reviewed material, which lent itself most organically to drama-based pedagogy, was closely linked with the 'real world' examples and case studies. Indeed, subjects such as law, tourism management and marketing and communications arguably have a strong emphasis on practice as part of their curriculum already. However, drama-based pedagogy may offer students more unconventional ways of accessing elements of real world learning, without leaving the classroom, as it creates powerful learning opportunities through imaginative, emotive and dynamic work.

In our case, tools such as activating dialogue, image work and role work were used to facilitate the process of learning and knowledge

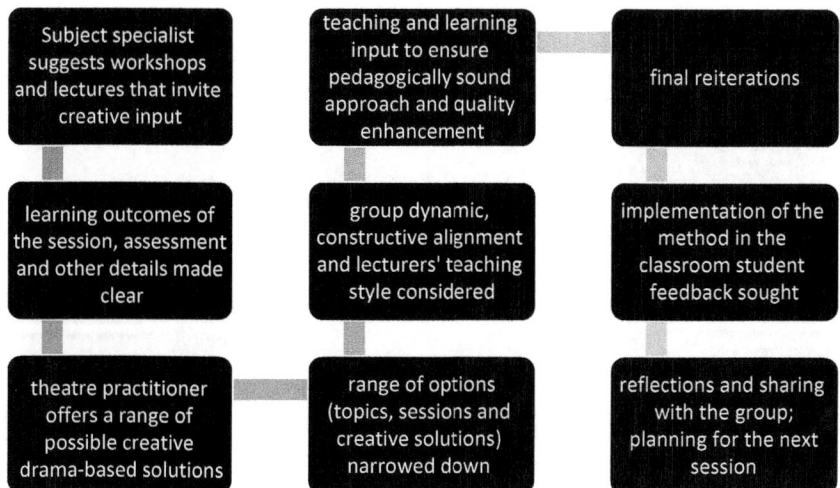

Fig. 12.3 Reiterative process of workshop development

construction. These tools were used in place of pair and group discussions—both effective active learning tools, but arguably less dynamic and interactive (from the embodied and affective learning domain point of view) than the drama-based methods. That said, it was important to scaffold the activity, by gradually increasing the interactivity, to make drama-based learning more comfortable for the students. Indeed, having an open mind with regards to how the subject is being taught may be a challenge for some students (as well as academics), as they may be coming with relatively fixed ideas about their discipline of choice, and, within that, learner identity, which presents "a stumbling block for learners in taking interdisciplinarity on board" (Dalrymple & Miller, 2006, p. 30).

For example, law students were asked to complete a series of activities, aimed at deconstructing, reconstructing and 'layering' their understanding of a legal case study presented to them. As this legal case study formed a part of their upcoming assessment, detailed understanding of the key facts as well as the context was crucial to the students' achievement. Each task was followed by a discussion, facilitated in the format of Socratic dialogue (questioning), to encourage reflection and create an opportunity for deeper learning. The model in Fig. 12.4 illustrates the activity.

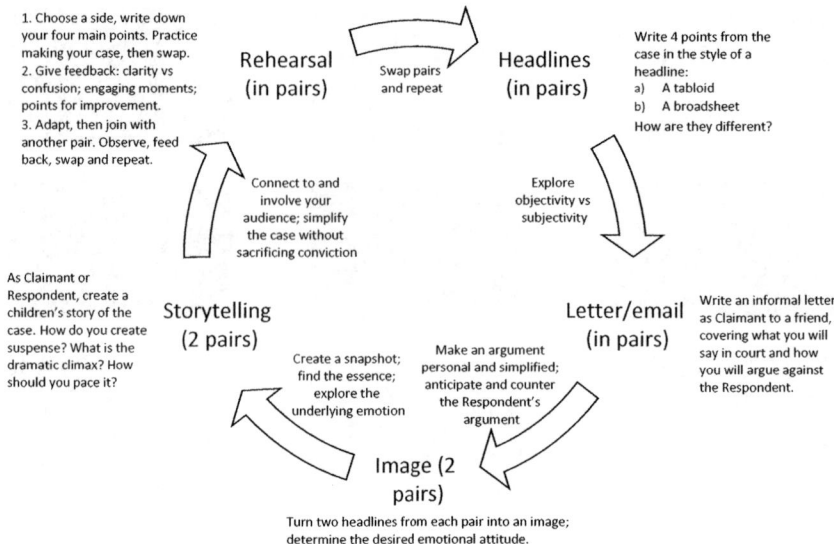

Fig. 12.4 Task-based reflection for assessment

Similarly, students studying marketing and tourism were offered to connect with the subject content through role play, activating dialogue, image play and even poetry. The activities were scaffolded, with each step building on the previous, and continuity of the imaginative process emphasised by the lecturer. The students were learning to connect with their discipline of choice through creating deeper and more personalised and therefore meaningful learning experiences. Although some were hesitant at first, they were surprised at the realisation that although 'it didn't feel like learning', they seemed to have retained a complex topic at the end of what seemed to be 'playing' that didn't appear to be directly related to their discipline.

Davis (2015) offers an explanation of this phenomenon, stating that transformative learning can occur through activities by which participants "come to see aspects of the world or themselves in new ways, and where the meaning making may lead to changes in consciousness, in beliefs and actions". After all, the students were using the methods that professional actors use in order to live and become the character they'll play on stage. It is important to mention here that although the students were offered an approach that went beyond their understanding of what their subject entails, the majority were positively surprised by their own as well as their classmates' creativity, and the feeling of 'learning while not learning'. The law students, who completed drama-inspired exercises in preparation for their assessment, stated that they felt more confident and prepared; the assessment results supported this suggested impact, which was a truly positive development. The success of this development was grounded in all parties' commitment to the cross-disciplinary partnership working, new learning and knowledge transfer, and willingness to innovate. Once developed, the approach and accompanying materials can be sustained by embedding them into the curriculum, thus pushing the 'beyond the subject' wave from 'event' level into 'course' and possibly even 'institution' level.

Collaboration and Construction: Beyond the Technology

Up to this point, community has been taken as a physical entity, its members interacting face to face and the networks of social relations having a tangible structure. Nevertheless, a learning environment can go beyond the physical classroom. Social constructivism holds that learning takes place when learners have the opportunity to explore, negotiate and construct their own understanding; it doesn't require that this takes place in person, simply that there is opportunity for learning to emerge through discussion.

Virtual learning environments (VLEs), like Moodle, are built on the principles of social constructivism (Moodle, 2012), and the collaboration this involves is mediated by the tools and affordances of the technology, within the necessary context of a community. Just as in a classroom setting the imparting of content is held to be inauthentic, so too in the online learning environment should learners be able to interact in a discursive context in order to negotiate meaning (Lambropoulos, Faulkner, & Culwin, 2012). Learning is therefore active rather than passive, with students engaged in an ongoing process of building, adjusting and consolidating knowledge based on what has gone before (Lindgren & McDaniel, 2011). As with all communities of practice, this can only succeed when the community members act as though they were members of a community (Stroh, 2015). If a VLE is set up as a community space, then its users are more likely to recognise it as such and act accordingly.

Case study 3 showcases the transformation of an institutional virtual learning environment (VLE) into a site for collaboration and discussion through the active participation of both staff and students in a learning community. For this to succeed required a change to the institutional culture, to bring that same student-centred approach to the learning space that existed in the classroom into the online environment.

Case Study 3

The SOL Baseline and authentic engagement beyond the technology (Carina Buckley, Instructional Design Manager, Solent University, UK)

In July 2016, Solent University introduced a goal for all courses to become 'Blended by Default', through a standardised approach to learning and teaching that would take full and seamless advantage of all the strengths of classroom and online learning. The first move towards this was the development of a template in Solent Online Learning (SOL), the VLE delivered in Moodle, that would be automatically applied to all modules each academic year. The initial purpose of the new template was to encourage greater consistency in the presentation of individual modules, to help ensure every student had access to the same online experience. However, it quickly became apparent that the move to a fixed template carried greater opportunities than originally anticipated. Accordingly, the SOL Baseline model emerged as a way to deepen and contextualise the template (Fig. 12.5).

The innovative approach came in how the Baseline imagines—and provides the potential for—each individual module to become a site for a collaborative learning community, in its own right and also as part of a networked web of modules encompassing a course, a programme or even a subject group. Up until that point, SOL had been used principally as a

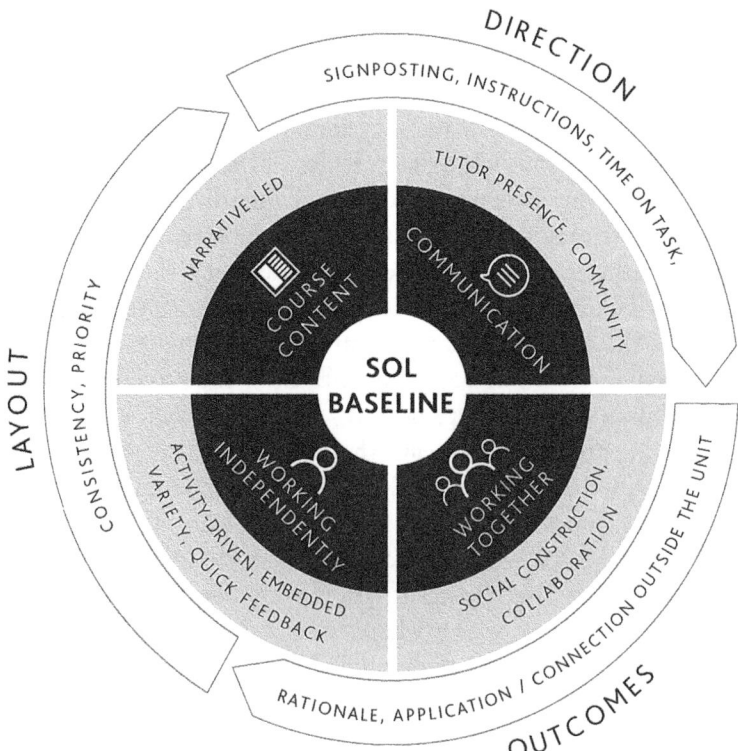

Fig. 12.5 The SOL Baseline

file repository and often viewed with mistrust by lecturers who saw it as a means for their replacement. It was a radical change, therefore, for the SOL Baseline, in contrast to those fears, to take a structured approach towards building a true learning community, where staff and students could interact and learn from each other. The ultimate goal was to provide a rich and valued learning experience beyond the classroom, with the focus becoming what the students were learning and how, rather than where. Real world learning in this instance, therefore, refers to authenticity in engagement.

For the SOL Baseline to break free of the technology and embrace the VLE as a site for pedagogic change and authentic learning, it would be necessary to make more coherent links with the physical teaching spaces and the people in them. As such, the whole direction of the SOL Baseline moved towards the relationships and interactions between tutor and student, and between peers, whether they were situated online in SOL or in the classroom. The VLE became engaged as a tool for challenging and changing learning and teaching culture across the university.

At the heart of the Baseline are four principles through which staff and student agency may be enacted: Communication, Course content, Working together and Working independently. By giving clear signposting through the unit, with rationales for each task or learning object, the lecturer can direct the students' learning and maintain their presence without needing to be physically present. The same precept is applied to the way course content is presented, with the Baseline endorsing a narrative-led approach. This means that files, videos and other resources are contextualised and linked, making SOL dynamic rather than static. The lecturer becomes a curator of teaching and learning materials, their expertise harnessed to create authentic, real world learning. In a world increasingly characterised by information overload, the Baseline asks lecturers to help students discover what is essential for their course.

Over time, the Baseline has developed further, through the exploitation of the affordances of the technological tools. Assessment briefs are now recorded as a video by lecturers, which is uploaded onto the module page but also shown in class and used for a discussion activity to check students' understanding of the assessment requirements. Originally introduced as part of a project to reduce the attainment gap between Black and minority ethnic (BME) and White students, it serves a greater and more holistic purpose in acting as a counter to the alienation students can feel from the community, in this case through the discourse of the academy.

The introduction of new interactive elements has likewise empowered students to take more control of their own learning and increase opportunities for peer engagement. SOL becomes a safe space in which to be challenged and supported, collating resources—including and especially people—that can help students achieve their goals. However, this is not to say that the value of the SOL Baseline is in the technology it uses. Authentic, real world learning means going beyond the technology, and for SOL that equally means the provision of texts or other resources that are explored by the students in their own time and made use of in the classroom, in a flipped approach. The overriding principle is the holistic nature of the SOL Baseline; it applies to the learning environment generally, whether that is online, in a classroom or out in the field. Its value lies in the social networks it embodies, rather than the medium through which it embodies them.

An innovation that was introduced at institutional level, the SOL Baseline has succeeded because it has gone beyond the technology to encompass the physical space and how the subject is taught there. In doing so, it has changed the conversation around teaching and learning at Solent University.

A Learning Development Approach to Real World Learning

A learning development approach is inherently student-centred, within a broader emancipatory context that recognises and, if necessary, challenges the social relations that together make up an institutional culture. Rather than replicate and reinforce systems that alienate the individual from the community, such as the deficit model that problematises the student's abilities, learning development instead looks to champion practices that go beyond the individual student to embrace the learning and teaching culture as a whole.

The three case studies outlined in this chapter all have a learning development perspective, putting the student at the centre of cross- and multidisciplinary practices. All three recognise that knowledge is constructed by each individual in collaboration with others. Knowledge becomes an activity rather than a possession; it becomes something that people do, rather than have. At the same time, knowledge is not "value-free, decontextualized, neutral and apolitical" (Morrice, 2009, p. 8, cited in Sinfield et al., 2011, p. 54) and therefore neither should the means of constructing it be considered in those terms. "Knowledge emerges only through invention and reinventions" (Freire, 1996, p. 53, cited in Sinfield et al.,

2011, p. 55) and it is the task of learning development to enable those reinventions if the students are to experience true authentic learning.

Thinking specifically about real world learning, these innovative approaches all constitute ways of achieving authenticity: collaboration through discourse, collaboration through shared meaning and collaboration through activity. These collaborations are not restricted to a classroom or a discipline group, but instead can take place at all levels of the institution, through a variety of modes.

The Writing Café in Case study 1 is a multidisciplinary space in which students can explore the discourse. It moves academic writing from an instrumental, skills-based task to a set of literacies and practices that must be embodied and performed. Even so, this is not something that is done to the students. Meaningful collaboration requires that hierarchic structures are flattened as much as possible (Sinfield et al., 2011) and in the Writing Café, this means peer-led support. The boundaries between expert and novice are blurred, and the student gets the chance to engage as an equal member of a community. By sharing the space with staff as well as students they get to participate legitimately, not simply peripherally but also centrally, in a professional, situated setting.

The collaboration in Case study 2 takes place amongst three expert groups of staff in an interdisciplinary enterprise. Working together, they create a space that engages students emotionally as well as intellectually, and which allows them to connect with each other and with the subject through the process of making meaning. The authentic nature of the activity comes through in the way that they, as Davis (2015) says, "come to see aspects of the world or themselves in new ways". More than that, it is argued from our Heideggerian perspective that by working authentically, they come to see aspects of the world *in* themselves. Through being given a chance to recognise their individuality in a personalised learning experience, it opens up the opportunity to see the community of which they are a part. Drama, and the taking on of another character or personality, is a way of exploring the world through alternative perspectives and being able to test out what feels 'true' or 'right' in a particular situation. In playing a role, they construct meaning for themselves but also for those who get to see the performance.

Finally, Case study 3 took a medium that arguably could, used badly, increase alienation and isolation (Holley, Burns, Sinfield, & Glass, 2011) and ameliorated the risk by providing for the development of a collaborative learning community that has the potential to reach far beyond the module. The biggest danger of this approach was that it would lock the student and the lecturer into a resource repository, knowledge and learning constrained by the technology. However, the emphasis on narrative and context counters this by bringing in the personal and showing the student that the lecturer shares the space. Those lecturers that use the space best do so by sharing their interests, pointing out problems or puzzles and encouraging students to share their ideas with each other. Students, in this enriched environment, gain power and choice in their learning; the emphasis shifts from where they learn to what they are doing and who they are with. They are fully embedded in the community, and the learning environment is a blend of the online and the physical.

The value and rewards of community-based authentic learning are what make these three strategies so worth pursuing. All of them contribute to an ethos of partnership working and crossing boundaries, and all of them work to normalise these innovative pedagogies and make them mainstream. That is not to say they are easy to institute. Good partnership working requires at least one like-minded other, as well as an institutional culture that allows them to work together. These pedagogies also require space: to plan and to enact. Physical space is inextricably linked to the subject and the technology, the degree determined by the level at which the innovation takes place, whether that is a single class or across the whole institution. To roll out these innovations and bring them into the mainstream means being able to see the interplay between the scale and domain. This is the site of the learning community, and this is where the opportunities reside that each provides.

Conclusion

We have proposed in this chapter an approach to viewing innovation as a mainstream activity, and in doing so have presented a way to increase student engagement through the dynamic flexibility of the innovation model, from a learning development perspective. We chose to do this for several reasons, not least because we felt that it was necessary. When we look at UK higher education, we take in a view of boundaries becoming increasingly blurred between learning spaces and places, and ever more emphasis placed upon the dynamic nature of learning and the growing focus on collaboration and knowledge exchange. In this environment, real world learning presents itself as a productive model to pursue as the boundaries between the university and the world outside become similarly porous.

We also saw the necessity from the point of view of the student as a person in the world. Our approach is a route to achieving authenticity in learning and therefore a stronger connection to it. Fully situated and contextualised tasks, within an ethos of partnership working, take students beyond the constraints of place and subject and into a broader and deeper learning space that takes in the whole person.

The model introduced in Fig. 12.2 presents learning as a non-linear event constituted by one or more domains and which may take place at one or more levels. It aims to reinforce the importance of recognising innovative approaches in higher education practice, and then identifying how these approaches can become part of mainstream activity. We argue that the three case studies presented here, while framed as innovative pedagogies, all have the potential to become mainstream and fully incorporated into what we understand as good learning and teaching. The main mechanism for doing so is via the learning development lens and its emancipatory emphasis on social relations.

The three case studies, all grounded in real world learning, were purposefully chosen for their differing nature and institutional application. They illustrate how innovative approaches can emerge from any corner of university practice, yet the underpinning rationale and methodology share the common learning development philosophy of building knowledge and practice exchange on the foundation of the shared commitment to student learning and development. For example, Case studies 1 and 2 both draw strength and purpose from a multidisciplinary methodology, which is operationalised in vastly different ways but which shares the same relationship between subject and space. Case studies 1 and 3 both prioritise communication and collaboration as a means of learning and take as a starting point the model of a community of practice, with novices and experts challenging each other.

The model is of value to educational and academic developers as well as learning development practitioners and can be used to spot innovation, as well as map it. The model has the capacity to encapsulate a broad range of activity and be used to explore how innovative activity can be grown and expanded, whether that is into another domain or up to a higher level.

More than anything, innovative pedagogies require confident teaching staff willing to take a risk, and there are a number of routes to gaining that confidence. In the spirit of this chapter, the first step has to be collaboration with a colleague.

References

ALDinHE. (n.d.). *About the association for learning development in higher education*. Retrieved from http://www.aldinhe.ac.uk/about/

Allan, J. (2013). Staged interventions: Deleuze, arts and education. In I. Semetsky & D. Masny (Eds.), *Deleuze and education* (pp. 37–54). Edinburgh, UK: Edinburgh University Press.

Ashforth, B. E. (2012). *Role transitions in organisational life: An identity-based perspective*. New York, NY: Routledge.

Barnett, R. (2011). Configuring learning spaces: Noticing the invisible. In A. Boddington & J. Boys (Eds.), *Reshaping learning: The future of learning spaces in post-compulsory education* (pp. 167–178). Rotterdam, Netherlands: Sense Publishers.

Barton, D., & Hamilton, M. (1998). *Local literacies: Reading and writing in one community*. London, UK: Routledge.

Bennett, S. (2006). First questions for designing higher education learning spaces. *The Journal of Academic Librarianship, 33*(1), 14–26. https://doi.org/10.1016/j.acalib.2006.08.015

Brundiers, K., Wiek, A., & Redman, C. L. (2010). Real-world learning opportunities in sustainability: From classroom into the real world. *International Journal of Sustainability in Higher Education, 11*(4), 308–324. https://doi.org/10.1108/14676371011077540

Callary, B., Werthner, P., & Trudel, P. (2012). The lived experience of a doctoral student: The process of learning and becoming. *The Qualitative Report* 17, article 86. Retrieved from https://nsuworks.nova.edu/tqr/vol17/iss43/2

Carnell, E., MacDonald, J., McCallum, B., & Scott, M. (2008). *Passion and politics: Academics reflect on writing for publication.* London, UK: Institute of Education.

Dalrymple, J., & Miller, W. (2006). Interdisciplinarity: A key for real-world learning. *Planet, 17*(1), 29–31. https://doi.org/10.11120/plan.2006.00170029

Davis, S. (2015). Transformative learning: Revisiting Heathcote and Vygotsky for the digital age. *p-e-r-f-o-r-m-a-n-c-e* 2 (1-2). Retrieved from http://www.p-e-r-f-o-r-m-a-n-c-e.org/?p=1835

Dawson, K., & Lee, B. K. (2018). *Drama-based pedagogy: Activating learning across the curriculum.* Bristol, UK: Intellect.

Fleer, M., Rey, F. G., & Veresov, N. (Eds.). (2016). Perezhivanie, emotions and subjectivity: Advancing Vygotsky's legacy. In *Perspectives in cultural-historical research* (Vol. 1). Springer.

Gardener, H. (2008). The five minds for the future. *Studies in Education, 5*(1/2), 17–24. Retrieved from http://centre.upeace.org/wp-content/uploads/2013/04/1.3-Gardner-5-Minds-of-the-Future.pdf

Gourlay, L. (2015). 'Student engagement' and the tyranny of participation. *Teaching in Higher Education, 20*(4), 402–411. https://doi.org/10.1080/13562517.2015.1020784

Haggis, T. (2009). What have we been thinking of? A critical overview of 40 years of student learning research in higher education. *Studies in Higher Education, 34*(4), 377–390. https://doi.org/10.1080/03075070902771903

Holley, D., Burns, T., Sinfield, S., & Glass, B. (2011). When worlds collide: The paradox of learning development, e-learning and the 21st-century university. In P. Hartley, J. Hilsdon, C. Keenan, S. Sinfield, & M. Verity (Eds.), *Learning development in higher education* (pp. 199–211). Basingstoke, UK: Palgrave Macmillan.

Hwang, G.-J., Chang, S.-C., Chen, P.-Y., & Chen, X.-Y. (2018). Effects of integrating an active learning-promoting mechanism into location-based real-world learning environments on students' learning performances and behaviors. *Educational Technology Research and Development, 66,* 451–474. https://doi.org/10.1007/s11423-017-9567-5

Jamieson, P., Dane, J., & Lippman, P. C. (2005). Moving beyond the classroom: Accommodating the changing pedagogy of higher education. *Refereed proceedings of 2005 Forum of the Australasian Association for Institutional Research* (pp. 17–23). Retrieved from http://www.aair.org.au/app/webroot/media/pdf/AAIR%20Fora/Forum2005/Jamieson.pdf

Jennings, G., Cater, C. I., Hales, R., Kensbock, S., & Hornby, G. (2015). Partnering for real world learning, sustainability, tourism education. *Quality Assurance in Education, 21*(4), 378–394. https://doi.org/10.1108/QAE-03-2015-0010

Kreber, C. (2013). *Authenticity in and through teaching in higher education.* London, UK: Routledge.

Lambropoulos, N., Faulkner, X., & Culwin, F. (2012). Supporting social awareness in collaborative e-learning. *British Journal of Educational Technology, 43*(2), 295–306. https://doi.org/10.1111/j.1467-8535.2011.01184.x

Lave, J., & Wenger, E. (1991). *Situated learning: Legitimate peripheral participation.* Cambridge, UK: Cambridge University Press.

Lea, M. (2004). Academic literacies: A pedagogy for course design. *Studies in Higher Education, 29*(6), 739–756. https://doi.org/10.1080/0307507042000287230

Lea, M., & Stierer, B. (Eds.). (2000). Student writing in higher education: New contexts. *Higher Education, 40*(3), 373–374.

Lea, M., & Street, B. (1998). Student writing and staff feedback in higher education: An academic literacies approach. *Studies in Higher Education, 23*(2), 157–172.

Lea, M., & Street, B. (2000). Student writing and staff feedback in higher education: An academic literacies approach. In M. Lea & B. Stierer (Eds.), *Student writing in higher education.* Buckingham, UK: Open University Press.

Lenten, A. P., Slabu, L., Sedikides, C., & Power, K. (2013). I feel good, therefore I am real: Testing the causal influence of mood on state authenticity. *Cognition and Emotion, 27*(7), 1202–1224. https://doi.org/10.1080/02699931.2013.778818

Lindgren, R., & McDaniel, R. (2011). Transforming online learning through narrative and student agency. *Educational Technology & Society, 15*(4), 344–355.

Lock, J., Kim, B., Koh, K., & Wilcox, G. (2018). Navigating the tensions of innovative assessment and pedagogy in higher education. *The Canadian Journal for the Scholarship of Teaching and Learning, 9*(1). https://doi.org/10.5206/cjsotl-rcacea.2018.1.8

McDonald, M., & Wearing, S. (2013). A reconceptualization of the self in humanistic psychology: Heidegger, Foucault and the sociocultural turn. *Journal of Phenomenological Psychology, 44*, 37–59. https://doi.org/10.1163/15691624-12341244

Molderez, I., & Fonseca, E. (2017). The efficacy of real-world experiences and service learning for fostering competences for sustainable development in higher education. *Journal of Cleaner Production, 172*, 4397–4410. https://doi.org/10.1016/j.jclepro.2017.04.062

Moodle. (2012). *Philosophy*. Retrieved from https://docs.moodle.org/29/en/Philosophy

Moore, S. (2003). Writers' retreats for academics: Exploring and increasing the motivation to write. *Journal of Further and Higher Education, 27*(3), 333–342. https://doi.org/10.1080/0309877032000098734

Murray, R., & Newton, M. (2009). Writing retreat as structured intervention: Margin or mainstream? *Higher Education Research and Development, 28*(5), 527–539. Retrieved from https://www.tandfonline.com/doi/full/10.1080/07294360903154126

Quigley, C. (2014). Expanding our view of authentic learning: Bridging in and out-of-school experiences. *Cultural Studies of Science Education, 9*, 115–122.

Repko, A., Szostak, R., & Buchberger, M. (2017). *Introduction to interdisciplinary studies* (2nd ed.). Los Angeles, CA: Sage. Retrieved from https://brandon.multics.org/library/macintyre/macintyre2002education.pdf

Rey, F.G. (2016). Vygotsky's concept of Perezhivanie in the psychology of art and at the final moment of his work: Advancing his legacy. *Mind, Culture, and Activity* 23(4): Symposium on Perezhivanie. Retrieved from http://www.tandfonline.com/doi/abs/10.1080/10749039.2016.1186196?journalCode=hmca20

Sagayadevan, V., & Jeyaraj, S. (2012). The role of emotional engagement in lecturer-student interaction and the impact on academic outcomes of student achievement and learning. *Journal of the Scholarship of Teaching and Learning, 12*(3), 1–30.

Sinfield, S., Holley, D., Burns, T., Hoskins, K., O'Neill, P., & Harrington, K. (2011). Raising the student voice: Learning development as socio-political practice. In P. Hartley, J. Hilsdon, C. Keenan, S. Sinfield, & M. Verity (Eds.), *Learning development in higher education* (pp. 53–63). Basingstoke, UK: Palgrave Macmillan.

Street, B. (1984). *Literacy in theory and practice.* Cambridge, UK: Cambridge University Press.

Street, B. (1993). *Cross-cultural approaches to literacy.* Cambridge, UK: Cambridge University Press.

Stroh, K. M. (2015). Intersubjectivity of Dasein in Heidegger's being and time: How authenticity is a return to community. *Human Studies, 38,* 243–259.

Temple, P. (2008). Learning spaces in higher education: An under-researched topic. *London Review of Education, 6*(3), 229–241. https://doi.org/10.1080/14748460802489363

Theodosiou, M., Rennard, J.-P., & Amir-Aslani, A. (2012). Theory to practice: Real-world case-based learning for management degrees. *Nature Biotechnology, 30*(9), 894–895.

Xerri, M. J., Radford, K., & Shacklock, K. (2018). Student engagement in academic activities: A social support perspective. *Higher Education, 75,* 589–605. https://doi.org/10.1007/s10734-017-0162-9

Zepke, N. (2015). Student engagement research: Thinking beyond the mainstream. *Higher Education Research & Development, 34*(6), 1311–1323. https://doi.org/10.1080/07294360.2015.1024635

13

'Getting to the Soul': Radical Facilitation of 'Real World' Learning in Higher Education Programmes Through Reflective Practice

Jo Trelfa

Introduction

Reflective practice, brought to life and popularised by Donald Schön, is "a rigorous, disciplined approach for noticing, attending to, and inquiring into aspects of practice" (Trelfa, forthcoming) and integral to real world learning pedagogy and practice in higher education (Bruno & Dell'Aversana, 2018). At its soul, so its principle of life, feeling, thought, and action, is the development of "artistry" (Schön, 1992) of, and for, post-degree professional practice. Schön defined artistry as the "artful practice" (Schön, 1983, p. 19) of "implementation and improvisation" (Schön, 1987, p. 13) involved in professional engagement in their settings. Through provision of, and engagement in experience of practices that mimic draw on, and are located in whatever is deemed ordinary within a particular profession (Lombardi, 2007), students develop

J. Trelfa (✉)
University of Winchester, Winchester, UK
e-mail: Jo.Trelfa@winchester.ac.uk

© The Author(s) 2021
D. A. Morley, M. G. Jamil (eds.), *Applied Pedagogies for Higher Education*,
https://doi.org/10.1007/978-3-030-46951-1_13

299

'artistry' as they work with complex problems, whether through.: 'in-class' activities such as role play; working with representative or unusual problem-based inquiry and case studies from a single or composite of actual events; and embedded fieldwork, including a virtual or physical community of practice in the form of placement, voluntary work, and industry experience as part of a higher education programme. Lucas, Claxton, and Spencer (2013, p. 21) refer to this as an "epistemic apprenticeship", where emphasis is on direct participation in the "ill-defined problems, sustained investigation, collaboration, and multiple and interdisciplinary sources and perspectives" that characterise daily professional life of a particular profession. Assessment of performance and learning is usually "woven seamlessly into the major tasks" (Lombardi, 2007, p. 3) with a focus on development of appropriate "behaviours, attitudes and habits" (Lucas et al., 2013, p. 21).

The current rise in popularity of real world learning infers that it was previously absent in higher education, a claim that pedagogues will (and should) take to task, but putting this aside for the purposes of this chapter, we can agree that acknowledgement of the epistemic (and ontological—as shall be seen) awareness of learning and being is important in ongoing education for learning, employability, and a critically reflective professional practice.

This chapter draws directly from my PhD research, specifically on one particular theme, applied here to real world learning: the contention that reflective practice is integral to real world or 'authentic' learning (Lombardi, 2007) but its 'soul' of artistry has been taken out. If real world learning is to live up to its ambition and aims then it needs the "soul putting back in" (Jeanette, *research participant,* cited in Trelfa, forthcoming) (all participants are referred to via pseudonyms).

Real World Learning

Even with this introduction in mind the label of 'real world' can sit uncomfortably in a teaching and learning context given its inference that other kinds of student learning and experience are excluded from imposed notions of 'real' because they are in some way inferior or insignificant. Instead, if we understand the term as a short-cut reference to the body of literature that establishes the *value* of experiential and authentic, applied, learning, it becomes meaningful. It is possible to discern at least five threads of bodies of work that have been responsible for 'moving' learning processes that facilitate 'connection-building' (Lombardi, 2007, p. 2) "from the periphery of education to the center" *[sic]* (Lewis & Williams, 1994, p. 5). The first is the historically influential work of, to select a fragment to illustrate, Dewey, Kolb, and Schön in their focus on experiential reflective learning and teaching. Second can be identified the more recent contributions of those explicitly adopting the term 'real world learning', such as the Expansive Education Network, a group of organisations, universities, schools, colleges, and individuals exploring "the point of education; the place where learning happens; the nature of intelligence; and the role of the teacher as a reflective practitioner" initiated by the Centre for Real-World Learning at the University of Winchester (Lucas & Claxton, 2011). A third thread is created by those who focus on the 'unique' opportunities and challenges of twenty-first-century teaching and its implications for notions of 'real world', such as through Strawser (2018) in his edited works. The fourth contributes to all the other threads through its appreciation of the phenomenological experience of real world learning, and the fifth and final thread is identified through the contributions of contemplative and radical pedagogy.

To convey a sense of those here, I will briefly take each thread in turn to briefly expand descriptions of their contribution to appreciation of real world learning.

• Experiential Education

Beginning with a broader focus on education Dewey (1920, p. 194) based his theories on adults actively experiencing the world through "initiative, inventiveness, varied resourcefulness, assumption of responsibility in choice of belief and conduct", that can be 'had' (unreflected), 'known' (reflected), and a 'method' (inquiry) (1929/1984, p. 194).

Kolb (1984, 2015) took Dewey's ideas into a model to underscore the way in which people "combin[e] experience, perception, cognition and behaviour" (Kolb, 2015, p. 31) in a continuous process (2015, p. 38) of learning. Referring to it as a "holistic, integrative perspective" rather than an 'alternative' theory (2015, p. 31) he articulated a process whereby adults learn from their experiences through the 'concrete' experience itself, followed by "reflective observation, abstract conceptualisation, and active experimentation".

Schön's (1983, 1987) contribution was to apply Dewey's work to professional contexts, initially concentrating on the real world decision-making and learning of architects, town planners, and science-based professions, but his ideas became quickly adopted by social professions, those that:

> comprise practitioners whose role it is to work with people who are regarded as in need of support, advocacy, informal education or control. They work within a shared set of values stressing a commitment to individual and social change, respect for diversity and difference and a practice that is participatory and empowering. (Banks & Nøhr, 2003 p. 8)

Schön articulated the way in which individuals reflect *in* and *on* experiences, albeit confusing and confounding the two, and focusing predominantly on reflection-on-action alone, a situation that has persisted in the vast literature related to reflective practice that has blossomed in the wake of his original work (see Trelfa, forthcoming for details).

- Real World Education

The second thread is essentially a more recent enhancement of the two above wherein real world learning has been specifically named and located in a frame of "expansive education" at all levels (Lucas et al., 2013, p. 3). To illustrate, Lucas et al. (ibid.) describe relevant education practices as being those that have the "core purpose" of "[giving] confidence and capacity to flourish in the world that [students] are going to inhabit".

- Twenty-First-Century Education

In the third thread, writers such as Strawser (2018) and the authors in his edited collection of work sets this within postmillennial education of 'generation Z' and the technological advances that offer different opportunities, sources, and contexts for real world learning.

• Phenomenology in Education

In parallel, another rich historical root to the present day in a fifth thread to the literature base to real world learning considers the phenomenology of real world learning as a lived experience, for instance, adding embodiment to the focus of perception, cognition, and behaviour of established education theories (e.g. see Friesen, Hendriksson, & Saevi, 2012). Bodied and embodied experience has contributed to understanding real world learning and its facilitation. To illustrate, Strawser, referred to above, grounds his edited collection in Mezirow's (1991, cited in Strawser, 2018) phenomenological concept of 'transformation' to consider the lived nature of change involved in real world learning in the twenty-first century.

• Contemplative and Radical Pedagogy

Finally, and more recently, others have taken these ideas into the project of contemplative pedagogy, the fifth thread, connecting processes that were previously solely associated with contemplative traditions to learning and teaching, a response to the fragmentation and atomisation of education (e.g. Ergas, 2017). In purpose and aims it has links to radical pedagogy, connecting an individual's learning to beyond themselves, an interdependency and critical consciousness that has a Freirean history (e.g. Freire, 1996; Giroux, 2004; Seal, 2019) and feminist standpoint (e.g. Foss & Foss, 1994; Mackinlay, 2016).

'Real World Learning'

The term 'real world learning' can be understood as a short-cut reference to this rich multiformed landscape created by these five threads and an articulation of it through concept mapping as follows:

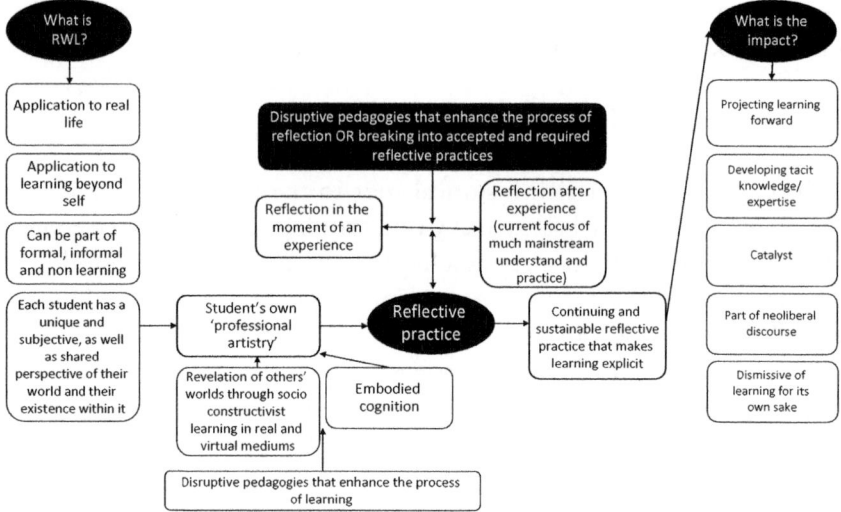

Fig. 13.1   Concept map from the author

applied and contextual formal, informal and non-formal learning, that encourages, facilitates and requires connection to one's individual unique and subjective perspective as well as connection to others, so a shared, diverse, *and* interdependent awareness and understanding, constructed by socio-political-historical discourse and structures. (Scott & Trelfa, 2019)

In sum, real world learning is critical consciousness of, as well as beyond, self through experiential learning (Fig. 13.1).

Reflective Practice and Real World Learning

To realise this opportunity and potential reflection that "[converts] action that is merely appetitive, blind and impulsive into intelligent action" (Dewey, 1933/2008, p. 125) can only be invaluable and, indeed, necessary to real world learning. To expand on the outline above, Schön famously took up Dewey's ideas about the uncertainty of the world and the way individuals engage with and make sense of it via control of self and situations through thought, and applied it to practitioners engaging with perplexing interactions in professional contexts and as a result find ways forward. An often-used example of this is from his popular and well-known *Educating the Reflective Practitioner* (1987) where he describes the "topography of professional practice":

> ...there is a high, hard ground overlooking a swamp. On the high ground, manageable problems lend themselves to solutions through the application of research-based theory and technique. In the swampy lowland, messy, confusing problems defy technical solutions. The irony of this situation is that the problems of the high ground tend to be relatively unimportant to individuals or society at large, however great their technical interest may be, while in the swamp lie the problems of greatest human concern. (1987, p. 3)

For Schön, then, reflective practice both describes how and enables someone to make sense of and control the "messy, indeterminate situations" (Schön, 1987, p. 4) of practice in professional settings in order to provide effective service to their users/clients. Schön's research identified that they do this in the two ways introduced above through 'reflection-in-action' and 'reflection-on-action'. Reflection-in-action refers to the process whereby practitioners "think about doing something while doing it" (Schön, 1983, p. 54), so in "a stretch of time within which it is still possible to make a difference to the outcomes of action" (Schön, 1995, np). Reflection-on-action refers to how,

> in the relative tranquillity of a post-mortem, [practitioners] think back on a project they have undertaken, a situation they have lived through, and they explore the understandings they have bought to their handling of the case. (Schön, 1983, p. 61)

It is this "fumbling act of discovery" (Hamilton, 2005, p. 288) leading to self and situation control that characterises 'artistry'. Fish (1998, p. 42) goes further, articulating artistry as a 'paradigm' that is about

> recognising and responding to, understanding and valuing, the artistry of professional practice [...] the appreciation and connoisseurship of good practice, with a view to making it generally possible to enable people to

'make such appreciation their own' (to experience that appreciation from the inside, rather than being dependent on the judgement of others).

However, reflective practice as part of the epistemic apprenticeship of higher education is such that it has been taken from Schön's exposition of what it is that professionals *do* and applied to what it is that students need to *learn* to do and perform successfully for qualification. Reflective practice features in Quality Assurance benchmarks for subjects at higher education; in notions of 'graduateness' for all, the "orientating framework of educational outcomes that a university community agrees its graduates should develop as a result of completing their studies successfully" (Hill, Walkington, & France, 2016, p. 156); and in National Occupation Standards for specific professions (Trelfa, forthcoming). As a result reflective practice has become embraced in a 'wave of euphoria' (Horgan, 2005, p. 33, cited in McGarr & Moody, 2010, p. 580) in education as part of real world learning, as "a natural fact of life that furnishes the 'fix', the 'this is it'" (Gergen & Gergen, 2008, p. 11), 'relied' on (Clegg, Saidi, & Tann, 2002, p. 131) as the 'promised land' (Papastephanou & Angeli, 2007, p. 604) of salvation for students as they strive towards professional practice development through real world learning.

As a consequence, therefore, substantial attention in related literature has focused on the nature, form, instruction, and assessment of activities that foster the scrutiny and control of self and situation in reflective practice. Through journals, diaries, reflective essays, facilitated peer dialogue, action learning sets, reflective practice groups, and fieldwork-based supervision students reflect "on the understandings which have been implicit" in their 'actions and understandings' (Schön, 1983, p. 61) whilst they are involved in learning 'for, through and at' (Lemanski, Mewis, & Overton, 2011) real world contexts.

The Soul of Reflective Practice

Having established the invaluable necessity of reflective practice to real world learning it follows that the practice of reflective practice at its core, so, its soul as defined above, must also be authentic, in other words a genuine and worthwhile deliberate, disciplined commitment and engagement. It is in *this* way that reflective practice enables learning for, through and in real world contexts.

This appreciation of reflective practice emerges from my own background in the social professions. Qualifying as a Youth and Community Worker, my early career of 12 years was in fluid and risky contexts of violence and abuse where reflective practice was the anchor to my practice. Therefore a passionate proponent of both reflective practice and real world learning, when I moved to lecture in higher education I took both into my teaching through expectation, content, process, and modelling, and it became the focus of my masters (Level 7) and then PhD (Level 8) research. At Level 7 it was a surprise when my research with students engaging in reflective practice revealed learning dominated by preoccupation with how to perform it and produce its artefacts (diaries, journals, and so forth) sufficient to pass their courses (Trelfa, 2010), as opposed to Schön's original exposition of it as development of professional artistry. Exploring that further in doctoral research, in effect the focus was if not that then what. The research participants, also students engaged in reflective practice as part of their higher education programmes whilst in real world contexts, express the same experiences I found in the Level 7 research. To illustrate, this Jeanette's experience was characteristic. A diligent student, she recalls keeping a reflective journal as part of her final term-length placement, recordings for each day and for which she received a first-class grade. She had gone through the diary highlighting words that described her emotions in pink and this was stressed in her lecturer's feedback as a strong positive feature that contributed to her excellent outcome. However, during the research she explains how as a single parent she had found juggling her studies with family commitments and a full-time placement extremely difficult. She had previously been able organise around a university-based day and attained consistently good grades, but fitting in a placement as well, one that often took place in evenings, was a task too much; the compromise was in making up her diary entries at the end of the placement period just prior to submission rather than the daily record it was supposed to involve. Based on some kind of association with her actual placement of course, it was still a work of fiction. So what of the highlighted elements that had been held up by her university assessor as a particularly strong feature that evidenced her real world learning? They were in fact "just words in pink" *(Jeanette, research participant)*. Jeanette explains "one, [names lecturer] was like, 'very good you've gone into a lot of effort', I used lots of different colours and highlighters, you know, but it's just that, she was marking the effort, it doesn't mean anything, like actually it doesn't mean anything". Rather than develop the skill of reflective practice and enhance and articulate real world learning, her experience was characteristic of all the participants, a preoccupation with formulating their accounts in such a way that the intended audience will be able to understand them. It involved stories with distinct beginnings, middles, and ends that do not match the messy, complex and rich reality of their actual experiences in their real world context. Added to this, of course, they want their stories to be judged positively: given that they are carrying out the task for the requirements of their course and professional qualification. So it is that they speak of their concern to provide "a version of us we want others to see" (Jeanette, *research participant*). Sadie likens this to "when someone comes round your house you kind of suddenly look round your house and go 'oh god' you know, like you want it to represent something about you and it's not going to be this you know [laughter]" *(research participant)*. She jokes, for example, that she wants to rush round 'her house' of her reflective diary and make sure there are "Educated books on the shelves!" As a pre-emptive response to such concerns, much attention is given to the instructional skills, guidance, and facilitation of reflective practice; however, this is clearly not impacting on *actual* experience of engaging in reflective practice. The participants speak of lying, exaggerating, censoring, and, Jeanette as established above, making the whole thing up. It is a conclusion borne out by other researchers, such as Hobbs (2007) and Powell and Gilbert (2006).

Therefore rather than an artistry paradigm my thesis understands current mainstream understanding and practices of reflective practice from an 'engineering science' paradigm (Soler, Zwart, Israel-Jost, & Lynch, 2014), an "input-output, additive, and cumulative" process (Vlair, 2008, p. 459). Through that analysis, and supported by wider theory, we can understand the additive and cumulative output as being driven by the nature and quality of the input, the instructional skills, guidance, and facilitation of reflective practice. The input must necessarily be standardised to ensure parity and equal possibility of output. This involves stipulation of reflective activities, so how they are to be engaged with, and the nature of outcome, which is followed by assessment, carried out by those who facilitated it in the first place. Judgements are made about the student output, so evidence of whether they have developed sufficiently against explicit and implicit notions of what 'sufficient' involves. To ensure this too has parity (otherwise how can equivalent 'sufficient' between individuals be judged), standardised assessment measurements are used. If all are to know what they need to produce and perform, and then re-present this appropriately, focus must necessarily centre on its 'administrable features' (Vlair, 2008, p. 448). Therefore significant attention from facilitators and students alike is dominated by expectations, requirements, pro forma, handbooks, checklists, SMART-ness (specific, measurable, achievable, relevant, timely/timeframe), and accessibility—delivered by facilitator-assessors such that students are enabled to access exactly the same information at the same time. Diversity in form of learning and nature of expression becomes a "noise that should be minimised through accountability mechanisms" (ibid.). Consequently, lack of reflective practice in real world contexts becomes the fault of students, their laziness, lack of engagement, non-reflection, or non-compliance and not the result of poor facilitator input, instruction, and administration.

Furthermore, to train students in this takes time; indeed, the deterministic significance of time to produce such effects is integral to the way that reflective practice is incorporated into real world learning. Higher education programmes 'tell' students what elements of reflective practice as part of real world learning they must know about at specified points in time in their degree programmes and specified times during their working week that they should engage in it, whether in university or home. It is therefore little wonder that emphasis on time proliferates the research participants in their experiences of reflective practice, time to learn and understand what is required, time to understand what they must perform and produce, and time to learn what and perform 'good' involves so they can do it well and get good grades. Thus in the spirit of being helpful, significant attention is given to *more* instruction, curriculum, and guidance and for a typical facilitator of reflective practice this is difficult to argue against: more instruction on how to approach and produce reflective journals, more guidelines concerning number, length, and content of the recordings, and more clearly specified Learning Outcomes, or better defined assessment rubrics, all make sense when it is understood this will be for the better of the practitioner/student. It is hard to argue against the hegemony of a good thing (see Trelfa, forthcoming).

Therefore, we can understand how this shapes and characterises student experience of and engagement in reflective practice for real world learning, "even though they are aware of this, and even when they can imagine it could be different" (Trelfa, forthcoming). It is striking to note how closely this matches Bella's (2003, p. 33) characterisation of an engineering paradigm as 'plug and chug' and 'cram and flush':

Plug and chug: procedural ways of solving problems and completing assignments that ~1. allow you to get by without wasting time thinking, ~2. do not require you to really understand what you are doing, and ~3. protect your own limited understanding from being exposed.
Cram and flush: a general approach to taking tests, completing assignments, and meeting deadlines that involves ~1. anticipating what the evaluators want, ~2. stuffing your mind with whatever fits the above requirement, and ~3. dumping this stuff out at the appropriate time and place.

At best, as Sadie puts it, one 'sorts thoughts out' but this does not equate or lead to learning (*research participant*) and Jeanette concurs, summing up that the 'soul' of artistry has been taken out of reflective practice in real world learning and needs to be 'put back in' (*research participant*).

Breaking-in

Their experience can be related to and understood through political philosopher Henri Lefebvre's (1992/2004) concept of 'breaking-in', part of his broader theory that I explore fully in my thesis, but used in this chapter to both better understand the state of affairs, and importantly, identify how the soul can be put back in to reflective practice in real world learning.

Lefebvre's concept of 'breaking-in' is a little-known scholarship (Elden, 2004). In his book *Rythmnalysis* Lefebvre compares 'breaking-in' or the "dressage of a horse to learning, which I apply to education. Like breaking in a horse, education that *breaks-in* 'presents [people] with the same situation, prepares them to encounter the same state of things'" and does so in 'ritualised, stereotyped rites' (1992/2004, p. 39). It is an "automatism of repetitions" (1992/2004, p. 40) in which those engaging need not be fully present: they are "absent, not present in the presentation" (1992/2004, p. 39). In this vein, the instruction and methods of dressage "fills the place of the unforeseen" (1992/2004, p. 40) through "phases", a "linear series" with 'a beginning and end' so reliance on "a general organisation of time" (1992/2004, p. 39) and is reinforced through "identification with the chief, the sovereign, the models that have great power and influence" (1992/2004, p. 42). It has an astonishing resonance with the students' accounts of reflective practice above. As Lefebvre puts it, "in the course of their being broken-in animals *work*" *[sic]* (1992/2004, p. 40): "under the imperious direction of the breeder or trainer, they produce their bodies [...] their bodies modify themselves, are altered" (1992/2004, p. 40), a telling metaphor for their experiences. Here, then, the dressage "determines" rhythms, it "is the training that counts: that imposes, that educates, that breaks in" (1992/2004, p. 41)—and in fact Lefebvre goes further, likening it to a "military model" (ibid.), where information "stocks up on itself, trades itself, sells itself" (1992/2004, p. 49).

So, it is in the process and outcome of being 'broken-in' that the soul of reflective practice—and therefore of real world learning—is lost. Or, put another way, student attention becomes dominated by a particular *kind* of real world learning, one that centres on compliance with imposed requirements, a façade of authentic performance, a soul-less experience.

Radical Facilitation of 'Real World' Learning in Higher Education Programmes Through Reflective Practice

Therefore, the concern of this chapter is with ensuring that real world learning lives up to its aims and intentions of being applied and contextual formal, informal, and non-formal learning, that encourages, facilitates, and requires connection to one's individual unique and subjective perspective as well as connection to others, so a shared, diverse, and interdependent awareness and understanding, constructed of socio-political-historical discourse and structures. In sum, how do we put the soul back in to real world learning so it (re)turns to being critical consciousness of and beyond self through experiential learning.

Such authentic real world learning necessarily requires its fundamental process of reflective practice to also be authentic. If real world learning *is* to be defined as such, then reflective practice needs radical attention to facilitate it differently.

The word and action of 'radical' is deliberately chosen here, but not in the sense of 'revolutionary' as might be understood through common usage of the term, but in the spirit of Neill (1960) and his 'radical approach' to learning and being, in addition to the 'radicalism' of education proposed by Freire (1996). They use it in light of its Latin origins, *radicalis* and *radix* meaning 'roots', so, getting to or expounding the roots (of learning, being, and education). To elaborate, Fromm's elegant foreword to Neill's (1960, p. iix) Summerhill refer to radical as "the true principle […] without fur". Here, then, concern is with getting real world learning back to its roots, to its 'true principle without the fur', this being artistry, and analysis of the research participants experiences suggests that the route to this will be through reclaiming it from appropriation by and drift into an engineering paradigm. In this chapter I offer two case studies, one that illuminates the current situation of 'breaking-in' and the other an example of a way in which it can be reclaimed (for further extension and examples, see Trelfa, forthcoming). By this I am not suggesting that the activity is a panacea to all the issues outlined above, but the overarching aim of this chapter has been to point up the need for radical attention to reflective practice if real world learning is to be authentic. The second case study is therefore offered as (soul) food for thought concerning ways out of the soul-less situation. It links the practice of object contemplation (Williams, 1984) with embodied experience (Ergas, 2017) in a 'real world' classroom-based activity focusing on the specific matter of early career lectures reflecting on and in practice differently about their students questions (Avnon, 1998; Bloom, 2018).

'Getting to the Soul': Radical Facilitation of 'Real World' Learning in Higher Education Programmes Through Reflective Practice

Rogers and Freiberg (1983, p. 18) remind us that learning should not be "lifeless, sterile and quickly forgotten stuff that is crammed into the mind of poor helpless individuals tied to their seat by ironclad bonds of conformity", and yet in this chapter we have seen how this has become the case for reflective practice. The soul of reflective practice and therefore real world learning being knocked out of it by, we assume, well-meaning practices that focus on 'breaking' learners in so they can perform required evidence. This chapter argues for and had promoted thinking about how we might radically (re)turn real world through facilitation of reflective practice back to its soul of artistry.

> **Case Study 1**
> **'Breaking a student in': Losing the soul of reflective practice in real world learning**

This actual case study illuminates the process by which students get 'broken in' to the practices of reflective practice and its impact on their real world learning.

Aphra is a student in the first year of a three-year social professional degree programme that requires its participants to engage in placements as part of their overall study to successfully be awarded with the qualification. Aphra's placement is for three months, part-time, in a statutory agency that works with adolescents who have been excluded from or have dropped out of compulsory education. Tracking her experience at the end of the day as required wherein she is expected to reflect on the session that she has been involved with, she has written:

> I can see a big gap between the theory that I'm learning at University and what actually happens on the ground at [the agency]. I observe and feel that my supervisor thinks I'm full of ideas about participation and empowerment, which I am, but for him supervising me it's a case of 'welcome to the real world'. I suspect he feels a bit threatened. At the beginning of the session I am handing out pens and paper to those who want to get involved, helping them [young people] come up with ideas of what to put on the walls, and after I'm having a discussion with him as to why they are not allowed to put more of themselves into the project of decorating the top floor. And the answer is that due to cuts the Local Authority is now going to turn the floor into offices and they want a certain standard of appearance, i.e. what's acceptable to the adult eye. Any idea of the young people owning their space by painting it their way is impossible. I feel really thrown by this. That was the whole point of my placement project. I find myself retreating into myself when the scope of what is possible gets smaller and smaller. Reduced by bureaucracy and cuts. I find it demoralising and demotivating.

She describes feedback from her university tutor who reads her diary half way through the placement period. The tutor says that her recording was "inappropriate and unprofessional, wrong, tactless, and very ill judged"; "highly critical, one-sided, judgemental, generally made from a place of ignorance and not seeing the bigger picture"; and that Aphra should consider "how [her] supervisor would feel if he read it". At the end the tutor reassures her that "as long as [she] adjust [her] style of writing from now on this will all be viewed as a valuable learning experience" and she should do this by "adopting a new or improved model" for her reflective diary.

Aphra is both bewildered and angry. She understood that her diary was hers, a place in which she should meaningfully record her own experience and reflect on it with emphasis on what *she* learns from that process, but now sees that she should write with an audience in mind, who will judge not only her writing but her as a person, with priority on the artefact less than the journey.

We could consider Aphra as naïve to expect otherwise, after all, every detail of the placement is mapped to course requirements—yet Aphra is a mature student who has run a successful business and has elected to create a career change for herself. She is new to higher education, and the social professional she is aspiring to join, but she is an excellent cue-seeker and is definitely not naive.

We might also take note of her observation and interpretation of the fieldwork supervisors comments, his conception of the 'real world' of the agency compared to hers, the inference being that Aphra's worldview is ideological and somehow not rooted in reality. Competing definitions and ownership of 'real' in real worlds can also be seen in the university tutor's (reported) too. Who calls these shots, the student who is doing the learning but is new to the profession and agency and comes from a business world, the supervisor who is experienced in the profession but has a fixed view of things and a perspective of 'seen it all, done it all', or the university tutor who knows what passing the higher education programme entails but may or may not be qualified in the social profession itself or have any significant critical understanding of reflective practice? Moreover, their notions of 'real' in real worlds are intersected by genders, economic class, culture, age, and the capital of academia or practice expertise.

We might also consider that the university tutor was overbearing, perhaps not understanding the position and role of reflective practice, or at the very least not modelling best practice. However, if we consider higher education frameworks and the way in which significant attention is given to *more* instruction (on how to approach their recordings, integrate with theory, map to Learning Outcomes, and occupational standards) and *more* guidance (regarding number, length and content, or more clearly specified Learning Outcomes, or better-defined assessment rubrics) in the spirit of being helpful, for a typical university lecturer this is difficult to argue against when couched in terms of being better for student experience. Even if not delivered in the same way as Aphra's tutor, subtly the message is the same, and divergence, whether student *or* lecturer, becomes a cautious affair if not avoided altogether. It is a wise student who knows where and how to seek out, interpret, and perform the implicit and explicit cues presented to them about reflective practice in order to re-present it for a favourable outcome and assessment; it is a process of being 'broken in' to understanding and practices of reflective practice.

Case Study 2
'Getting to the Soul' of Reflective Practice

This second case study offers food-for-thought to prompt ideas of get-ting back to the soul of reflective practice. It links the practice of object contemplation with embodied experience in the moments of a 'real world' classroom-based activity aimed at supporting early career lectures on post-graduate teaching course to appreciate their students' questions differently during the classes they teach. 'Breaking them in' to that end could include prior instruction and guidance, followed by observation as they try it out in practice contexts and feedback that may be overtly or subtly heavy-handed in terms of expected compliance.

Instead, as a way to get (back) to the soul of reflective practice to develop professional artistry in real world learning, an experiential activ-ity follows along with discussion of its impact.

The participants are invited to pair up and then one of each pair leaves the room. Those remaining are asked to find an object that they have with them of personal significance, explaining that the things we choose to carry around with us are not there by chance, some are there for practi-cal reasons, some purely personal, some both, but all have significance. They are asked to spend time reflecting on the object and its personal significance. So, without interaction with anyone else, they are invited to observe it thoughtfully, carefully, thoroughly; recall vividly the memories, feelings, and emotions it holds for them; let their associations with their object wash over them like waves. They are asked to treasure the treasures the object brings to them.

Before their pair partners return back in to the room, it is explained that they are to give the object to them to explore once they have sat down. They are not going to share their stories and associations with the object with them. Indeed, they are not going to tell them anything about it at all—but nothing more is told to them about what will happen.

When the partners return and the pairs are back together, it is explained that "your partner is going to give you an object. Your task is to hold it, explore its textures, surfaces, shape, smell and as you do verbalise your thoughts, associations with that object, memories that arise as a result, and voice your feelings and emotions that come with them. Your partner will listen".

Following the activity, the individuals who stayed in the room (those who owned the object) are asked to describe their feelings, emotions, and thoughts as they watched and listened to their partner exploring their object that has such personal significance to them. I remind them that I had asked them not to share their own stories about their objects and ask if they had been able to do that. I ask how it was to not tell their reason for having that possession with them. I ask if they paid attention to similarities in stories/feelings/associations—and if they heard differences in stories/feelings/associations in the same way.

After the discussion I point out that this activity has been a focused, intense—and therefore more exaggerated—version of what happens when a student asks a lecturer a question in class. In that question they are sharing something of significance to them. Their question might be very brief, or long; it might be rambled, unclear, seem unrelated; we might even be unable to discern a clear question within it at all. But either way it has personal significance to them and always will, and as lecturers we don't know the extent, or in what way. As they are speaking, brief or not, our own thoughts, associations, judgements, feelings, arise, crowd in, and we select what we tune in to in the question and its presentation from that background, in certain ways and with differing results and consequences, and all this is fleeting, fast. This might not feel like 'select'—so it might not feel deliberate—but with their felt experiences from the in-class 'real world' activity just carried out they can now consider the impact this might have on their students. As they witnessed someone else receiving their personal object and react and respond to it from their own frames of reference, and the feelings this created as a result, so they receive students' questions.

I ask for illustrations from their own practice. I extend by pointing out that these do not always have to be negative, that is, when we hear a student's question we might be aiming to respond in ways that communicate our empathy, however I explain how empathy can be uncomfortable, troubling, tip in to being 'all about me' in terms of a flight-or-fight response—and no longer be about the student.

So, we discuss compassion, connection, and what that involves, in the moment, with the invitation to experiment with the fleeting in-the-moment of student questions differently in the real world contexts of their teaching practice.

Having done so the early career lecturers speak of the impact this simple activity in terms of how they appreciate students' questions differently. They recount the way that they now consider how they both facilitate *and* receive questions differently, through an experience of attentive encounter, silence, and dialogue. The real world learning in the in-class activity applied to real world learning in their own practice settings catalysed a 'turning' in Buber's (Avnon, 1998) terms, from separation to deep connection, which they then went on to write about in assessed work.

In this, then, the activity in and for real world learning gets to the soul, of both reflective practice and authentic learning, whilst also fitting higher education frameworks such as the need of assessment for award purposes. The nature and quality of that experience in process and outcome are entirely different to the 'words in pink' learning in the main chapter and to Aphra's experience in case study 1. By getting to the soul of reflective practice, learning in real world contexts can indeed become real.

References

Avnon, D. (1998). *Martin Buber. The hidden dialogue*. Lanham: Rowman & Littlefield.

Banks, S., & Nøhr, K. (2003). *Teaching practical ethics for the social professionals*. European Social Education Training/Formation d'Educateur Sociaux Européens.

Bella, D. A. (2003, January). Plug and chug, cram and flush. *Journal of Professional Issues in Engineering Education and Practice*, 32–39. https://doi.org/10.1061/(ASCE)1052-3928(2003)129:1(32)

Bloom, P. (2018). *Against empathy: The case for rational compassion.* London: Vintage.

Bruno, A., & Dell'Aversana, G. (2018). 'What shall I pack in my suitcase?' The role of work-integrated learning in sustaining social work students' professional identity. *Social Work Education, 37*(1), 34–48. https://doi.org/10.1080/02615479.2017.1363883

Clegg, M., Saidi, S., & Tann, J. (2002). Reflecting or acting? Reflective practice and continuing professional development in higher education. *Reflective Practice, 3*(1), 131–146.

Dewey, J. (1920). *Reconstruction in philosophy.* New York: Holt & Co.

Dewey, J. (1929/1984). The quest for certainty. In J. A. Boydston (Ed.), *John Dewey: The later works, volume 4—1929.* Carbondale: Southern Illinois University Press.

Dewey, J. (1933/2008). How we think: A restatement of the relation of reflective thinking to the educative process. In J. A. Boydston (Ed.), *John Dewey: The later works, 1925–1953.* Carbondale: Southern Illinois University Press.

Elden, S. (2004). Rhythmanalysis: An introduction. In H. Lefebvre (1992/2004) (S. Elden & G. Moore, Trans.). *Rhythmanalysis: Space, time and everyday life* (pp. vii–xv). London: Continuum.

Ergas, O. (2017). *Reconstructing 'education' through mindful attention: Positioning mind at the center of curriculum and pedagogy.* London: Palgrave Macmillan.

Fish, D. (1998). *Appreciating practice in the caring professions: Refocusing professional development and practitioner research.* Oxford: Butterworth Heinemann.

Foss, K. A., & Foss, S. K. (1994). Personal experience as evidence in feminist scholarship. *Western Journal of Communication, 58*(Winter), 39–43.

Freire, P. (1996). *Pedagogy of the oppressed* (R.M. Bergman, Trans.). London: Penguin Books

Friesen, N., Hendriksson, C., & Saevi, T. (Eds.). (2012). *Hermeneutic phenomenology in education: Method and practice.* Rotterdam: Sense Publishers.

Gergen, M., & Gergen, K. C. (2008). *Social construction: A reader.* London: Sage Publications Ltd.

Giroux, H. (2004, March). Cultural studies, public pedagogy, and the responsibility of intellectuals. *Communication and Critical/Cultural Studies, 1*(1), 59–79. https://doi.org/10.1080/1479142042000180926

Hamilton, D. (2005). Knowing practice. *Pedagogy, Culture & Society, 13*(3), 285–290. https://doi.org/10.1080/14681360500200229

Hill, J., Walkington, H., & France, D. (2016). Graduate attributes: Implications for higher education practice and policy. *Journal of Geography in Higher Education, 40*(2), 155–163. https://doi.org/10.1080/03098265.2016.1140128

Hobbs, V. (2007). Faking it or hating it: Can reflective practice be forced? *Reflective Practice, 8*(3), 405–417. https://doi.org/10.1080/14623940701425063

Kolb, D. A. (1984). *Experiential learning: Experience as the source of learning and development.* New Jersey: Prentice-Hall.

Kolb, D. A. (2015). *Experiential learning: Experience as the source of learning and development* (2nd ed.). New Jersey: Pearson Education Inc.

Lefebvre, H. (1992/2004). *Rhythmanalysis: Space, time and everyday life* (S. Elden & G. Moore, Trans.). London: Continuum.

Lemanski, T., Mewis, R., & Overton, T. (2011). *An introduction to work-based learning.* York: The Higher Education Academy/UK Physical Sciences Centre.

Lewis, L. H., & Williams, C. J. (1994). *Experiential learning: Past and present. New Directions for Adult and Continuing Education, 62*(Summer), 5–16.

Lombardi, M. M. (2007). *Authentic learning for the 21st century: An overview.* Education Learning Initiative paper 1 [online]. Retrieved from https://www.educause.edu/ir/library/pdf/ELI3009.pdf

Lucas, B., & Claxton, G. (2011). Who we are. The Expansive Education Network. Retrieved from http://www.expansiveeducation.net/aboutus

Lucas, B., Claxton, G., & Spencer, E. (2013). *Expansive education: Teaching learners for the real world.* Victoria, Australia: Acer Press.

Mackinlay, E. (2016). *Teaching and learning like a feminist: Storying our experiences in higher education.* Rotterdam: Sense Publications.

McGarr, O., & Moody, J. (2010). Scaffolding or stifling? The influence of journal requirements on student's engagement in reflective practice. *Reflective Practice, 11*(5), 579–591. https://doi.org/10.1080/14623943.2010.516968

Neill, A. S. (1960). *Summerhill: A radical approach to education.* London: Pelican.

Papastephanou, M., & Angeli, C. (2007). Critical thinking beyond skill. *Educational Philosophy and Theory, 39*(6), 604–621.

Powell, J. L., & Gilbert, T. (2006). Performativity and helping professions: Social theory, power and practice. *Critical Journal of Social Welfare, 16,* 193–201. https://doi.org/10.1111/j.1468-2397.2006.00459.x

Rogers, C., & Freiberg, H. J. (1983). *Freedom to learn* (3rd ed.). New York: Merrill.

Schön, D. (1992). The Crisis of Professional Knowledge and the Pursuit of an Epistemology of Practice. *Journal of Interprofessional Care, 6*(1), 49–63. https://doi.org/10.3109/13561829209049595

Schön, D. (1995, November/December). The new scholarship requires a new epistemology. *Change, 27*(6), 27–34 [online, non-paginated]. Retrieved from http://bonnernetwork.pbworks.com/w/file/fetch/59896448/Schoen%2520 Scholarship%2520New%2520Epistemology.pdf

Schön, D. A. (1983). *The reflective practitioner: How professionals think in action.* London, Hants: Avebury.

Schön, D. A. (1987). *Educating the reflective practitioner.* San Francisco: Jossey-Bass.

Scott, C., & Trelfa, J. (2019). Concept-mapping, *discussion.*

Seal, M. (2019). *The interruption of heteronormativity in higher education: Critical queer pedagogies.* London: Palgrave Macmillan.

Soler, L., Zwart, S., Israel-Jost, V., & Lynch, M. (2014). Introduction. In L. Soler, S. Zwart, M. Lynch, & V. Israel-Jost (Eds.), *Science after the practice turn in the philosophy, history and social studies of science* (pp. 1–43). Oxon: Routledge.

Strawser, M. G. (Ed.). (2018). *Transformative student experiences in higher education: Meeting the needs of the 21st century student and the modern workplace.* London: Lexington Books.

Trelfa, J. (2010) *Emperor's new clothes? Exploring student experiences of reflective practice.* Submitted to the University of Exeter as a dissertation towards the degree of Master of Education: Professional Development (unpublished).

Trelfa, J. (forthcoming). *Facilitating reflective practice in higher education professional programmes: Reclaiming and redefining the practices of reflective practice.* Submission to the University of Winchester as a requirement for a postgraduate research degree.

Vlair, G. (2008, April). Can we administer the scholarship of teaching? Lessons from outstanding professors in higher education. *Higher Education, 55*(4), 447–459.

Williams, P. B. (1984, Winter). Object contemplation: Theory into practice. *Museum Literacy: Ideology and Methodology, 9*(1), 10–12.

14

Real World Learning and Authentic Assessment

Melenie Archer, Dawn A. Morley,
and Jean-Baptiste R. G. Souppez

Introduction

As students increasingly adopt a consumerist lifestyle academics are under pressure to assess and mark more students' assignments in quicker turn around periods. In no other area is the marketisation shift between student and academic more apparent in the accountability that academics now need to demonstrate to students in their grading and feedback (Boud & Molloy, 2013). When evaluating their higher education experience students are most likely to complain about their grading or

Case studies: Melenie Archer and Jean-Baptiste R. G. Souppez.

M. Archer (✉)
Solent University, Southampton, UK
e-mail: melenie.archer@solent.ac.uk

D. A. Morley
School of Sport, Health and Social Sciences, Solent University, Southampton, UK

J.-B. R. G. Souppez
Aston University, Birmingham, UK

© The Author(s) 2021
D. A. Morley, M. G. Jamil (eds.), *Applied Pedagogies for Higher Education*,
https://doi.org/10.1007/978-3-030-46951-1_14

feedback (Boud & Molloy, 2013) and National Student Survey results consistently indicate that this category, more than any other, has the highest student dissatisfaction rates (Race, 2014).

Real world learning (RWL) encourages the development of student attributes for employment and lifelong learning. Over recent years the ethos in higher education has started to move towards a real world learning approach and student-led curriculum where a socio-constructivist positioning of students' learning invites students to be active partners in their higher education experience. The increasing incidence of group assessment and peer review is indicative of this change and traditional methods of marking have also been touched by this changing ethos (Nicol, Thomson, & Breslin, 2014). Students are encouraged to lessen their dependency and increase their pro activity in negotiating and building their academic and personal journey through higher education (Nicol & Macfarlane-Dick, 2006). Feedback has started to be positively repositioned as feed forward where students are encouraged to build on feedback for future development.

The recognition that academics need to be smarter about the time they spend marking (Race, 2014) supports a re-examination of assessment and feedback especially as traditional written feedback encourages passivity in students rather than a personal hunger to feed forward their learning into future development. It makes sense that academics step out of present practice to embrace assessment that actively engages students not only with their learning but the means to use feedback constructively for future learning and employability.

What Is Real World Learning and How Does It Relate to Assessment?

This concept map was produced during a session to identify what RWL is and where it fits into higher education teaching and assessment frameworks (Fig. 14.1). The map explores the learning outcomes in relation to employability, understanding of the industry sector and identifies the opportunities for personal development and self-awareness. Recognising RWL as an authentic assessment experience, which can be personalised to

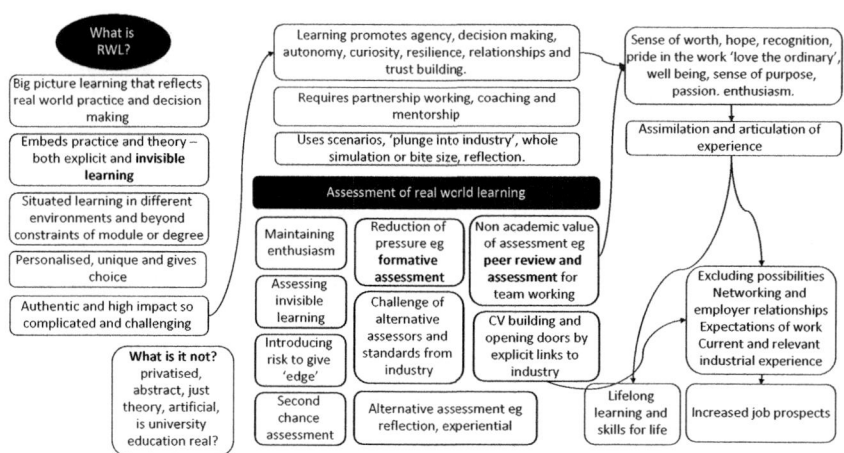

Fig. 14.1   Concept map from the authors

create challenging and unique learning, the concept map also ascertains that *formative* and *group peer review and assessment* will allow students to develop personal traits such as resilience, reflection and team working.

Designing Authentic Assessment

Real world learning requires student assessment to replicate as close as possible the authenticity of real world experiences. Gulikers, Bastiaens and Kirschner (2004) in their examination of STEM subjects present the idea that authentic assessment requires students to use the same competencies, or combinations of knowledge, skills and attitudes that are applied in the criterion situated in professional life. The assessment criteria may necessarily differ according to the discipline area and Shulman (2005) argues that educators should try to develop signature pedagogies that link not only to ideas, practices and values, but also the behaviours adopted in inherent uncertainty. Authentic assessment may involve increased challenge and risk that initiate student affective engagement and reflection on the consequences of the decisions made. Traditional assessment, dominated by examinations and essays, risks creating a schism between theory and practice while assessment remains dominated by academic procedure. Carefully designed assessment, that enhances work readiness as well as measuring learning, encourages a bridging of university learning and its practical application (Morley, Bettles, & Derham, 2019).

The case studies, presented in this chapter, are drawn from the different disciplines of yacht design and festival management. They are good examples of the differing signature pedagogies that Shulman (2005) presents; both courses require different pedagogies to suit each discipline.

In order to ensure assessment and feedback are relevant to RWL, practitioners must decide on the desired outcomes for the course. From the outset the module must fit with the title of the course. The BA (Hons) Yacht Design course focuses on the technical elements of the design process and the assessment would not be solely based on the model boat race, as described in the case study, but also based on other simulated and controlled environments that prepare students for working within the yachting industry. In contrast, the BA (Hons) Festival and Event Management course assessments focus on the management competencies required during the delivery stage of an event. This is assessed through tutor observation and peer assessment reflecting real world practice and decision making. Both courses require students to demonstrate how they would perform, act and react in a work environment thus providing the student with an enriched learning experience relevant and beneficial to their chosen career path.

Kolb (1984), Honey and Mumford and Lewin have all linked theory to practice when decoding the experiential learning process, presenting a cyclical method (Beard & Wilson, 2006). The design of this approach allows for reflection on experience during the formative feedback stages; however, the use of the model may not always be applicable in the summative stages of assessment when the physical action is the end product. Assessment design and timing should, therefore, be considered if the student is to benefit from the formative feedback experience in the RWL environment.

Academics must consider if there are enough steps in the assessment process to assist the delivery of an RWL programme—to build in reflective elements and to establish if these actually meet the learning criteria. As a result of trying to make learning explicit and 'usable' for students, courses may need extra formative assessments, formal or informal, to give the students the best chance of performing to their best ability during a 'live' assessment through the feed forward gained en route.

The importance of dialogue is key to shifting feedback away from the notion of *telling* to students playing an active role in using the information presented to them. Hounsell (2008) reinforces the need for sustainability in feedback where feedback moves from the short-term gain to becoming embedded in the students' understanding of what constitutes acceptable work and within a framework, what needs improving. This can then be transferred to the world of work where students can engage meaningfully in their lifelong learning.

Group meetings, one-to-one support and online surveys are currently used to monitor students' progress throughout a course to give feedback on predicted academic outcomes. This would be an ideal opportunity to give the student time to reflect on how they will behave in the real world assessment by adding simulated tasks or problem-based activities, so the mid-term progress meetings would subsequently focus on academic and personal development in relation to the real world environment.

The use of Kolb's experiential learning cycle (1984) helps to counteract another challenge of using RWL assessment in that all student learning is not always accounted for in the specified learning outcomes of the teaching session. Assessment of experience, particularly in the disciplines of art and performance, is an example of these invisible learning outcomes. Described by De Bono (1976), logical and analytical thinking demonstrated and practised throughout the study process also interact with 'lateral' thinking or 'out of the box thinking' (Bladen & Kennell, 2014). Often the explicit and invisible learning is so inextricably linked that a physical action that they may cause an emotional reaction therefore affecting the outcome of the assessment. Students may behave differently during a simulation assessment, whereby the emotional effects of working under pressure or creative problem solving may impact student performance. However, the student responses to stress, group conflict or problems are skills essential in the workplace, and the individual's attitude and approach to learning should be considered in the assessment process. This authentic learning experience creates very personal outcomes for the student, and the use of formative feedback, coaching and peer assessment can provide an enriched learning experience.

Designing Real World Assessment

Peer Review as Assessment of Real World Learning

The process of peer review had been defined as the process by which students give feedback on their peers and receive feedback from their peers (Nicol et al., 2014). Peer review will contribute to the formative feedback process by allowing students the opportunity to rate performance and reflect on a formative assessment ahead of the summative task. Peer assessment is the process by which students can grade each other as part of the final assessment. Both stages of the use of peer grading could be designed as a simple comparison of work whereby students grade as if they were the tutor or a more complex approach with set criteria and weightings on the results. Peer assessment allows for discussion and reflection on the assessment and is an important tool where the assessment may be an event or simulation. Evidence of contribution during group work can also be assessed using peer assessment, enabling the students to recognise where they fit into the group dynamic and how others view their work. The positive effect of this approach to learning is that the students contribute to the assessment and feedback process establishing ownership and a deeper understanding of their learning journey. Nicol et al. (2014) discuss using peer review to close the gap between feedback and assessment, allowing students an element of control and autonomy over their own learning and deepening student understanding of how to succeed in the summative assessment.

Case Study 1 is an example of how peer review and assessment can support the students to develop the invisible outcomes associated with experiential learning. Bladen and Kennell's (2014) 'out of the box' thinking is assessed with criteria such as attitude and leadership skills during the assessment cycle.

Case Study 1

Live Event Assessment (Melenie Archer, Lecturer Festival and Event Management. Solent University, UK)

Students on the BA (Hons) Festival and Event Management course are required to fill out a group peer assessment at both the formative and summative stages of assessment and case study 1 explains this process in more detail. Students are also asked to grade themselves as part of this process, the peer assessment criteria are:

1. Ideas and suggestions
2. Leadership and administration of group
3. Event logistics (e.g. risk management and crowd management)
4. Staging (e.g. theming, décor and special effects)
5. Customer care (e.g. appearance, name badge and attitude)

Solent University Festival and Events students are required to host two live events at levels 4 and 5 to demonstrate their understanding of the specific industry disciplines during their three-year BA (Hons) course. When starting the academic year students are asked to choose an event team of up to eight students to work with for the duration of the unit, simulating working in an event or festival team in the workplace. It is recognised that group work poses its own problems in an academic setting, some students will want more control of their grades and prefer individual assessment and others may rely on their group to achieve their best work. For this reason, the core assessment is broken into three elements per year, the event manual (group work), the live event (group work) and a reflective essay (individual). This assessment format is the same for both the live event units, allowing the students to build a deeper level of knowledge by using the skills and theory learned in level 4 and applying them to level 5. This gives the students a clear understanding of expectations at each level and develops more a complex approach to problem solving as the course progresses.

In level 4 the students are given the opportunity to run a practice event before their assessed live event, this takes place in the classroom as it is a low-risk environment allowing students to concentrate on the very basics of running an event. Students host the event for the rest of the class and have sole responsibility for the theme, style and format of the event. Due to the safe environment student's focus on making the event fun and engaging, and the formative assessment is an enjoyable experience for all involved. Students understand that this practice event is part of the formative assessment process and are supported to try new concepts and develop practical skills they have not had experience of previously. The formative assessment is very much a nurturing process where students are given verbal, written and peer feedback timed a few months before the final live event assessment to give students time to reflect and adapt.

The first 'real' assessment is the event manual where students must divide the workload to produce one piece of group work which is graded by the tutor, and the group is given a collective grade mark. As the whole group has contributed to the project the students are given the opportunity to award their peers individual grades based on five criteria, ideas and suggestions, leadership and administration, event logistics, staging and customer care. The final grade is a 50% split contribution between the tutor and the student peer assessed grade. The tutor has the authority to override an unbalanced peer grade if they think the decision is not based on academic effort.

When the final event manual grades are released, students are told the grade the tutor initially awarded and their final peer assessed grade. This gives the students a balanced indication of how well they did according to the tutor (the client) and their peers (workmates). Often this is not taken well, and one-to-one tutorials are offered to support students who did not do as well as they thought or who may feel they have to justify their performance to the tutor.

Introducing peer assessment to the students from the very beginning gives them the opportunity to reflect and improve on their performance by using it as a formative assessment tool. By the time the second part of the assessment, the live event, comes around the students are well aware of their tutor expectations as well as what their event group expect from them.

Annie (anonymised) underperformed in her first year, she rarely attended seminars and group meetings and her contribution to group work in all her level 4 units was poor. She received a lower score to her peers in her first-year core unit and blamed everyone else in her reflective essay. At this stage of Annie's learning she was not ready to acknowledge that she was responsible for her own learning and performance. Annie passed the first year and returned still blaming the rest of her previous group for her poor grades. It was only when the class were asked to choose their event groups for the second year that Annie started to realise the effect this would have when in seminar time the whole class had chosen their groups and Annie sat on her own group less. The tutor intervened and both groups said they did not want her in the group due to her repu-tation for freeloading in group work. Annie had to make a case to each group as to why they should give her another chance and she was made to sign a group contract. Annie over delivered to all parts of the group work as she realised that it was her own attitude to learning that was holding her back. Annie graduated with a 2:1 in 2018.

Peer assessment is successful on this course as it opens a dialogue on individual and group performance between the student and tutor, reflect-ing the world of work and the structure of the festival and event industry.

When grading themselves for the first time, students will often inflate their own grade overestimating their contribution to group work. Falchikov (2005) argues that in the peer assessment process there will always be an element of over and under rating of peer performance; this can be monitored through the formative feedback process. As in Case Study 1, the student was not aware of her own shortcomings and when evaluating the assessment in a reflective essay still believed that the rest of the group were to blame. In this instance, the formative feedback did not have an instant effect on Annie's behaviour as she needed more proof that her own behaviour and approach to the task was the problem, triggering an emotional response to the situation. Beard and Wilson (2006) con-firm the significance of emotions in student engagement and response to learning. The feed forward process resulted in a positive outcome in this instance by allowing the student time to reflect on her actions, increasing awareness of self.

Boud and Molloy (2013) comment that the use of self and peer assess-ment seemed to accentuate students' critical processes and their ability to make judgements about their work. Both self and peer assessments were predominantly given in 'real time' with no delay to feedback and at best required some facilitation by the academic through, for example, an assessment handout for students to structure their responses. This sort of academic intervention addresses Carless' (2008) concerns that an element of trust and credibility needs to be built between peers if peer assessment is to be successful and for educationalists to work in a climate where review is valued, where they can share practice which is both celebrated as well as requiring change.

This self-reflection process is in contrast to the students participating in the BEng (Hons) Yacht and Powercraft Design and the BEng (Hons) Yacht Design and production. In Case Study 2 the students are given a clear end goal, to be the winner of the model yacht race. Students on these courses learn in a simulated environment throughout the year, outside of the traditional classroom set up. The students receive formative feedback throughout the learning journey, as described by Hattie and Timperley (2007) as a feed forward process.

Case Study 2

Model Yacht Assessment (Jean Baptiste Souppez, Senior Lecturer in Yacht Design and Composite Engineering, Solent University, UK)

The first year of a degree typically covers all the underpinning knowledge on which the rest of the course will be built but is often not appreciated as such by the students, overwhelmed with theory and missing on the practical applications. Consequently, it is vital to provide a real world and tangible learning outcomes, involving decision making and unique choices, in the form of an engaging assessment. To demonstrate the practical applications of all the knowledge and skills acquired in the first year of the BEng (Hons) Yacht and Powercraft Design and BEng (Hons) Yacht Design and Production at Solent University, students compete in a model yacht design, build and race.

In this piece of coursework, students are issued a design rule and are tasked with entirely designing their 70 cm long, 1.8 m tall model boats, building them and eventually racing them, making numerous informed decisions driven by their acquired theoretical understanding of naval architecture along the way. The race itself takes place in the very last week of the year and as such is a nice social event to showcase the student's achievements; nonetheless, the ranking is worth 20% of the assessment: the winner scoring full marks, and the sinkers none! Anecdotally, one's victory in the model yacht race is considered a terrific achievement, owning to prestigious yacht designers having won this particular event, and in one instance, one's victory was mentioned over 20 years later when being awarded an honorary PhD.

Throughout the academic year, this particular unit is focussed on building towards this final assessment and inherent deliverables and thus is structured in a manner that supports the students in successfully reaching the model yacht assessment. Firstly, the unit is only taught in seminar session, where students have a dedicated work station and work on an individual task. This allows the lecturer to assist and support each student individually, thus creating a more learner-centred environment, with room for personalised advice and practice.

Secondly, blended learning is utilised as part of the unit when looking at the use of specialist software, by either utilising existing online courses (Lynda.com) and videos tutorials made in-house. The students can therefore follow those at home, with the seminars being focussed on the practical application of the knowledge gained. With each session having a clear objective in the bigger picture of the overall coursework, a patchwork assessment style is adopted, keeping the students on track while providing ample opportunities to make their own design decisions.

Feedback is conceptualised by Hattie and Timperley (2007) who imply that the feedback is a consequence of a performance, and therefore comes too late to allow the learner to make the necessary progresses. This led to the feed forward concept which, coupled with formative assessments, will provide students with the valuable support they need in prevision of the summative assessment. This is the rationale behind the unit's structure: each summative assessment occurs after a similar formative one has been undertaken, with formative feedback given and opportunities for self-assessment and reflection, allowing the students to assess their own performance and critically evaluate changes to be made for the summative one. This strategy has proven to significantly reduce the pressure of the assessment and build student confidence. Eventually, the race also provides students with more than just the final assessor's comments, but a physical realisation of how their model boat compares to the rest of the class.

Lastly, the unit aims to build a skill set that will support a final tangible outcome: in this instance, the design, build and race of a model yacht. This represents a perfect example of an authentic learning activity, as defined by Ashford-Rowe, Herrington and Brown (2013), and a tremendous tool to boost engagement, but also motivates the students to achieve their best, and materialise their skills into designing and building their first yacht. The physical nature of the deliverable and the friendly, yet competitive, peer pressure of the race allows to build up the knowledge throughout the year with the model yacht as a clear objective. Furthermore, the highly social nature of the construction and race has proven a key strategy to ensure a strong cohesion across the cohort, building trust but also introducing peer mentoring. Indeed, as all students face similar challenges in the process, they will naturally support each other.

Over the decades, the model yacht assessment has become a flagship assessment of the Yacht Engineering courses at Solent University thanks to its real world nature, providing the students with a clear learning journey, building towards a physical assessment that is engaging, challenging and fun and draws together the whole of the first year's theory into the first yacht of their career as naval architects.

Use for Formative Feedback and Assessment to Enhance Real World Learning

Boud and Molloy (2013, p. 704) applaud "an approach to feedback that not only respects students' agency in their own processes of learning but can develop the dispositions needed for identifying and using feedback beyond formal educational structures". A student must be able to translate academic feedback into a form that is meaningful to themselves so that it can subsequently be used (Nicol, 2009). Feed forward provides a valuable alternative strategy to assessment and feedback for the emphasis is placed on active student engagement in the use of their feedback to encourage their own self-regulation (Murtagh & Baker, 2009). This has important potential benefits to students' learning and academics' time trying to support it.

The very nature of the assessment simulates the real work environment, and, in this instance, there is a tangible outcome. The exposure of students to learning within simulated environments where the feed forward activity contributed to the ongoing development of students' familiarity, and therefore their professional identity, within that setting. Any opportunity that allows students to learn and be critiqued by experts potentially adds to what Polanyi (1966) identifies as students' learning through the tacit dimension of learning found to contribute to students' fluency and criticality of their performance in practice (Benner, 1984).

The use of feed forward, in familiarising students with potentially complex environments that they will have to perform in a professional role in the future, embeds tacit knowledge into students' learning for future recall and builds confidence for the world of work, as long as the educationalist can articulate, against specific criteria, exactly how the student can improve.

Students are supported to achieve with constant and structured formative feedback, where the students are set online learning to complete at home and feedback and guidance are delivered through timetable tutorial and seminar classes. Students are given the framework and structure of the content of sessions therefore giving them the ownership and agency to develop themselves combining partnership working, coaching and mentorship.

The concept of an assessment being a competition as a standalone measurement of student learning would be neither fair nor productive; however, the feed forward structure of this course enables the students to develop their reflective practice in this learner-centred environment. The idea of winning and losing as an assessment replicates the risks involved within the industry, and to give students the opportunity to practise managing risk gives this assessment value and purpose. Shulman (2005) identifies that without a certain amount of anxiety and risk, there are limits to how much learning occurs. As a result of the structure of the assessment, overcoming hazards and dealing with unplanned situations heighten the students' sense of achievement and passion for their subject, and the excitement on race day embeds RWL in the process of making assessments fun, meaningful and memorable.

Taking a more active stance in their learning requires students to be tutored in new processes and attitudes that extend to students taking a more active role in their assessments (Boud & Molloy 2013). Academics themselves therefore need to be cognisant of a wider range of assessment methods and design, as well as their own personal practice that will encourage students to actively learn from previous performance. Boud and Molloy (2013) reinforce that the majority of publications on feedback in higher and professional education concentrate on the micro-skills of the educator in feedback. Whilst all teaching staff bring their own personal style to the giving of feedback, Carless, Salter, Yang and Lam (2011, p. 2) view feedback as a much wider skill set and offer characteristics of sustainable feedback that involve the student in the process of learning from the feedback given:

1. Involve students in dialogues about learning which raise their awareness of quality performance
2. Facilitating feedback processes through which students are stimulated to develop capacities in monitoring and evaluating their own learning
3. Enhancing student capacities for ongoing lifelong learning by student development of skills for goal setting and planning their learning
4. Designing assessment tasks to facilitate student engagement over time in which feedback from varied sources is generated, processed and used to enhance performance.

The literature therefore highlights two ways that students may use feed forward in their work. The first is a focused version of feed forward when the formative assessment shapes and drives the performance of students towards the summative assessment (Sadler, 1989; Hounsell, 2008). The second offers a broader interpretation of Carless et al.'s (2011) characteristics of sustainable feedback when a longitudinal view on student feed forward is used outside the specific boundaries of the formative-summative continuum for ongoing self-development. In other words, the feedback is used beyond the assignment for the development of future academic or professional skills. If students can attain self-regulation skills (Murtagh & Baker, 2009) through real world learning pedagogy, that allow them to interpret their feedback, these skills will work for them across courses and longitudinally during their academic careers.

The feed forward method gives the student the opportunity to reflect and grow both academically and emotionally, and the concept of a two-step assessment approach allows for a second chance approach to achieving the final grade mark, Sambell, McDowell and Montgomery (2013) describe the process as opening up a space where students can learn through failure and be supported to develop. Students do not always respond well to group assessment feedback and may seek to blame others when group work fails, as emphasis is often placed on individual academic achievement within an assessment framework (Boud & Hawke, 2004). By receiving detailed formative feedback from peer and tutors, the student can process and understand in more depth what they need to do in order to succeed, as this dual approach to feedback will also mimic the workplace.

To get the most positive results from this process, the assessment criteria must be transparent from the outset; students need to understand what it is exactly that they are being assessed on and, just as importantly, what they will not be graded on. For instance, simulated assessed tasks can involve pressurised scenarios with the added challenges associated with observation assessments. There may not be a physical product produced during the course of the assessment therefore tutors must establish and communicate to students what success looks like. How invisible outcomes can be assessed, such as, atmosphere and enjoyment must be communicated to the students and the complexity of the nature of the assessment will require an increased amount of coaching and mentoring. Again, the use of formative peer and tutor assessments will give the individual student a greater comprehension of how to succeed and what they will need to deliver in the summative assessment. To avoid marking students on personality traits or emotional response, and for formative feedback to be fair and constant, it must be based on the criteria the tutor has co-constructed with the class.

Formative assessment and feedback deepen students' understanding of the assessment particularly when the assessment criteria are complex and have the potential for the outcomes to be influenced by individual or group physical and emotional responses to a task. It was felt that common complaints of students only focusing on assessment-driven learning (Koen, Bitzer, & Beets, 2012) could start to be addressed if a balance was taken between two forms of feed forward when it was specifically placed within modules of learning as a formative activity as well as being used as a wider ethos for students' self-development.

Conclusion

Assessment emphasis on long-term development is currently at odds with the immediate approach to assessment and feedback to which students and universities have become accustomed. This chapter argues that academics designing learning programmes can identify the twin components of peer and formative review as a means of developing real world and unique assessment methods. Embedding practice and theory together are essential elements of RWL and authentic assessment.

It is also recommended that real world learning assessment needs to incorporate reflection as part of the formative or summative assessment. If reflection is not at a formative stage, students should go through the assessment cycle with reflection at the end. This can be addressed by inserting a 'What if?' stage which could be adopted into the assessment framework. A formative sample of 'what if?' scenarios would challenge the students to address the potential pitfalls of the summative assessment task and their personal and professional response to problems. For example, students in the BA (Hons) Festival and Event Management course could be presented with 'What if?' situations such as 'the venue cancels the day of your event' or 'adverse weather conditions affects staff transport to the venue' to prepare them for the Real World Assessment. Student reflection has to be part of authentic assessment whether implicitly or explicitly and course design and structure are key to the RWL framework.

The case studies present examples of development and sequential assessment, the use of other assessors other than the academic and an increasing co-constructive element between student and academic as described by Boud and Soler (2016). Consensus understanding by the teaching staff and the student of the meaning of assessment standards and their application and interpretation are an essential element to this co-constructive responsibility for feed forward. Student literacy needs to be supported by "meta-dialogues [to] discuss processes and strategies for assessment and feedback rather than the specifics of a particular piece of work" (Carless & Boud, 2018, p. 8).

Complaints as to the sometimes subjective nature of marking and grading of assignments will only be mitigated against if academic staff can articulate the strengths and limitations of any one assignment and in particular to express themselves well in identifying the way forward for students. The underlying ethos of Duncan, Prowse, Wakeman and Harrison (2003/2004) project could be built upon and named members of academic teams assist students to collate the essence of the feed forward recommendations and help the students to plan these into their next year's study. In this way, feed forward could be built into undergraduate courses early on rather than students arriving at it by chance or by the preference of individual academics.

References

Ashford-Rowe, K. J., Herrington, J., & Brown. (2013). Establishing the critical element that determine authentic assessment. *Assessment & Evaluation in Higher Education,* *39*(2), 205. https://doi.org/10.1080/0260293 8.2013.819566

Beard, C., & Wilson, J. (2006). *Experiential learning. A best practice handbook for educators and trainers* (2nd ed.). London and Philadelphia.: Kogan Page Limited.

Benner, P. (1984). *From novice to expert. Excellence and power in clinical nursing practice.* Menlo Park, CA: Addison-Wesley Publishing Company.

Bladen, C., & Kennell, J. (2014). Educating the 21st century event management graduate: Pedagogy, practice, professionalism and professionalisation. *Event Management,* *18*(1), 5–14. https://doi.org/10.3727/152599514X 13883555341724

Boud, D., & Hawke, G. (2004). *Sustainable assessment.* Sydney: The Australian Centre for Organisational, Vocational and Adult-Learning, University of Technology. (online).

Boud, D., & Molloy, E. (2013). Rethinking models of feedback for learning: the challenge of design. *Assessment and Evaluation in Higher Education, 38*(6), 698–712. https://doi.org/10.1080/02602938.2012.691462

Boud, D., & Soler, R. (2016). Sustainable assessment revisited. *Assessment & Evaluation in Higher Education, 41*(3), 400–413. https://doi.org/10.1080/02602938.2015.1018133

Carless, D. (2008). Trust, distrust and their impact on assessment reform. *Assessment and Evaluation in Higher Education, 34*(1), 79–89. https://doi.org/10.1080/02602930801895786

Carless, D., & Boud, D. (2018). The development of student feedback literacy; enabling uptake of feedback. *Assessment and Evaluation in Higher Education, 43*(8), 1315–1325. https://doi.org/10.1080/02602938.2018.1463354

Carless, D., Salter, D., Yang, M., & Lam, J. (2011). Developing sustainable feedback practices. *Assessment and Evaluation in Higher Education, 34*(1), 79–89. https://doi.org/10.1080/03075071003642449

De Bono, E. (1976). *Teaching thinking*. London: Penguin.

Duncan, N., Prowse, S., Wakeman, C., & Harrison, R. (2003/2004). *"Feed-forward": Improving students' use of tutors' comments.* Centre for Learning and Teaching. [online].

Falchikov, N. (2005). *Improving assessment through student involvement*. London: Routledge Falmer.

Gulikers, J. T. M., Bastiaens, T. J., & Kirschner, P. A. (2004). A five-dimensional framework for authentic assessment. Educational technology. *Research and Development, 52*(3), 67–87. https://doi.org/10.1007/BF02504676

Hattie, J., & Timperley, H. (2007). The power of feedback. *Review of Educational Research, 77*(1), 81–112. https://doi.org/10.3102/003465430298487

Hounsell, D. (2008). The trouble with feedback. New challenges, emerging strategies. *TLA Interchange* [online], Spring (2).

Koen, M., Bitzer, E. M., & Beets, P. A. D. (2012). Feedback or feed-forward? A case study in one higher education classroom. *Journal of Social Science, 32*(2), 231–242. https://doi.org/10.1080/09718923.2012.11893068

Kolb, D. (1984). *Experiential learning. Experience as the source of learning and development*. Englewood Cliffs, NJ and London: Prentice Hall Inc.

Morley, D., Bettles, S., & Derham, C. (2019). The exploration of students' learning gain following immersive simulation—The impact of feedback. *Higher Education Pedagogies, 4*(1), 368–384. https://doi.org/10.1080/23752696.2019.1642123

Murtagh, L., & Baker, N. (2009). Feedback or feed forward? A case study in one higher education classroom. *Journal of Social Science, 32*(2), 231–242.

Nicol, D. (2009). Assessment for learner self-regulation: Enhancing achievement in the first year using technologies. *Assessment and Evaluation in Higher Education, 34*(3), 335–352. https://doi.org/10.1080/02602930802255139

Nicol, D., & MacFarlane-Dick, D. (2006). Formative assessment and self regulated learning: Model and seven principles of good feedback practice. *Studies in Higher Education, 31*(2), 199–218. https://doi.org/10.1080/0307 5070600572090

Nicol, D., Thomson, A., & Breslin, C. (2014). Rethinking feedback practices in higher education: A peer review perspective. *Assessment and Evaluation in Higher Education, 39*(1), 102–122. https://doi.org/10.1080/0260293 8.2013.795518

Polanyi, M. (1966). *The tacit dimension*. London: Routledge and Kegan Paul.

Race, P. (2014). *Making learning happen. A guide for post-compulsory education* (3rd ed.). London, California, New Delhi, and Singapore: Sage Publications Ltd.

Sadler, D. R. (1989). Formative assessment: Revisiting the territory. *Assessment in Education, 5*(1), 77–84. https://doi.org/10.1080/0969595980050104

Sambell, K., McDowell, L., & Montgomery, C. (2013). *Assessment for learning in higher education*. London: Routledge.

Shulman, L. S. (2005). Signature pedagogies in the professions. *Daedalus* [online] (Summer), 52–59.

15

Using Educational Technology to Support Students' Real World Learning

Edward Bolton and Roger Emery

Introduction

Technology-enhanced learning (TEL) is the process of utilising information and communication technologies to support teaching and learning (Kirkwood & Price, 2014), with the aim of enhancing the learning experience for the student. This can be achieved by providing the learner with more flexibility with the pace, place and mode of learning that best suits them (Gordon, 2014). Learning, rather than reading or being told about a subject, can be experienced through different media such as video, simulation and augmented reality that gives context to the materials (Cook, Anderson, Combes, Feldman, & Sachdeva, 2018; Ahmet,

Case studies: Dawn A. Morley, Beth Gordon, Steven Bookman, Roger Emery, Tom Simons, Martina Brown, and Edward Bolton.

E. Bolton (✉) • R. Emery
Solent Learning and Teaching Institute, Solent University, Southampton, UK
e-mail: edd.bolton@solent.ac.uk

© The Author(s) 2021
D. A. Morley, M. G. Jamil (eds.), *Applied Pedagogies for Higher Education*,
https://doi.org/10.1007/978-3-030-46951-1_15

Gamze, Rustem, & Sezen, 2018). TEL also allows students and staff to communicate and collaborate beyond the physical teaching space by facilitating different modes of synchronous and asynchronous forms of communications such as webinar, online chat, forums, blogs and wikis.

We are currently in the throes of the fourth industrial revolution, where data are now becoming the natural resources that are fuelling economic growth. Digitisation is profoundly reshaping the way that we work and communicate with each other (OECD, 2019). Its effects are seen in almost every industry globally (Schwab, 2015). This rate of change of technology means that business is unable to keep up. The British Chamber of Commerce (Marshall, 2017) identified over 75% of UK companies experiencing a digital skills shortage in their employees of which 24% is a significant skills shortage. This skill deficit has been attributed to hampering productivity (Marshall, 2017) and a low proficiency to problem solve in technology-rich workplace (OECD, 2016). This may account for over half of graduates believing that higher education (HE) did not prepare them for their career (Pearson, 2019).

As educators in HE we have a duty to our graduates to prepare them for this rapidly changing world of work (Pearson, 2019). It is not simply training them on specific software but making them prepared for a digital landscape. No one technology learned will be future proof, but a range of software and experiences will make students more resilient to deal with continuous change:

> Workers in a digital environment are more likely to maintain or improve the skills they develop during their studies or in past professional experiences, because digitisation widens the variety of tasks they perform. (OECD, 2019, p. 56)

Technology in education has mirrored the evolution of the web. With Web 1.0, tutors would support their teaching by placing courses online for student to access and consume in their own time. However, technology can also be used to support the move away from a didactic transmission model of learning, where the expert imparts their knowledge, to a more collaborative active learning process whereby the students can build, test and adapt their knowledge (Kolb, 1984). This is reflected in

Web 2.0, which focuses on the communications aspects supporting a social constructivist model of learning (Wenger, 1998).

Web technology could now be considered as moving to Web 3.0 in reaction to the fourth industrial revolution through its use of data analytics and provision of the personalised experience. This is reflected in educational technology through the implementation of progress tracking and learning analytics in an attempt to 'measure learning' but also to provide the student with a personalised learning experience and evidence of their progress.

Effective learning technology integration requires that this is done as part of the learning design process and not as an afterthought (National Academies of Sciences, 2018). Simply replacing one technology for another, for example, moving a document online to cloud storage, does not necessarily result in learning enhancement. The user would certainly gain productivity benefits that they are now able to access the document from any internet-enabled device and they know that they are always working on the most up-to-date version. Impact on learning may come if an activity is designed where the document is shared from that cloud storage to other students or a tutor. The collaborative conversations and feedback, made significantly easier and convenient through technology, help learning happen.

This chapter will explore several tools and processes where technology has been essential to enhancing the learning process in a real world environment. The concept map (Fig. 15.1) visualised the key themes of the chapter. The chapter will start with light-touch TEL solutions that are relatively easy to implement to explore real world scenarios progressing through more substantial curriculum change and complex technologies that increasingly represent or emulate the workplace more authentically.

The technologies that attempt to represent or simulate the real world equip learners with the tools that will enable them to seamlessly transition between study and the workplace. Those learners will have been able to take their theory and apply it in practice in a safe environment. When they enter the workplace, students will be entering a new community, not of learners but now of practitioners. The learner has now to balance the process of becoming part of that community of practice

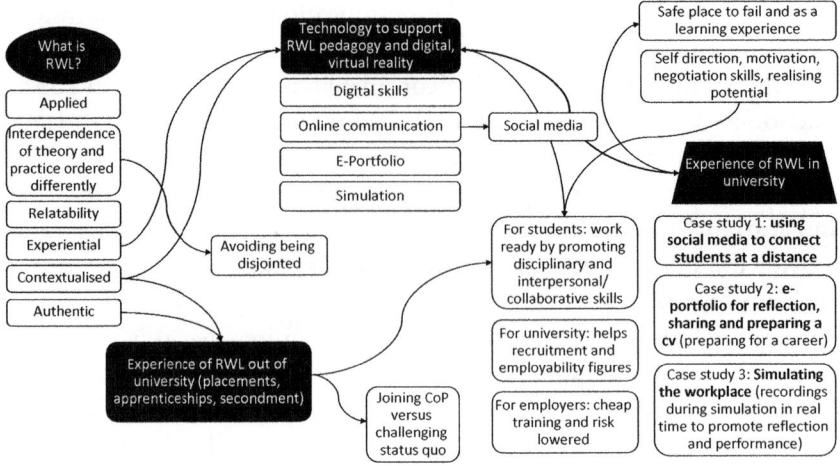

Fig. 15.1 Concept map from the authors

(Wenger, 1998) and being accepted as part of that community by the already established practitioners whilst on the other hand challenging current practices with the latest developments in academia.

Removing Technological Barriers to Develop Real World Skills

This chapter will explore technology from two aspects: the first is learning the technology and the second is learning through the technology. The first focuses more towards training, furnishing students with the technical knowledge by which they are to operate the technology that will be used to learn. This is essential, no matter how engaged the student is and how much they want to contribute; without the technical skills they will be unable to do so. It is also presumptive to assume that because the students are of a particular generation (Prensky, 2009) they already have the required skill set of, for example, using social media tools (discussed later in this chapter). Knowledge of one system does not necessarily translate to another, and learning discussions through technology may be seen as being more high stakes than a casual social situation, so the barrier of technology needs to be completely removed. The most effective way that this can be facilitated is within the classroom setting: tutors demonstrate and emulate desired behaviours, and the students practise this with guidance from the tutor. It is also worth pointing out that it is a necessity for the tutor to be comfortable with the technology, first to support their students, and second, if tutors value the technology themselves, this is picked up by students who will also value and engage with the technology (Morley, 2012).

Once the technological barriers have been overcome, the second step of learning through the technology can take place. This can develop a culture of learning: what the students are contributing, how this is adding value and whether this fits into the social norms that are expected in their future workplace. These two themes will run through all the technologies that we explore throughout this chapter.

Relevance of the Virtual Learning Environment in Relation to Real World Learning

Information technology, digital by its nature, is not limited to a physical location, thus provides the learner with more flexibility. The virtual learning environment (VLE), also referred to in some regions as a learning management system (LMS), supports learning by providing spaces outside the classroom for the learning to continue. For many students, use of the university's VLE is the primary online interaction with the institution (Phipps, Allen, & Hartland, 2018). This means that the student can continue their learning through directed activities without the tutors' direct intervention and feedback as this can be partially automated. As in simulations, VLEs give the ability for students to express their ideas, through blogs and fora in a safe space, reducing the consequence or repercussions of misconceptions and mistakes. The focus of learning is now about what the student is doing and not where they are. VLEs enable the learner to work at their pace, in a place and time that suits them.

To successfully utilise the VLE as an educational tool partly relies on the curation of appropriate content, but more importantly, it is the narrative that the students follow that deepens their knowledge and tests their ideas. Content is important, but the students need to be told why the resources are important and worth engaging with and connected to the knowledge they are learning. By using directive activities, students can be led to test their understanding in an automated quiz, asked to write a reflection on how it applied to their practice or articulate the arguments in their own words. The directed activity takes the place in lieu of the tutors' presence and allows the student to take action at a time and place of their choice.

The problem with the VLE is that it is a system that for the most part only exists in the realm of academia and does not represent any real world equivalent. For this reason, there are arguments that suggest it could be replaced with more authentic work-orientated tools such as online project management tools, especially Microsoft Teams (Phipps, 2019). There is, however, a growing interest in the use of online learning systems for employee training evidenced in the marketing of adapted VLEs for the commercial sector such as Moodle Workplace (Moodle, 2019) and Totara (Totara Learning, 2019). Many corporations are beginning to use VLEs to upskill their staff in a developing digital environment (Totara, 2020; Enlyft, 2020).

Platforms, originally marketed to the corporate sector, are finding traction in educational settings such as Trello, Microsoft Teams and MeisterTask. These incorporate two elements discussed earlier; social interactions between users and storage and management of collaborative work. They are based on Kanban boards, which visualise the work in progress related to a project (Rose, 2018). They comprise cards defining tasks that make their way across the board as members complete them. From the learners' perspective the 'project' is represented by the assignment and cards are the defined learning activities that will achieve this. Students interact and discuss by using the '@mentioning' function to alert other members of activity, which is recorded on the cards. Unlike the VLE, this cannot support individual self-directed learning and does not provide a structured narrative. Educators, therefore, have to balance technology that facilitates and enhances learning by exposing and training students to function effectively in the workplace.

Discussion and Collaboration Online Emulating Workplace Culture

This area of discussion considers the digital workplace, with a stonger focus on students becoming effective practitioners and a lesser focus on conveying understanding of a particular academic subject. Two key skills that are required in the world of work are: collaboration in online documentation and online discussion.

A key aspect of social constructivism is the ability of participants to build on and communicate their ideas with one another (Wenger, 1998). Technology has allowed to transcend the physical four walls of the classroom and continue without geographical borders into the online space. However, this is not a simple case of moving from one medium to another. Due to its nature, the discussion could be high-paced and low structured (Garrison, Anderson, & Archer, 2009). Conversely, Garrison goes on to say that online discussions provide a totally different environment. The importance of this is the lack of synchronicity; points can be articulated in an educated and considered fashion allowing the student to assimilate, reflect and respond. From these online discussions 'higher-order cognitive learning' is achieved when a student actively contributes to the discussion (Garrison et al., 2009).

Since these discussions are asynchronous the participants do not have to be engaged at the same time as their peers, allowing for much more flexibility (Patel & Aghayere, 2006). This is significant to the non-traditional student who may be balancing other pressures such as work. For students with disabilities, for instance a hearing impairment, or registered for additional learning support, synchronous discussions, whether online or face to face, can be challenging, which limits engagement with the group. A possible solution to overcoming barriers to engagement is the use of distributed and asynchronous learning technologies such as online forums (Anderson & Kanuka, 1997). This allows the participant time to digest the topic of conversation and construct their contribution. Unlike the real world context, the asynchronous online communication gives students the opportunity to be more reflexive about their inputs allowing them a level of protection in their participation—what Lave and

Wenger (1991) would term 'legitimate peripheral participation' and is a useful step towards their practice in authentic real world following graduation.

A discussion is a two-way process that through the contributions of peers can develop ideas and come to a shared sense of understanding. Palmer, Holt and Bray (2008) qualify that this happens when contributions to the discussions are made and not from those who simply read the material. These students, 'lurkers', do not add to the community of learners (Honeychurch, Bozkurt, Singh, & Koutropoulos, 2017), and due to the lack of contribution, it is difficult to track whether the student has indeed read the material or has learned from it. Salmon (2011) suggests a few reasons for the learner not contributing: a lack of skill or confidence, communication overload, the public nature and permanence of posts, and nothing additional to add to the post. This follows the theory of the "1% rule" of internet culture, where 1% create content, 10% interact with that content and the other 89% will just view it (Arthur, 2006).

Contribution begets contribution, so students who do not receive replies to their online post will not see the value and stop contributing themselves. Social validation and reciprocity are influencing factors in computer-mediated communications (Guadagno, Muscanell, Rice, & Roberts, 2013). Tutors can provide guidance for students on how to interact, provide encouragement to students and reward the students who communicate (Sun, Rau, & Ma, 2014).

As so much more communication is now being facilitated by technology, it is crucially important that learners are encouraged to embrace this medium of communication. Learning activities can be designed with collaborative documentation and communication giving the students these crucial technical skills. Applying real world problems can breathe life into otherwise more abstract and less engaging aspects of the curriculum and gives them context (Light, Cox, & Calkins, 2009). Comments and discussion features allow students to interrogate initial problems, and collaborative documentation allows students to work together to generate ideas and refine a solution.

Businesses are taking advantage of continuous internet connectivity, by moving documentation from local devices to centralised cloud storage (Coles, 2016). Applications are also embracing the cloud with the majority of providers making the switch in the coming years (IBM, 2018). As these services grow, we will see their reliability, security, expressivity and sustainability improve in the future (Varghese & Buyya, 2018). Benefits to users, and students, allow data created on one device and sent to the cloud, which becomes available on any other device with an internet connection. Backups are now automated, reducing the effects of human error and providers, such as Google Drive and Microsoft OneDrive, provide version control.

Use of Social Media for Learning and Working

Earlier, this chapter has discussed the facilitating conditions of online communication. Social media really gained mainstream popularity with the launch of Facebook in 2004, initially just to college and university students but then to the wider population allowing users to easily create and curate their own groups and networks. This marked the transition from Web 1.0 to 2.0, and presently there are around 2.45 billion users on the platform (Statista, 2019). Due to its popularity media advertising is shifting online to platforms such as Google and Facebook (Guttmann, 2019; eMarketer, 2018a, 2018b). The real world implications are two-fold, first as a medium where companies can communicate with their customers. Second, social media are now the platforms by which individuals build their professional identities (Beckingham, 2019).

Academics have been tempted to utilise social media platforms as they are familiar to students; they represent a real world environment and the students are already there. About 77% of UK students use social media to connect with other students, and 46% use platforms to support their learning (Pearson, 2019). These platforms do not present as much of a technological barrier and, therefore, have less of a training implication (Rowell, 2019). However, the transition of students from using social media as a professional space can have its repercussions. For example, health care students, such as nurses, have been advised to follow professional guidelines following high-profile cases of breaches of confidentiality (Morley, 2014). This is explored in depth in the first case study.

Before learners use social technologies in a learning context, they will likely have experienced them in a social context. As such their experiences may be varied. Critiques of social media claim that these platforms are in a race to the bottom for our attention, as time spent on the platform drives advertising revenue (Harris & Lewis, 2018). Algorithms promote the posts that drive engagement on that platform; those posts that elicit outrage have the most engagement more than any other emotion, leading to over sensationalised contributions (Vaidhyanathan, 2019). Students themselves may have experienced adverse actions from other users including trolling and callouts in their attempts to undermine individuals and their points of view (Marantz, 2019). These perceptions may inhibit meaningful engagement online, although on the learning platform, participants are known and interactions are monitored by academics.

However, private groups in social platforms such as Facebook do provide some level of protection. Students may themselves organise their own groups independently. Other services that students would want to consider on their journey towards becoming a professional are LinkedIn and Twitter LinkedIn boasts the largest professional network with over 660 million users (LinkedIn, 2020), giving them the opportunity to connect with industry professionals, and build a professional profile to find employment.

There is a difference between organic groups arising and explicitly using these platforms as a learning environment. Institutionally, supported systems will provide protection in terms of General Data Protection Regulation (GDPR), safe harbour and data protection. Student data are only used for the purpose of their learning and nothing else. Social media platforms are free at point of use exactly because user data are sold to other companies (Hardy, MacRury, & Powel, 2018), so it would be unethical to require students to sign up to these platforms to be part of the learning process. With the continuous progression towards 'online', the duty of educators is to prepare students so that they can make informed decisions on what personal data they share and how and what they communicate. Anything that is placed online will be searchable forever, potentially impacting future job opportunities.

Case Study 1

Facebook—Using Social Media to Connect Students at a Distance (Dr Dawn A. Morley, Principal Academic in Adult Nursing, Bournemouth University, Bournemouth UK)

As a personal tutor to adult nursing students, I experienced first-year student nurses returning from placement with stories of challenging treatment. The academic nursing team had carefully supported students through their first semester of academic study by placing them in the same seminar groups as their personal tutor groups. As students geographically dispersed to their first placements the support networks, accessible at university, were not called upon by students to make sense of their new learning environment or to seek advice on how best to learn.

It was clear some student nurses were communicating through Facebook, but this was not inclusive to all their group. In nursing, there are also underlying professional issues of students naively communicating on their personal Facebook accounts without realising the risk of breaching patient confidentiality—one of the cornerstones of the Nursing and Midwifery (NMC) code of conduct and punishable by exclusion from the professional register. It seemed that students when put 'at a distance' reverted to their social media accounts for support but the scale and risk of this were unknown.

Students had been using wikis as an online collaborative learning tool for two of their first semester modules and this included an introduction to netiquette in relation to the NMC code of professional conduct. Having successfully trailed online, group communication as part of their academic learning, I sought the informed consent of two first year tutorial groups who were about to leave on placement. I wanted to conduct a mixed method study of 52 first year students (Morley, 2014) whereby each of the two groups were divided into their original online groups that they had communicated with at university. On this occasion, each group was given the option of continuing their communication on placement through an allocated online medium—that of email communication with their personal tutor, use of the established wiki and a newly set up

Facebook account for the purposes of professional communication. The personal tutor acted as an e. Moderator for each of the groups trying to ensure enough space was given to students to respond to students in the first instance.

During the placement, students' access and use of their online tools were monitored. They were encouraged to reflect deeper on their learning experiences through their allocated medium. However, students across all groups only used the new communication routes for asking specific questions about the course or expressing immediate anxiety about starting the placement or frustration when their supernumerary status was threatened. The latter led to some immediate advice from the personal tutor although students, despite their briefing, resorted to naming their placements which immediately had to be taken down from the Facebook page as previously agreed with the students. Students' reflex to communicate in the same manner as their personal Facebook pages was clearly very strong.

Overall, out of all the communication routes it was Facebook that was used the most and this seemed to occur predominantly during the 2-week settling in period of the placement. No student took up the option of personal communication with their tutor for difficulties that they wished to discuss individually (Morley, 2014).

As a result of the research study, a comprehensive eLearning online training package was designed by academics that recognised students' Facebook usage and prepared them for the differences of communicating online in a professional context. The third-year students that piloted the training enthused how much they had learnt and how it would alter their online communication behaviour both personally and professionally. The training package, e. Smart, was launched in the first semester for nursing and occupational therapy degree courses and was eventually adapted by the University of Southampton for their medical degree courses.

Research findings were disseminated to academics in three internal workshops and interest was high in finding more immediate and student friendly ways of communicating. As part of the workshop, academics were assisted in setting up a Facebook account for their usage in the professional setting. The long-term success of this was limited as no academic was naturally active on their Facebook accounts.

With the progression of time, the use of 'WhatsApp' and 'Twitter' have provided more accessible and immediate routes for group communication. Twitter provides a way of sending 'breaking news' to students that may be relevant to their academic or professional development. As a way of summarising academic sessions, it provides a way for students to informally feedback their views on their day's teaching. This provides a more immediate and qualitative route for student course feedback which proves useful for academics as they move to the next week of delivery.

Capturing Real World Learning Through e-Portfolios

An e-portfolio is an electronic resource created by the learner. This is a collection of digital artefacts articulating their experiences, achievements and learning. Behind any product, or presentation, lie rich and complex processes of planning, synthesising, sharing, discussing, reflecting, giving, receiving and responding to feedback (JISC, 2008).

As with other technologies explored so far, the technical skills that are developed for the learner to engage with learning do not necessarily translate directly into the workplace. Despite this, they offer the same enhancement with online communication and collaboration and logistical benefits over physical paperwork. This chapter will explore how these portfolios can be shared with (potential) employers or capture experience from employment. As with other technologies, academics need not only support their students in their learning journey but also support them in the use of the system (Eynon & Gambino, 2016). They also provide accessibility and usability anywhere, at any time, for students, academics and employers.

Portfolios support a social constructivist (Web 2.0) style of learning through reflection. Unlike simulation they do not attempt to mimic real life, but through evidence collected in them, they draw upon it as part of learners' prior learning (Brown & Thoroughman, 2017). Unlike written assignments, reports and exams that test a student's point-of-time understanding, portfolios are a means by which student can demonstrate the path they have taken in their learning. For this reason they are considered a truer demonstration of their learning (Parker White, 2004). In real world learning the journey is as important as the final destination as, by its nature, it is an ongoing process of evidence collected through a variety of mediums (Eynon, Gambino, & Kuh, 2017). Learners continuously create links between the theory and real world concerns—as students grapple with lived experiences and try to make sense of them in the context of the theory (Lombardi, 2007). As a result, e-portfolios support the development of lifelong learners, and this ability to reflect on one's achievements, values and beliefs enables participants to make links to professional development better equipping them for a varied life of employment (Hartnell-Young & Morriss, 2007). An example of this developmental use can be seen in the Pace Pathway case study, where students use an e-portfolio all through their university programme and beyond into their careers.

Students' reflections show how their experiences and learning have impacted their decision making and future actions. The important addition of reflection gives "meaning to the student lived experienced, and delivered learning" (Buyarski, Oaks, Reynolds, & Rhodes, 2017, p. 7) adding value to learning. This action repeats in a cyclical process, and the learning theory is underpinned by reflective practice (Kolb, 1984; Moon, 2004; Schön, 2009; Gibbs 1988; Driscoll, 1994). Students thus curate their evidence into a final portfolio showcasing the milestones in their learning journey. The connections that they make deconstructing, analysing, reflecting and summarising these different experiences deepen the learning process (Sutherland, Brotchie, & Chesney, 2011; Eynon et al., 2017), and the portfolio platform is the tool that provides the personal learning space for this to happen.

Portfolios can be a powerful tool if used correctly; however, the process can be easily undermined. Students who are goal orientated will see the portfolio as a means of showing all of their work rather than a curated selection (Robin & Bair, 2018).

Deadlines drive action, which is in direct conflict with the ethos of the portfolios of sustained effort and reflection over time. To counter this academics may need to design in regular formative assessment points to drive engagement and provide feedback reinforcing the cyclical reflective process. A far more structured approach is required when students must evidence development or get 'signoff' when working towards a professional competency.

Conceptually the idea of collection and curation can be difficult for students to grasp, compounded by technical aspects of the online system that supports it. Software such as Mahara and PebblePad have two sections: first, the ability to input content, upload documentation, write blogs, create actions plans and write reflections all of which are private to the individual. The second is the portfolio, which resembles a webpage; this is where the student curates content from the pool of materials they have collected and generated. This becomes the 'public' presentation that best demonstrates the journey they have undertaken and what they have learned from the process.

The following case study looks to overcome the teaching investment both technically and conceptually by using portfolios as a tenant that runs through the entire course, rather than the burden placed on one module and the skills developed never utilised again.

> **Case Study 2**
>
> **The Pace Path (Dr Beth Gordon, Assistant Vice President for ITS, Academic and Administrative Services, Pace University, New York, USA; Steven Bookman, Adjunct Assistant Professor, Pace University, New York, USA; and Roger Emery, Head of Learning Technologies, Solent University, Southampton, UK)**

Pace University is a comprehensive institution in the New York, USA, metro area with approximately 13,000 students spread across six academic schools. Pace has been developing an e-Portfolio project, using the Mahara platform since 2010, which now is a mature and embedded provision to support students through their studies and on into employment.

The Pace Path was launched in 2014 and is a programme designed to provide all students with a competitive edge by setting them on a course to not only pursue their academic work but to also encourage them to pursue co-curricular work, advisory mentoring and networking from the very start of their university career. The Pace Path has been realised through the use of the e-portfolio platform to provide students with a tool to highlight certain competencies that tie in not only to their coursework but also to their co-curricular work (e.g., managing and evidencing their interpersonal relations and organizational awareness) and by tracking these competencies early on from their first semester of Pace University. This is designed to help students better understand the areas to develop in order to be successful not only as students at Pace but also successful in their careers beyond Pace.

Introducing first-year students to the e-portfolio through the Pace Path program provides a firm foundation of reflective practice, even if it is not required for other modules later in their courses. First-year students are introduced to the process, using a template in the e-portfolio to guide them; however, students quickly develop beyond the template adding dynamic content, such as examples of videos developing through various stages of production during an internship placement.

Another key aim is to develop a positive online presence and develop a complete personal professional branding in an era of social media. Students follow a set of guidelines, which come from videos from recruiters, a lecture from Career Services, and the professor's experience in the subject discipline, including conducting the assessment. This provides the students with the tools to write for a social media audience and, in particular, potential employers.

Creating an e-portfolio has opened students' eyes to how they will be viewed by future recruiters and employers. Many students see their accomplishments differently, and they mean more to them having them on the e-portfolio. They feel much more comfortable in the search for internships and jobs after having created an e-portfolio. These rich dynamic e-portfolios provide students with evidence of their employability beyond a CV and LinkedIn profile. Developing the language to prepare for the world of searching for jobs or internships helps students prepare for employability even if students do not use their e-portfolio during their interview process. By creating an e-portfolio, they build the language for discussing their strengths and weaknesses, their goals and aspirations. As a career development tool, it is extremely powerful.

The academic team did not want access to end when the student graduated after four or five years at Pace, so they worked together to ensure that alumni had lifelong access to their e-portfolio, which has also been a key to maturing the e-portfolio initiative and supporting the Pace Path. It also helps Pace because they maintain contact with their graduates and helps the students because e-portfolios, for employability, are critical not only right when they graduate but also six months to a year after when they are often searching for either graduate work, first jobs, second jobs or new opportunities. To have access to the e-portfolio allows students to show evidence of what they are capable of. They may not have a whole slew of professional experience behind them, but they have a lot of great academic and co-curricular work, perhaps an internship too, which just does not come across as clearly through something like LinkedIn alone. However, through e-portfolio, there is concrete evidence. Many students see their accomplishments differently and having developed an e-portfolio helps visualise their skills and qualities to feel much more comfortable in the search for internships and jobs. Creating an e-portfolio has opened students' eyes, as to how they will be viewed by future recruiters and employers.

Research carried out by Pace with employers in the area has shown that employers are really looking for this evidence. Dr Beth Gordon reflects: "It can make the difference by showing a technological proficiency and a certain savviness that our better students knew all along. However, we are trying to make it, so that all of our students have this same opportunity to show their best selves and do it in a powerful way through the e-portfolio".

Simulating the Workplace

Simulations allow learning to imitate real-life situations reducing real-life risk whilst still giving students the experience of it. Due to this they are used in situations of high economic, social, environmental or life-endangering risks of failure, for example, coxing an oil tanker or intubation on a patient. A level of immersion that is comparable to the real situation develops reflexive knowledge and skills, and this is especially crucial in high-stress, demanding environments as this will trigger processes developed in simulations enabling the student to act.

In previous sections it has been discussed that students are required to learn additional technical skills in order to engage with eLearning. In contrast with simulations, technical skills developed often directly translate to skills and behaviours required in the workplace. For example, a simulation of a ship's bridge will attempt to replicate what will be found on a real ship. Academics can then focus on the skills, attitudes and behaviours desirable to a practitioner of that given occupation (Cook et al., 2012). Not all simulations require the use of information technology, but with recent developments it has allowed an enhanced experience through the use of augmented reality and virtual reality (Holley & Hobbs, 2020). This gives the user a greater level of immersion without the cost of custom-made facilities, and this technology is further explored in the next chapter.

Information technologies have also enabled the capture of the simulation providing the student with a tool to review their performance, analyse, reflect, and learn and develop from it. The subsequent case study explores how this is implemented with students. Students can rewind, replay and scrutinise their verbal language, body language and ability to listen and develop professional skills without feeling embarrassed or judged in real world settings (MacLean, Geddes, Kelly, & Della, 2019). With this they are able to reflect and create action plans for their areas of development to work on to better their performance at the next simulation.

Case Study 3

Adult Nursing Simulation Scenario (Tom Simons, Lecturer in Adult Nursing, Edward Bolton, Learning Technologies, and Martina Brown, Senior Lecturer in Nursing, at Solent University, Southampton, UK)

Solent University is proud of being an institution that teaches vocational skills and gives students real world experience to better enable them to succeed in the workplace. The nursing degree is one such example. The university has designed the teaching space to mimic a real hospital ward, including adjustable beds, monitoring equipment, intravenous and oxygen supply. In place of patients the beds are filled with anatomically realistic dummies (Laerdal nursing Anne high fidelity simulators), who have skin real to the touch, breathe and have a pulse. The simulator allows the operator to directly interact with the student using their voice or a pre-recorded response/sound effect, such as vomiting. Students will have the opportunity to practice techniques, procedures and turn theory into practice. This gives them the opportunity to familiarise themselves with the setting and the dynamic of the space. In addition to the standard ward equipment, these rooms are also fitted with cameras, microphones and a computer.

Data feeds are taken from these devices along with a mock phone line and ECG monitor (displaying the vitals of the dummy patient) and fed into a capturing system installed on the computer. The ward telephone is connected to the system and can be used to ring the GP room for handover that would take place in the community or between wards in the hospital. Students will be asked to practice various scenarios where they will implement their knowledge. They assume different roles required to work as a team in their given scenario, which is aimed to test their practical competency but also the demands and stresses of the busy environment of the workplace. An operator will remotely control symptoms of the dummy patient and be able to call and directly talk to the students via the internal phone. As the scenario progresses complications are added to the scenario aimed at testing the students' resourcefulness, resilience and communications skills.

In one such scenario the students may be conducting a routine blood extraction when the operator simulates the dummy having a heart attack. Each of the students working individually, or in small groups, is encouraged to collect and interpret patient physiological data, establish a provisional nursing diagnosis and propose a nursing care plan, all to prevent the patient's condition from further deterioration. As the students progress, more complexities are added with additional time and resource pressures.

As the simulation is taking place the computer is capturing every aspect of the event. The video of the student and their movement actions, phone calls to the nurse students, ECG monitor of the dummy patient and all the conversations that the student has with the patient and other staff. The student is given the recording at the end of the simulation and is required to reflect on their actions. From this they then develop an action plan on areas to work on. With the benefits of such a system the students can revisit and better analyse the nuances of their actions and model them against best practice to see what area they should work on to develop.

To mimic the workplace and induce some panic and adrenaline, the tutor will run a real time scenario where they will inject a bit of urgency to stimulate an energetic response. The students can then get used to how they react and how to react to situations in the future.

The prospect of this can be daunting to a lot of students. An alternative for them is to attend other beds in the ward to practice routine tasks. The fact they are still in the room will offer the opportunity to watch the simulation unfold. At the end of it they are included in the debrief with the video where they are then asked to feedback their thoughts and feelings. This provides the simulation of a real-life experience that they have observed and which might help alleviate some of their fears of taking part in the future.

Not all the students are comfortable with cameras, so it is important to try to embed those concepts slowly. They know the CCTV is there, but it is not mentioned until the second module of the first year. When the students know they are being recorded there is a risk that they start concentrating on how they are perceived on camera rather than concentrating on the task in hand. This can be detrimental to their learning.

Simulating and recording major incidents is an effective way of showing the students the communication chain of command which is pivotal to deal with the situation. iPads record bed spaces and students are allocated patients. Students focus on the treatment for their allocated patients and here is also an overarching camera to capture the whole environment. The first time the student is given no structure to deal with the patients and their skills. This is done purposely in order to promote a level of chaos. Tutors can then use the overarching cameras to demonstrate how the chaos affects the whole room. The individual iPads record how the individual students react to the situation.

The students have an assignment where they must reflect on their practice and their conversation that has been recorded. This forces the student to go back and engage with the video recording. Whereas if this were a formative assessment not all learners will necessarily engage with reviewing the situation because they may not feel comfortable watching themselves and reviewing themselves.

Conclusion

This chapter has explored numerous ways that technology can be uniquely used to support learning in real world experiences looking at 'light-touch' TEL solutions before moving on to explore real world scenarios that are enabled through more complex technologies to attempt to authentically emulate the workplace. The increasing need for digital literacy as part of future employability (Pearson, 2019) can be addressed at university through a better orientation to the increasing availability and functionality of technology. The chapter has also presented three case studies, where technology has enhanced pastoral support, the use of portfolios and simulation by adding an additional dimension to existing, traditional learning.

However, a word of caution with the use of TEL: it must be remembered that these are just tools, as with any tools its acquisition does not provide success. Academics need to model appropriate practice so that students develop confidence and increasing professionalisation with the technology (Morley & Carmichael, 2020). The eLearning process needs to be carefully planned and how this will emulate real world experience. From the perspective of the academic, a real world approach needs to be cultivated continuously and integrated seamlessly into the narrative of the learning process that students will follow.

References

Ahmet, A., Gamze, K., Rustem, M., & Sezen, K. A. (2018). Is video-based education an effective method in surgical education? A systematic review. *The Journal of Surgical Education, 75*(5), 1150–1158. https://doi.org/10.1016/j.jsurg.2018.01.014

Anderson, T., & Kanuka, H. (1997). On-line forums: New platforms for professional development and group collaboration. *Journal of Computer-Mediated Communication, 3*(3). https://doi.org/10.1111/j.1083-6101.1997.tb00078.x

Arthur, C. (2006, July 20). What is the 1% rule? *The Guardian*. Retrieved from https://www.theguardian.com/technology/2006/jul/20/guardianweeklytechnologysection2

Beckingham, S. (2019). Developing a professional online presence and effective network. In C. Rowell (Ed.), *Social media in higher education: Case studies, reflections and analysis* (pp. 21–34). Cambridge: Open Book Publishers. Retrieved from https://doi.org/10.11647/OBP.0162

Brown, G., & Thoroughman, K. (2017). Authentic learning: Eportfolios across the divide. In T. Batson, T. L. Rhodes, E. Watson, H. L. Chen, K. S. Coleman, & A. Harver (Eds.), *Field guide to eportfolio* (pp. 25–31). Washington, DC: Association of American Colleges and Universities.

Buyarski, C., Oaks, S., Reynolds, C., & Rhodes, T. L. (2017). The promise of eportfolios for student learning and agency. In T. Batson, T. L. Rhodes, E. Watson, H. L. Chen, K. S. Coleman, & A. Harver (Eds.), *Field guide to eportfolio* (pp. 7–13). Washington, DC: Association of American Colleges and Universities.

Coles, C. (2016). *Office 365 adoption and risk report*. Online. Retrieved from https://www.skyhighnetworks.com/cloud-security-blog/7-charts-reveal-the-meteoric-rise-of-office-365/

Cook, D. A., Andersen, D. K., Combes, J. R., Feldman, D. L., & Sachdeva, A. K. (2018). The value proposition of simulation-based education. *Surgery, 163*(4), 944–949. https://doi.org/10.1016/j.surg.2017.11.008

Cook, D. A., Brydges, R., Hamstra, S. J., Zendejas, B., Szostek, J. H., Wang, A. T., … Hatala, R. (2012). Comparative effectiveness of technology-enhanced simulation versus other instructional methods: A systematic review and meta-analysis. *Simulation in Healthcare: Journal of the Society for Simulation in Healthcare, 7*(5), 308–320. https://doi.org/10.1097/SIH.0b013e3182614f95

Driscoll, J. (1994). Reflective practice for practise. *Senior Nurse, 14*(1), 47.

eMarketer. (2018a). Media advertising spending in the united states in 2019, by medium.

eMarketer. (2018b). Data suggests surprising shift: Duopoly not all-powerful. Retrieved from https://www.emarketer.com/content/google-and-facebook-s-digital-dominance-fading-as-rivals-share-grows

Enlyft. (2020). Companies using moodle. Retrieved from https://enlyft.com/tech/products/moodle

Eynon, B., & Gambino, L. M. (2016). Professional development for high-impact eportfolio practice (ANALYSIS)(report). *Peer Review, 18*(3), 4.

Eynon, B., Gambino, L. M., & Kuh, G. D. (2017). *High-impact ePortfolio practice* (1st ed.). Sterling, Virginia: Stylus.

Garrison, D. R., Anderson, T., & Archer, W. (2009). Critical thinking, cognitive presence, and computer conferencing in distance education. *American Journal of Distance Education, 15*(1), 7–23. https://doi.org/10.1080/08923640109527071

Gibbs, G. (1988). *Learning by doing.* London: FEU.

Gordon, N. (2014). *Flexible pedagogies: Technology-enhanced learning.* Retrieved from https://www.advance-he.ac.uk/knowledge-hub/flexible-pedagogies-technology-enhanced-learning

Guadagno, R. E., Muscanell, N. L., Rice, L. M., & Roberts, N. (2013). Social influence online: The impact of social validation and likability on compliance. *Psychology of Popular Media Culture, 2*(1), 51–60. https://doi.org/10.1037/a0030592

Guttmann, A. (2019). Media advertising spending in the united states from 2015 to 2022. Retrieved from https://www.statista.com/statistics/272314/advertising-spending-in-the-us/

Hardy, J., MacRury, I., & Powell, H. (2018). *The advertising handbook* (4th ed.). Abingdon: Routledge.

Harris, T., & Lewis Helen. (2018). *How tech has hijacked our brains.* London: Intelligence Squared.

Hartnell-Young, E., & Morriss, M. (2007). *Digital portfolios: Powerful tools for promoting professional growth and reflection* (2nd ed.). Thousand Oaks, CA: Corwin Press.

Hobbs, M., & Holley, D. (2016). Using augmented reality to engage STEM students with an authentic curriculum. EAI Endorsed Transactions on E-Learning, 3, 151447. https://doi.org/10.4108/eai.15-6-2016.151447

Holley, D., & Hobbs, M. (2020). Developing an authentic curriculum using augmented reality tools: An action research approach. *Research in Learning Technology.*

Honeychurch, S., Bozkurt, A., Singh, L., & Koutropoulos, A. (2017). Learners on the periphery: Lurkers as invisible learners. *European Journal of Open, Distance and E-Learning, 20*(1), 191. https://doi.org/10.1515/eurodl-2017-0012

IBM. (2018). Cloud computing: A complete guide. Retrieved from https://www.ibm.com/cloud/learn/cloud-computing

JISC. (2008). *Effective practice with e-portfolios.* Bristol: University of Bristol. Retrieved from https://issuu.com/jiscinfonet/docs/jisc_effective_practice_with_e-portfolios_2008

Kirkwood, A., & Price, L. (2014). Technology-enhanced learning and teaching in higher education: What is 'enhanced' and how do we know? A critical literature review. *Learning, Media and Technology, 39*(1), 6–36. https://doi.org/10.1080/17439884.2013.770404

Kolb, D. A. (1984). *Experiential learning.* Englewood Cliffs, NJ: Prentice-Hall.

Lave, J., & Wenger, E. (1991). *Situated learning. legitimate peripheral participation.* Cambridge: University Press. Retrieved from http://www.fachportal-paedagogik.de/fis_bildung/suche/fis_set.html?FId=741925

Light, G., Cox, R., & Calkins, S. (2009). *Learning and teaching in higher education* (2nd ed.). London: Sage. Retrieved from http://digitool.hbz-nrw.de:1801/webclient/DeliveryManager?pid=1915182&custom_att_2=simple_viewer

LinkedIn. (2020). About LinkedIn. Retrieved from https://about.linkedin.com

Lombardi, M. (2007). Authentic learning for the 21st century: An overview. ().EDUCAUSE. Retrieved from https://library.educause.edu/resources/2007/1/authentic-learning-for-the-21st-century-an-overview

MacLean, S., Geddes, F., Kelly, M., & Della, P. (2019). Video reflection in discharge communication skills training with simulated patients: A qualitative study of nursing students' perceptions. *Clinical Simulation in Nursing, 28*, 15–24. https://doi.org/10.1016/j.ecns.2018.12.006

Marantz, A. (2019). *Antisocial.* New York: VIKING.

Marshall, A. (2017). *UK companies are facing a shortage of digital skills in their workforce which is hampering productivity.* London: British Chambers of Commerce. Retrieved from https://www.britishchambers.org.uk/media/get/BCC%20Digital%20Survey%202017%20Summary-2.pdf

Moodle. (2019). Moodle workplace: Online training, onboarding and development. *Moodle.* Retrieved from https://moodle.com/workplace/

Moon, J. A. (2004). *Handbook of reflective and experiential learning: Theory and practice.* London: RoutledgeFalmer.

Morley, D. (2012). Enhancing networking and proactive learning skills in the first-year university experience through the use of wikis. *Nurse Education Today, 32*(3), 261–266.

Morley, D and Carmichael, H. (2020). Engagement in socio constructivist online learning to support personalisation and borderless education. *Student Engagement in Higher Education Journal, 3*(1), 115–132

Morley, D. A. (2014). Supporting student nurses in practice with additional online communication tools. *Nurse Education in Practice, 14*(1), 69–75. https://doi.org/10.1016/j.nepr.2013.06.005

National Academies of Sciences, E. M., Division, H. M., Health, B. G., Education, G. F. I. H. P., Forstag, E. H., & Cuff, P. A. (2018). *Improving health professional education and practice through technology: Proceedings of a workshop*. National Academies Press. Retrieved from https://books.google.co.uk/books?id=bOF0DwAAQBAJ

OECD. (2016). *Skills for a digital world, policy brief on the future of work*. Paris: OECD Publishing. Retrieved from https://www.oecd.org/els/emp/Skills-for-a-Digital-World.pdf

OECD. (2019). *OECD skills outlook 2019*. Paris: OECD Publishing. https://doi.org/10.1787/df80bc12-en

Palmer, S., Holt, D., & Bray, S. (2008). Does the discussion help? the impact of a formally assessed online discussion on final student results. *British Journal of Educational Technology, 39*(5), 847–858. https://doi.org/10.1111/j.1467-8535.2007.00780.x

Parker White, C. (2004). Student portfolios: An alternative way of encouraging and evaluating student learning. *New Directions for Teaching and Learning, 2004*(100), 37–42. https://doi.org/10.1002/tl.169

Patel, J., & Aghayere, A. (2006). *Students' perspective on the impact of a web-based discussion forum on student learning*. Paper presented at the 36th Annual Conference Frontiers in Education, 26–31 October. https://doi.org/10.1109/FIE.2006.322600. Retrieved from https://ieeexplore.ieee.org/document/4117225

Pearson. (2019). *Global learner survey*. London: Pearson. Retrieved from https://www.pearson.com/content/dam/one-dot-com/one-dot-com/global/Files/news/gls/Pearson_Global_Learner_Survey_2019.pdf

Phipps, L. (2019). Thinking aloud: MS teams, domain of one's own and EdTech. Retrieved from http://lawriephipps.co.uk/?p=9393

Phipps, L., Allen, R., & Hartland, D. (2018). *Next generation [digital] learning environments: Present and future*. Bristol: JISC. Retrieved from http://repository.jisc.ac.uk/6845/1/JR0090B_NDGLE_REPORT_EXECUTIVE_SUMMARY_SINGLE_PAGE_MAY18.pdf

Prensky, M. (2009). H. Sapiens digital: From digital immigrants and digital natives to digital wisdom. *Innovate* [online], *5*(3), 1–11.

Robin, A. M., & Bair, H. (2018). Deconstructing the notion of ePortfolio as a 'High impact practice': A self-study and comparative analysis. *The Canadian Journal for the Scholarship of Teaching and Learning, 9*(3), 1–16. https://doi.org/10.5206/cjsotl-rcacea.2018.3.6

Rose, D. (2018). *Stay lean with kanban*. Carpenteria, CA: linkedin.com.

Rowell, C. (2019). From a tweet to a blog, to a podcast, to a book. In C. Rowell (Ed.), *Social media in higher education: Case studies, reflections and analysis* (pp. 3–20). Cambridge: OpenNook Publishers. https://doi.org/10.11647/OBP.0162

Salmon, G. (2011). *E-moderating* (3rd ed.). New York: Routledge. Retrieved from http://bvbr.bib-bvb.de:8991/F?func=service&doc_library=BVB01& local_base=BVB01&doc_number=022628568&sequence=000001&line_ number=0001&func_code=DB_RECORDS&service_type=MEDIA

Schön, D. A. (2009). *The reflective practitioner* (Paperback ed., reprinted ed.). Farnham: Ashgate. Retrieved from http://bvbr.bib-bvb.de:8991/F?func= service&doc_library=BVB01&local_base=BVB01&doc_number= 017750199&sequence=000003&line_number=0001&func_code=DB_ RECORDS&service_type=MEDIA

Schwab, K. (2015, December 12). The fourth industrial revolution. *Foreign Affairs*. Retrieved from https://www.foreignaffairs.com/articles/2015-12-12/ fourth-industrial-revolution

Statista. (2019). Number of monthly active Facebook users worldwide as of 3rd quarter 2019 (in millions). Retrieved from https://www.statista.com/statis-tics/264810/number-of-monthly-active-facebook-users-worldwide/

Sun, N., Rau, P. P., & Ma, L. (2014). Understanding lurkers in online commu-nities: A literature review. *Computers in Human Behavior, 38*, 110–117. https://doi.org/10.1016/j.chb.2014.05.022

Sutherland, S., Brotchie, J., & Chesney, S. (2011). *Pebblegogy* (1st publ. ed.). Telford: Pebble Learning. Retrieved from http://bvbr. bib-bvb.de:8991/F?func=service&doc_library=BVB01&local_ base=BVB01&doc_number=024955948&sequence=000001&l ine_number=0001&func_code=DB_RECORDS&service_type=MEDIA

Totara learning. (2019). Totara learning—Freedom to learn. Retrieved from http://www.totaralearning.com/node/10

Totrara. (2020). Customer stories. Retrieved from https://www.totaralearning. com/customer-stories

Vaidhyanathan, S. (2019). *Antisocial media*. Oxford: Oxford University Press.

Varghese, B., & Buyya, R. (2018). Next generation cloud computing: New trends and research directions. *Future Generation Computer Systems, 79*, 849–861. https://doi.org/10.1016/j.future.2017.09.020

Wenger, E. (1998). *Communities of practice* (Reprint. ed.). Cambridge: Cambridge University Press.

16

Real-Time, Real World Learning— Capitalising on Mobile Technology

Keith D. Parry, Jessica Richards, and Cameron McAuliffe

Introduction

This chapter explores the adoption of Web 2.0 technologies to promote active learning by students and to both mediate and enhance classroom instruction. Web 2.0 refers to open source, web-enabled applications (apps) that are driven by user-manipulated and user-generated content (Kassens-Noor, 2012). These apps are often rich in user participation, have dynamic content, and harness the collective intelligence of users (Chen, Hwang, & Wang, 2012). As such, these processes create "active, context based, personalised learning experiences" (Kaldoudi, Konstantinidis, & Bamidis, 2010, p. 130) that prioritise learning ahead of teaching. By putting the learner at the centre of the education process

K. D. Parry (✉)
Bournemouth University, Bournemouth, UK
e-mail: kdparry@bournemouth.ac.uk

J. Richards • C. McAuliffe
Western Sydney University, Sydney, Australia

© The Author(s) 2021
D. A. Morley, M. G. Jamil (eds.), *Applied Pedagogies for Higher Education*,
https://doi.org/10.1007/978-3-030-46951-1_16

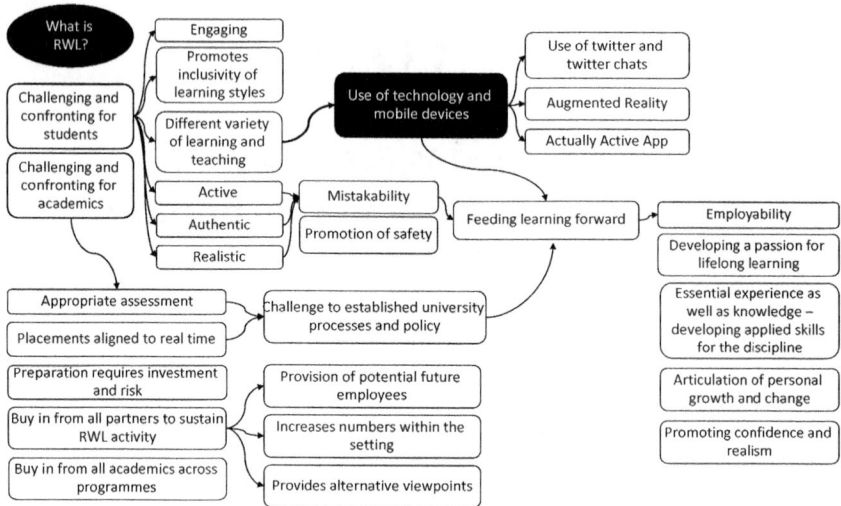

Fig. 16.1 Concept map from the authors

educators can provide environments that enhance employability prospects and spark a passion for learning that, hopefully, lasts a lifetime.

As such, we critique an active learning approach that makes use of technology such as mobile applications (apps), Twitter, and augmented reality to enhance students' real world learning. Dunlap and Lowenthal (2009) argue that social media can facilitate active learning as they recreate informal, free-flowing communications that allow students and academics to connect on a more emotional level. Furthermore, their use upskills students in the technical complexities of the digital world and also the specialised discourses that are associated with online participation, suitable for real world learning and working (Fig. 16.1).

Three case studies explore the benefits of Web 2.0 processes. The first details the use of Twitter chats to connect students, academics, and industry professionals via online synchronous discussions that offer a number of benefits such as encouraging concise writing from students and maintaining on-going relationships between staff, students, and industry contacts. The second details a location-based mobile app that delivers content to students when they enter a defined geographical boundary linked to an area of a sports precinct. Finally, we explore the use of augmented reality apps to enhance teaching in Human Geography and Urban Studies.

Engaging Students

Academic engagement, which can be defined as active involvement in learning, is linked to high achievement. According to Park et al. (2012) it has been identified by educational researchers as a primary predictor of high levels of achievement in high school in particular. Students who are highly engaged at school are more likely to learn more, earn higher grades, and pursue higher education (Sciarra & Seirup, 2008). Yet, too often, students are apathetic, lack interest, and only engage superficially with learning; leading Newmann (1992, p. 2) to argue that "the most immediate and persisting issue for students and teachers is not low achievement, but student disengagement".

Newmann (1992) contrasts engagement with the above conditions that have become (too) common in many education settings. Herrmann (2013) identifies that the higher education sector is now aware that undergraduates are often passive in teaching sessions and suggests that a solution to this is active learning, which is capable of motivating students to engage meaningfully in their courses and in their classes. Such an approach engages students in high-level thinking strategies and develops improved cognitive skills (Stolk & Harari, 2014). Stevens (2015) claims that when students process information in meaningful ways they are transformed from 'consumers of content' to 'producers of knowledge'. Building on Biggs and Tang's (2011) discussion of constructivism, we argue that students should indeed become producers of knowledge rather than consumers of content (Stevens, 2015).

As far back as the late 1990s researchers were beginning to advocate for active learning techniques to replace passive classroom activities and it has now been highlighted as a good practice in undergraduate teaching (Kassens-Noor, 2012). According to Moore (2013) even seemingly 'traditional' institutions have developed activity-based learning courses. It can include "lively debates between instructors and students, peer-to-peer discussions, reflective writing and team work" (Kassens-Noor, 2012, p. 9), but increasingly more innovative active learning practices are being employed.

In many Western societies, students are now bringing a variety of mobile electronic devices into the classroom and it can be challenging to maintain their interest and engagement when they can be connected to the world outside the classroom via these devices (Kuznekoff, Munz, & Titsworth, 2015). In a review of the use of mobile electronic devices in classrooms, Kuznekoff, Munz, and Titsworth (2015) concluded that when such devices were used for non-relevant activities, they were a distraction for not only the user but also those students seated in close proximity. As a result, the typical practice for educators is to ask students to switch off phones or to at least to put them away during teaching sessions. The fear that mobile devices, and the access that they provide to external content (and people), will disrupt the flow and control of information may explain the reluctance of many educators to embrace them. Indeed, it can be both daunting and challenging to step away from traditional practices based on face-to-face instructions where the teacher conveys and arranges the learning and knowledge flow (Nincarean, Alia, Halim, & Rahman, 2013). Furthermore, in a survey of higher education faculty members, it was found that while over 90% of academics are using social media in the courses they teach or their professional careers the vast majority believed that social networks take more time than they are worth (Moran, Seaman, & Tinti-Kane, 2011).

Nevertheless, it is now recognised that social media sites offer value for teaching practices in higher education, affording particular benefits for collaborative learning (Moran, Seaman, & Tinti-Kane, 2011), which resultantly allows students to construct knowledge. Web 2.0 technologies and practices are now being introduced into teaching and learning activities around the world (Dohn, 2009). Dohn (2009) notes that Web 2.0 technologies and educational practices must be reshaped to fit each other and so the time and effort needed to successfully and effectively combine the two should not be underestimated. Yet, when the two are integrated effectively it is possible to create innovative teaching and learning environments that engage students. Moreover, the introduction of technology "provides an exciting opportunities [sic] to design learning environment that are realistic, authentic, engaging and extremely fun" (Nincarean et al., 2013, p. 658). It is the realistic aspect of these innovative learning environments that is of particular interest to this chapter.

In the early twenty-first century, the integration of learning technologies has been at the forefront of innovation in learning experiences. In particular, the ability to co-create content via Web 2.0 technologies positions them as ideal tools to facilitate an active learning approach where students create both content and knowledge. Whereas traditional forms of media have used one-directional communication models, web-mediated communication practices such as social media applications permit two-way communication between the site and users that allows them to create their own content and the interact with other users. One way to produce active and productive learners is through the use of Web 2.0 technologies and more specifically Web 2.0 practices (such as blogging and using social media platforms) that create collaborative and participatory learning environments (Tambouris et al., 2012). Web 2.0 has even been specifically described as "a collaborative medium" by the inventor of the World Wide Web, Tim Berners-Lee (1997) and it offers solutions to a number of the problems that beset higher education.

For example, with large-group teaching sessions there are a number of challenges, amongst which is the ability of teachers to assess the degree to which the information being presented is retained by learners (Fisher, Exley, & Ciobanu, 2014). Furthermore, these large-group sessions can be daunting as it can be difficult to identify what the audience is thinking. The use of electronic audience response systems can transform a passive audience into active learners (Boscardin & Penuel, 2012, Raux, 2012, Keogh & Wang, 2010). Early clicker-based systems have been replaced with web-based audience response system such as GoSoapBox and PollEverywhere. One simple benefit to these systems is that they can provide immediate and anonymous feedback. They allow the teacher to analyse student comprehension and learning during sessions (Konstantinidis, Bamidis, & Kaldoudi, 2009). Regardless of whether it is because of their collaborative nature or not, student interest and satisfaction has been shown to increase when Web 2.0 tools are implemented in the curriculum (Rogers-Estable, 2014). However, many of these integrated practices are still based on traditional campus-based models of instruction with technological support.

There is an increased expectation that learning should be available on demand, reflective of entertainment habits in a modern consumer society. The "anytime, anyplace" nature of such connected devices allow learners to study at times and locations that are convenient to them and, crucially, when driven to do so by curiosity or in response to an external stimulus. In addition, they facilitate informal learning, building on the "previous experiences that net generation learners have with social networking" (Williams & Chinn, 2009, p. 165). Young people are using Web 2.0 technologies voluntarily in their own time so the integration of these into teaching and learning practices in HE settings can help to motivate and reassure students (Dohn, 2009). As technology becomes increasingly interconnected and ubiquitous in everyday life there may even be an expectation from students that their learning experiences will reflect their real world practices and feature Web 2.0 technologies. Such technologies also provide a more learner-controlled environment as users can obtain information quickly and efficiently via mobile devices and mobile Web 2.0 apps. A form of "highly active and participatory experiences" that today's students are searching for (Brill & Park, 2008, p. 71) is thus created.

In addition, incorporating social media into learning process has the added benefit of upskilling students for future jobs that will increasingly require competence in the use of Web 2.0. It is naïve to assume that all digital natives are technologically sophisticated and comfortable with using technology. However, for successful engagement in education and the wider world it is essential that students develop the skills and knowledge that enable them to engage in "the new literacies of the internet" (Nicholson & Galguera, 2013, p. 7). Therefore, the integration of Web 2.0 into HE practices can further enhance the employability prospects of students. In addition to preparing students to be work ready in the twenty-first century, technology-rich learning environments have the potential to create lifelong learners and citizen-scholars possessing "global awareness, creativity, collaborative problem-solving, self-directed learning" (Groff, 2013, p. 1). These twenty-first century skills improve "learning and innovation skills, life and career skills, information and media skills" (Papanastasiou et al., 2018, p. 2). Therefore, As Dohn (2009) puts it, effective use of Web 2.0 can provide a "lifelong, life-wide" set of skills and weaken boundaries between formal and informal learning.

Social Media

Social media has been defined as "a group of internet-based applications that build on the ideological and technological foundations of Web 2.0, and that allow the creation and exchange of User Generated Content" (Kaplan & Haenlein, 2010, p. 61). Social media has recently been adopted by a number of academics to promote active learning by students and to both mediate and enhance classroom instruction (Tess, 2013). Dunlap and Lowenthal (2009) argue that Twitter can facilitate this form of learning as it recreates the

> informal, free-flowing, just-in-time banter and chit-chat that we [academics] have with students in our on-campus courses—the banter that helps us get to know each other, experience our personalities, and connect on a more emotional level.

Informal learning, as facilitated by both Twitter and active learning, is an essential component of education that enhances academic performance (Kassens-Noor, 2012). To facilitate this process, it is important that students are provided with out-of-class opportunities to interact with each other, with academic staff, and, potentially, industry professionals. Junco, Heiberger, and Loken (2011) found that the use of Twitter increased engagement in the learning process by both staff and students and increased communication, through the creation of non-traditional classroom activities. In a controlled experimental study of first year students a class Twitter account was used to continue in-class discussions, to provide a "low-stress way to ask questions", to provide information on class and campus activities, as an optional assessment task, and as part of compulsory assessments (Junco, Heiberger, & Loken, 2011, p. 122). Twitter also provides individual students (particularly less vocal ones) with a voice in large classrooms settings (Kuznekoff, Munz, & Titsworth, 2015) and may increase student contact with staff outside of class (DeGroot, Young, & VanSlette, 2015), both of which may reduce feelings of isolation and foster a sense of community. Twitter has also been shown to increase the informal communications between staff and students that have been found to "positively influence student perceptions of trust and feelings of instructor immediacy, as well as student motivation" (DeGroot, Young, & VanSlette, 2015, p. 2).

Yet contrary to the findings of Jacquemin, Smelser, and Bernot (2014), students are not necessarily au fait with the use of all social media platforms and Twitter may be less commonly adopted by students than other platforms. Lin, Hoffman, and Borengasser (2013) found that students require education on how to use Twitter as many were not using it, while DeGroot et al. (2015) that even those who do use it may need educating on how to use it in a professional manner.

Bennett et al. (2012) evaluated six Web 2.0 implementations in Australian higher education and found that many students had little prior experience with the technologies involved and struggled to see the worth of Web 2.0 technologies in learning and teaching. In addition, some students, particularly those who are not currently using it, can be quite sceptical of Twitter and experience an "information overload" when they begin using it (DeGroot et al., 2015; Nicholson & Galguera, 2013). Nicholson and Galguera (2013) suggest that using Twitter requires students to learn the technical complexities of the digital world and also the specialised discourses that are associated with online participation.

Case Study 1

#Tweaching: Using Social Media to Increase Student Engagement (Jessica Richards, Lecturer, Western Sydney University)

This case study presents the use of Twitter with Sport Management students in the School of Business at Western Sydney University, Australia. The university is located in the Greater Western Sydney region, which has a large multicultural population of more than two million people from 170 nations. It is often referred to as working-class and has been identified as having average levels education, income and employment that are lower than the rest of Sydney (Lodewijks, 2013). The demographics of these students vary, with 50% of students at Western Sydney University being first in family to attend university and 23% of the students coming from low SES backgrounds. The unit in this case study is a first-year unit with approximately 125 students across two campuses. The unit is titled "Sport Entertainment" and explores the relationship between sport organisations and social media engagement.

During the week prior to semester starting students are sent a hashtag (e.g. #WSUSport) allowing the lecturer to track tweets and respond to questions being posed by students within and outside of the class setting. The lecturer also encouraged students to use Twitter to begin following sporting organisations and media channels that would be tweeting stories of interest over the course of semester. However, whilst the use of Twitter as a tool to enhance student engagement has been discussed within academic circles (see Chawinga, 2017; Mollett et al., 2011) the use of live tweeting within the classroom remains under explored. Live tweeting refers to the lecturer and students using the platform to respond to course material in real time within the teaching setting.

The lecturer would show the cohort a type of stimulus material that related to the weekly module (this could be an online video, new story, or sport report). For example, a short video advertisement by Australia's national sport governing body Sport Australia titled "*make your move*", which was accessed via YouTube. The students watched the advertisement and then were asked to reflect on the message it was promoting and to assess its effectiveness. Immediately after watching the video, students were encouraged to ask the cohort questions (via the unit hashtag) or to tweet their opinions on the material. This proved to be an effective activity which not only engaged different groups of students within the teaching session, but also e-connected students from different campuses to the weekly content. As the students were able to see what other students had asked and posted they were then able to respond, "like", or further discuss the trigger material with peers who may be sitting one metre away or with those being taught in another suburb. Additionally, students were shown how to "mention" organisations as part of this discussion, resulting in an increase to the breadth of the tweet's audience. This use of mentions creates a direct link between the organisation and the student that then will appear on the thread.

In a similar manner, Twitter Chats were used to further connect students with the real world. In place of some weekly sessions, staff and students "met" online and made use of an agreed hashtag to discuss a series of questions. The questions were published online in advance and were numbered to allow all participants to follow the discussion. Unlike a face-to-face session, there was no requirement for students to attend class and while some were at various locations on campus others were at home or their place of work. Industry contacts, alumni, and academics were also invited to participate to provide real world insights and examples.

The School of Business at Western Sydney University have adopted the flipped delivery model, which refers to a blended learning pedagogy that transforms the traditional learning environment by delivering instructional content online and outside of the classroom (Simko et al., 2019). However, one of the challenges of delivering content in this way is the lecture being able to gauge if the students have (1) understood the course material and (2) whether they were stimulated by what was chosen to reflect the topic of the module.

Using Twitter within class sessions provided the lecturer the capacity to create a poll to gauge how the content was being delivered and the level of interest from the students. The poll was utilised multiple times throughout the semester, particularly when the content was considered challenging. However, the most significant benefit to students utilising Twitter within the class setting was that it provided an opportunity for those more comfortable communicating digitally rather than verbally to engage with the lecturer and other members of the cohort. It was observed that this translated later in the semester to a more engaged and vibrant classroom, where students often referred back to tweets as a discussion point.

This approach also allowed students to engage with peers within the classroom and at other campuses, the lecturer, as well as sporting organisations. As a micro-blogging tool Twitter (now) has a limit of 280 characters, which means students must be considered about how they tweet, further promoting the importance of responding in a concise and engaging manner. Overall, the use of Twitter enhances the student experience by providing a fun and engaging tool to enhance interaction and promote discussion.

Augmented Reality Apps

Augmented reality, which merges or overlays digital information with real world settings, has been described as bringing "truly unlimited possibilities for teaching and learning process" (Sural, 2018, p. 566). Most significantly, mobile augmented reality (MAR) situates users in the real world, providing natural and authentic experiences and environments for learning. As described by Papanastasiou et al. (2018, p. 6) augmented reality (AR) "dramatically shifts the location and timing of education and training" and thus solves some of the space-time challenges that higher education institutions are currently facing. AR has been used in a variety of educational settings (e.g. increasing awareness of recycling, teaching the history of cities, and training in the use of electrical machines) and, in the last decade, a number of educational games have even been developed to enhance the learning experience of students in a fun manner (Huizenga et al., 2009; Nincarean et al., 2013). Embedding AR in teaching practices has been found to increase learner immersion and engagement, positively impact motivation, and even encourage experimentation (Sural, 2018). Papanastasiou et al. (2018, p. 1) provide a more extensive list of benefits: promoting self-learning, enabling multi-sensory learning, enhancing spatial ability, confidence and enjoyment, promoting student-centred technology…and decreasing cognitive load". The widespread use of mobile internet-enabled devices has paved the way for a rise in MAR technology. As noted, the "unique" benefit of MAR comes with the ability to embed learning in authentic environments that promote and encourage learning outside formal education settings (Huizenga et al., 2009).

Recently, the rise of Pokémon GO, where players wander around the real world to unlock imaginary creatures via a location-based mobile app, using Geocaching (Tabacchi et al., 2017), highlighted that popularity of immersive, augmented reality games (Adlakha et al., 2017; Rauschnabel, Rossmann, & Dieck, 2017) and the effectiveness of gamification of health behaviours and social life (Kaczmarek et al., 2017). Players used their mobile phones to locate and then "collect" virtual characters that are overlaid onto prominent public locations, known as "Poke-stops", via augmented reality technology (Clark & Clark, 2016; Tabacchi et al., 2017). The game also included elements of social interaction, often chance encounters with other players at Poke-stops, and exchanges of knowledge between users. While virtual mobile games and games that require physical play/activity have been around since the 1990s, Pokémon GO connected users to urban (physical) spaces in ways that previous games had not (Adlakha et al., 2017).

> **Case Study 2**
>
> **Mobile Augmented Reality Case Study: Pyrmont AR Field Trip (Cameron McAuliffe, Senior Lecturer, Western Sydney University)**

Our cities are constantly changing to accommodate population growth, and to replace the old with the new. But while urban forms continue to change, sometimes the processes that drive these changes shift, with new processes emerging to influence the type of cities we live in. In Sydney, a "global city" of 5 million people, becoming enmeshed in a global economy has produced new patterns of urban development. Urban geographers and urban planners need to understand and be sensitive to these dynamic patterns, to disentangle the processes that drive change in our cities. As part of an introductory undergraduate unit in the Urban Planning degree at Western Sydney University (WSU), mobile augmented reality (MAR) has been successfully implemented to facilitate learning through the analysis of urban forms and processes in the field.

Urban geography, as a sub-discipline of human geography, is a field-based discipline. As an applied social science, field trips are a key tool in the pedagogical toolbox of human geographers. In this case, a MAR element was designed into an existing field trip to the inner city harbourside suburb of Pyrmont. The pedagogical principle of experiential learning (Kolb, 2014), along with a commitment to a pedagogical approach to technological integration (Brill & Park, 2008), influenced the development of the MAR component of the field trip. The redesign of the field experience around mobile augmented reality was intended to extend and intensify the embodied experience of the field trip, helping to embed analytical connections between theory and the urban environment.

The Pyrmont AR Field Trip is structured as a small group self-guided field exercise for students enrolled in the unit, *Cities: Introduction to Urban Studies*. Students enrolled in this unit are typically beginning their degree pathway as an urban planner or geographer or progressing a geography teaching specialisation in their education degree. On the day, the students attend a briefing lecture onsite that provides information about the urban processes that students will be looking to identify, including urban consolidation, gentrification, and urban regeneration, along with evidence of de-industrialisation and the presence of a new post-industrial economy. Following the briefing lecture students head out into the urban landscape of Pyrmont in allocated small groups on one of eight preset self-guided field trips. During the field trip they observe historical change in the landscape at five different locations through an open-access commercial AR app. The AR app allows students to overlay archival images of the former waterfront industrial and trading urban landscape over the contemporary urban environment.

Mirroring processes happening in cities in developed economies elsewhere, Sydney's working harbour has been reborn as a place of tourism and leisure. The dirty, working-class industrial suburb of Pyrmont has been replaced by newly gentrified residential communities, living in new high-density residential towers and the repurposed warehouses of the former industrial waterfront. Mobile augmented reality allows the students to see these changes as a function of new processes through direct observation of the shift from the historical maritime core of the nineteenth and twentieth century city to newer post-industrial functions.

During the field trip students observe urban change using the AR app on their mobile devices at a selection of the more than 20 sites that have been setup for the field trip. They also observe and collect their own evidence of urban processes from the landscape, in the form of visual data (photographs and videos), which are then used for analysis and reflection in a debriefing lecture on the day and associated post-field trip assessments on the impact of global processes on Sydney's urban landscape. Using MAR in this field trip, urban geography and planning students can peel back the history of these places, to observe and experience *in situ* how new urban processes have led to a new type of urban landscape in their city. Additionally, those students training to become geography teachers in secondary education gain insights into the use of immersive technologies in the field as a tool for experiential learning.

Feedback from students has consistently indicated that they have found the field trip "fun" and "engaging". Beyond this, students report that the field trip has helped "implement learning" and "put into practice key concepts", as they use MAR to "see the changes in the landscape over time". Importantly, the immersive technologies used in the field trip have been reported to complement and support learning, rather being merely tokenistic. As one student commented at length in general feedback on the unit:

> The field trip to Pyrmont was a perfect example of why this unit was so good. It married concepts in the unit with the real world and I really enjoyed that. It was a unit which had plenty of theory but was applied in a way that I have not experienced before in tertiary study. The use of technology was pretty advanced which is great because it did not feel tokenistic or forced. The use of [the AR app] HP Reveal was genuinely interesting and a fantastic way to drive home how much Sydney has changed (or hasn't) over the years. For someone who has not done a geography or planning subject it was a real revelation.

The use of mobile augmented reality in the Pyrmont AR Field Trip has been influential in teaching and learning at WSU and beyond, informing best practice in the pedagogical use of technologies in flexible learning and teaching. The Pyrmont AR Field Trip has been recognised as a best practice case in the geography discipline in research on the development of national Teaching and Learning Outcomes for Australian first year tertiary students (Luzia et al., 2015). In 2020, the AR field trip is moving into the next stage of its development to integrate advances in AR and VR technologies, along with better integration of geolocation to improve the efficacy of the student experience.

In line with the principles of experiential learning, students have been able to use MAR to reflect on the complex ways theoretically informed classroom discussions might play out in "real-life". The field trip consistently receives positive feedback, with students recognising how this technology helps them see the world through a critical social scientific lens, providing the basis for the critical interpretation of urban landscapes and the processes that underpin urban change that is central to their professional development as urban geographers and planners.

Actually Active Learning

Pokémon GO has proved to be successful, in the first week of its release it broke the Apple App Store's record for the most downloads in a week and generated approximately US$600m (£470m) in global revenue in its first three months (Adlakha et al., 2017). Yet, more significantly, the application has been found to increase levels of physical activity, particularly in groups that traditionally have lower levels of activity, such as teens, preteens, and younger men (Clark & Clark, 2016; Gabbiadini, Sagioglou, & Greitemeyer, 2018; Ma et al., 2018; Marquet, Alberico, & Hipp, 2018). Users were encouraged to walk up to 10 kilometres in some instances and daily step levels increased by an average of 25% per day in the first stages of adoption (Gabbiadini, Sagioglou, & Greitemeyer, 2018).

Case Study 3

The Development of an "Actually Active Learning" Mobile Application (Keith D. Parry, Senior Lecturer, Bournemouth University and Western Sydney University)

This recent case study also features the Sport Management programme in the School of Business at Western Sydney University. Within one particular unit, students study sports fans to gain an understanding of their behaviours and the different types of fans that may be observed. Academic studies of sports fans and teaching in this area traditionally rely on theoretical discussions of fans, highlighting their behaviours or possibly using a video or two if the academic is adventurous. However, sports fans are not dry academic constructs, they are living, breathing people and the subject is a dynamic and rich area that is of interest to many students. There is a disjuncture between the active, engaging environment of sport fandom and traditional teaching in this area. It was identified that a real world setting, where learning could take place just in time when students were observing sports fans in a real-life setting would provide a more engaging learning environment.

Contacts with professional sports clubs allowed students access to elite level sports matches but the challenge of delivering timely content while they were able to view sports fans remained. With these consideration in mind, a location-based mobile app, inspired by the popularity and principles of Pokémon GO was developed that delivers learning materials related to sports fans when students are actually at sporting venues. The app consists of a map of the sports precincts, video content with short descriptions, and a user guide. It was made freely available for both iOS and Android devices with students allowed to download it during an earlier contact session using the University's Wi-Fi network.

Using the GPS functionality of a student's mobile device, content is released when the student enters a defined geo-fenced boundary linked to an area of a sports precinct, in this case Sydney Olympic Park. The app delivers content to explain what the students are seeing in and around the various stadiums. They are required to visit different areas of the precinct, walking between locations indicated on the in-built map on the app. As they move around the venue new content is released, gamifying the learning process.

The content consists of short lecturer-created videos that provide academic commentary and industry insights on topics related to the location and theoretical discussions on sports fans. To ensure that an active learning approach was followed, the videos were supplemented with short tasks (such as capturing a photograph or posting on social media) that allows students to immediately apply their learning and which further engages the students in the learning process. Attendance at these venues replaced traditional face-to-face sessions and allowed students to experience a match while studying sports fans and a variety of sport-related issues first-hand.

Feedback from students indicated that attendance at the stadium was both entertaining and educational. In some instances, it was their first sports match and attending in person brought the content "to life". There was an initial excitement at the use of a mobile app for educational purposes and the novelty of the app itself heightened this feeling. Students found the app easy to use and initial feedback indicates that the immediacy of the content delivery enhanced their understanding of the concepts. In addition, the app also allowed those who were not able to attend a specific game to attend an alternative event at a more convenient time.

Active learning refers, typically, to the active mental engagement of students with learning and generally does not require physical activity. This actually active learning approach not only motivates students to engage meaningfully in their learning but also encourages them to be physically active, increasing their physical activity levels. Early measures of the physical activity of users indicate that while students did not walk the 10 kilometres that Gabbiadini, Sagioglou, & Greitemeyer (2018) found Pokémon GO users to do, they averaged approximately 2.5 kilometres each match. As such, this form of learning improves educational potential and also the health of students.

Conclusion

The emergence of Web 2.0 tools on the internet have resulted in a growing number of interactive and socially constructed resources, which are often available for free, that teachers can use to support learning. The proliferation of internet enabled mobile devices and the increases in availability and quality of mobile data allowances means that mobile-based learning environments are becoming increasingly common. The ability of these Web 2.0 technologies to create active learning environments is further enhanced by their immediacy, allowing learning to be delivered in real time in addition to real world contexts.

The use of social media platforms to enhance student engagement and interest remains a growing area of academic inquiry in higher education research. With higher education institutions increasingly directing resources to developing online or blended/flipped teaching environments, the use of social media in the classroom has never been timelier. In large teaching workshops/lectures social networking platforms yield great benefits as an additional way for students to engage and have a digital voice and platform to express themselves.

More generally, Web 2.0 tools provide a variety of benefits for students that traditional approaches to teaching and learning may not offer. They can enhance critical abilities, increase employability prospects, stimulate curiosity, and encourage learning outside of traditional settings. Furthermore, with a degree of innovation, they can also be used to create actually active learning environments.

Finally, the integration of such tools into educational practices can create lifelong learners and citizen-scholars that are ready and motivated to actively engage in global discussions. Educators should be encouraged to embrace mobile technologies within the classroom rather than seeing them as a threat to their control over the learning environment.

References

Adlakha, D., Marquet, O., Hipp, J. A., & Tully, M. A. (2017). Pokémon GO or Pokémon Gone: How can cities respond to trends in technology linking people and space? *Cities & Health, 1*(1), 89–94. https://doi.org/10.108 0/23748834.2017.1358560

Bennett, S., Bishop, A., Dalgarno, B., Waycott, J., & Kennedy, G. (2012). Implementing Web 2.0 technologies in higher education: A collective case study. *Computers & Education, 59,* 524–534. https://doi.org/10.1016/j. compedu.2011.12.022

Berners-Lee, T. (1997). *Realising the full potential of the web.* Retrieved from https://www.w3.org/1998/02/Potential.html

Biggs, J. B., & Tang, C. (2011). *Teaching for quality learning at university* (4th ed.). Berkshire: McGraw Hill, Open University Press. Retrieved from http:// UWSAU.eblib.com.au/patron/FullRecord.aspx?p=798265

Boscardin, C., & Penuel, W. (2012). Exploring benefits of audience-response systems on learning: A review of the literature. *Academic Psychiatry, 36*(5), 401–407. https://doi.org/10.1176/appi.ap.10080110

Brill, J. M., & Park, Y. (2008). Facilitating engaged learning in the interaction age taking a pedagogically-disciplined approach to innovation with emergent technologies. *International Journal of Teaching and Learning in Higher Education, 20*(1), 70–78. https://doi.org/10.12691/education-4-1-9

Chawinga, W. (2017). Taking social media to a university classroom: Teaching and learning using Twitter and blogs. *International Journal of Educational Technology in Higher Education, 14*, 3. https://doi.org/10.1186/s41239-017-0041-6

Chen, Y.-C., Hwang, R.-H., & Wang, C.-Y. (2012). Development and evaluation of a Web 2.0 annotation system as a learning tool in an e-learning environment. *Computers & Education, 58*(4), 1094–1105. https://doi.org/10.1016/j.compedu.2011.12.017

Clark, A. M., & Clark, M. T. G. (2016). Pokémon GO and research: Qualitative, mixed methods research, and the supercomplexity of interventions. *International Journal of Qualitative Methods, 15*(1), 1609406916667765. https://doi.org/10.1177/1609406916667765

DeGroot, J. M., Young, V. J., & VanSlette, S. H. (2015). Twitter use and its effects on student perception of instructor credibility. *Communication Education, 65*(4), 1–19. https://doi.org/10.1080/03634523.2015.1014386

Dohn, N. (2009). Web 2.0: Inherent tensions and evident challenges for education. *International Journal of Computer-Supported Collaborative Learning, 4*, 343–363. https://doi.org/10.1007/s11412-009-9066-8

Dunlap, J. C., & Lowenthal, P. R. (2009). Tweeting the night away: Using Twitter to enhance social presence. *Journal of Information Systems Education, 20*(2), 129–135. Retrieved from http://search.proquest.com/docview/200135030?accountid=36155

Fisher, A., Exley, K., & Ciobanu, D. (2014). *Key guides for effective teaching in higher education: Using technology to support learning and teaching.* Florence, KY: Taylor and Francis.

Gabbiadini, A., Sagioglou, C., & Greitemeyer, T. (2018). Does Pokémon GO lead to a more physically active life style? *Computers in Human Behavior, 84*, 258–263. https://doi.org/10.1016/j.chb.2018.03.005

Groff, J. (2013). Technology-rich innovative learning environments. *OECD Working Paper.*

Herrmann, K. J. (2013). The impact of cooperative learning on student engagement: Results from an intervention. *Active Learning in Higher Education, 14*(3), 175–187. https://doi.org/10.1177/1469787413498035

Huizenga, J., Admiraal, W., Akkerman, S., & Dam, G. t. (2009). Mobile game-based learning in secondary education: Engagement, motivation and learning in a mobile city game. *Journal of Computer Assisted Learning, 25*(4), 332–344. https://doi.org/10.1111/j.1365-2729.2009.00316.x

Jacquemin, S. J., Smelser, L. K., & Bernot, M. J. (2014). Twitter in the higher education classroom: A student and faculty assessment of use and perception.

Journal of College Science Teaching, 43(6), 22–27. Retrieved from http://ezproxy.uws.edu.au/login?url=http://search.ebscohost.com/login.aspx?direct=true&db=ehh&AN=96434846&site=ehost-live&scope=site

Junco, R., Heiberger, G., & Loken, E. (2011). The effect of Twitter on college student engagement and grades. *Journal of Computer Assisted Learning, 27*(2), 119–132. https://doi.org/10.1111/j.1365-2729.2010.00387.x

Kaczmarek, L. D., Misiak, M., Behnke, M., Dziekan, M., & Guzik, P. (2017). The Pikachu effect: Social and health gaming motivations lead to greater benefits of Pokémon GO use. *Computers in Human Behavior, 75*, 356–363. https://doi.org/10.1016/j.chb.2017.05.031

Kaldoudi, E., Konstantinidis, S., & Bamidis, P. (2010). Web 2.0 approaches for active, collaborative learning in medicine and health. In S. Mohammed & J. Fiaidhi (Eds.), *Ubiquitous health and medical informatics: The ubiquity 2.0 trend and beyond* (pp. 127–149). Hershey, PA: IGI Global.

Kaplan, A., & Haenlein, M. (2010). Users of the world, unite! The challenges and opportunities of social media. *Business Horizons, 53*, 59–68. https://doi.org/10.1016/j.bushor.2009.09.003

Kassens-Noor, E. (2012). Twitter as a teaching practice to enhance active and informal learning in higher education: The case of sustainable tweets. *Active Learning in Higher Education, 13*(1), 9–21. https://doi.org/10.1177/1469787411429190

Keogh, P., & Wang, Z. (2010). Clickers in instruction: One campus, multiple perspectives. *Library Hi Tech, 28*(1), 8.

Kolb, D. A. (2014). *Experiential learning: Experience as the source of learning and development* (2nd ed.). Upper Saddle River, NJ: Pearson Education.

Konstantinidis, S., Bamidis, P., & Kaldoudi, E. (2009). *Active blended learning in medical education—Combination of WEB 2.0 problem based learning and computer based audience response systems.* Paper presented at the 22nd IEEE International Symposium on Computer-Based Medical Systems, Albuquerque, NM.

Kuznekoff, J. H., Munz, S., & Titsworth, S. (2015). Mobile phones in the classroom: Examining the effects of texting, twitter, and message content on student learning. *Communication Education, 64*(3), 344–365. https://doi.org/10.1080/03634523.2015.1038727

Lin, M.-F., Hoffman, E., & Borengasser, C. (2013). Is social media too social for class? A case study of twitter use. *TechTrends, 57*(2), 39–45. https://doi.org/10.1007/s11528-013-0644-2

Lodewijks, J. (2013). Political Economy in Greater Western Sydney. *The Journal of Australian Political Economy, 72*, 80–105.

Luzia, K., Cole, B., Allen, P., Clark, J., Jones, A., Lawrence, J., ... Wallace, J. (2015). *Geography—Good practice guide*. Sydney: Office for Learning and Teaching.

Ma, B. D., Ng, S. L., Schwanen, T., Zacharias, J., Zhou, M., Kawachi, I., & Sun, G. (2018). Pokémon GO and physical activity in Asia: Multilevel study. *Journal of Medical Internet Research, 20*(6), e217. https://doi.org/10.2196/jmir.9670

Marquet, O., Alberico, C., & Hipp, A. J. (2018). Pokémon GO and physical activity among college students. A study using ecological momentary assessment. *Computers in Human Behavior, 81*, 215–222. https://doi.org/10.1016/j.chb.2017.12.028

Mollett, A., Moran, D., & Dunleavy, P. (2011). Using Twitter in university research, teaching and impact activities. In *Impact of social sciences: Maximizing the impact of academic research*. London, UK: LSE Public Policy Group, London School of Economics and Political Science.

Moore, D. T. (2013). *Engaged learning in the academy challenges and possibilities*. New York: Palgrave Macmillan.

Moran, M., Seaman, J., & Tinti-Kane, H. (2011). *Teaching, learning, and sharing: How today's higher education faculty use social media*. Retrieved from Boston http://www.pearsonlearningsolutions.com/educators/pearson-social-media-survey-2011-bw.pdf

Newmann, F. M. (Ed.). (1992). *Student engagement and achievement in American secondary schools*. New York: Teachers College Press.

Nicholson, J., & Galguera, T. (2013). Integrating new literacies in higher education: A self-study of the use of Twitter in an education course. *Teacher Education Quarterly, 40*(3), 7–26. https://doi.org/10.1002/ncr.20069

Nincarean, D., Alia, M. B., Halim, N. D. A., & Rahman, M. H. A. (2013). Mobile augmented reality: The potential for education. *Procedia—Social and Behavioral Sciences, 103*, 657–664. https://doi.org/10.1016/j.sbspro.2013.10.385

Papanastasiou, G., Drigas, A., Skianis, C., Lytras, M., & Papanastasiou, E. (2018). Virtual and augmented reality effects on K-12, higher and tertiary education students' twenty-first century skills. *Virtual Reality, 23*, 425–436. https://doi.org/10.1007/s10055-018-0363-2

Park, S., Holloway, S., Arendtsz, A., Bempechat, J., & Li, J. (2012). What makes students engaged in learning? A time-use study of within- and between-individual predictors of emotional engagement in low-performing high schools. *Journal of Youth & Adolescence, 41*(3), 390–401. https://doi.org/10.1007/s10964-011-9738-3

Rauschnabel, P. A., Rossmann, A., & tom Dieck, M. C. (2017). An adoption framework for mobile augmented reality games: The case of Pokémon Go. *Computers in Human Behavior, 76*, 276–286. https://doi.org/10.1016/j. chb.2017.07.030

Raux, D. J. (2012). An effective active approach for teaching accounting in the 21st century: Using active learning, an on-line course management system, and a student response system. (Report). *Review of Business Research, 12*(4), 86.

Rogers-Estable, M. (2014). Web 2.0 use in higher education. *European Journal of Open, Distance and E-Learning, 17*, 130–142. https://doi.org/10.2478/ eurodl-2014-0024

Sciarra, D. T., & Seirup, H. J. (2008). The multidimensionality of school engagement and math achievement among racial groups. *Professional School Counseling, 11*, 218–228. https://doi.org/10.5330/PSC.n.2010-11.218

Simko, T., Pinar, I., Pearson, A., Huang, J., Mutch, G., Patwary, A. S., … Ryan, K. (2019). Flipped learning—A case study of enhanced student success. *Australasian Journal of Engineering Education, 24*(1), 35–47.

Stevens, R. (2015). Role-play and student engagement: Reflections from the classroom. *Teaching in Higher Education, 20*(5), 481–491. https://doi.org/1 0.1080/13562517.2015.1020778

Stolk, J., & Harari, J. (2014). Student motivations as predictors of high-level cognitions in project-based classrooms. *Active Learning in Higher Education, 15*(3), 231–247. https://doi.org/10.1177/1469787414554873

Sural, I. (2018). Augmented reality experience: Initial perceptions of higher education students. *International Journal of Instruction, 11*, 565–576. https:// doi.org/10.12973/iji.2018.11435a

Tabacchi, M. E., Caci, B., Cardaci, M., & Perticone, V. (2017). Early usage of Pokémon GO and its personality correlates. *Computers in Human Behavior, 72*, 163–169. https://doi.org/10.1016/j.chb.2017.02.047

Tambouris, E., Dalakiouridou, E., Tarabanis, K., Ryberg, T., Buus, L., Peristeras, V., … Porwol, L. (2012). Enabling problem based learning through Web 2.0 technologies: PBL 2.0. *Educational Technology & Society, 15*, 238–251.

Tess, P. A. (2013). The role of social media in higher education classes (real and virtual)—A literature review. *Computers in Human Behavior, 29*, A60–A68. https://doi.org/10.1016/j.chb.2012.12.032

Williams, J., & Chinn, S. (2009). Using Web 2.0 to support the active learning experience. *Journal of Information Systems Education, 20*, 165–174.

17

Conclusion: Real World Learning— Researching and Co-constructing Working Definitions for Curriculum Development and Pedagogy

Dawn A. Morley

Introduction

During 2019, the lead editor for an open-access edited collection 'Applied pedagogy for higher education. Real world learning and innovation across the curriculum' consulted with 15 groups of authors whose chapters had been selected for submission. The authors and case studies presented expertise on applied pedagogies from a variety of disciplines, and higher education specialisms, from eight universities from across the UK.

Overall, the research study followed the methodology of concept mapping by engaging authors in a collaborative exercise to co-construct the emerging pedagogic issue of 'real world learning' within their own sectors. Previous studies (Ornellas, Falkner, & Stalbrandt, 2019) used qualitative methodology to establish a theoretical framework to build on authentic learning for employability, but the choice of concept mapping for this study hoped to address two purposes. The first was to facilitate a

D. A. Morley (✉)
School of Sport, Health and Social Sciences, Solent University, Southampton, UK

© The Author(s) 2021
D. A. Morley, M. G. Jamil (eds.), *Applied Pedagogies for Higher Education*,
https://doi.org/10.1007/978-3-030-46951-1_17

deep and immersive critique of authors' real world learning approaches for the purposes of thematic analysis. The second gave authors a visual route map of their own reflections on real world learning to assist them with the writing of their own chapters.

Concept mapping is a 'graphic organisational technique' designed to help individuals (and groups) explain and explore their knowledge and understanding of a topic…

1. The concepts that an individual deems important in illustrating their personal understanding of a topic are placed in text boxes and arranged hierarchically…
2. Concepts are then linked with arrows that are annotated with 'linking statements' to explain the nature of the link
3. Concepts may be listed only once, but any number of links may be made between any number of concepts at any number of conceptual links. (Hay & Kinchin, 2006, p. 129)

The authors were viewed as experts but were also all working within changing higher education environments and could therefore reflect from a wider, rich and socially constructed perspective. For the purposes of this study, the research was concerned with "clarifying, validating or building a theory" (Gray, 2017, p. 3) of real world learning for the explicit intention of being of use in the design of curriculum and pedagogy within higher education. The first purpose of its usefulness was to give authors a tangible framework of their own definition of real world learning in order to build the narrative of their chapters.

Methodology

For the purposes of this study, authors' discussions of the concept of real world learning and a description of their own educational context and situation occurred in their chapter groups and through concept mapping. This followed a technique of enhancing the construction of concept maps through a facilitated narrative reflection between the lead editor and authors (Kinchin et al., 2018). The resultant visual "networked" concept maps, where concepts link in multiple directions (Hay & Kinchin, 2006) from each author group, demonstrated the complexity of the concept of real world learning. These are included in the relevant, associated chapters.

Following focus groups with 15 groups of authors the transcriptions of discussions on real world learning were thematically analysed using Nvivo 11.

Real World Learning Analysis

Although three main themes emerged from the data analysis, all authors began by providing examples of what they defined as real world learning. Some universities had already gained advanced expertise on negotiated work-based learning frameworks (Chap. 2) with the majority of authors naming overt initiatives within the curriculum where students were prepared for employment by being exposed to the world of work through, for example, placements (Chap. 7). Others named pedagogies that enhanced skills which were also seen as useful to the workplace, for example, innovative pedagogies (Chap. 12) and project-based learning (Chap. 8). At the early stages of discussion alternative approaches to learning were mooted. These included better use of the online environment (Chaps. 15 and 16) and less traditional access routes to real world learning such as the volunteering opportunities discussed in Chap. 5 through civic engagement (Chap. 4) as well as greater use of students' own co-creation of the curriculum (Chap. 3).

> I think rooting it in these ideas of co creation is one of the ways because that's giving students ownership of the design of whatever they're doing—projects scenario or what have you—… it's still not real world it's sort of real world-esque.

As authors reached a deeper level of collaborative discussion between themselves and the researcher, more nuanced themes began to be discussed and, when thematically analysed, produced the three themes of fidelity, individuality and mutuality.

Theme One: Fidelity

Authors believed that creating a situated learning context, that replicated as close as possible the authentic world of work, could manifest itself both in curriculum design and the manner of learning. "Without the context … the risk is students' learning is quite fragmented" and "if you're too abstract, and talk about theory, you don't get the context around it".

As a result of real world learning's fidelity to simulate, replicate or exist in authentic work settings, authors identified the close association of students developing employability skills with this type of situated learning. Simply students can "increase job prospects, employee relationships and networking" but many authors felt that this employability link was much more subtle and required deeper development to be effective on students' work readiness. Authors identified the development of identities and attributes, as opposed to simply a set of skills, that started at the beginning of the degree course building work readiness, as well as theoretical knowledge, as learning progressed

> it isn't just about university as a factory for employability. It is about the person, it's about rethinking, well it's just trying to do a lot more within the university framework.

Exposing students to situations that they will meet again in their professional lives starts to build confidence as students gain tangible proof of their abilities.

> 'I might have a degree in the theory behind this, but I have run my own event.' What it's doing is, it's opening more doors.

Students begin to appreciate the holistic nature of employment where attributes and skills mix and blend dependent on the situation. Theory is enhanced by a foundation of soft skills that employers are increasingly expected to have been developed at university. To achieve this, authors identified a need for a repositioning of the employer-university relationship where there is closer communication on what is expected of graduates and how this can be achieved through the course. Fidelity needs to be co-constructed by a partnership of all three so the end point, when students leave university, is not too late to address the employers' needs.

> employers always complain that they get these graduates who have got all this knowledge, but they don't know how to function in the workplace. And they don't prepare their students for the workplace, and I think perhaps, having this real world learning maybe lowers that risk for the employer.

This greater building of a collaborative partnership is supported in the study by Ornellas et al. (2019).

It was believed that learning with greater fidelity was an element of the curriculum that could be simplified or made more complex according to the students or the focus of the learning.

> Fidelity is how you can validate against the real world. Verisimilitude is an area of fidelity. It's more about how you perceive the real world, how you perceive what you're doing to correspond to the real world, rather than the actual.

Authors argued that students could begin their studies with low fidelity design and pedagogy, for example, the use of case studies introducing them to the real world context. In order to avoid a "double switch off" academics need to be attuned to examples that will engage students. Following this, employability skills can be grown through medium fidelity examples, such as simulation and gaming (Chap. 9), to full immersion into the authentic context of work where students learn through live briefs or find themselves fully participating in the work environment at university and beyond. A greater level of learning control is presented lower in the fidelity spectrum which may be appropriate for learners naive to the work environment, for the lecturer to take a particular learning focus or when an alternative problem base is needed for the more experienced practitioner.

you could argue that simulations might be a better aid to learning than something that's totally real world because it helps to simplify things, make it slightly more abstract than real world that takes you part way to that abstract conceptualisation that you need to fully understand a problem or situation.

Most significantly, the level of immersion impacted the affective engagement of students. What was viewed as the ideal trajectory from low to high fidelity learning situations increased not only the novelty of the learning, but students were stretched to a more expansive type of learning—deeper and more problem-based synonymous with "graduate-ness" (Holbery, Morley, & Mitchell, 2019).

High fidelity learning was associated with greater risk, "there is risk, there is consequence, there's responsibility" and mistakability—a concept spoken about by many authors as a powerful way of students learning from their noncritical mistakes as students are situated at university rather than the real world itself, "And if they fell over, then it would be a poor mark and a learning experience with feedback, which you don't get later". Taking a real world learning approach gives "students a safe space to fail. They need to learn to fail and understand why they've failed, without additional pressure of they've just cost some business some money".

In turn, students have the potential to develop resilience and better preparation for employment by engaging attributes, such as leadership, critical thinking and collaborative working—"those won't develop, unless [students] are challenged, but what goes beyond ... a traditional, safe, HE environment". In effect, students' real world learning scaffolds them to reach their potential and the incremental building of this experience, reflected in Bruner's spiral curriculum (1960), continues to integrate an ongoing tension of personal achievement into the curriculum.

> [Students] are on the periphery of a community, and they've got access into it. But they're meant to be a little bit grittier and a bit more asking questions. It's giving students permission to do that.

The balance of fidelity against academic content, for example, student participation in a complex business strategy game with the understanding of business theory, was important so students' clarification of their learning remained explicit. Authors also recognised that academics must be cognisant of the time to step in to rescue projects, or how much to offer students in the first instance, so the quality and timing of delivery were not compromised.

> if there's too much fidelity, [that is] it represents the thousands of decisions you can make—a student wouldn't see the wood for the trees. You need to have simplification of reality which is complex enough to make those causal connections, but not too complicated that they can't do that.

Fidelity was enhanced by structures and pedagogy that increased students' awareness of their learning. Having the ability to reflect and articulate authentic learning experiences was important (Ornellas et al., 2019) as was the careful connection of the fidelity learning experience through the curriculum to an end point such as real-life practice or assessment (Morley, Bettles, & Derham, 2019). It was possible to implement fidelity through all stages of the curriculum, but notable comment was made by authors on the importance of introducing an authentic assessment brief that used students' time purposely towards real world attributes and identities. Emphasis moved away from the confines of traditional summative assessment to one where the process of assessment was paramount, and it was important that the element of risk had no effect on the credit bearing of the course and students' ability to meet learning outcomes.

Authentic assessment, explored more fully in Chap. 14, had two purposes of creating opportunities for ongoing and longitudinal feedback that replicated that of the workplace "it's being able to recognise feedback and delays between decisions and actions, consequences" but also started to create a culture of self-regulation. With multiple and ongoing assessment points, students prioritised feedforward to their next assessment and had a greater awareness of their individual, ipsative development (Hughes, 2011, 2014). Authors advocated assessment methods that both cultivated success, irrespective of the starting point, but with enough room for the acknowledgement and extension of a priori knowledge. Students were more likely to transition from simple, single loop learning to more complex double loop solutions (Argyris & Schon, 1974) as they could envisage the wider scope of their assessments. Again, assessments that were associated with greater prestige or risk were more likely to promote the affective engagement of students.

> you're going to be doing things like generating assignment, which is real world, which could have been written for the outside world, rather than the sort of stuff that you would churn out for your A-levels just to get a grade.

In a "first steps" approach to real world assessment authors were more likely to use multi-faceted and innovative approaches to assessment, such as peer review and assessment, that recognised and reflected the links to the world of work. Learning technology was used significantly to enhance the fidelity of the assessment, feedback and the situation of the learning itself as presented in Chaps. 12, 15, and 16.

Theme Two: Individuality

Authors emphasised the individuality of students' personal trajectories as they travelled through higher education and the individuality of students' real world constructions where "they don't necessarily grasp how everything could make a difference to their own journey". Authors highlighted differences in age, experience of work and study, outside commitments and levels of confidence yet felt that students were often infantilised and "historically, is just solve it—treat everybody like they're the same, actually the same shape and size". Students developed at different stages necessitating a pedagogy that differentiated and built on students' individual experience "to do with personal development, as much as sort of professional pedagogy".

> if you're going to make it real world, everybody's different. Everybody's come from a different place, and they might be heading in a different direction. And you've got enough scope, to be able to calibrate what you're doing to enhance that.

Authors offered different stories of being part of the individual, transformational development of students. This was further enhanced when students' needs were considered holistically, and students were encouraged to develop an instinct for lifelong learning and preparation for employment going forward.

> It's all going to be preparing them for work that doesn't exist now. So, what is it about real-world learning that's really going to enable them to leave confident and resilient ...?

The pedagogic theory that enhances real world learning therefore takes an individual, developmental ethos "it's almost as if you're taking a lot of the approaches, practices, philosophical underpinnings, and power relationships for andragogical university education and implanting it in a more traditional pedagogic environment". It is the antithesis of the short-term immediacy that dominates traditional higher education, "things are changing over time and it's ongoing. That's what some students embrace, but others don't necessarily like that idea, they want things to be terminal" and builds on the work of theorists such as Kolb (1984), Dewey (1938) and Knowles, Holton and Swanson (2005). Real world learning requires a different mindset for longitudinal development that projects past students' university experience, rather than the achievement of short-term goals and traditional, linear learning.

> we can provide the support, but they have to be the people who kind of go away and make the connections between all the different things that help them step through. One of the things they don't do, is they don't saturate themselves with inputs.

Those authors running degree apprenticeship programmes (Chap. 11), as opposed to traditional degrees, noted the difference in student experience and how it impacted their learning. The differentiation within the student body meant that a pedagogy needed to be used that drew on the student experience as a starting point and allowed for these differences.

[Students] need to be in a place where they can be reflective practitioners, they can be agile, they can be critical decision makers, so, it's pulling upon, I think probably just that agile element that we see from our real-world students.

Networking, (Chap. 3) and mentoring (Chap. 11 in the context of degree apprenticeships) were significant employability skills highlighted by authors but ones not naturally accessible to all students.

giving [students] the opportunity to network and establish contacts within that field, because it is so difficult to generate a career immediately coming out of an academic setting … what we try to encourage the students to understand is that every time you're in a new situation, you're exposing yourself to a new group of people [and] to make everything count.

Student mentorship for employment trod a fine balance between encouragement and control that real world learning was trying to overcome.

As with leading more authentic assessments, authors articulated strategies where students' own individual development was made explicit and clear to them.

what we try and do behind it is to support them in mapping what they're doing. So, we see a lot of students that leave our programmes that don't necessarily capture everything that they've done over their time, they don't see the relevance of it. But the moment you sit down with them and say, 'well, you did this, you ran this particular event, which incorporated leadership, which incorporated management, the commitment, that control.' 'Oh, yeah, I didn't think about that. I just saw myself as running an event.' So, it's encouraging people from what we see at the start, to when we get to the end point. What does their journey look like? And how have they showed themselves as individuals to get that end goal?

This was supported by pedagogies that promoted "student agency, making decisions, wiser students, autonomy, motivation, curiosity". Real time feedback from a range of facilitators, not just academics, strengthened the learning connections that students may miss in the present and "the real world element that they should see that that they're taking it forward into something else". Opportunities for students to reflect on their learning, presented in greater detail in Chap. 13 and interspersed throughout the chapters, allowed them to attend to their learning more instead of being hurried through imposed teaching schedules.

> I think that's one of the reasons why the assessment based on reflection is important, rather than performance. Because they might crash and burn, but they'll have learnt a lot from it. It's often easier to reflect on what went wrong, than what went right.

Individuality also encompassed giving students choice over critical paths within degrees, and when students had greater opportunity to make assessment more personal to their interests, culture and needs, their motivation and enthusiasm were increased.

Theme Three: Mutuality

Mutuality involves a greater collegiality between student and facilitator—the facilitator could be either internal or external to the university including alumni and peer students themselves. In some instances, this created a flattening of the traditional power dynamics between student and academic. In the opinion of authors, the loosening of these boundaries allowed students the opportunity for the co-creation of new knowledge, a greater voice and the development of confidence while speaking to other professionals, usually with more experience. Through the proximity to real world practitioners, students learnt at first-hand about professional responsibility, "in the film industry, it's about daylight. So, you've got to be there early, you've got to be there on time, you've got to be unpacked and ready to go" and students "get real exposure on how to communicate with those people". Working with external experts allowed students a vicarious route into real world practice and access to the "war stories" and experience of current practitioners.

it should be an opportunity to learn from people who have been where the students are heading for or might be heading for. It's a way to get insights and learn by doing and learn from people who have expertise.

Mutuality was defined differently by authors depending on their experience within higher education teaching. An influence was the introduction of degree apprenticeships and the perceived stronger relationship between student, higher education provider and the workplace facilitator that has resulted.

the direction should be two way, we should be upskilling industry in terms of knowledge exchange, but the practicality of what the students learn out in the field should be coming back and informing theory. There should be that two-way process.

Authors reflected on the need for three-way partnerships as a conduit for students attaining a real world education. Increasingly, external partners were taking more diverse roles in higher education from the more traditional workplace mentor and assessor to being actively involved in course design.

we're here to service the needs of the business region, so, it's working with them and actually doing that. And that's where we have to be agile, we have to be connected to the customer that we serve, and the customer being the industry that we provide the talent to help gear that and make it happen.

Authors noted that engaging students in "mutuality" came with increased responsibility. Academics had to ensure support systems were in place, regulatory commitments were met and students gained appropriate experience to both their future professional and personal needs. Authors also commented on the challenge mutuality could bring to the workplace.

we have got apprentices that have grown so much in themselves confidence wise, knowledge wise, and they're now starting to question the capability, the management style, the quality and level of decision making that's happening above them through the organisation. So, in many ways for organisations adopting this real-world learning approach and looking at nurturing talent and using these apprentice opportunities, you're almost creating a great wealth for energy within an organisation. But unless it's driven from the top-down, this can be quite challenging from a change model perspective.

With the increased acceptability of outsourcing teaching, learning strategies were heightened and more clearly thought through on how to successfully bridge the divide of students working and learning in different settings. Connecting theory and practice is a recognised and perennial issue within higher education learning (Evans, Guile, & Harris, 2009) and many authors commented upon this and saw it as important to the success of real world learning. The interdependency between the two was either enhanced inductively when students were in practice first, and then had a foundation of experience to base their theory around, or deductively when theory was taught first and practice applied later.

Authors talked of several learning strategies that encompassed mutuality. Peer learning was a popular choice where students worked with each other's individual abilities to build teams with the possibility of extending this to assess group dynamics.

And when students receive their grades, they will receive their grades from the tutor, and we will say overall as a group, you've got a B. Now go away, peer assess each other. So, the students then can compare the two, and see, okay, so my tutor saw this, but my colleagues didn't: what am I doing differently, and vice versa.

Conclusion

Real world learning focuses on developing attributes towards employability and lifelong learning—those mentioned were challenge, cultural competence, competition, leadership and professional networking—not usually associated with traditional university education. It reflects "shifting expectations about what universities are for in the last ten, fifteen, twenty years". Instead of focusing on the traditional learning methods that systematically build knowledge or community, real world learning looks for impact that can be carried and developed by the individual student as they journey through university, and then into employment and lifelong learning. Ornellas et al. (2019) argue for a

> broadened notion of authentic learning [that] incorporates not only the epistemological dimension—what students are expected to know and be able to do—but also the ontological—who students are becoming and learning to be.

The difficulties of the integration of employability skills, and the disjunction within the curriculum experienced by students, could go some way to be resolved through a greater real world learning approach.

> You're taking something and you're recalibrating it—it's not totally different … there's a subtle but really important change of direction and purpose for it.

There were many suggestions as to the scale of a real world learning approach "we're talking about effectively, totally reengineering your whole curriculum. So that pretty much every experience the student takes part in has some real world and focus" and the issues of integration "so it's not an add on" and an "undercut for the local industry". The study found that most authors were able to isolate different areas of curriculum design and pedagogies that took a real world learning approach suggesting that, irrespective of discipline, this emerging ethos has resonance across the higher education sector.

Some universities, recognising a difference in their real world ideology and approach, used this as a competitive advantage to attract students. Others realised that strategies, such as the creation of internal companies for placements presented in Chap. 7, increased control and the ability to offer work experience to many students in disciplines where finding placement experience was challenging.

From speaking to authors, all active practitioners and passionate advocates of real world learning, and "high investment education", the discussed real world learning strategy takes time, effort and considerable creativity.

> Real world learning is a lot harder to set up than just writing a lecture you write a lecture you do some powerpoint slides—job done. Real world learning takes a lot more thought …

As well as the efforts of individuals and teams, it was recognised that the commitment required for real world learning may be challenging to adopt with the "need to break down those separate silos" and "… to seriously start connecting bits of … universities together in a way that can help create something different, new, and which is going to take HE to the next level".

It was anticipated that "[blurring] of the power relationship" may draw resistance from academics and the nuances of "the lecturer [being] there to facilitate the learning rather than deliver the content". Many academics are either uncomfortable or unpractised adopting a coaching style with students so suggestions of broadening the net of facilitators to ones within industry, alumni networks and retired professionals could also expose students to the valuable experience of different styles of support and management.

> you need the confident facilitator for that, and not everyone will feel comfortable. And not all the students will feel comfortable either, which is a challenge, convincing the students that this could be a benefit to them—if they're going to feel exposed or vulnerable

Many authors had been frustrated in persuading quality processes at universities to take a more open approach to learning outside of the curriculum when, for example, sports placements were available. An allowance for greater flexibility with deadlines and enrolment due to students' real work commitments were concerns that "the quality processes that we have don't impede these initiatives … we certainly would need to ensure that we have got proper quality procedures that address work-based learning initiatives".

A factor not mentioned by authors was the move in higher education towards a greater quantitative measurement of student course evaluation. Traditionally student evaluation has prioritised the "fire alarm function" (Edstrom, 2008) where audit, the measurement of the "here and now" of teaching quality, has taken precedence over examining how evaluation can be used as a catalyst for future development. Taking a more reflective approach to evaluation encourages students to be "more considered, they interrogate their own engagement in the learning context, and they are more likely to demonstrate reconstructive thought" (Ryan, 2015, p. 1142). Nestel et al. (2012, p. 9) believe that the use of alternative methods could contribute to an "evaluation culture" where students felt "valued, respected and heard". A sense of engagement in the moment of the evaluation, and the encouragement of greater ownership with fellow students, seems possible using the professional networks discussed in Chap. 3 which provides suggestions for collaborative discussion between student and academic more in keeping with a real world learning approach.

Overall, authors spoke with enthusiasm of their real world learning initiatives which had motivated their students but also inspired their own professional practice.

> the students are challenged a lot of the times—the activities can be difficult for them, but I think they do enjoy the fact that they're different and all get some other things from it. From a staff perspective it's nice to do different things rather than just have four thousand-word reports to mark across every module … it just brings a bit of variety into it.

Most importantly, it charged both staff and students with an educational approach that goes beyond the university experience and one that is more pertinent to students' employability requirements. It instils a learning ethos that "[tries] to dig deeper and wider perhaps than some of us have courage to do" and "creating these lifelong learners so it's not just about the skills it is about a passion for learning too … they're motivated because they enjoy it … it has the ability to get people hooked into learning".

Chapter authors demonstrated a multiplicity of ways that the three themes of the research could be integrated into curriculum design and pedagogy. By the discovery of alternative routes through the traditional higher education systems (Chaps. 2, 4, 5, 10, and 11) and a re-emphasis on the pedagogies of what authors termed real world learning (Chaps. 3, 7–9, and 12–16) authors saw at first hand the benefits of more carefully considered curriculum that addressed changing student needs.

References

Argyris, C., & Schon, D. (1974). *Theory in practice: Increasing professional effectiveness*. San Francisco: Jossey Bass.

Bruner, J. (1960). *The process of education*. Cambridge, MA: The President and Fellows of Harvard College.

Dewey, J. (1938). *Experience and education*. London: Collier-Macmillan Ltd.

Edstrom, K. (2008). Doing course evaluation as if learning matters most. *Higher Education Research and Development, 27*(2), 95–106.

Evans, K., Guile, D., & Harris, J. (2009). *Putting knowledge to work: Integrating work-based and subject-based knowledge in intermediate level qualifications and workforce up skilling*. Retrieved from https://thecet.org/wp-content/uploads/2018/10/Book-of-Exemplars.pdf

Gray, D. E. (2017). *Doing research in the real world* (4th Kindle ed.). London: Sage Publications.

Hay, D., & Kinchin, I. (2006). Using concept maps to reveal conceptual typologies. *Education and Training, 48*(2/3), 127–142.

Holbery, N., Morley, D., & Mitchell, J. (2019). Expansive learning. In D. Morley, K. Wilson, & N. Holbery (Eds.), *Facilitating learning in practice – A research based approach to challenges and solutions*. Abingdon; New York: Routledge.

Hughes, G. (2011). Aiming for personal best: A case for introducing ipsative assessment in higher education. *Studies in Higher Education, 36*, 353–367.

Hughes, G. (2014). *Ipsative assessment. Motivation through marking progress*. Palgrave Macmillan.

Kinchin, I., Heron, M., Hosein, A., Lygo-Baker, S., Medland, E., Morley, D. A., & Winstone, N. E. (2018). Researcher-led academic development. *International Journal for Academic Development, 23*(4), 339–354. https://doi.org/10.1080/1360144X.2018.1520111

Knowles, M., Holton, I. E., & Swanson, R. (2005). *The adult learner* (6th ed.). Elsevier.

Kolb, D. (1984). *Experiential learning. Experience as the source of learning and development.* Englewood Cliffs, NJ/London: Prentice Hall Inc.

Morley, D., Bettles, S., & Derham, C. (2019). The exploration of students' learning gain following immersive simulation – The impact of feedback. *Higher Education Pedagogies, 4*(1), 368–384. https://doi.org/10.108 0/23752696.2019.1642123

Nestel, D., Ivkovic, A., Hill, R. A., Warrens, A. N., Paraskevas, P. A., McDonnell, J. A., & Browne, C. (2012). Benefits and challenges of focus groups in the evaluation of a new graduate entry medical programme. *Assessment and Evaluation in Higher Education, 37*, 1–17.

Ornellas, A., Falkner, K., & Stalbrandt, E. (2019). Enhancing graduates' employability skills through authentic learning approaches. *Higher Education, Skills and Work-Based Learning, 9*(1), 107–120. https://doi.org/10.1108/ HESWBL-04-2018-0049

Ryan, M. (2015). Framing student evaluations of university learning and teaching: Discursive strategies and textual outcomes. *Assessment and Evaluation in Higher Education, 40*(8), 1142–1158.

Index

A

Andersen, P., 165, 166
Argyris, C., 154, 201
Augmented reality, 343, 360, 372, 381–385

B

Baker, N., 335, 337
Barnett, M., 191
Barnett, R., 42, 117
Biggs, J. B., 231, 373
Billett, S., 4, 136–138
Bloom, B. S., 192
Boud, D., 324, 331, 334, 336, 337, 339
Bourdieu, P., 169
Breslin, C., 324
Bruner, J., 139

C

Carless, D., 332, 336, 339
Cicmil, S., 163, 165, 167
Collaborative online international learning (COIL), 119
Communities of practice (CoP), 10, 44, 49, 52, 59, 120, 121, 147, 163, 164, 171, 271
Cooke-Davies, T., 165

D

De Laat, M., 44
Degree apprenticeships, 2, 11, 58, 136, 150, 245, 246
Dewey, J., 23, 69, 70, 301, 302
Double-loop learning, 201

© The Author(s) 2021
D. A. Morley, M. G. Jamil (eds.), *Applied Pedagogies for Higher Education*,
https://doi.org/10.1007/978-3-030-46951-1_5

E

Ellstrom, P.-E., 6, 145
E-portfolios, 358, 359
Eraut, M., 26, 52, 140, 141, 154
Espoused theories, 154

F

Facebook, 351–355
Feed forward, 324, 327, 331, 333,
    335, 339
Freire, P., 69, 70, 289, 303

G

Gibbons, M., 24, 70
Gibbs, G., 356
Giddens, A., 169

H

Hawke, G., 337
Heidegger, M., 273, 274
Higher Degree Apprenticeships
    (HDAs), 243–264
Hodgson, D. E., 163, 167
Hounsell, D., 327, 336

I

Illeris, K., 3, 4

K

Knowledge Exchange Framework
    (KEF), 136
Knowles, M., 26
Kolb, D. A., 69, 301, 326, 327, 344,
    356, 382

L

Lam, J., 336
Land, R., 69, 216, 222
Lave, J., 49, 276, 349
Learning gain, 1, 110, 112,
    128, 200
Lefebvre, H., 12, 310
Legitimate peripheral participation,
    44, 276, 350
Lindgren, M., 167

M

MacFarlane-Dick, D.,
    192, 324
Maslow, A.H., 50
Meyer, J. H. F., 69, 216, 222
Mezirow, J., 69, 70, 303
Molloy, E., 324, 331,
    334, 336
Moon, J. A., 356
Murtagh, L., 335, 337

N

National Student Survey
    (NSS), 3, 67,
    136, 324
Nicol, D., 324, 328, 335
Nicol, D. J., 192

P

Packendorff, J., 167
Pavlov, P. I., 192
Peer assessment, 326,
    328–332
Perezhivanie, 280
Polanyi, M., 140, 335

R

Race, P., 324
Reflection-on-action, 305
Research Excellence Framework
(REF), 70

S

Sadler, D. R., 336
Salter, D., 336
Schön, D., 6, 140, 153, 154, 201,
299, 301, 302, 305, 306
Schön, D. A., 356
Shulman, L. S., 126, 325, 326, 336
Single-loop learning, 201
Skinner, B. F., 192
Smith, C., 165
Soler, R., 339
Svejvig, P., 165, 166

T

Tang, C., 231, 373
Teaching Excellence Framework
(TEF), 3, 33, 42, 67, 136
Theories in use, 154

Thomson, A., 324
Threshold concepts, 216,
222, 223
Trayner, B., 43, 44
Twitter, 355, 372, 377–380

V

Vygotsky, L., 192, 280

W

Web 1.0, 344
Web 2.0, 345, 355, 371, 372,
374–378, 387, 388
Web 3.0, 345
Wenger, E., 4, 43, 44, 49, 69, 122,
141, 150, 163, 164, 276, 279,
345, 349
Wenger-Trayner, E., 43,
170, 171
Winter, M., 165–168

Y

Yang, M., 336

Printed by Printforce, the Netherlands